How Ireland V

How Ireland Voted 2007: The Full Story of Ireland's General Election

Edited by

Michael Gallagher
Michael Marsh

First published 2008 by
PALGRAVE MACMILLAN
Houndmills, Basingstoke, Hampshire RG21 6XS and
175 Fifth Avenue, New York, N.Y. 10010
Companies and representatives throughout the world

PALGRAVE MACMILLAN is the global academic imprint of the
Palgrave Macmillan division of St Martin's Press LLC and of
Palgrave Macmillan Ltd.
Macmillan® is a registered trademark in the United States,
United Kingdom and other countries. Palgrave is a registered
trademark in the European Union and other countries.

ISBN-13 978–0–230–50038–9 hardback
ISBN-10 0–230–50038–2 hardback
ISBN-13 978–0–230–020198–9 paperback
ISBN-10 0–230–20198–9 paperback

This book is printed on paper suitable for recycling and made from
fully managed and sustained forest sources. Logging, pulping and
manufacturing processes are expected to conform to the
environmental regulations of the country of origin.

A catalogue record for this book is available from the British Library.

A catalogue record for this book is available from the Library of Congress.

10   9   8   7   6   5   4   3   2   1
17 16 15 14 13 12 11 10 09 08

Printed and bound in Great Britain by
Antony Rowe Ltd, Chippenham and Eastbourne

Contents

Appendices
Liam Weeks

List of Tables and Figures

Tables

Figures

Notes on Contributors

Heinz Brandenburg (PhD, Trinity College Dublin) is a lecturer in Politics at the University of Aberdeen. His teaching and research focuses on the field of political communication. His interests include the application of quantitative methods to the study of electoral campaigns and political rhetoric, the relationship between the military and the media, and the alleged value of online media for political deliberation.

Patrick Butler is Associate Professor of Marketing at Melbourne Business School, University of Melbourne, Australia. Formerly based at Trinity College Dublin, he remains fascinated by Irish politics and elections.

R. Kenneth Carty is Professor of Political Science and Brenda and David McLean Chair in Canadian Studies at the University of British Columbia. He recently served as Director of Research for the first Citizens' Assembly on Electoral Reform. The author of many studies of party organisation, political leadership and electoral institutions, his first book was *Party and Parish Pump: Electoral Politics in Ireland* (Ontario, 1981).

Neil Collins is Professor of Government at University College Cork. He has written extensively on Irish politics. His most recent book is *Modernising Irish Government: the Politics of Administrative Reform* (Dublin, 2007), co-authored by Patrick Butler and Terry Cradden.

Rory Costello is a doctoral candidate in the Department of Political Science, Trinity College Dublin, and an IRCHSS Government of Ireland Scholar. His research interests include decision-making in the European Union and Irish politics. His PhD dissertation focuses on legislative competition between the European Parliament and the Council of Ministers.

Michael Gallagher teaches Irish politics and is Professor of Comparative Politics at Trinity College Dublin. He is co-editor of *The Politics of Electoral Systems* (Oxford, 2008) and *Politics in the Republic of Ireland* (Abingdon, 2005), and co-author of *Representative Government in Modern Europe* (New York, 2006) and *Days of Blue Loyalty* (Dublin, 2002).

Gail McElroy is a lecturer in the Department of Political Science at Trinity College, Dublin. Her research interests include legislative politics and party organisation, with a particular focus on the European Union.

Michael Marsh is Professor of Comparative Political Behaviour and head of the School of Social Sciences and Philosophy at Trinity College Dublin. He is a co-author of *The Irish Voter* (Manchester, 2008) and a principal investigator on the 2002–07 Irish election studies.

Gary Murphy is Associate Professor of Government in the School of Law and Government at Dublin City University. He has published extensively on Irish politics, most notably in the areas of interest group influence and political corruption, and is a former editor of *Irish Political Studies*. He is currently engaged in research on political lobbying in representative democracies.

Eoin O'Malley is a lecturer at the School of Law and Government, Dublin City University. His main research interest is political power in and of parliamentary executives. He has published a number of articles on this topic in *International Political Science Review, British Journal of Politics and International Relations* and *Government and Opposition*.

Theresa Reidy is a lecturer in the Department of Government at University College Cork where she teaches Irish politics and political economy. Her research interests are in the field of economic performance and elections.

Robert Thomson is a lecturer at the Department of Political Science, Trinity College Dublin. His previous research includes a study of the fulfilment of election pledges in the Netherlands. His current research focuses mainly on decision-making in the European Union.

Liam Weeks is a lecturer in the Department of Government, University College Cork. His research interests include electoral systems, political parties and Irish politics. He is currently researching Independent politicians, and has published work in *New Parties in Government* (forthcoming), *Irish Political Studies* and *How Ireland Voted 2002*.

Zbyszek Zalinski is a PhD student in the Department of Political Science, Trinity College Dublin. He is working on a thesis on media agenda-setting during general elections in Ireland and Britain. His research interests include political communication, media and elections.

Preface

Political parties in most countries these days operate on a cycle defined by the incidence of elections. Policy development, membership recruitment and personnel changes all seem to be means to the end of performing well at the next election, and performance in 'second order' contests such as local or European Parliament elections is significant mainly for what it tells us about the party's prospects in, and what lessons the parties learn for, the next election that really matters: the election to the lower house of parliament, which will determine who gets into government. Parliamentary elections loom so large in the thinking of those who are involved in politics or who closely observe the political process that they can be anti-climactic when they arrive, and many elections are dismissed as 'not as exciting as elections used to be'.

No one said that about Ireland's 2007 election. Whereas the 2002 contest had amounted almost to a walkover for the incumbent government in the face of a dispirited and disunited opposition, in 2007 there was a fierce head-to-head confrontation between two opposing teams which looked for most of the campaign to be evenly matched. Smaller parties that had made significant advances in 2002 were expected to gain further territory. If the make-up of the next parliament was uncertain, the composition of the next government seemed to be anyone's guess, with five or even six parties having credible expectations of being in office after the election and a mind-boggling range of possible combinations being discussed as feasible scenarios.

Not only was the outcome in doubt until the end, but the campaign had a life of its own. In 2002 Fianna Fáil devised and was able to impose a trajectory for the campaign that was characterised by spin, agenda-setting and successful media manipulation. In 2007 the media was determined not to be so pliant again and, besides, events derailed any plan that Fianna Fáil's head office might have had. It all began with the bizarre initiation of the campaign not long after dawn on a Sunday morning, proceeded to a press conference where the Taoiseach's launch of his party's manifesto was rendered almost irrelevant by tough questions about his finances from a high-profile journalist, and continued with the coalition teetering on the brink of collapse as the junior partners, the PDs, wrestled, ultimately successfully, with their consciences about pulling out of government. It took place against a backdrop of a dispute with the country's nurses, who were engaged in industrial action over claims for higher pay and a shorter working week, and of a series of set-piece events concerning the Northern Ireland peace process, at which the presence of the Taoiseach, Bertie Ahern, reminded voters of his central role in that process.

And, finally, the government to emerge was one that very few people had expected, with some of the new ministers being as surprised as anyone else to find themselves in office. If policy, let alone ideological, conflict between the parties was still hard to spot, then at least the election had pretty much everything else.

An election generates certain inevitable consequences, and we like to think that by now part of the unavoidable 'collateral damage', so to speak, of every Irish general election is the production and appearance of another book in the *How Ireland Voted* series. Several volumes in the series were published or co-published by the Political Studies Association of Ireland (PSAI), and we acknowledge and appreciate the support given by the PSAI to the study of politics in and of Ireland. The first volume, *How Ireland Voted 1987*, examined the aftermath of the collapse of Garret FitzGerald's second government and the failure of Charles Haughey, for the fourth time, to win an overall majority for Fianna Fáil. The dramatis personae of Irish politics has changed a good deal since then, and the approach that political scientists take to analysing elections has also evolved but within a fairly stable framework. In short, this book is modelled on the format of its predecessors, but as usual there are innovations.

The first four chapters analyse pre-election developments. Chapter 1 sets the scene by reminding, or informing, readers of relevant political developments since the 2002 contest. Chapter 2 contains analysis, for the first time in a *How Ireland Voted* book, of the extent to which the incumbent government delivered on its promises. Chapter 3 examines the campaign strategies of the parties, while chapter 4 focuses on an important but usually hidden aspect of this, namely the way all the parties selected their Dáil candidates. In chapter 5, four candidates convey the agony and the ecstasy of the campaign.

Chapters 6 and 7 analyse the results; the former establishing, broadly speaking, what happened, and the latter analysing the available survey data to try to answer the question of why it happened. One of the unexpected features of the 2002 election was what was perceived to be a poor performance by the opinion polls, and chapter 8 asks whether they did any better this time. Chapter 9, in another first for the series, examines the relationship between the election and the betting markets – not to advise readers how to make money but to ask whether the markets offered a guide to what would happen. Chapter 10 examines the interaction between the media and the election campaign and discusses the extent to which the media itself became the story. In Chapter 11 the low-visibility but high-intensity election to the Seanad, the upper house of parliament, is analysed, and chapter 12 tells the story of how the three-party coalition government, one that few people had expected when they voted, emerged from the post-election negotiations. Finally, chapter 13 places the election, and the position of Fianna Fáil in particular, in a long-term and comparative context, while the appendices contain the full election results, information on all 166 TDs, and other useful information.

At the front of the book we have included, for the first time, a chronology of the election campaign, which should help readers puzzled by references throughout the book to 'Bertiegate', 'the Rumble in Ranelagh', 'the Great Debate', the *'Late Late'* or 'Meltdown Manor'. This is followed by what some will feel is the most fascinating feature of the book, a selection of photographs and campaign literature that conveys, perhaps even better than words, the spirit of election 2007. We thank the *Irish Independent* for permission to reproduce these photos, and Gerry Mulligan and Brian Bergin for helping us to obtain them, and we appreciate the great work of Séin Ó Muineacháin in sourcing the campaign literature. We would also like to thank Fine Gael and the *Wexford Echo* and *Connacht Tribune* for jpeg files of Fine Gael vote management advertisements that appeared in those newspapers.

As always, we thank our contributors, who responded with the appropriate combination of cooperation, patience and alacrity to the demands of a book being produced on a very tight schedule. We are pleased that this volume, like its predecessor, is being published by the major international publisher Palgrave Macmillan, and in particular we would like to thank Alison Howson for her enthusiastic response to our initial proposal and Amy Lankester-Owen for fast-tracking it through the production schedule.

Michael Gallagher and Michael Marsh
Dublin, October 2007

Glossary

Áras an Uachtaráin, residence of the President of Ireland
ard-fheis (plural ard-fheiseanna), national conference (of a political party)
Ceann Comhairle, speaker or chairperson (of the Dáil)
Dáil Éireann, directly-elected lower house of parliament to which the Irish
    government is answerable
Fianna Fáil, largest party in Ireland
Fine Gael, second largest party in Ireland
Leinster House, seat of houses of parliament
Oireachtas, parliament (has two houses: Dáil and Seanad)
Seanad Éireann, indirectly-elected upper house of parliament
Sinn Féin, republican party
Tánaiste, deputy prime minister
Taoiseach, prime minister
Teachta Dála, Dáil deputy

List of Abbreviations

DUP	Democratic Unionist Party
EP	European Parliament
ESB	Electricity Supply Board
ETF	Electoral Task Force (committee in Green Party)
FF	Fianna Fáil
FG	Fine Gael
GAA	Gaelic Athletic Association
Grn	Green Party
Ind	Independent
Lab	Labour Party
MEP	Member of the European Parliament
MW	Mid-West
N	North
NC	North-Central
NE	North-East
NW	North-West
OCSC	Organisation of Candidate Selection Committee (in Fine Gael)
OECD	Organisation for Economic Cooperation and Development
OMOV	one member one vote
OSC	Organisation Sub-Committee (in Labour)
PbP	People before Profit
PDs	Progressive Democrats
PR-STV	proportional representation by means of the single transferable vote
RTÉ	Radio Telefís Éireann, the national broadcasting station
S	South
SC	South-Central
SDLP	Social Democratic and Labour Party, second largest nationalist party in Northern Ireland
SE	South-East
SF	Sinn Féin
STV	single transferable vote
SW	South-West
TD	Teachta Dála

Chronology of 2007 Election Campaign

Sun 29 Apr   At 8 a.m., Taoiseach Bertie Ahern calls on President McAleese and advises her to dissolve 29th Dáil. Election set for Thursday 24 May. PDs publish their manifesto within hours of the announcement.

30 Apr   Mahon tribunal, established to investigate incidence of corruption in Irish public life, announces that it will suspend its hearings until the election is over, thus ensuring that potentially damaging new allegations against the Taoiseach, to which he would have been unable to respond, are not aired.

1 May   Green Party launches its manifesto.

3 May   FF and Labour launch manifestos; FF launch hijacked by further questions to the Taoiseach about his finances (the affair known generically as 'Bertiegate') from journalist Vincent Browne.

4 May   PD leader Michael McDowell announces that he needs to reflect on issues relating to Bertie Ahern's finances.

5 May   PD leadership group meets. Amidst speculation that the party is on the verge of withdrawing from the government, the leadership decides not to do that but instead to consult wider parliamentary party.

Sun 6 May   Michael McDowell says he has come into information that suggests information he was given by Ahern last autumn about his finances was 'selective at best', and requests further 'clarification' from Ahern.

7 May   FG launches its manifesto.

8 May   Closing date for nomination of election candidates.

      Campaign overshadowed by events at Stormont, where the Northern Ireland Executive is re-established after more than four years, with Ian Paisley (DUP) as First Minister and Sinn Féin's Martin McGuinness as Deputy First Minister. Much coverage of Bertie Ahern, who was present as one of the architects of the event. Meanwhile, at FF press conference in Dublin several FF ministers emphatically rule out possibility of coalition with SF after election under any circumstances.

11 May   First opinion poll since recent controversy over Ahern finances shows FF support up slightly since last poll in same TNS mrbi/*Irish Times* series. Campaign overshadowed by historic visit by Bertie Ahern and Ian Paisley to site of the 1690 Battle of the Boyne in Co. Meath.

Sun 13 May   Taoiseach issues detailed statement regarding his finances; Michael McDowell pronounces himself satisfied.

14 May   Brian Cowen says that with their economic policies FG and Lab are trying to foist a 'con job' on the Irish people.

15 May   Bertie Ahern delivers an address to the joint houses of parliament at Westminster, the first Taoiseach to do so.

16 May   Sinn Féin launches manifesto. TV debate between leaders of Labour, PDs, Greens and SF, in which Gerry Adams of SF is generally perceived to

	have fared worst. Michael McDowell delivers the most quoted soundbite, saying 'I'm surrounded by the left, the hard left and the leftovers'.
17 May	Pat Rabbitte says that as far as he's concerned there's no prospect of Labour doing business with FF after the election. Two FF ministers, Brian Lenihan and Willie O'Dea, again rule out any arrangement with SF after election.

TV debate between leaders of FF and FG, which Bertie Ahern is generally perceived to have won.

The so-called 'Rumble in Ranelagh', probably the most photogenic event of the campaign, takes place. Michael McDowell stages a media event, putting a poster on a telegraph pole as in 2002, but the event is gatecrashed by senior Green politician John Gormley, who disputes McDowell's criticisms of his party's policies.

18 May	Bertie Ahern says that while he'd be happy with continuation of present government, he'd 'have no difficulty' doing business with Labour; Pat Rabbitte says 'forget it, Bertie'.

RTÉ's flagship *Late Late Show* features three prominent commentators – Eamon Dunphy, Eoghan Harris, John Waters – discussing the election, and the latter two endorse FF. Some complaints that the programme was biased, and some post-election analyses attach importance to the role of the debate given the programme's huge viewership.

19 May	Pundits' predictions concur on a figure of around 68 seats for FF, with FG at around 50, Labour at around 20, SF and the Greens at around 10 each, and the PDs in the 1–4 range. Kathy Sheridan, writing in *Irish Times*, says some staff working in FF campaign headquarters have dubbed the building 'Meltdown Manor'.
Sun 20 May	RED C and Millward Brown IMS opinion polls in agreement that FF is heading for poor result.
21 May	New TNS/mrbi opinion poll in *Irish Times* shows surge in FF support, leading pundits to revise forecasts.
23 May	Nurses' dispute, which has been running for over seven weeks, is effectively resolved after the main union agrees to settlement proposals.
24 May	**Election day**
25 May	Counting of votes begins, finishes early hours 27 May. PD leader and Tánaiste Michael McDowell, having lost his seat in Dublin SE, dramatically announces that he is quitting politics with immediate effect.
28 May	Mahon tribunal resumes, with its counsel outlining a series of damaging allegations against the Taoiseach, which his lawyers vigorously reject.
3 Jun	FF and Green Party open discussions on possible coalition government after exchange of position papers.
7 Jun	In High Court, Mr Justice Frank Clarke dismisses a case brought by Finian McGrath and Catherine Murphy, both Independent TDs in the 29th Dáil, to the effect that the Oireachtas was in breach of its constitutional obligations by its failure to revise the constituency boundaries following the publication of the 2006 census figures.
8 Jun	After six days' talks FF and Greens say they've been unable to reach agreement. Both parties say good progress was made and breakdown isn't necessarily final. It's known that FF held meetings with several Independent TDs during this time; there are rumours (later established as inaccurate) that it has also been in contact with Labour.

12 Jun	FF–Green talks, having resumed, conclude with an agreement.
13 Jun	In accordance with its constitution, Green Party puts the agreement to a hastily-convened conference, held in Dublin's Mansion House, of all its members. Programme needs approval of two-thirds of members and achieves 87 per cent: 508 members vote, and it's passed by 441 to 67. Party leader Trevor Sargent announces that while he supports the programme, he's now standing down as leader and won't accept a cabinet post if offered one, given that he said before the election that he wouldn't lead the party into government with FF.
	Meanwhile, FF parliamentary party unanimously approves programme; by this stage, FF has concluded agreements with Independent TDs Healy-Rae, Lowry and McGrath.
14 Jun	The 30th Dáil meets for the first time, elects Bertie Ahern as Taoiseach, and approves the nomination of members of the government, who come from FF (12 ministers), the Green party (2) and the PDs (1).
22 Jun	Closing date for nomination of Seanad candidates.
10 Jul	Tom Parlon, the front-runner to become the next PD leader, announces that he is leaving politics to become chief executive of the Construction Industry Federation, deepening the doubts about the survival of the PDs.
17 Jul	John Gormley succeeds Trevor Sargent as leader of Green Party by winning 65 per cent of the votes cast by party members.
23 Jul	At 11 a.m. the poll closes in Seanad elections and counting of the votes begins.
27 Jul	Counting of votes in Seanad election ends: 43 senators from panels, and 6 returned by university graduates, have been elected to the 23rd Seanad.
3 Aug	Taoiseach announces the names of his 11 nominations to the 60-member Seanad, thus finalising the composition of the Oireachtas.
23 Aug	Pat Rabbitte announces his resignation as leader of the Labour Party, thus becoming the third party leader to step down in the wake of the election.
6 Sep	Éamon Gilmore is elected unopposed as the new Labour leader and, four weeks later, Joan Burton is elected as deputy leader.

Illustrations

Except where it is indicated otherwise, or is campaign literature, all photographs are reproduced by courtesy of the *Irish Independent*.

Bertie Ahern, FF leader, launches the party's campaign and its manifesto, 3 May ...

... but the event was dominated by Vincent Browne's questions on 'Bertiegate'.

One of several FG posters highlighting
failure in a public service.

Enda Kenny with FG Education
spokesperson Olwyn Enright.

Posters in Dublin SE constituency for Michael McDowell (PD), Rory Hearne
(People before Profit), Ruairí Quinn (Lab), Jim O'Callaghan (FF),
Lucinda Creighton (FG), John Gormley (Greens) and Chris Andrews (FF) –
as well as a couple for the Rathmines Festival.

Joe Higgins (Dublin W), the lone Socialist Party deputy in the 29th Dáil, details the evils of 10 years of FF–PD government and asks working people for a No. 1 or the 'highest possible preference' (the small print). Higgins was a surprise election loser.

Election literature from Niall Blaney (FF, Donegal NE),
the latest member of a Dáil dynasty dating back to 1927.

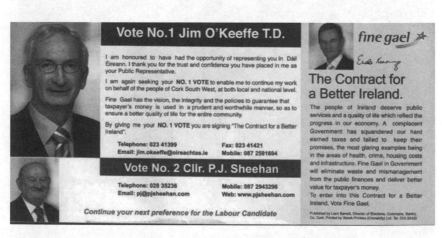

Jim O'Keeffe asks for your No.1 vote in Cork SW, as well as a No. 2
for his redoubtable running mate P. J. Sheehan and the next
preference for the (unnamed) Labour candidate.

The standard PD candidate literature came with a cartoon on the reverse side.

Jeff Aherne (PD, Kildare N) warns of the dangers posed by Labour and the Greens.

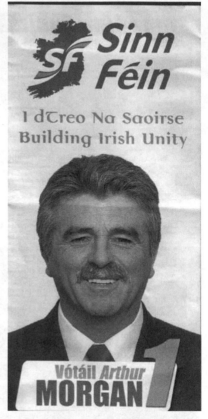

New candidate but well known businessman Brody Sweeney (FG, Dublin NE) introduces himself to the electorate.

Sinn Féin TD Arthur Morgan (Louth) reminds voters in his border constituency of the party's traditional message.

Finian McGrath TD (Dublin NC) makes a successful pitch for re-election.

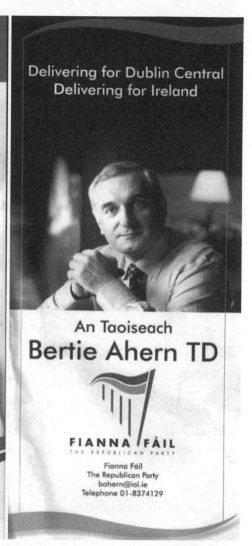

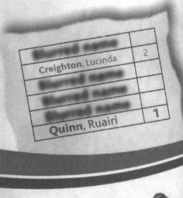

A Special Message from Ruairi Quinn

To all those who believe it's time for change:

If you want me to continue working for you in the Dáil, I need your Number 1 Vote. Remember, last time I only just won the last seat, so every vote counts.

If you think it's time for a real change, I ask that, when you have given me your Number 1 vote, you give your next preference to the Fine Gael candidate to ensure that Dublin South East delivers, along with me, representatives who will be a force for change.

Labour

Delivering for Dublin Central
Delivering for Ireland

An Taoiseach
Bertie Ahern TD

FIANNA FÁIL
THE REPUBLICAN PARTY

Fianna Fáil
The Republican Party
bahern@iol.ie
Telephone 01-8374129

Ruairí Quinn assures voters that his seat is not safe and asks his supporters to give their second preference to the FG candidate.

Bertie Ahern reminds his constituents – as if they needed reminding – that he is not just Taoiseach but also the local TD.

Joanne Spain (SF, Dublin MW) and party leader Gerry Adams promise to deliver.

Another PD cartoon. The party ended up in government with one of the crocodiles.

FG poster that was designed to attack FF's record but on a superficial glance
seemed to be promoting that party.

Charlie Flanagan (FG, Laois–Offaly) won back the seat he lost in 2002.

Carrying Bertie Ahern and his team to the top of the hill: near Tuam, Galway East.

Tony Gregory, long-serving independent TD for Dublin Central, has to put up his own posters in Phibsborough as the campaign gets under way.

'You're fired!': Enda Kenny with cut-out copies of FF ministers.

'Vote No. 1 Fergus O'Dowd' car hides poster for FG running mate in Louth.

Enda Kenny signs his contract with the Irish people for the photographers.

Independent, FF, Labour and SF posters together on a bridge in Dublin NC.

Enda Kenny places a bet that these two FG candidates, Regina Doherty and footballer Graham Geraghty, will be elected in the Meath constituencies, but the FG leader would lose his money as neither was successful.

Enda Kenny campaigning with party candidate
Ann Marie Martin (right) in a hairdresser's in Dublin SC.

Enda Kenny up for a tune from a Romanian accordion player, Kildare South.

Enda Kenny in positive mood on the trail.   Enda Kenny with a winning FG leader.

Bertie Ahern campaigns in Dublin's Moore Street market with running mates Cyprian Brady and Mary Fitzpatrick.

Door to door in Dublin Central: Bertie on the canvass with his wife Miriam Ahern.

Tánaiste and Taoiseach with First Minister Ian Paisley at the Battle of the Boyne site.

Bertie Ahern is 8/11 to be next Taoiseach too, according to Paddy Power.

Michael McDowell showing the strain as
he is asked to explain why he decided to
stay in government (again).

On 17 May Liz O'Donnell, Michael
McDowell and Tom Morrissey try
to repeat history with a new poster
in Ranelagh ...

... but it turns into 'the rumble in Ranelagh' as the Greens' John Gormley gatecrashes
the PD photo op and confronts Michael McDowell, to the delight of the media.

An Taoiseach addresses the British Parliament at Westminster. Enda Kenny listens, along with the SDLP's former leader John Hume and current leader Mark Durkan.

Guide dog Neff poses for photographers in
Paddy Power bookmakers beside a famous friend.

Pat Rabbitte rides out, watched by
Kathleen O'Meara (Lab, Tipperary N).

Enda Kenny and FG's deputy leader
Richard Bruton give the government
its marching orders.

Three faces of Labour leader Pat Rabbitte.

Green deputy leader and future TD Mary White (Carlow–Kilkenny) with a burned-out car dumped at her home.

Green party leader Trevor Sargent on safari, followed by Ciarán Cuffe with future leader John Gormley bringing up the rear.

Hard questions? SF's Mary Lou McDonald, MEP and candidate in Dublin Central, at her party's press launch.

Men in suits: the leaders of the smaller parties line up before their four-way TV debate in the RTÉ studio, 16 May. From left: Pat Rabbitte (Lab), Gerry Adams (SF), Michael McDowell (PD), Trevor Sargent (Grn).

Bertie Ahern and Enda Kenny prepare to make their opening addresses to start the Great Debate on 17 May, which was watched by almost two-thirds of voters.

Vote management advice for FG supporters in Wexford, who are asked in this newspaper advertisement to give their No. 1 to Michael D'Arcy in the light-shaded areas, Liam Twomey in the south-east of the constituency (Wexford town and south-eastern New Ross electoral area) and Paul Kehoe in Enniscorthy and north-western New Ross.

Putting You First in Galway East

Dr. John Barton   Senator Ulick Burke   Paul Connaughton T.D.   Councillor Tom McHugh

The Contract For A Better Ireland

- Free Health Insurance for all children under 16.
- 2,3000 more hospital beds.
- 2,000 more Gardai on the streets.
- Tougher sentences, tougher bail for criminals.
- Appoint Minister to take charge of immigration.
- Your money well spent, by sacking wasteful Ministers.
- Dramatic reduction in Stamp Duty for all buyers.
- Lower income tax for every taxpayer.

fine gael

For a winning Fine Gael team in Galway East, I ask you to

Vote 1–2 In the order of your choice for
Paul Connaughton
and
Cllr. Tom McHugh
IN THE NORTHERN HALF OF THE CONSTITUENCY
and continue your preferences for
Dr. John Barton and Ulick Burke.

Enda Kenny, T.D. Leader of Fine Gael

Vote 1–2 in order of your choice for
Dr. John Barton
and
Ulick Burke
IN THE SOUTHERN HALF OF THE CONSTITUENCY.
and continue your preferences for
Paul Connaughton and Cllr. Tom McHugh.

Together we're better – *Vote Fine Gael*

Fine Gael advertisement in the *Connacht Tribune* 18 May, spelling out the party's vote management scheme in Galway East. Supporters in the northern half were asked to vote 1 – 2 (in any order) for Paul Connaughton and Tom McHugh, while those in the south were asked to support John Barton and Ulick Burke, again in any order, before going on to support the other FG candidates. Burke and Connaughton were elected.

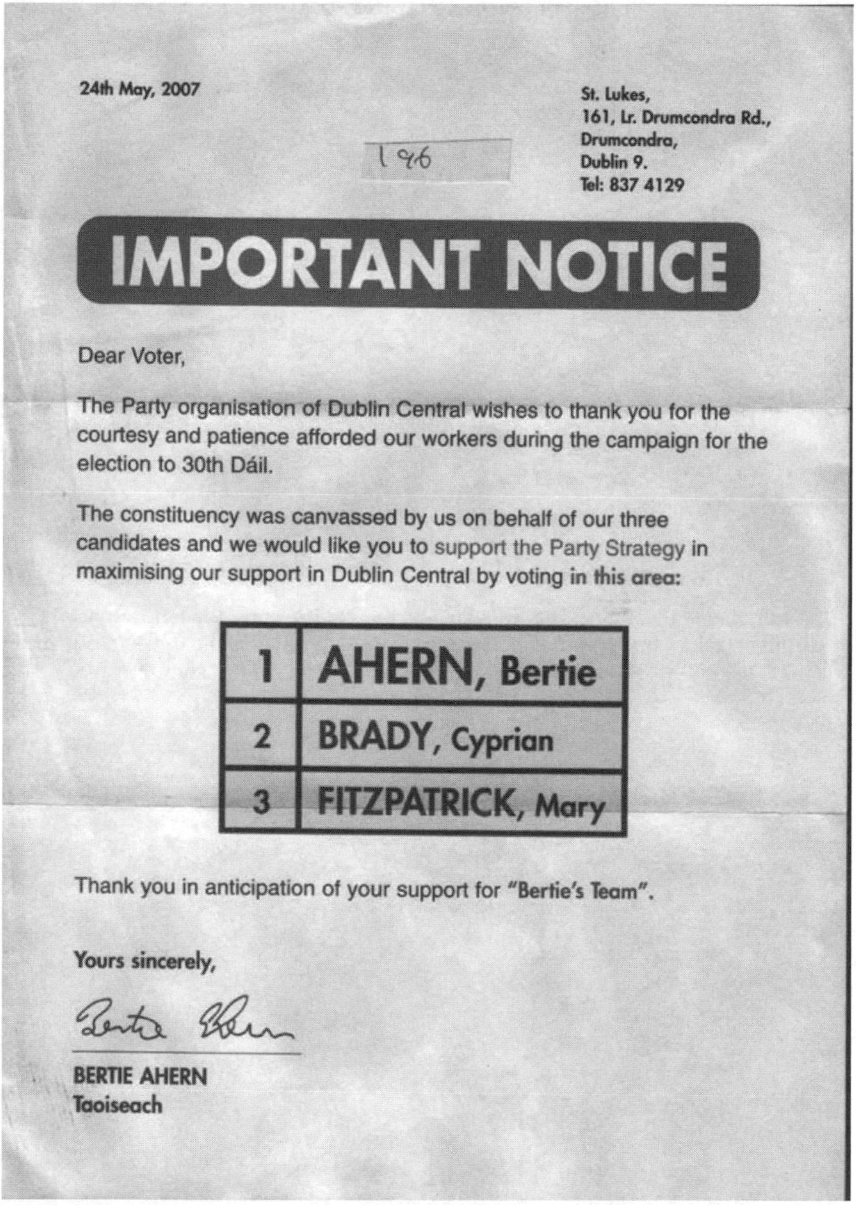

24th May, 2007

St. Lukes,
161, Lr. Drumcondra Rd.,
Drumcondra,
Dublin 9.
Tel: 837 4129

| 96 |

IMPORTANT NOTICE

Dear Voter,

The Party organisation of Dublin Central wishes to thank you for the courtesy and patience afforded our workers during the campaign for the election to 30th Dáil.

The constituency was canvassed by us on behalf of our three candidates and we would like you to support the Party Strategy in maximising our support in Dublin Central by voting in this area:

1	AHERN, Bertie
2	BRADY, Cyprian
3	FITZPATRICK, Mary

Thank you in anticipation of your support for "Bertie's Team".

Yours sincerely,

[signature]

BERTIE AHERN
Taoiseach

The famous last-minute letter circulated by Fianna Fáil in Dublin Central. Despite a very small first preference vote Cyprian Brady was elected thanks to receiving a large number of Ahern's surplus votes. Mary Fitzpatrick, who lost out, was not impressed at being ranked last of the three FF candidates (see p. 99 below).

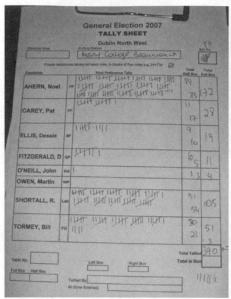

A tallyman's sheet from Dublin NW, keeping track of first preferences for the candidates in individual polling districts.

Counters on the left watched by tallymen on the right, in one of the Dublin count centres.

Counters and tallymen in Galway East, New Inn.

Opening a box of votes in Tymon North, Dublin.

Checking the votes in the RDS, Dublin: the tallyman with his clipboard looks on.

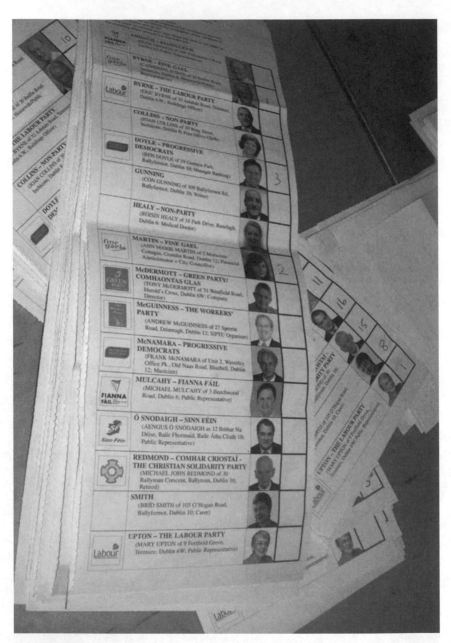

Completed ballot paper from Dublin SC: 1 Byrne FG, 2 Martin FG, 3 Doyle PD.
The ballot paper visible below indicates a full list of preference votes, with
Ó Snodaigh SF being ranked number 16. Few ballots are completed fully in this way.

Celebrating victory in Dublin NE: new TD Terence Flanagan FG (see chapter 5)
and 10-term veteran Dr Michael Woods, FF.

New FG TD Lucinda Creighton and Ruairí Quinn, former Labour leader,
are elected in Dublin SE.

I'm in again! Tommy Broughan (Lab, Dublin NE) makes it four in a row.

Those who thought P. J. Sheehan (FG, Cork SW) was lost to the Dáil after his 2002 defeat were proved wrong, as the 74-year-old returns to Leinster House on 14 June.

Seán Connick (FF, Wexford), the first
wheelchair user to be elected to the Dáil.

Minister Martin Cullen (FF) tops the
poll in Waterford.

SF's Seán Crowe (Dublin SW) accepts commiserations on his shock defeat.

Tánaiste and PD leader Michael McDowell, having lost his seat in Dublin SE,
stuns television viewers and his own party by announcing his retirement
from politics with immediate effect.

Three FF members of the Dáil are siblings: brothers Tom Kitt (Dublin S) and Michael
Kitt (Galway E), both ministers of state, and new TD sister Áine Brady (Kildare N).
Their father Michael, and Áine Brady's husband Gerry, were also TDs.

Green negotiators Donal Geoghegan, Dan Boyle and John Gormley smile for the cameras at the start of negotiations with FF on 4 June.

FF negotiator and Minister for Finance (and next leader?), Brian Cowen, 4 June.

Richard Boyd Barrett (People Before Profit candidate in Dun Laoghaire), with the Irish Anti-War Movement outside the Green party conference on 13 June, calls on Green members not to support another Ahern government.

Green members endorse their party's participation in government and the leadership celebrates: Dan Boyle (left) with leader Trevor Sargent (centre), who has promised that he would not serve in a FF-led cabinet and so resigned his position.

The members of the new government, holding their seals of office, pose for pictures with President Mary McAleese.

1
The Background to the Election

Gary Murphy

The end of the 29th Dáil and the calling of the election

At 11 p.m. on Saturday 28 April 2007, journalists from the main news organisations received a call from government press secretary Mandy Johnston to be on standby to go to Áras an Uachtaráin at two hours' notice. At 6 a.m. the following morning the same journalists were alerted via text message or phone call from Ms Johnston advising them to meet her between 7 a.m. and 7.30 am at the Áras, the official residence of the President of Ireland. Just before 8 a.m., the Taoiseach Bertie Ahern turned up wearing his Sunday best at this rather unusual hour and went in to ask President Mary McAleese to dissolve the 29th Dáil. He re-emerged at 8.10 a.m. and left without taking any questions. In the meantime news organisations had been issued a statement on behalf of 'An Taoisech' (sic) announcing that the general election would take place on Thursday 24 May, thus heralding a three and a half week campaign, unusually long by Irish standards. The misspelling of the title 'Taoiseach' was symptomatic of the rather frayed nerves of the government heading into what looked like being an extremely tight general election. The rather bizarre behaviour of the Taoiseach in calling the election in this manner was to continue a number of hours later when he made a brief statement in Fianna Fáil election headquarters at Treasury Buildings and refused to take any questions. In his short statement the Taoiseach said that, once again, the moment had arrived for the people to decide Ireland's future: 'No one knows what the outcome of this election will be. The people have a real choice and two very different alternatives before them. That choice will frame Ireland's future, and the consequences of this election will be felt for many years to come', stated Ahern before he promptly left the stage.[1] The Taoiseach's admission that there was a clear choice for voters and that there was an alternative government on offer with a chance of winning the election betrayed the nervousness within government as to the outcome of

Leabharlanna Fhine Gall

the election. It was all remarkably different from the astonishingly confident launching of the 'showtime' 2002 general election.[2]

There was speculation that the timing of the Taoiseach's decision to dissolve the Dáil, and his refusal to answer questions, were connected with the fact that the Mahon tribunal, which had been investigating certain planning matters and payments for nigh on ten years, was due to open its public inquiry on Monday 30 April into the Quarryvale affair. The tribunal announced before Easter that it would begin its public session on Quarryvale (a large development in west Dublin) and would continue to sit in public until two weeks before the election. Mr Ahern, his former partner Celia Larkin, and those known to have given him money in 1993/94 were listed as witnesses at the tribunal.

Ahern had delivered on his promise made back in 2002 to serve a full five years as Taoiseach, leading a Fianna Fáil–Progressive Democrat coalition government. Unlike 2002, the outcome of this general election would be in doubt until right up to polling day. The incumbent government would face an opposition that offered an alternative to an electorate which, after ten years of Ahern with his unique consensual style, might have been in the mood for change. Moreover, by the time Ahern actually called the election, discussion of his personal finances had been a significant political news story (dubbed, inevitably, 'Bertiegate') ever since the *Irish Times* revealed in September 2006 that as Minister for Finance in 1993 and 1994 he had accepted payments of between €50,000 and €100,000 from a variety of business people and that the matter was being investigated by the Mahon tribunal.[3] The inquiries into Mr Ahern's finances began after allegations were made about supposed payments to him by property developer Owen O'Callaghan in relation to Quarryvale. Both Ahern and O'Callaghan stated publicly that no such payments had been made. On the day the election was called a spokesperson for Ahern was forced to reiterate this point, stating that the 'Taoiseach did not seek any monies, he received no monies, nor was he offered any monies from Mr O'Callaghan or by anybody connected with him … He never received money in connection with any tax designation for Quarryvale or anywhere else.'[4] The odd nature of Ahern's personal finances – apparently, while Minister for Finance in the first half of the 1990s he had had no bank account and had kept large amounts of cash in his office safe – would dominate the first half of the election campaign and cause significant difficulties that the Progressive Democrats in particular would not be able to shake off.

Up to the astonishing revelations on Ahern's financial situation, the Fianna Fáil–Progressive Democrat coalition that took office after the 2002 election proved remarkably stable. It was quickly established after the election despite the then Attorney General and PD candidate Michael McDowell's bitter denunciation of the dangers of single party Fianna Fáil government during the 2002 campaign when he complained that Fianna Fáil's plan for a national stadium, the so-called 'Bertie Bowl', had echoes of the Ceausescu regime in

Romania. After the election, which saw Fianna Fáil come agonisingly close to an overall majority, winning 81 of the 166 seats, Ahern quickly moved to establish a Fianna Fáil–Progressive Democrat government.[5] The Progressive Democrats had, against all media predictions, won eight seats, thereby doubling their representation and ensuring a comfortable majority for the incoming government. This was in contrast to the 1997–2002 coalition, which had relied on the support of four Independents for its existence. The 2002–07 Programme for Government was negotiated without any great drama. The major commitments on the economy were to continue the budgetary and economic strategy that had delivered general prosperity while keeping the public finances in a relatively healthy state. Specific commitments were given to remove all those on the minimum wage from the tax net, to ensure that 80 per cent of all earners paid tax only at the standard rate and to increase the state pension to €200 per week by 2007.

While the government's economic targets were broadly met (see chapter 2 for a detailed assessment of pledge fulfilment), it did have a rather awkward start to its tenure as it emerged after the 2002 election that the economy was not in as good a shape as Fianna Fáil in particular had suggested during the campaign. In September 2002 a secret memorandum was exposed in which the Minister for Finance Charlie McCreevy, shortly after the election, warned his cabinet colleagues of the need for major cutbacks and possible increases in taxation.[6] This led to calls for his resignation from the opposition, and accusations of deception proved rather difficult for the government to overcome. Such charges hung over the heads of both Fianna Fáil and the Progressive Democrats for the first half of the Dáil in particular. The failure of the government to complete other commitments over the course of its duration such as increasing the number of gardaí to 14,000 or the ludicrous and much-derided undertaking, voiced during the 2002 election campaign by Micheál Martin, to end hospital waiting lists allowed the opposition to point to a number of broken promises. In that context the 2007 campaign between two alternative coalitions, the outgoing Fianna Fail–Progressive Democrat government and the alliance for change of Fine Gael and Labour, with both the Greens and Sinn Féin also hoping to be in government in some shape or form, was set to be one of the most competitive in recent memory.

Party competition

Entering into the 2007 general election Fianna Fáil had been in power for 18 of the previous 20 years. While it had traditionally governed alone, often in minority governments, the party had broken one of its core values by going into coalition with the Progressive Democrats in 1989.[7] Fianna Fáil's commitment to coalition was copperfastened when, after a particularly poor election in 1992 where it dropped below 40 per cent of the first preference for the first time since the 1920s, it entered into another coalition, this time with the Labour Party. Once Fianna Fáil accepted the politics of coalition, party competition became more volatile and unstable, which was signified in 1994 by the change in government during the 27th Dáil when the Fianna Fáil–Labour government collapsed and was replaced by a coalition of Fine Gael, Labour and Democratic Left.[8] The 1997 election saw the return of Fianna Fáil to government, this time in partnership with the Progressive Democrats again, but also on a first preference share of the vote below 40 per cent. With most commentators assuming that the 1992 and 1997 results meant that Fianna Fáil would struggle to gain over 40 per cent of the vote in an increasingly congested political arena, there was much surprise in 2002 when the party received over 41 per cent of the vote and only barely missed out on an overall majority. The one persistent feature of Irish politics has been Fianna Fáil's hegemonic position (see chapter 13 for further discussion). Its decision to abandon its opposition to coalition government has presented it with a variety of new strategic opportunities and the party has unquestionably learned to take advantage of these. Ultimately, the core feature of the Irish party system remains Fianna Fáil dominance.[9]

The re-election in 2002 of the Fianna Fáil–Progressive Democrat coalition was especially noteworthy as this had been the first time in over 30 years that an outgoing government was returned to office. Moreover, both of the incumbent parties managed to increase their share of seats in the Dáil.[10] Ever since their foundation in 1985 as a small economically right-wing and socially liberal party, the Progressive Democrats had been confounding various media commentators who had constantly predicted their demise. With their re-election into a coalition government and a doubling of their seats from four to eight, the future looked extremely rosy for them. With an increased parliamentary party and two cabinet positions, they faced the post-2002 election landscape with bullish confidence. It would prove to be misplaced.

For Fine Gael, the 2007 election was an opportunity to lay the ghost of their disastrous outing in 2002. The early 1980s saw Fine Gael get to within five seats of Fianna Fáil and gain over 39 per cent of the first preference vote, being the dominant party in two coalition governments with the Labour Party. This, however, proved to be something of a false dawn, as by accepting coalition in 1989 Fianna Fáil opened itself up to alliances that would once have been the sole preserve of Fine Gael. The 2002 election was nothing short of a catastrophic disaster for Fine Gael. It won just over 22 per cent of the vote, down over 5 per cent on its 1997 showing, but lost 23 seats, leaving it with only 31 deputies in a parliamentary cull that saw many high-profile members lose their seats. By teatime on the day of the counting of votes in 2002 the Fine Gael leader Michael Noonan announced his resignation, stating on RTÉ television that the election result was 'beyond our expectations and beyond our worst fears. It's been a seriously bad election for our party.'[11] In the light of this result Fine Gael's position as the second party of the state was in jeopardy. Its reaction to the election over the course of the 29th Dáil could see it either rejuvenate itself or potentially collapse into irrelevance.

Crucial to the idea of an alternative government in 2007 was the Labour Party. In December 1998 Labour and Democratic Left (DL) merged into a new entity still to be called the Labour Party. It was hoped that the newly strengthened party would transform the fortunes of left-wing politics in Ireland, but this was dashed by the reality of the 2002 election when there was little change in Labour's strength. Some criticised Labour for failing to offer the electorate an alternative government by more firmly committing itself to a coalition with Fine Gael. Given Fine Gael's meltdown, such criticism was probably somewhat unwarranted. Yet with the failure of the party to make any electoral breakthrough after the merger, the 29th Dáil would present a serious test of Labour's ambitions for government.

The 2002 election had seen significant breakthroughs for two smaller parties with ultimate ambitions for government; the Green Party and Sinn Féin. The Greens came into the 29th Dáil with six seats, while Sinn Féin had five. Both hoped that their increased representation – up from two and one respectively – would enable them to significantly strengthen their TDs come the next election and allow them to be possible coalition partners for Fianna Fáil or part of an alliance led by Fine Gael and Labour. Added to this increasingly confusing mix was the startling success of Independents in the 2002 election, winning over 10 per cent of the vote and 8 per cent of the seats, rising from 7 to 14 seats. In essence the 2002 election returned an opposition that was much more fragmented than it had been in over half a century.[12] Another symptom of this was that voter volatility in 2002 was three times the level recorded in the early 1980s.[13] In this context political competition up to the calling of the 2007 election would remain fiercely competitive.

Leadership elections in Fine Gael and Labour

Faced with the prospect of five more years of opposition, both Fine Gael and Labour went for new leaders to revive their fortunes. Michael Noonan's resignation on election count night presented Fine Gael with a clean opportunity to elect a new leader. Labour's was to be a bit messier. Fine Gael party rules dictated that following the resignation of the party leader, its successor was to be elected within 30 days. The electoral body was limited to members of the Fine Gael parliamentary party, and in the summer of 2002 that meant 49 individuals: the depleted Dáil group, members of the outgoing Seanad and Members of the European Parliament. Despite some rumblings about the way to proceed, with a view expressed by some members that the party would do better to wait until the autumn, the opposite view best expressed by outgoing senator Maurice Manning prevailed: 'This is going to be the most competitive opposition in the history of the State. If Fine Gael is a bystander with no leader during the early formative life of this Dáil then we would risk having permanent damage inflicted upon us.'[14] Four names ended up on the ballot paper: Enda Kenny, a minister in the 1994–97 Rainbow coalition and a TD for Mayo since 1975; Richard Bruton, also a minister in the Rainbow government and a TD for Dublin North-Central since 1982; Gay Mitchell, a junior minister in the Rainbow government and a TD for Dublin South-Central since 1981; and Phil Hogan, briefly a junior minister in the Rainbow government and a TD for Carlow–Kilkenny since 1989. During the campaign there was a deliberate attempt to ensure that there would be no public bloodletting as there had been in the upheaval that ended John Bruton's tenure as leader in January 2001. The main focus of all four candidates was on the necessity to rebuild the Fine Gael organisation and rejuvenate the morale of the party faithful after its crushing election defeat. Gay Mitchell was the only candidate to spell out his message in any clear ideological way, placing Fine Gael firmly in the European Christian democratic tradition. This, however, did not go down too well with the parliamentary party constituency, which wanted a promise of better electoral days ahead. In that context they went for Enda Kenny, the Mayo TD who, while he had been in the Dáil for 27 years, would, according to one of his proposers, 'look well on posters and had a nice fresh face'.[15] The results were not made public, although it was reported that Kenny was ahead on the first count and after the elimination of Hogan and Mitchell, he easily saw off the challenge of Richard Bruton.[16] Kenny, who had previously lost out to Noonan, was 51 years of age on his election, and was faced not only with a decimated political party but with having to oppose a Taoiseach who had just led a government to re-election for the first time since 1969 and was reckoned to be the most popular politician of his generation. In these circumstances Kenny faced a gargantuan task to make Fine Gael relevant. It was a job he would prove to be up to.

Things were not so clear cut in the Labour Party. With its genuine high hopes for office scuppered by the revival of the Progressive Democrats, Labour faced a period of introspection immediately after the election. Its leader Ruairí Quinn initially indicated that he would be staying on but had changed his mind over the summer and in late August announced he was resigning the position he had held since late 1997. Quinn's election as leader had taken place under rules that allowed only those who were members of the parliamentary party and Labour's national administrative council to vote. In the intervening period, however, the voting mechanism had changed with the election of the new leader to take place under a one-member-one-vote system. This allowed members 'of good standing' for a minimum of two years who had paid their €5 party subscription for the previous year, to vote by post. In total, 3,942 members were entitled to vote. There were four candidates for the leadership: Brendan Howlin, the party's deputy leader from Wexford who had served in government between 1992 and 1997 and had lost out to Quinn for the leadership in 1997; Róisín Shortall, first elected in Dublin North-West in the Spring tide of 1992 and without ministerial experience; and two former

Democratic Left members, Eamon Gilmore of Dun Laoghaire and Pat Rabbitte of Dublin South-West. All four were pretty much agreed on policy issues but differed significantly in regard to political tactics. Shortall was the most hostile to coalition, advocating that the party remain outside government until it had a minimum of 40 seats. Given that in its history Labour had never even once reached this figure, such a stance might well result in its never entering government again. Howlin and Gilmore expressed their opposition to Fianna Fáil but did not rule out the possibility of going into government with it. Rabbitte was more clear cut in opposing coalition with Fianna Fáil and was widely seen as a critic of the Quinn–Howlin electoral strategy of keeping this option open. There was a view within the party that Rabbitte's background in Democratic Left might lessen his appeal among long-standing Labour Party members as there were only approximately 250 former DL members in the total electorate. However, his declaration prior to the general election that he would not serve as a Labour minister in a government involving Fianna Fáil gave him the status of challenger to the status quo within the party and the candidate for change.[17] This 'anti-Fianna Fáilism' was one of the key distinguishing factors between Rabbitte and Howlin, who quickly emerged as the front-runners.

Ultimately Rabbitte was comfortably elected, having been over 500 votes ahead of Howlin on the first count. Another former Democratic Left member, Liz McManus from Wicklow, was elected deputy leader, leaving some in Labour wondering whether they had been the victims of a Democratic Left takeover. On his election as leader Rabbitte pledged that his aim was to make Labour the great national voice of popular opposition to the government. With Fine Gael, Sinn Féin and the Greens all attempting to do the same thing, the Rabbitte–McManus leadership faced a severe task in not only trying to do this, but also trying to get Labour into government after the next general election.

The 2004 European and local elections

The 2004 local and European elections would be the first test of both Kenny and Rabbitte as party leaders. Both Fine Gael and Labour had participated in the second referendum on the Treaty of Nice held on 19 October 2002. Held some 16 months after the defeat of the original referendum, Fine Gael opted to fight a somewhat low-key campaign on which it spent some €150,000. Fine Gael's campaign for a Yes vote was unofficially spearheaded by former Taoiseach, the then 76-year-old Garret FitzGerald. Indeed, Fine Gael's commitment to the European Union as a defining principle of its domestic politics was put in some doubt by various media stories that it was willing to compromise on Nice to create a possible alternative coalition for government with the Greens.[18] The referendum coincided with the Labour leadership campaign, but this did not stop the party from advocating a Yes vote, despite some protests from individual members that it should oppose the Treaty. Politically, the main interest in the referendum was the performance of the government parties. The defeat of the first Nice Treaty had certainly come as an embarrassment to the government, particularly after the Minister for Community, Rural and Gaeltacht Affairs, Éamon Ó Cuív, declared he had voted against, even though he had campaigned for a Yes vote, while Minister for Finance Charlie McCreevy welcomed the No outcome on the basis that it showed the independent-mindedness of the electorate in the face of so much advice from the establishment to vote Yes. In the second referendum Fianna Fáil campaigned much more enthusiastically for a Yes vote. The final result saw a comfortable win for the Yes side, which gained just under 63 per cent of the vote on a significantly increased turnout of nearly 50 per cent compared to a turnout of less than 35 per cent in the first Nice referendum. With the referendum out of the way, the domestic political focus turned towards the local and European elections to be held in the summer of 2004.

The adoption of the Nice Treaty had one significant electoral consequence in that Ireland's representation in the European Parliament was reduced from 15 to 13. There were four constituencies: Dublin (four seats), East (three seats), North-West (three seats) and South (three seats). The European Parliament election was to prove a difficult one for the governing parties. The Progressive Democrats were unable to persuade anyone with a high public profile to run and so decided not to contest any of the constituencies, which left Fianna Fáil to take the brunt of any disgruntlement that the voters might be harbouring. With government satisfaction running at only 34 per cent in the opinion polls in the lead-up to the election, and the reduction in seats, Fianna Fáil faced an uphill battle to retain its six seats. The party's campaign was marred by internecine conflicts between its candidates in three of the constituencies. In South, sitting MEPs Brian Crowley and Gerard Collins clashed over canvassing strategy.[19] Dublin saw similar problems between Eoin Ryan and new boy on the block Royston Brady who was seen as Bertie Ahern's favourite candidate but whose campaign imploded under an unforgiving media spotlight. Meanwhile, North-West saw an unseemly nomination controversy involving Donegal TD Jim McDaid and sitting MEP Seán Ó Neachtain, who had gained his seat as a replacement for Pat 'The Cope' Gallagher after the latter had returned to national politics and taken up a junior ministry following his election as a TD in the 2002 general election.

With all the other parties hoping to do well at Fianna Fáil's expense, there was a surprisingly high turnout of 59 per cent on polling day, 11 June 2004, due partly to the decision to hold a simultaneous referendum on removing the automatic right to citizenship conferred by birth in Ireland. This was approved by 79 per cent of the electorate. Fine Gael was the big winner in the European elections, gaining a seat and overtaking Fianna Fáil, with five MEPs to that party's four. Its result in the East constituency was especially outstanding, as it took two of the three seats with newcomer Máiréad McGuinness topping the poll. Labour retained its seat in Dublin but failed to make an impact elsewhere. The Greens had a disastrous election, losing both their seats, including that of their two-term MEP Patricia McKenna in Dublin. McKenna's loss in Dublin came as a result of the spectacular rise in the Sinn Féin vote there; Mary Lou McDonald polled over 14 per cent of the vote, taking in excess of 60,000 first preference votes.

Fine Gael's electoral revival was mirrored in the local elections held on the same day. The local elections were seen by the political parties as an opportunity to blood potential new Dáil candidates, as the importance of a strong local profile has been an enduring feature of the Irish political system. This was particularly important for Fine Gael and Labour. The general expectation was that Fianna Fáil and Fine Gael would lose seats, especially considering their relatively strong performances in the 1999 elections, and that Sinn Féin would make significant gains, particularly in Dublin, building on its winning of two Dáil seats in the capital at the 2002 general election. The election was seen as a crucial test of Pat Rabbitte's leadership given the challenge on the left from Sinn Féin and the Greens. Again the high turnout led to some dramatic changes in voting patterns, with Sinn Féin and Labour increasing their votes and seats, particularly in Dublin. Fine Gael, although its share of the vote went down slightly to just over 27 per cent, succeeded in winning an extra 13 seats, bringing its overall total to 293. It won close to 19 per cent of the vote in Dublin and increased its seats from 25 to 27 and, more importantly, again elected a number of councillors who would fare well in the 2007 general election, such as Lucinda Creighton in Dublin South-East and Leo Varadkar in Dublin West – the latter gained almost two quotas and received the highest number of first preferences in the country.

For Fianna Fáil the results were nothing short of disastrous, as it lost 80 seats and just held off Fine Gael as the largest party of councillors. Its share of the vote fell to just 32 per cent nationally and 24 per cent in Dublin. Overall, the elections marked the lowest share of the vote that Fianna Fáil had won in a national election since 1927. Its partners in government, the Progressive Democrats, lost six seats and had a disappointing election, especially considering that they were not running any candidates in the European elections. Sinn Féin had an excellent election, gaining 33 seats, bringing its total to 54, and its 18 percentage share of the vote in Dublin seemed to presage great things for the party come the next general election. The local election results were satisfying for Labour, especially in Dublin where its vote held up in the face of the surge for Sinn Féin. Labour managed to win 18 extra seats nationally to break the 100 barrier mark by one, and emerged as the largest party in Dublin, winning nearly 20 per cent of the vote and 34 of 130 seats. The Greens won 18 seats, doubling their 1999 result, but this could not compensate for their disastrous European election result. Ultimately, though, what the local election results did raise was the possibility of an alternative government of Fine Gael, Labour and the Greens emerging to, at the very least, challenge the hegemony of Fianna Fáil and the Progressive Democrats at the next general election.[20]

There was the possibility of a presidential election in 2004 as President McAleese's seven-year term came to an end. Fine Gael, having had bitter experience in losing the 1990 and 1997 elections, had no interest in putting up a candidate against the popular incumbent. Labour leader Pat Rabbitte began 2004 by proclaiming that he wanted Labour to contest the presidential election, but later changed his mind about a Labour candidacy. As the closing date for nominations loomed there was some uncertainty as to whether Labour's veteran former minister Michael D. Higgins was interested in seeking a nomination to contest the presidency. The Greens later got in on the act and their Dublin South TD, Eamon Ryan, announced in September his intention to seek a nomination, which Pat Rabbitte stated that Labour would facilitate and support. In the course of a rather frantic week, President McAleese declared that she was to seek re-election, Labour's national executive voted by 13 to 12 not to contest the election despite intensive canvassing from Higgins for a nomination, and Ryan withdrew his name from the race after the Greens decided not to run a candidate. Independent candidate Dana Rosemary Scallon then failed to secure the requisite nominations from county councillors with the result that President McAleese was deemed re-elected as the only candidate.[21] The parties were able to keep their powder dry for the election that really mattered, the election to the 30th Dáil.

The Mullingar Accord and changes within government

September 2004 also saw Fine Gael and Labour publicly commit themselves to begin negotiations for an alternative government to be put before the people at the general election. Speaking at Belvedere House in Mullingar in County Westmeath, both Kenny and Rabbitte said that the message from the public after the local and European elections was that there should be such an alternative. In a joint statement, they welcomed what they called the 'Mullingar Accord'. They travelled to Mullingar to hail a power-sharing agreement between their parties on Westmeath County Council as 'a good indicator of how enhanced co-operation among the main opposition parties could produce a meaningful and decent alternative to the failed policies of the present Government'.[22]

The Mullingar pact was of little significance in itself. The two parties already cooperated with each other on a number of other councils, and both had also done similar deals with Fianna Fáil on other local authorities. However, the two leaders decided to use the Westmeath arrangement to build on the European and local election results to move towards presenting themselves jointly, perhaps together with the Greens, as an alternative government in the next general election campaign. Indeed, Rabbitte said that the only reason the Green Party was not involved in the initial accord was that it had no councillors in Westmeath – which may have been news to the Greens, who would hold steadfast to an independent line all the way to the 2007 general election. At the same time that Fine Gael and Labour were committing themselves to their accord, Fianna Fáil's parliamentary party was meeting in Inchydoney, west Cork, to review its own electoral performance and plan strategy not only for the coming Dáil term, but also for the looming general election. These September meetings had been a feature of Bertie Ahern's leadership and featured a number of prominent guest speakers. The star guest on this occasion was Father Seán Healy, the head of the Conference of Religious in Ireland, who had sharply criticised all of the government's budgets since Fianna Fáil and the Progressive Democrats had taken office in 1997. While acknowledging that the economy had done very well, he pointed to the large number of individuals who he claimed had been left behind. He demanded that social welfare rates should rise, extra money should be spent on community employment schemes, all children should have medical cards, and tax credits should be refundable.[23] Father Healy's demands seemed to have a somewhat peculiar impact on Bertie Ahern in particular, as by November he was declaring himself to be 'one of the few socialists left in Irish politics'.[24]

Three weeks after the Inchydoney think-in, Bertie Ahern reshuffled his cabinet. Back in July Ahern had announced his Minister for Finance, Charlie McCreevy, as Ireland's nomination to the European Commission. Despite protestations from both Ahern and McCreevy that they had agreed on this move as far back as September 2003, there were few who saw McCreevy's nomination as anything other than a demotion out of the Department of Finance for political reasons. In essence McCreevy had become the fall guy for Fianna Fáil's local and European electoral difficulties, with rumblings within the party that its national electoral future could be salvaged only if McCreevy was moved and a new, more caring image adopted. Ahern's new cabinet, announced on 29 September, saw McCreevy replaced as Minister for Finance by Brian Cowen. After the reforming zeal of McCreevy, Cowen would prove to be a cautious minister whose aim would be to direct more resources towards the lower paid and less well-off. His first budget would, for instance, see social welfare payments, tax bands and credits all significantly increased. The other major significant shift in the cabinet was the appointment of the Progressive Democrats' leader, Mary Harney, as Minister for Health. To general political astonishment Harney revealed that she had actually volunteered for the post, memorably termed 'Angola' by Cowen as a place where landmines can go off without warning. With the state of the health services seen as a crucial issue in the forthcoming general election, it was a brave decision which could have either perilous or rewarding consequences. McCreevy's departure to Brussels and John Bruton's appointment as EU ambassador to the United States necessitated by-elections in Kildare North and Meath respectively. Fianna Fáil lost McCreevy's seat to the Independent left-wing candidate Catherine Murphy, while Fine Gael held Bruton's seat with first-time candidate Shane McEntee holding off the Fianna Fáil challenge. This was an important result for Fine Gael in its continuing battle to convince the national electorate that it was a serious contender for government.[25]

The Progressive Democrats had polled poorly in both elections, and a month later in April 2005, at their annual conference, Harney declared that the party was not tied to a coalition with Fianna Fáil and would be willing to serve in government with Fine Gael and Labour, but notably, given the ultimate outcome of the 2007 general election, not with the Greens whose economic policies she described as 'crazy'.[26] The removal of McCreevy had not only deprived the Progressive Democrats of a valuable ally in government, it had also taken away the one senior cabinet member who in effect had straddled both coalition partners. In that context Harney's conference speech served as a reminder that the Progressive Democrats were an independent party who might well have a choice as to whom to share government with after the election. Harney had made similar utterances in June 2004, warning Fianna Fáil not to take the Progressive Democrats for granted. Fianna Fáil for its part had been maintaining contact with a number of Independent TDs, two of whom, Jackie Healy-Rae and Niall Blaney, had explicitly stated that they would be willing to support a minority Fianna Fáil administration if the party wished to end its coalition with the Progressive Democrats.

Politically, things hotted up considerably within the Progressive Democrats when, in the summer of 2006, Minister for Justice and party president Michael McDowell pressed Harney to honour what he perceived to be a commitment to step down as leader – and, presumably, make way for him. McDowell, long seen as the leading intellectual force within the party, had been somewhat of a crusading minister for justice and came forward with a whole range of ideas, including so-called Asbos for young offenders, café-style bars as replacement for traditional public houses, and the creation of a garda reserve force. He tackled with enthusiasm the vexed question of overtime in the prison service and had also successfully steered through the controversial citizenship referendum in June 2004 which tightened the citizenship rules for immigrants. Michael McDowell's main political achievement as Minister for Justice came in relation to Northern Ireland. In the ongoing negotiations on the northern settlement he fought an extremely strong rearguard action to ensure that the ending of IRA criminality had to be part of any political deal. Despite huge pressure from Sinn Féin in particular, the rather ambiguous position of Fianna Fáil, and the desire of the British government to actually ignore the issue, McDowell eventually prevailed and was instrumental in persuading the Democratic Unionist Party (DUP) to accept power-sharing in the North. This was no mean feat in the light of the Northern Bank robbery of December 2004, the IRA murder of Robert McCartney in January 2005 and ongoing Sinn Féin attempts to get the government to order the release of the IRA killers of Detective Garda Jerry McCabe. Ultimately, though, it was clear to all political observers that McDowell longed for the leadership of his party and was putting pressure on Harney to step aside.

Harney resisted such pressure amid media reports that suggested that the residue of personal bitterness and enduring divisions between members of the parliamentary party were threatening the very survival of the Progressive Democrats.[27] The divisions within the party may have been to do with both personality clashes and the fact that its flagship policy, tax cuts for the middle class, had become to all intents and purposes redundant due to the steady lowering of taxes over successive budgets. McDowell's ambition for the leadership of the party was not to be denied, however, and he duly became leader on 11 September 2006, just four days after Harney had stepped down as leader, stating that she felt her decision was in the best interests of the party. No other candidates emerged to challenge him and he was elected unopposed as party leader. He also became Tánaiste (deputy prime minister) in the government. Within two weeks McDowell would be thrown head-first into the most sensational controversy in Irish politics in the nine years of Bertie Ahern as Taoiseach with the *Irish Times* revelation about Ahern's finances.

Given the significant controversy that the first Fianna Fáil–Progressive Democrat coalition had been mired in, from revelations at the various tribunals of inquiry to the Philip Sheedy affair and the nomination of Justice Hugh O'Flaherty to the European Investment Bank,[28] the coalition elected in 2002 was remarkably serene, with very few political controversies until the payments to the Taoiseach were revealed. The tribunals into various aspects of alleged corruption had continued to work away, almost as part of the background to Irish politics, rarely commanding the headlines. There was an exception in September 2002 when the Flood tribunal issued a stinging interim report, concluding that former senior Fianna Fáil minister Ray Burke had received corrupt payments from a number of builders. The report also stated that during his time as Minister for Communications Burke had made decisions that were not in the public interest after receiving what Mr Justice Flood considered to be a corrupt payment from Oliver Barry of Century Radio in 1989.[29] Burke was eventually jailed for six months in January 2005 for failing to make tax returns on over £100,000 over a ten-year period between 1982 and 1991, becoming the first person to be jailed as a result of tribunal investigations and the first ex-minister in the history of the state to be imprisoned on criminal charges.[30]

The profile of the work of the tribunals was also raised dramatically in September 2006, due to the political controversy that followed the *Irish Times* revelations about the Taoiseach's finances. The opposition parties launched fierce attacks on Ahern's behaviour, and for a brief period it looked as if Michael McDowell might pull the Progressive Democrats out of government. Fianna Fáil let it be known that if this did happen it would carry on in government anyway. The party came out strongly in defence of the Taoiseach, with senior figures robustly defending him in a variety of media outlets. The turning point in the controversy came when Ahern gave a long television interview to RTÉ's Bryan Dobson on 26 September, broadcast in full on the 6.01 News, in which he gave details of payments totalling IR£39,000 made to him by friends during difficult personal circumstances in the early 1990s while he had been Minister for Finance.[31] Ahern also revealed that he had received a further payment of IR£8,000 after a personal trip to Manchester to watch a football game and attend a dinner. He explained that the payments were in effect a 'dig-out' from friends during a period of personal difficulty for him in relation to the break-up of his marriage. This went down well with the general public and in the first opinion poll after the controversy there was a dramatic eight-point rise in support for Fianna Fáil, with Ahern's own ratings also improving slightly, even though, rather contradictorily, 64 per cent of those polled thought that he had been wrong to take the money.[32] The startling result of this poll, which saw both Fine Gael and Labour support drop while the Progressive Democrats rose slightly, seemed to settle any frayed nerves in government and both parties settled down to prepare for the budget. This poll would also have the consequence of making Fine Gael and Labour very wary of raising the issue of the Taoiseach's finances during the election campaign itself. The lure of power, it seems, was too much for McDowell to walk out on. He salved his conscience by announcing that he had secured an agreement from the Taoiseach that an ethics bill would be drafted to cover the issue of gifts or loans from friends in the future, and on that basis he stayed in government.

Countdown to the election

The 2007 election would see the Irish electorate vote in the traditional manner, by writing numbers on paper. Electronic voting, first used in three constituencies in the 2002 general election,[33] had proved controversial. The voting machines were again used in some constituencies in the second Nice referendum, with plans to roll them out to all constituencies in future national elections. In February 2004, amidst rising public concern about electronic voting, the government announced plans to establish an independent commission to verify the security of the machines, which were due to be used in the June local and European elections. The government also decided to introduce legislation to ensure that e-voting results could not be challenged in the courts. By April 2004 it was reported that over 90 per cent of submissions to the commission stated that the system was flawed, and by the end of the month plans to use the machines for the June elections were dropped when the commission stated that the security of the system could not be guaranteed come polling day.[34] In July 2006 the commission issued a further report stating that while the machines should not be used as they stood, they could be used after suitable modifications. However, the government made it clear that it was in no hurry to take the machines out of storage, and in political terms it seemed that the assessment of the chairman of the Dáil's all-party Public Accounts Committee, former Fine Gael leader Michael Noonan, was more realistic, when he declared that he was sure the machines would never be used and that e-voting was 'a dead duck'.[35]

Throughout the various political events of 2002–07 the issue of Northern Ireland remained constantly to the forefront of Bertie Ahern's thinking, and his record here was to be highlighted during the first two weeks of the 2007 election campaign (see the Chronology at the front of the book). Ever since he became Taoiseach in 1997 he had striven to seek a solution to the so-called Northern Ireland problem. October 2002 saw the British Secretary of State Dr John Reid announce that he was suspending the Northern Ireland Assembly, bringing about the return of direct rule from London. This was due to a seemingly irretrievable breakdown in trust between the various Northern Ireland political parties with attempts made to have Sinn Féin excluded from the Assembly after allegations of a massive IRA spying ring within Stormont.[36] Elections to the Assembly in November 2003 saw large gains for both the DUP and Sinn Féin, leading to a further sharp polarisation of views on how best to restore the Assembly. The ultimate result was a continuation of the state of suspension following this election. This situation continued until another Assembly election was held in March 2007. With the DUP and Sinn Féin copperfastening their leadership of unionism and nationalism respectively, an agreement was finally reached between both parties to share power in a new Northern Ireland government as from 8 May 2007. More than nine years after the Good Friday Agreement, which the DUP opposed, the four main parties in the north – the DUP, Sinn Féin, the Ulster Unionists and the SDLP – had for the first time agreed to govern collectively. Helping to bring this situation about was widely seen as Bertie Ahern's finest achievement. The following week he became the first Taoiseach to address both houses of the British parliament. In the middle of a hectic and closely fought election campaign, both events were a fitting tribute to his perseverance in finding a solution to the Northern Ireland problem.

The months up to the calling of the 2007 general election saw much shadow boxing. During the 2006 party conference season all the political parties pretty much set out their stall. The Progressive Democrats had reiterated their stance of running without any pre-election agreement with Fianna Fáil, the Greens likewise ruled out any such agreement with any other party, while Labour, albeit with some dissenting voices, endorsed the leadership's position on the Mullingar Accord with Fine Gael. The Constituency Commission report issued in January 2004 had recommended significant and unexpected changes, with almost two-thirds of the Dáil constituencies being revised, with the result that there was much uncertainty as to how some of these changes would impact on election day. Over the last 16 months before the election was called, there was no great change in the support of the parties (see Figure 1.1). In percentage-point terms, Fianna Fáil fluctuated between the mid-30s and the low 40s,

Fine Gael remained in the 20s throughout, and the smaller parties showed no consistent signs of growth or decline. The final TNS mrbi poll published in the *Irish Times* two days before the Taoiseach called the election showed government satisfaction had dropped to 43 per cent, five points lower than registered in a January 2007 poll and nine points lower than in November 2006. Support for Fine Gael was up five points to 31 per cent while Fianna Fáil was down three to 34 per cent.[37] Fine Gael had managed to narrow the gap to three points in May 2006, only to see Fianna Fáil pull away once again after the payments to the Taoiseach were revealed. This eve-of-election poll also saw Labour and Sinn Féin both on 10 per cent, the Greens on 6 per cent, the Progressive Democrats on 3 per cent and Independents/others at 6 per cent. With the polling margins this tight, two distinct coalitions on offer, and both the Greens and Sinn Féin also eyeing up possible government entry, the election promised to be a close and brutally fought contest.

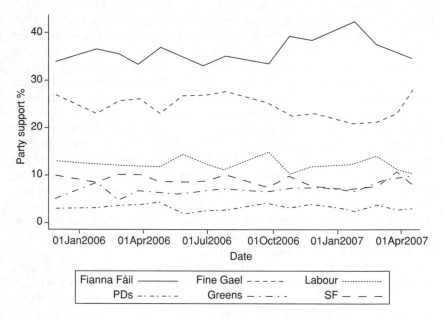

Figure 1.1   Party support in opinion polls, November 2005–April 2007

Source: RED C monthly polls.

Notes

1. *Irish Times*, 30 April 2007.
2. Gary Murphy, 'The background to the election', pp. 1–20 in Michael Gallagher, Michael Marsh and Paul Mitchell (eds), *How Ireland Voted 2002* (Basingstoke: Palgrave Macmillan, 2003).

3. *Irish Times*, 21 September 2006.
4. *Irish Times*, 30 April 2007.
5. For the formation of the government in 2002 see Paul Mitchell, 'Government formation in 2002: you can have any government as long as it's Fianna Fáil', pp. 214–29 in Gallagher et al., *How Ireland Voted 2002*.
6. *Sunday Tribune*, 22 September 2002.
7. Michael Laver and Audrey Arkins, 'Coalition and Fianna Fáil', pp. 192–207 in Michael Gallagher and Richard Sinnott (eds), *How Ireland Voted 1989* (Galway: PSAI Press, 1990).
8. John Garry, 'The demise of the Fianna Fáil/Labour "Partnership" government and the rise of the "Rainbow" coalition', *Irish Political Studies* 10 (1995), pp. 192–9; Brian Girvin, 'Political competition 1992–1997', pp. 3–28 in Michael Marsh and Paul Mitchell (eds), *How Ireland Voted 1997* (Boulder, CO: Westview and PSAI Press, 1999).
9. Michael Laver, 'The Irish party system approaching the millennium', pp. 264–76 in Marsh and Mitchell, *How Ireland Voted 1997*; Peter Mair and Liam Weeks, 'The party system', pp. 135–59 in John Coakley and Michael Gallagher (eds), *Politics in the Republic of Ireland*, 4th edn (Abingdon: Routledge, 2005).
10. Fiachra Kennedy, 'The 2002 general election in Ireland', *Irish Political Studies* 17:2 (2002), pp. 95–106, at p. 95.
11. Quoted in ibid., p. 103.
12. Mitchell, 'Government formation in 2002', p. 220.
13. Mair and Weeks, 'The party system', p. 156.
14. Quoted in the *Irish Times*, 5 June 2002.
15. Michael Ring TD, quoted in the *Irish Times*, 6 June 2002.
16. Kevin Rafter, 'Leadership changes in Fine Gael and the Labour party, 2002', *Irish Political Studies* 18:1 (2003), pp. 108–19, at p. 114.
17. Peter Fitzgerald, Fiachra Kennedy and Pat Lyons, 'The Irish Labour Party leadership election, 2002: a survey of party members', *Journal of Elections, Public Opinion & Parties* 14:1 (2004), pp. 230–44, at p. 231.
18. Katy Hayward, 'If at first you don't succeed … The second referendum on the Treaty of Nice', *Irish Political Studies* 18:1 (2003), pp. 120–32, at p. 125.
19. Aodh Quinlivan and Emmanuelle Schon-Quinlivan, 'The 2004 European Parliament election in the Republic of Ireland', *Irish Political Studies* 19:2 (2004), pp. 85–95, at p. 89.
20. For a comprehensive account of the local election of 2004 see Adrian Kavanagh, 'The 2004 local elections in the Republic of Ireland', *Irish Political Studies* 19:2 (2004), pp. 64–84.
21. See the *Irish Times* between Saturday 11 September 2004 and Tuesday 21 September 2004.
22. *Irish Times*, 7 September 2004.
23. *Irish Times*, 7 September 2004.
24. See Ahern's interview with the *Irish Times*, 13 November 2004.
25. See Adrian Kavanagh, 'The 2005 Meath and Kildare North by-elections', *Irish Political Studies* 20:2 (2005), pp. 201–11.
26. *Irish Times*, 11 April 2005.
27. See for instance the *Irish Times*, 22 June 2006, *Sunday Business Post*, 2 July 2006.
28. See Murphy, 'Background to the election', pp. 9–12, for these events.
29. Gary Murphy, 'Payments for no political response? Political corruption and tribunals of inquiry in Ireland, 1991–2003', pp. 91–105 in John Garrard and James

L. Newell (eds), *Scandals in Past and Contemporary Politics* (Manchester: Manchester University Press, 2006), p. 100.

30. *Irish Times*, 25 January 2005.
31. The full interview can be seen on the RTÉ website at www.rte.ie/news/2006/0926/ ahernb.html. One Irish pound has the same value as 1.27 euros.
32. This *Irish Times* TNS mrbi poll can be seen in the *Irish Times*, 13 October 2006.
33. Liam Weeks, 'Appendix 6: electronic voting', pp. 265–7 in Gallagher et al., *How Ireland Voted 2002*.
34. References to electronic voting here are taken from Liam Weeks, 'Data section – Republic of Ireland', *Irish Political Studies* 21:1 (2006), pp. 26–8.
35. *Irish Times*, 28 April 2006.
36. For events in Northern Ireland see Jonathan Tonge, *The New Northern Irish Politics?* (Basingstoke: Palgrave Macmillan, 2005), and annual overviews in data section of *Irish Political Studies*.
37. This *Irish Times* TNS mrbi poll can be seen in the *Irish Times*, 27 April 2007.

2
The Fulfilment of Election Pledges

Rory Costello and Robert Thomson

The televised debate on 17 May between the two candidates for Taoiseach, Bertie Ahern and Enda Kenny, was one of the more high-profile events of the 2007 election campaign. During the debate, each leader espoused the merits of his party's election pledges, while attempting to undermine the credibility of those made by his opponent's party. For example, when Kenny outlined the Fine Gael promise to provide 2,300 extra hospital beds, Ahern responded by saying that this was not feasible without cutting back on essential medical services. When Ahern discussed a plan for 2,000 extra gardaí, Kenny argued that a similar commitment made by Fianna Fáil in the previous election had not been met and so there was no reason to believe it this time. Ahern defended the government's record by pointing to promises that had been fulfilled, such as the increase in the old age pension to over €200 per week. This pattern was repeated in relation to a wide range of issues, as both leaders sought to convince the viewers that the pledges made by their party were more attractive and more reliable than those of the other party.

The debate between the party leaders illustrates the prominence of election pledges in the campaign. Election pledges are an important part of election campaigns in two respects. First, politicians make specific promises to take particular actions or to achieve particular aims if they are returned to office. Such promises are intended to convince voters that their personal circumstances and those of the country would improve if the party behind the promises were to receive sufficient votes. Specific pledges also deflect criticism that a party is light on policy. Second, parties that were in government prior to the campaign are held accountable for their record of pledge fulfilment during the previous period of government. If a governing party did not fulfil the promises it made during the previous election campaign, then the pledges it makes during the present campaign are less credible.

This chapter examines as a backdrop to the 2007 campaign the fulfilment of election pledges made in 2002 on socio-economic issues. We examine the detail of the election manifestos for the 2002 election, and compare this with the record of government policies and performances up to the 2007 campaign. We use a strict definition of an election pledge. We consider statements to be pledges if they are specific, in the sense that they identify particular policy actions or outcomes that can be tested on the basis of clear evidence. We examine a broader range of pledges than those highlighted during the campaign. As we have seen in the example of the leaders' debate, opposition parties draw attention to pledges on which they can attack the government's record, and governing parties highlight the pledges they managed to keep. Such heated exchanges in the thick of the campaign are necessary and valuable for the information they provide voters. However, without a more systematic study covering a broader range of pledges, we have no way of knowing whether these examples are typical of the government's performance as a whole. Our study is as systematic and objective as possible, covering a wide range of pledges, rather than focusing on a few opportunistically chosen ones. Moreover, we study election pledges from 2002 in the same way as other researchers have studied other government periods in Ireland and in other countries. This allows us to make comparisons.

The chapter is structured as follows. The next section describes the socio-economic pledges made in the 2002 election manifestos. The analysis examines the extent to which there were differences between the pledges made by different parties. We then report our findings on the fulfilment of these pledges. The analysis focuses first on average percentages of pledges fulfilled, and then on explanations of variation in pledge fulfilment. In the conclusion, we compare our findings with research on other periods of government in Ireland and other countries.

Looking back at election pledges made in 2002

When researchers study election pledges, the first two issues they must resolve are where to find election pledges and what statements qualify as pledges. We examine the election manifestos published by parties before the election. Party manifestos provide detailed and authoritative accounts of where each party stands on a broad range of issues. Manifestos are the basis of the positions taken by party candidates and leaders during the election campaign. Although very few voters may read all manifestos in detail, these documents contain the most definitive statements of the policies put forward by parties during the campaign.

We consider a statement to be a pledge if it contains unequivocal support for a specific action or outcome that is testable. Unequivocal support usually takes the form of words such as 'we will' or 'we promise to'. Whenever a statement in a manifesto implies that the action or outcome referred to will be realised during the next government period, we record this statement as a pledge. For a statement to be recorded as a pledge it has also to refer to a specific and testable action or outcome. In other words, manifesto writers must provide us with criteria on the basis of which we can examine whether the pledge is fulfilled. Thus, pledges are quite distinct from other statements found in manifestos, such as evaluations of the past government's record in office, or statements of the general principles to which a party would adhere when in government. For example, the statement 'we will introduce a fairer system of taxation' would not be recorded as a pledge according to our definition, while the statement 'we will reduce the top rate of income tax to 40 per cent' would be. By applying this definition, we are able to compare our findings with previous research on pledge fulfilment in Ireland and other countries.[1]

We examined the election manifestos published by all of the parties for the 2002 general election. Readers might wonder why we examined the manifestos of all parties, rather than only those of Fianna Fáil and the Progressive Democrats. After all, only these two parties were in government and so only these two could be expected to have acted upon their pledges. There are two reasons for including the manifestos of opposition parties in the study. First, elections are supposed to be about choices between alternatives. We need to include the manifestos of all parties to identify the nature and extent of those choices. If all parties promised more or less the same things, this would certainly affect how we look at figures on pledge fulfilment. Second, election pledges made by parties that do not enter government after elections may also be fulfilled. Indeed, some studies of other government periods found rates of fulfilment of pledges made by opposition parties that did not differ markedly from those made by governing parties. We will return to this point later. For now, we note that whether governing parties fulfil more of their own pledges than pledges made by opposition parties is an open question. Answering it requires that we include the manifestos of all parties in the study.

Due to the large numbers of pledges made by parties, rather than studying all of the pledges we concentrate instead on the fulfilment of pledges made on socio-economic issues, broadly defined. This covers pledges that fell under the jurisdiction of seven government departments: the Department of Finance; the Department of Social and Family Affairs; the Department of Health and Children; the Department of Education; the Department of Environment and Local Government; the Department of Enterprise, Trade and Employment; and the Department of Justice, Equality and Law Reform. We examine 401 pledges made by the six main political parties that fought the 2002 election. This covers approximately half of the total pledges made by each of these parties. A previous study compared the rate of fulfilment of pledges made by Irish parties in the area of economics with pledges from all other policy areas, and found no significant difference between them.[2] It is therefore reasonable to assume that the pledges selected for this study are a representative sample of all pledges.

Table 2.1 identifies the total numbers of socio-economic pledges found in each election manifesto and the relationships between the pledges in different manifestos. Each column refers to the pledges made by a particular party, while the rows provide information on the relationship between these pledges and the pledges of the other parties. A pledge made by a particular party can be classified as being in consensus with, in disagreement with, or unrelated to, the pledges made by another party.[3] The first clear finding is that all parties are prolific in the numbers of election pledges they make. Manifestos are not confined to general statements of approval for lofty goals, nor to tirades against, or praise for, the last government's performance. Manifesto writers clearly feel the need to give substance to the general principles supported by their parties by elaborating policies in some detail. This does not mean that the quantity of pledges made by a party is related to its subsequent electoral performance; as Table 2.1 shows, the largest party (Fianna Fáil) actually made the fewest number of pledges on socio-economic issues.

Table 2.1 Election pledges on socio-economic issues from the 2002 manifestos

	Sinn Féin	Greens	Labour	Fine Gael	Fianna Fáil	PDs
Consensus with SF	–	10 (18%)	23 (21%)	14 (23%)	9 (18%)	6 (9%)
Disagreement with SF	–	1 (2%)	1 (1%)	0 (0%)	1 (2%)	4 (6%)
No relation with SF	–	46 (81%)	87 (78%)	48 (77%)	39 (80%)	58 (85%)
Consensus with Greens	10 (19%)	–	12 (11%)	9 (15%)	9 (18%)	7 (10%)
Disagreement with Greens	1 (2%)	–	2 (2%)	2 (3%)	2 (4%)	2 (3%)
No relation with Greens	43 (80%)	–	97 (87%)	51 (82%)	38 (78%)	59 (87%)
Consensus with Labour	22 (41%)	12 (21%)	–	24 (39%)	20 (41%)	21 (31%)
Disagreement with Labour	1 (2%)	2 (4%)	–	3 (5%)	2 (4%)	4 (6%)
No relation with Labour	31 (57%)	43 (75%)	–	35 (57%)	27 (51%)	43 (63%)
Consensus with FG	10 (19%)	9 (16%)	22 (20%)	–	15 (31%)	16 (24%)
Disagreement with FG	1 (2%)	2 (4%)	3 (3%)	–	2 (4%)	4 (6%)
No relation with FG	43 (80%)	46 (81%)	86 (78%)	–	32 (65%)	48 (71%)
Consensus with FF	8 (15%)	7 (12%)	20 (18%)	15 (24%)	–	19 (30%)
Disagreement with FF	1 (2%)	2 (4%)	2 (2%)	2 (3%)	–	1 (2%)
No relation with FF	45 (83%)	48 (84%)	89 (80%)	45 (73%)	–	48 (71%)
Consensus with PDs	6 (11%)	5 (9%)	17 (15%)	17 (27%)	15 (31%)	–
Disagreement with PDs	5 (9%)	2 (4%)	4 (4%)	4 (7%)	1 (2%)	–
No relation with PDs	43 (80%)	50 (88%)	90 (81%)	41 (66%)	33 (67%)	–
Total	54	57	111	62	49	68

Notes: For example, the second column labelled 'Sinn Féin' indicates that SF's 2002 manifesto contained a total of 54 election pledges. The row labelled 'Consensus with Greens' indicates that 10 of these 54 Sinn Féin pledges (19%) were consensually related to pledges made by the Greens. The row labelled 'Disagreement with Greens' indicates that one of these 54 Sinn Féin pledges (2%) was in direct disagreement with a Green pledge. The row labelled 'No relation with Greens' indicates that 43 of these 54 Sinn Féin pledges (80%) bore no direct relation to Green pledges.

A second finding from the quantitative evidence presented in Table 2.1 is that most pledges are not directly related to the pledges made by other parties. This can make it difficult for voters to identify exactly how the parties differ from each other on policies. In some cases it is clear that, if a pledge is made by only one party, it is likely that none of the other parties support implementing it in the next government period. For example, the 2002 Progressive Democrat party's manifesto contained pledges to privatise most of the ESB, Bord Gáis and sea ports. None of the other parties stated explicitly whether or not they would keep these companies in public ownership, but it is unlikely that they would have supported these privatisations. In other cases pledges are not explicitly supported or opposed by other parties, but it is unclear what the positions of other parties were on the basis of the information in the manifestos. For example, the 2002 manifesto of the PDs also contained a more detailed pledge to increase tobacco taxes. While none of the other parties took a position on this issue, it is conceivable that they were in favour of this measure. Despite the ambiguity caused by the absence of clear relationships between the pledges of different parties, unrelated pledges still provide information about where the priorities of different parties lie.

When pledges are related to those of other parties, they are generally related in terms of agreement rather than disagreement. For example, Fianna Fáil, the Progressive Democrats, Fine Gael, Labour and Sinn Féin all supported relaxing the eligibility criteria for the carer's allowance. Some parties were more ambitious in relation to this issue than others. Labour, Sinn Féin and the Progressive Democrats all pledged to abolish the means test for the carer's allowance altogether. Fine Gael simply stated that it would relax the means test, while Fianna Fáil specified that the eligibility criteria would be increased to include all carers whose joint family income was at the average industrial wage. Despite these real differences, the fulfilment of Labour, Sinn Féin and the Progressive Democrats' pledges would mean that the pledges of Fine Gael and Fianna Fáil would be at least partially fulfilled. They are therefore coded as being consensually related. Similarly, Fianna Fáil, Fine Gael and the Progressive Democrats all pledged to cut hospital waiting times and Fianna Fáil, Fine Gael and Labour all pledged to increase the number of hospital beds.

The relatively large number of pledges that are in agreement illustrates the importance of what is sometimes referred to as 'valence' politics. The traditional view of party competition is that parties take different positions on issues and voters choose the party that is closest to their own position. Valence politics, on the other hand, refers to issues where there is widespread agreement among the parties and the electorate as to what should be done, and voters choose the party that they believe to be the most competent. An important part of electoral competition therefore involves parties attempting to convince voters that they would deliver commonly agreed policies most effectively.

Nevertheless, on a small number of key issues, the manifestos provide clear alternatives. These involve pledges that, if fulfilled, by definition would mean that pledges of other parties were unfulfilled. For example, on income tax, Fine Gael and Labour pledged to freeze rates. The Progressive Democrats, by contrast, pledged to reduce the top rate from 42 per cent to 40 per cent. The Greens also pledged to reduce taxes on labour, but in coordination with increases in environmentally-friendly taxes. Fianna Fáil did not make a specific pledge on tax rates, but did make pledges on the overall tax burden.

So far, we have shown that parties made a considerable number of pledges in their 2002 manifestos. These pledges were on specific issues that are of importance to broad groups of citizens. Moreover, each party made many pledges that differed from those made by other parties. In that respect, voters were offered a choice between different sets of policies. However, the choice was made more difficult by the fact that parties usually did not take clear stances in their manifestos on each other's manifesto pledges. Moreover, when a party's pledge was related to a pledge made by another party, it usually agreed with that other pledge. In that respect, the choice faced by voters was limited.

The government's record of pledge fulfilment, 2002–07

We now turn to the government's record of pledge fulfilment in the period 2002–07. For each of the pledges examined, we referred to relevant legislation, ministerial decisions, spending allocations, Dáil records and official reports.

What constitutes the fulfilment of a pledge? The answer to this question is implicit in our definition of a pledge. Recall that we defined a pledge as unequivocal support for a particular action or outcome, specified in enough detail to enable researchers to test whether or not the action or outcome was realised. In other words, the pledges themselves tell us what evidence we would need to judge the pledge to be fulfilled. For example, we judged as fully fulfilled Fianna Fáil's pledge to establish a training fund of up to €2,500 per person for unemployed people facing serious barriers to employment. The 'High Support Process' was introduced by FÁS, the National Training and Employment Authority, in 2003. This measure is designed to assist FÁS Employment Officers to better meet the needs of clients who, because of health, literacy or other difficulties, are experiencing major barriers to finding employment. In 2006, a total of €2,500 per person was available under this scheme to resource the relevant interventions such as counselling and supplemental training.[4] Our strict definition of what a pledge is makes the study of pledge fulfilment easier than it would be if we were to include more general statements as pledges. Although our research design makes our study of pledge fulfilment as objective and replicable as possible, we still had to make judgement calls on difficult cases in which we had to balance partly conflicting evidence.[5]

In line with previous research on pledge fulfilment, we use three categories to describe the fulfilment of pledges: 'fully fulfilled', 'partially fulfilled' and 'not fulfilled'. The partially fulfilled category is necessary because there may be some policy change in the direction indicated by the pledge that falls short of full fulfilment. For example, the Progressive Democrats' pledge to reduce the top rate of income tax from 42 to 40 per cent was only partially fulfilled because the top rate had been reduced to 41 per cent by 2007.

Table 2.2 summarises our findings on pledge fulfilment quantitatively. If we include as fulfilled all those pledges that were even partly fulfilled, we can say that a majority of the pledges made by Fianna Fáil and the Progressive Democrats in their 2002 manifestos were fulfilled. Fianna Fáil realised 76 per cent (37/49) of its pledges while the Progressive Democrats realised 66 per cent (45/68). If we adopt a stricter definition of fulfilment, limiting it to include only 'fully fulfilled' pledges, then Fianna Fáil fulfilled 45 per cent (22/49) of its pledges, while the Progressive Democrats fulfilled 47 per cent (32/68) of theirs.

Table 2.2 The fulfilment of socio-economic election pledges in the 2002–07 government period

	Opposition				Government		
	Sinn Féin	Greens	Labour	Fine Gael	Fianna Fáil	PDs	Prog. for Govt.
Fully fulfilled	13 (24%)	10 (18%)	30 (27%)	17 (27%)	22 (45%)	32 (47%)	25 (58%)
Partially fulfilled	10 (19%)	9 (16%)	21 (19%)	15 (24%)	15 (31%)	13 (19%)	8 (19%)
Not fulfilled	31 (57%)	38 (67%)	60 (54%)	30 (48%)	12 (24%)	23 (34%)	10 (23%)
Total	54 (100%)	57 (100%)	111 (100%)	62 (100%)	49 (100%)	68 (100%)	43 (100%)

On taxation, the government continued the policy of low taxes on income. As mentioned above, the top rate was reduced from 42 to 41 per cent, partially fulfilling the Progressive Democrats' pledge. In addition, increases were made to tax credits, which had the effect of bringing those on the minimum wage out of the tax net.[6] This change fully fulfilled another pledge made by the Progressive Democrats. Fine Gael, Labour and Sinn Féin also made the same pledge. We also judged Fianna Fáil's pledge to 'keep down personal tax levels' to be fully fulfilled. Although still testable, this pledge is somewhat more general and easier to fulfil. Other tax pledges were not fulfilled, such as the Progressive Democrats' commitment to raise the exemption limits for Capital Gains Tax from €1,270 per annum to €10,000 per annum.

On health care, progress was made on reducing waiting times. Responsibility for monitoring hospital waiting times was transferred to the National Treatment Purchase Fund (NTPF) in 2004. According to the NTPF's 2006 report, average waiting times for the most common surgical procedures fell from two to five years in 2002 to two to five months in 2006.[7] On the basis of this evidence, we described Fianna Fáil's pledge to 'permanently end waiting lists in our hospitals within two years' and the Progressive Democrats' pledge to 'end waiting lists' as partially fulfilled. Fine Gael's pledge to cut waiting times to a maximum of six weeks was also judged to be partially fulfilled on the basis of this evidence. However, another of Fianna Fáil's pledges, that to end waiting lists for people with disabilities, was classified as not fulfilled. Waiting lists for services for people with disabilities actually increased over the period.[8]

On education, one of the main challenges faced by government is to reduce class sizes. Class sizes remained at roughly the same level throughout the 2002–07 government period. Fianna Fáil, Labour, the Greens and Sinn Féin all promised substantial reductions in class sizes. In 2002, the average class size in Irish primary schools was 24.2. The Department of Education's figures indicate that average size was still 24 in 2006.[9] Therefore, these pledges were coded as not fulfilled. The Minister for Education is reported to have acknowledged that the fulfilment of this pledge was not possible because of an expanding population and a greater focus on children with special needs.[10] Fianna Fáil also pledged to expand state-funded early education places, with the priority being given to a new national system of funded early education for children with intellectual disabilities and children in areas of concentrated disadvantage. We judged this pledge as not fulfilled. There is an early-start pre-school scheme in selected disadvantaged schools. This scheme was set up in 1994, and by 2002 was carried out at 40 schools. We found no evidence that this scheme was extended during the 2002–07 government.

Four of the parties pledged to increase state pensions to at least €200 a week. This was realised in 2007. This increase fully fulfilled the commitments made by Fianna Fáil and the Progressive Democrats. These two parties did not specify a particular time by which this increase would be made, but the clear implication of the manifesto is that it would be done before the end of the government period. Both Fine Gael and Labour promised to make the increase earlier. Therefore, we judged their pledges to be partially fulfilled.

The main finding from this section is that a clear majority of the pledges made by Fianna Fáil and the Progressive Democrats in their 2002 manifestos were partially or fully fulfilled by the time of the 2007 campaign. Although such systematic evidence as reported here did not feature in the 2007 campaign, Fianna Fáil and the Progressive Democrats were able to provide clear examples of policy actions in line with the promises they had made in 2002. The substantial numbers of pledges that were not fulfilled or were only partially fulfilled provided an opportunity for the opposition to criticise the government's record.

Explaining pledge fulfilment

Clearly, some promises are more likely to be met than others. This section examines factors that affect the likelihood of a pledge being fulfilled. Some of these explanatory factors involve the position of the party that made the commitment: for example, did the party enter government, and did it receive the relevant ministerial post? Other factors refer to the nature of the pledges themselves: for example, did the pledge receive cross-party support, and did it involve a continuation of existing policy or a new policy measure? All of these factors play a role in explaining pledge fulfilment.

The information in Table 2.2 makes clear that parties that enter the government are far more likely to fulfil their pledges than are parties that enter the opposition. The two governing parties partially or fully fulfilled an average of 70 per cent of their election pledges. Of the pledges made by the four parties that entered the opposition, 44 per cent were partially or fully fulfilled. Therefore, control over government office explains some of the variation in the likelihood of different pledges being fulfilled. The realisation of commitments made by opposition parties can be explained partly by the fact that many of them are in agreement with promises made by those of governing parties. In addition, some of the opposition parties' pledges, even those not explicitly supported by the governing parties, refer to actions or outcomes that are supported by or may be taken up by at least one of the governing parties.

The division of ministerial posts between government parties explains only a small part of the inter-party variation we found in pledge fulfilment. If a governing party that made a pledge secured the ministerial post relevant to that pledge, then the pledge was somewhat more likely to be partially or fully fulfilled. To illustrate this, we consider only the 117 pledges made by the two governing parties. Considering pledges even partially fulfilled as met, 72 per cent (52/72) of the pledges made by a governing party that received the relevant ministerial post were met, as against 67 per cent (30/45) of pledges made by a governing party that did not receive the relevant ministerial post.

Agreement among parties also increases the likelihood of pledge fulfilment. Of the 34 pledges made by Fianna Fáil and the Progressive Democrats on issues on which they explicitly agreed, 28 (82 per cent) were partially or fully fulfilled. Of the 83 commitments made by Fianna Fáil and the Progressive Democrats on which they did not agree explicitly, 54 (only 65 per cent) were partially or fully enacted. Interestingly, this is also the case when it comes to agreement between the government and the opposition. Fianna Fáil and the PDs made 59 pledges that were in agreement with those made by one or more opposition party, and 58 pledges that were not shared by any of the opposition parties; 46 (79 per cent) of the former were at least partially fulfilled, compared to 36 (61 per cent) of the latter.

The formulation of the Programme for Government is an important stage of the political process, and this has a noteworthy impact on pledge fulfilment. If a party secures support for its pledge in the Programme for Government, there is a higher likelihood that the pledge will be fulfilled (Table 2.2). The 2002 Programme for Government is a detailed document that contains many of the promises copied verbatim from the manifestos of the two coalition partners. Of the governing parties' pledges that were copied exactly into the 2002 Programme for Government, 77 per cent (33/43) were partially or fully fulfilled between 2002 and 2007 as against 67 per cent (49/74) of the governing parties' pledges that were not copied exactly into the programme for government.

Commitments to achieve ambitious policy outcomes that are not directly under the control of any government are of course less likely to be fulfilled than promises not to change certain policy arrangements. Almost all of the governing parties' commitments to keep the status quo on particular measures were met (11/12). For example, Fianna Fáil, supported by other parties, pledged to set aside, as required by law, 1 per cent of GNP for future pension obligations. Legislation was introduced in 2000 that placed a statutory obligation on the government to pay 1 per cent of GNP into a fund each year. The law was not changed and the government adhered to it, thereby fulfilling the promise. By contrast, pledges to achieve policy outcomes, such as reducing class sizes, require more than simply changing or not changing a piece of legislation. Such commitments are more difficult to meet.

This section has identified some general patterns in the likelihood of pledge fulfilment in line with general explanations of pledge fulfilment. The findings are in line with previous research on pledge fulfilment in Ireland.[11] In general, a party's promises are more likely to be fulfilled if that party receives more control over the levers of policy, and if its commitments are more responsive to broadly-shared societal demands. The identification of these general patterns is not inconsistent with the particular stories behind the fulfilment or non-fulfilment of individual pledges. For example, the commitment to complete the rail link to Dublin airport by 2007 was not fulfilled because of the delays caused by planning appeals. This is an example of a pledge that did not receive explicit cross-party support, which indicated that there was considerable disagreement about the rail link among the communities affected by it.

Conclusion

We began this chapter by noting that election promises were an important part of the 2007 campaign. All parties made a large number of commitments covering a wide range of policy issues. In addition, the government's record of pledge fulfilment came under scrutiny, with claims and counter-claims regarding pledge fulfilment made by candidates of the governing and opposition parties. Our research on the fulfilment of election promises on socio-economic issues confirmed that the 2002 manifestos contained substantial numbers of election pledges. The governing Fianna Fáil–Progressive Democrats coalition that was in office during 2002–07 partially or fully fulfilled on average 70 per cent of the pledges made by these parties. We conclude this chapter by drawing out some implications of the findings for key questions about the quality of democracy in Ireland.

To what extent are voters offered choices at elections? The findings indicate that in addition to offering voters choices between alternative leaders and general principles, parties offer voters different sets of specific policies. Each of the parties made large numbers of specific pledges of substantive importance to broad groups of citizens. This is an important conclusion. If parties did not offer voters policy choices, elections would lose their significance as crucial junctures in the democratic process. Our findings on the numbers of election promises are not unusual. Lucy Mansergh conducted the most comprehensive study of election pledges in Ireland.[12] Her study examined election promises made by all the main parties from 1977 up to and including the 1997 election. She reports similar numbers of promises in these manifestos. Similarly, research on election pledges in the Netherlands, the United States and the United Kingdom indicates that Irish parties are not unique in making large numbers of commitments.[13]

We also pointed out that the choice is constrained. Most of the pledges made by each of the parties did not relate directly to one made by any of the other parties. When there was a relationship between pledges made by different parties, these commitments were usually similar. This of course makes it difficult for voters to identify clear differences between parties on policies. This pattern of parties 'talking past' each other has also been identified in many other political systems, and in the other studies of election pledges referred to above. In response to this phenomenon, political scientists have formulated the 'saliency theory of party competition'.[14] The essence of this theory is that parties compete indirectly with each other, mainly by the extent to which they emphasise or de-emphasise different policy themes relative to each other. Saliency theory posits that parties avoid taking direct stances against each other. Instead, in order to distinguish themselves from their opponents, they emphasise themes on which they have an advantage over their opponents. Saliency theory is not undisputed. In particular, some of its proponents have in the past underestimated the extent to which parties make specific promises. Nonetheless, saliency theory does correctly identify the indirect nature of competition that typifies much of parties' policy statements during the campaign.

Are enough election pledges fulfilled? The findings reported in this chapter and by other studies make clear that it would be inappropriate to state blithely that parties do not keep their election promises. We found at least some policy action in fulfilment of clear majorities of pledges made by Fianna Fáil and the Progressive Democrats in 2002. Furthermore, it does matter which parties enter government office, because a pledge is more likely to be fulfilled if the party that made it entered government office after the election. This is also a noteworthy conclusion. One of the most important justifications for holding elections is that it provides voters with some influence over the way in which the country is run. If there were no congruence between election pledges and subsequent government actions, this justification would not be credible.

The percentage of commitments met in the 2002–07 period compares favourably with previous periods of government in Ireland. Recall that on average 70 per cent of pledges made by Fianna Fáil and the Progressive Democrats were at least partially fulfilled. Mansergh's research on the period 1977–2002 found that on average 50 per cent of governing parties' pledges were at least partially fulfilled. Her study covers commitments in all policy areas, not only socio-economic policy. The governing period 1997–2002 offers a particularly interesting comparison. During that period, Fianna Fáil and the Progressive Democrats were also in power, but they did not have a clear majority of seats. We might expect, therefore, that the Fianna Fáil–Progressive Democrats coalition would have fulfilled fewer of its pledges in the 1997–2002 government than did the 2002–07 government. However, Mansergh reports that in the period 1997–2002 Fianna Fáil partially or fully fulfilled 68 per cent of its 228 pledges, while the Progressive Democrats partially or fully fulfilled 64 per cent of their 85 pledges. Undoubtedly, both governments from 1997 to 2007 had the benefit of being in power during a time of great economic prosperity and growth. Previous governments, particularly those of the 1980s, faced far more difficult economic conditions.

The rate of pledge fulfilment we find for the 2002–07 government period also compares favourably to those of other countries where parties share power. Dutch governments, for example, are also coalitions of at least two parties. Research on pledge fulfilment in the Netherlands found that on average 57 per cent of commitments made by parties that entered governing coalitions were partially or fully fulfilled. In the United States, Royed reports that, on average, 60 per cent of the commitments made by the Republicans were partially or fully fulfilled during the 1980s when Ronald Reagan was in the White House. The US system also compelled inter-party cooperation during this period since the Democrats controlled Congress part of the time. The single-party governments of the United Kingdom offer a very different point of comparison. Single-party governments in Westminster typically fulfil high percentages of their election pledges. Royed reports that the Conservative Party partially or fully fulfilled 84 per cent of its pledges when Margaret Thatcher was in power in the 1980s. Similarly high percentages have been reported for other time-periods in the UK.[15]

It may seem intuitively obvious to most voters and politicians that parties that enter government should fulfil their promises: indeed, that they are under some moral obligation to at least attempt to do so. However, liberal democratic theory offers a more nuanced view. William Riker, one of the world's most renowned liberal democratic theorists, is famous for noting that no election result provides an unequivocal message encapsulating 'the will of the people'.[16] Election results generally do not provide clear messages about what 'the people' want. When the largest party receives a plurality of around

40 per cent of the votes, it might still be argued that a clear majority of votes did not support that party. Some variants of liberal democratic theory take this argument to the extreme, by arguing that election results provide no message on policies whatsoever. At best, elections provide a chance for voters to select leaders rather than policies, and to 'throw the bums out' for gross incompetence. We take a different view. We acknowledge that democratic theory does not provide a specific number for the percentage of pledges fulfilled that would qualify as being 'enough'. We also acknowledge that it would be inappropriate to evaluate the quality of a democracy simply by the percentage of pledges fulfilled. In other words, a higher rate of pledge fulfilment does not necessarily mean better democracy. Nonetheless, with today's parties, it is not possible for voters to disentangle their support for particular leaders from their support for particular policies. Furthermore, voters and politicians generally hold the view that parties that enter the coalition should attempt to carry out what they promise. Therefore, without specifying a particular number for adequate pledge fulfilment, we consider a substantial linkage between election pledges and subsequent government actions to be one of the signs of a healthy functioning democracy.

Notes

1. Lucy E. Mansergh, 'Do parties make a difference? The relationship between government intention and government output in the public policy sphere: the case of governments in Ireland 1977–1997', PhD thesis, Trinity College Dublin, 2004; Lucy E. Mansergh and Robert Thomson, 'Election pledges, party competition and policymaking', *Comparative Politics* 39:3 (2007), pp. 311–29; Terry J. Royed, 'Testing the mandate model in Britain and the United States: evidence from the Reagan and Thatcher eras', *British Journal of Political Science* 26:1 (1996), pp. 45–80; Robert Thomson, 'The programme-to-policy linkage: the fulfilment of election pledges on socio-economic policy in the Netherlands, 1986–1998', *European Journal of Political Research* 40 (2001), pp. 171–97. The studies referred to also report 'reliability tests' for the identification of pledges. Although we have a clear definition of what a pledge is, researchers must judge whether or not a statement qualifies as a pledge. Mansergh, Royed and Thomson tested the reliability of their coding procedure for identifying pledges by comparing their judgements with those of second readers. Of the hundreds of statements recorded as pledges, there was usually agreement on well over 80 per cent of cases, and no evidence of systematic biases.
2. Mansergh, 'Do parties make a difference?'
3. A pledge made by one party is considered to be consensually related to a pledge of another party if the fulfilment of the latter would automatically result in the partial or complete fulfilment of the former. Given that some pledges are more specific than others, it is possible for one pledge to be consensually related to a second pledge, while the second pledge is not consensually related to the first. For example, Fine Gael pledged to increase the amount put aside for the Pension Reserve Fund and the Progressive Democrats simply pledged not to raid that fund. Clearly, if the Fine Gael pledge were fulfilled, this would automatically fulfil the Progressive Democrats' pledge. Therefore, the Progressive Democrats'

pledge is consensually related to·the Fine Gael pledge. However, the reverse is not true, because the fulfilment of the Progressive Democrats' pledge would not automatically fulfil the Fine Gael pledge.

4. FÁS Annual Report 2003; *Dáil Debates* 623: 1596, 6 July 2006.
5. Previous research using the same procedure for studying pledge fulfilment showed high levels of reliability. Thomson's study of Dutch parties, for instance, reports a high level of agreement between his judgements on pledge fulfilment and the judgements of independent experts (Thomson, 'The programme-to-policy linkage)'.
6. The entry point to the tax net was increased under the 2005 budget, so that minimum wage earners were exempt. Subsequent increases to the minimum wage reversed this, but this was rectified following the Budget 2007.
7. National Treatment Purchase Fund, 'A Report on the Patient Treatment Register', December 2006.
8. National Physical and Sensory Disability Database Committee, Annual Report 2004, 2005, 2006; National Intellectual Disability Database Committee, Annual Report 2003, 2004, 2005, 2006. While the numbers on waiting lists for services for intellectual disability dropped slightly over the period, the numbers on waiting lists for physical disabilities increased substantially.
9. *Dáil Debates* 630: 1468, 1 February 2006; OECD, *Education at a Glance* (Paris: OECD, 2004).
10. *Irish Times*, Wednesday 11 April 2007.
11. Mansergh, 'Do Parties Make a Difference?'
12. Ibid.
13. Royed, 'Testing the mandate model in Britain and the United States'; Thomson, 'The programme-to-policy linkage'.
14. Hans-Dieter Klingemann, Richard I. Hofferbert and Ian Budge, *Parties, Policies and Democracy* (Boulder, CO: Westview Press, 1994).
15. Royed, 'Testing the mandate model in Britain and the United States'; Thomson, 'The programme-to-policy linkage'.
16. William H. Riker, *Liberalism against Populism: A Confrontation between the Theory of Democracy and the Theory of Social Choice* (San Francisco: Freeman, 1982).

3
Campaign Strategies and Political Marketing

Neil Collins and Patrick Butler

We have created 600,000 jobs in the last ten years. This country is finally in a position to say to its own people, 'We can have a good living in our own country' ... That's progress.

Brian Cowen's assertion constitutes both a defence of government and an attack on the economic manifestos of the opposition parties; it captures the election in a single soundbite. Voting in the 2007 general election was influenced by the campaigns of the political parties and there seems to have been a significant change in public opinion during the final week. Nevertheless, the bulk of voters remained loyal to the parties and, where possible, to the candidates they had chosen in 2002 (see chapter 7 for full exploration of voting behaviour). In this chapter we will look at the campaign, how it went for the various parties, how it was perceived from within the campaign headquarters of the parties and how central strategy played out at the local level (see also the Chronology at the front of the book for an overview of the campaign).

Party campaigns as political marketing

Many accounts of elections stress the formal campaign – an atypical period of limited impact on the outcome. In reality, political campaigns, rather than being periodic, are 'permanent'.[1] As Bertie Ahern told RTÉ: 'I very much believe in the Seán Lemass view of life that elections start the day after the count. So it just goes on all the time.'[2] Thus, the period from the calling of the election on 29 April to polling on 24 May was simply a phase of the campaign, albeit one of most heightened intensity. Party headquarters were gearing up and formulating their strategies for years before the final push.

What is different about recent Irish elections is the degree to which parties and candidates consciously employ marketing techniques drawn from business with strategies directly influenced by professional marketing, communications and media personnel. The *Irish Times* journalist Fintan O'Toole commented ruefully: 'The use of professional election strategists, who run campaigns across the globe, is now so well established that it is scarcely noticed. American consulting firms are now as central to Irish elections as back-slapping and promises.'[3]

Even as politicians publicly downplay opinion polls, focus groups and other marketing research techniques, each party's headquarters was employing them and analysing the results. The era of 'smoky back-rooms' may literally be gone following the ban on smoking in the workplace introduced in 2004 but, for the 2007 election, there was the same intense behind-the-scenes effort to manipulate events. There are good reasons for the increased reliance on marketing professionals. One is competition – and not just with other parties. Party activists, political analysts and others caught up in the dynamics of elections generally overestimate the public's interest in politics and under-assess the importance of the competition for the attention of voters/consumers from commerce, sport and entertainment. In 2007, all politicians had to compete with the public interest in the kidnapping of a young English girl in Portugal, which generated massive media coverage, and in the final of the European Champions League the day before polling.

Another less obvious cause of an increased reliance on professionals is the decline in party membership which, in part, dictates a less labour intensive strategy to the parties. Fianna Fáil claims an impressive 55,000 members and Fine Gael 34,000, but these numbers may mask a long-term decline in political activism.[4] An internal Fianna Fáil report in 2005 put its activist numbers at between 15,000 and 20,000 and found that 'party officer membership was predominantly middle-aged and elderly'.[5] Those closely involved in politics do not often recognise that, especially outside the formal campaign period, politics can be of very marginal interest to most citizens. Only 3 per cent of Irish residents over 15 years old reported having 'taken an active part in any political campaign' at any time in the past three years when questioned in April 2005.[6]

Party campaign strategies

The campaigning of all parties and candidates may be understood in terms of how they perceived themselves when positioned in relation to the electorate's preferences and their competitors. In this section, we examine the approach of each party in turn.

Fianna Fáil

It was clear from the outset that Fianna Fáil would face the dilemma of retaining its position by defending its record in government while promising to introduce further and better levels of service provision. An inherent problem for Fianna Fáil was the reconciling of apparent conflicts among its voters: tax concessions to middle-class property owners, for example, and high welfare provision for the less well-off. This theme permeated its communications, and reflects the classic situation for the market leader in the commercial world. The leader is subject to continual attack though the scale and intensity increases during the formal election campaign.

Fianna Fáil was genuinely concerned at the prospect of a viable challenger. Bertie Ahern explicitly noted at the outset that 'the people have a real choice and two very different alternatives before them',[7] indicating clearly that his party's leadership position in the market was under threat. Fianna Fáil's national strategy was to use the Taoiseach's discretion to stay in office for the full five-year period and to engineer a sense of well-being among its wide support base. This allowed it to have certain policies mature within months of the election and to give credibility to its slogan – 'the next steps forward'. Potentially the most influential policy concerned the special savings interest accounts, known as SSIAs, which were opened in the period May 2001 to April 2002 and which matured between May 2006 and April 2007 with a 25 per cent bonus for savers. As an example of a long-term strategy that anticipates future market demands, it was politically highly astute, and would have paid political dividends regardless of the state of the economy at the time – a real unknown when first initiated. Other areas in which policies were designed for conspicuous successes leading up to the election were road-building, garda numbers, and the level of social welfare payments. In the final period of the campaign these successes were trumpeted and further improvements promised at both national and local levels. Thus, Fianna Fáil's main critical strategic decision was to emphasise its appeal to the electorate exemplified by another of its marketing slogans: 'Protect the prosperity that the Irish people have worked so hard for'.

As in all competitive markets, the leader is vulnerable to counter offers so the Fianna Fáil list of promises was somewhat reactive, especially in the final period. The problem for the party was to match its opponents' offers while also presenting itself as the prudent management team. Tensions over the prudence/promises dilemma were clear even during the final weeks of the campaign. In late March, the Taoiseach seemed to 'outbid' the opposition parties' promises of higher public provision and lower taxes of various kinds, though a senior colleague had just scotched the idea of auction politics as lacking probity. Séamus Brennan, Minister for Social Affairs and a former general secretary of the party, had publicly advised his party only four days earlier to 'promise less and deliver more'. Brennan had been a leading, albeit youthful, party strategist in 1977 when it won a landslide on the back of extravagant promises.

Party strategists devised a timetable of policy announcements for April and May but prioritised the so-called 'pre-election economic policy' as the first major initiative of the campaign for a launch in mid-April to pre-empt its rivals by highlighting Fianna Fáil's strongest asset – the state of the economy. Though economists might argue that the government was overheating the economy in a period of full employment, precipitating inflation and depressing manufacturing, Fianna Fáil focus groups were assuring the party of public approval for its economic management. At the same time, its opponents were aware that criticism on this topic came across as begrudgery, thereby leaving considerable space for the government on this front.

With the advantage of timing, Fianna Fáil should have been in pole position to roll out an orchestrated agenda-setting and photo-opportunity-rich final few weeks. Certainly, the party organised daily news conferences at which it sought to ensure that attention was directed at some aspect of its policies. Initially, however, media attention was on the Taoiseach's personal finances. Indeed, the major set-piece manifesto launch on 3 May was completely hijacked by a journalist, Vincent Browne, who interrogated the Taoiseach about the mysteries of his personal finances during the mid-1990s (the so-called 'Bertiegate' affair, described in more detail in chapter 1 and illustrated in the photo section of this book). Fianna Fáil's plans for the final weeks appeared in disarray. For the first two weeks after the dissolution of the Dáil, the party headquarters in Treasury Buildings was unnerved by the persistence of the media focus. Party headquarters' staff felt that the journalists would never have treated their opponents as roughly.

In the first two weeks of the official campaign, even the most inscrutable ministers were flustered at press conferences into contradicting each other and occasionally advisors intervened to clarify inconsistencies. For a party with competence as a central electoral plank this looked increasingly dangerous. Slowly, however, order returned and two tendencies seemed to account for the restoration of confidence. Feedback from the canvassers around the country gave persistent evidence that voters were not bringing up the 'Bertiegate' issue that seemed to dog headquarters so much. At the same time, the party was improving in the polls. In fact, the perceived media attack on the Taoiseach seemed to galvanise Fianna Fáil loyalists and its mood was reflected back to headquarters. Party workers compared the mood with that displayed in the 1990 presidential election when the party candidate Brian Lenihan topped the poll on the first count in the face of very unfavourable press coverage.

Central to the party's campaign in 2007 was the decision to defend every existing seat vigorously. Particular attention was paid to those seats under threat and Fianna Fáil headquarters worked from a confidential assessment of vulnerable but winnable seats. The internal campaign for resources was intense, as candidates under threat sought support from campaign headquarters. As regards vote management, running the same number of candidates as targeted seats in the constituency with the intention of splitting the votes between them worked exceptionally well in most cases. Few observers expected the kind of outcome achieved in 2002 to be repeated, but the local strategies paid off.

Fine Gael

In business strategy, the role of the challenger is to depose the leader, and this is how Fine Gael cast itself in 2007. Challengers attack; their basic strategic objective requires an aggressive approach. For Fine Gael, the critical strategic decision was not to attack its main competitor for the role of challenger, the Labour Party, but to form an alliance with it. It identified its advantage as being the promise of renewal in the face of Fianna Fáil's lengthy period in office. The poor performance of some ministers and suggestions of a lack of probity surrounding some prominent figures associated with the governing party would lend credibility to its serious intention as challenger. This 2007 campaign strategy was crucial because Fine Gael had suffered its worst election result for over 50 years in the 2002 general election, declining from 54 TDs to 31; another poor performance would seriously erode its challenger status. Fine Gael's core message is summarised by the Alliance for Change agreed with Labour in 2005.

Fine Gael certainly took a permanent campaign view, and its approach and performance in 2007 reflected earlier decisions on positioning the party at national and local levels. Soon after 2002's poor performance Director of Elections Frank Flannery, the party's main strategist, called for new appointments to coordinate policy and communications. Similarly, his long-term perspective involved the new party leader in systematic moves to restore party morale through local rallies. His strategy received a fillip with the successful local and European elections in 2004 (see chapter 1), which were also used to groom new Dáil talent – of 91 candidates in 2007, 37 were running for the first time. Flannery prepared detailed predictions, based on extrapolations from a series of opinion polls, for substantial gains from as early as the summer of 2006 and recommended a continued strategy of market penetration through augmented vote transfers and targeting vulnerable Fianna Fáil seats. Clearly, Fine Gael did not declare its hand in terms of gains from Labour but regarded all PD seats as potential gains.

Critical to Fine Gael's plan to neutralise Fianna Fáil's advantages as market leader was the presentation of Enda Kenny as more competent and more honest than the Taoiseach and, crucially, capable of being a winner. In other words, the strategy was to present Fine Gael under its new leader as the core of an alternative government. Enda Kenny's constant touring and glad-handing showed a common touch and party morale was high at the ard-fheis at the end of March, where his address gave significant hope to party stalwarts. Kenny's youthful appearance was also played upon, though a running private joke between the Fine Gael leader and journalists centred on how much this was due to his hair stylist.

In contrast to Fianna Fáil headquarters, the final weeks in Fine Gael's central offices were much calmer and more controlled. Press briefings did not feature so many senior party figures and were taken in part by Frank Flannery himself. This was a deliberate attempt to get away from what Fine Gael strategists called the 'talking heads' approach. The calculation was that television coverage of the leader, if necessary highlighting that day's targeted topic, was more useful than the morning set-piece for journalists in Dublin. Indeed, the leader's tour was the central focus of the final weeks of campaigning. Enda Kenny was in every constituency, in the bailiwick of every candidate bar one and was made available to the local media on the day. He was portrayed each day in a 'dynamic context' chosen to be as television-friendly as possible.

The party sought to capitalise on its opponent's perceived failure to deliver on some policies and the failure of any minister to take direct responsibility for clear errors of judgement. For two years before the 2007 election, Fine Gael used focus groups extensively and came to the conclusion that the government was perceived as doing well on the economy but as being weak on health, crime, transport, infrastructure and other service delivery issues. The party's prime target was the government's record on health and it presented the election as a 'referendum on health'. The focus groups also pointed to a perception that Fine Gael had no policies, so it developed poster and media campaigns to highlight its distinctive commitments on health, education and crime. Within the party there were critics of the decision to avoid the economy as an issue, but the headquarters team was firm on this tactic.

Fine Gael strategists claim they did not consciously borrow the idea, but Enda Kenny's 'contract with the Irish people' did mirror a successful tactic of the Republican Party in the US. The 'Contract with America' was a document released by Republicans during the 1994 Congressional election which committed the party to specific legislative measures. The Fine Gael 'contract' was similarly constructed and publicly signed by the leader. In the leaders' televised debate and on other occasions the contract was attacked by Fianna Fáil. Indeed, the Taoiseach was quoted as charging that 'in your contract with the people, you left out jobs, you left out pensions, you left out schools'. Initially, however, Fine Gael's opponents were reluctant to attack it as to do so invited direct comparisons. The drama of the offer was increased by Enda Kenny's promise to resign as Taoiseach if he did not achieve his targets – again highlighting the conspicuous reluctance in the market leader's ranks to accept ministerial responsibility.

Post mortems suggest that a number of topics received rather more emphasis than matched the electorate's real anxieties. The concern with stamp duty received considerable attention earlier, but proved less critical as the campaign went on. Similarly, critics contend that there was not enough focus on the longevity of Fianna Fáil in power – 24 of the last 30 years. But again headquarters' fear was of giving the appearance of begrudgery or drawing attention to the issue of the party's lack of experience in office.

Labour

In strategic terms, the Labour Party's critical decision was whether to attempt an aggressive strategy of market development by appealing beyond its existing base to challenge either the market leader or Fine Gael, its main rival for the role of challenger. Its choice was the conservative one of market penetration – it calculated that the potential of its existing policies had not been fully exhausted. Labour judged that better vote management through a formal pact with Fine Gael would maximise its support. This assessment was in contrast to the party's stance in the 2002 election when it adopted a more independent line and viewed formal alliances as problematic. Labour strategists, however, considered the party's poor 2002 performance as reflecting voters' assessment that in practice there was no choice but Fianna Fáil. Before the 2004 local elections, Pat Rabbitte had approved a vote transfer pact with Fine Gael and this was extended in the 'Mullingar Accord' in 2005 (see chapter 1). The alliance strategy was formulated by the party leadership to emphasise a clear electable alternative to Fianna Fáil. In line with this strategic direction, steps were taken to outline a shared vision as well as clear goals and responsibilities for the new alliance. A particular effort was made to win the backing of party members and to build a plan for realistic and proportionate gains and risk-sharing. Labour presented the strategy as a vehicle for achieving more of its objectives because, though the smaller partner, it was the author of more of the policies in the agreed programme and its ranks contained more senior political figures with ministerial experience, an important asset when competence was being stressed. For its traditional supporters, it characterised the strategy as ensuring a framework for a centre-left government to replace the centre-right one in place.

Green Party

In contrast to Labour, the Green Party felt able to adopt a more adventurous strategy. The party pursued new supporters and developed new policy areas through a process of internal reorientation. That is, in some equivalence to a commercial brand extension strategy, the Greens had been strategically extending their interests beyond the rather narrow understanding held by the general population, and attempting to draw support from a broader base of voters. In a sense, the Green Party is akin to a market innovator that goes out ahead of current market demands, and promotes products and services which it believes in passionately, and for which it is prepared to go against the grain in the belief that the market will come around to its way of thinking. The party's position was greatly helped by wider international promotion of the issues with which it was associated, with one comment from a rival party strategist that 'every news programme was like a Green political party broadcast'. Nevertheless, the Greens remained primarily a niche player.

At the 2002 election the Green Party had nearly doubled its vote share and increased its seats from two to six. The party also made gains at the 2004 local elections that allowed it to broaden its appeal beyond its established Dublin base. It used its youth wing, formed in March 2002, to broaden its appeal both geographically and in terms of issues. In effect it moved from the position of a rather undisciplined protest movement to that of a niche political party with a more professional approach at parliamentary and organisational levels. By eschewing formal alliances, the Greens were not constrained in taking risks and developing new products targeting small businesses, working parents and the elderly.

In 2007, the Greens completed a change, which the party's leadership had been signalling for some time but which its opponents had discounted, from protest movement to a potential party of government. The party's new post-election position as a coalition partner with Fianna Fáil will present fresh marketing challenges but ones already faced by similar parties in other parts of Europe where Green ministers share power and responsibility.

Progressive Democrats

The Progressive Democrats (PDs) represent a curious strategic position. As part of government, the party had to defend its position and behave in ways typical of the market leader, but, as a small party, the marketing strategy that it adopted was that of a niche player. Interestingly, the party's rhetoric presented it as a national party with candidates in 30 constituencies, a decision that also increased its campaign expenditure limits (see appendix 5). The critical success factor for the nicher is carefully defining and successfully targeting a market segment where it specialises in serving the needs of those customers. The dilemma for the PDs was that they could not differentiate themselves from Fianna Fáil except by playing up their influence in government, and they faced the danger of underpositioning, whereby the party is perceived as not taking a strong, defining, stance on any important issue. Voters in different special interest segments may be significantly, if not fundamentally, opposed to each other on basic principles. So the niche party's strategy has to be particularly finely honed. This can suit the candidate in an individual constituency but leads to confusion in national strategy. These difficulties were clear in the PDs' approach to the 2007 election, which was marked by obvious tensions within the party, a change of leadership only eight months before the election and two public threats to pull out of government. The PDs' main election theme in 2007 was 'don't throw it all away', which suggested that the alternative governments on offer would endanger the recent economic success of the Republic by high spending, high taxes and poor management.

The renewed controversy about the Taoiseach's finances during the final weeks of the campaign unsettled the PDs and briefly threatened the governing coalition but suggestions of ministerial resignations came to nothing. Michael McDowell appeared to take a censorious stance on the issue without consultation with his colleagues. Those candidates, including very senior party members, who calculated that their re-election was dependent on vote transfers from Fianna Fáil, made their views known very forcefully to party headquarters and, after a damaging delay, the party leader gave his backing to Ahern. In the final weeks of the campaign, PD headquarters' activity was relatively muted and press briefings were low key. The party launched various policy documents in Dublin city centre but the main concentration of its senior figures was on their own constituency fortunes.

The PDs were formed with a distinct ideological position and astute strategic direction. Their appeal was essentially to middle-class voters but, as is the danger for niche players, the other parties moved into their space. For example, Labour proposed to cut the basic rate of tax substantially and to widen tax bands. The tax-cutting agenda became less distinctive and the PDs countered with promises of more spending on social welfare and childcare. The party pointed to the substantial surpluses in the government's accounts, but may have miscalculated the impact on its core vote. Similarly, the party's power to influence government policy on taxation was weakened by the absence of reform in stamp duty to which it had committed itself well before the most recent Budget. Even more than for the larger parties, the key campaigning for the PDs was in the individual constituencies. Indeed, even the issue of stamp duty illustrates the link between national strategy and local campaigning, as Michael McDowell, party leader and main advocate of stamp duty reform, stood in a Dublin constituency in which it was a significant local issue. McDowell's constituency fight with Green leader John Gormley also led to one of the more amusing incidents in the final weeks when the two rivals exchanged insults on the street. The 'Rumble in Ranelagh' was a big hit on YouTube and gave sub-editors a chance for mocking headlines.

Their niche strategy was illustrated by the PDs' choice of celebrity candidates in some constituencies, such as Dublin South-Central where it put up Frank McNamara, music director of the *Late Late Show*[8] for 20 years and the arranger and producer of two consecutive winners at the Eurovision Song Contest, but with no political profile. A similar tactic was used in 2002 when, for example, Tom Parlon, former president of the Irish Farmers' Association, was chosen at a late stage to run in Laois–Offaly despite having no previous connection with the party. Parlon obviously had a ready-built network in the farm organisations but McNamara brought wide name recognition and substantial campaign resources.

Sinn Féin

Sinn Féin enjoyed a substantial reputation as a well-organised party. Though a major player in Northern Ireland, the party made similar strategic decisions in the Republic where it was in a much more marginal position with just five TDs. Its electoral success in Northern Ireland is based in part on support from previous non-voters and new voters. Gerry Adams's personal influence, and, in the past, support for the IRA's military campaign, help to account for Sinn Féin's mobilisation of these voters. In the Republic, Sinn Féin's critical decision was to implement the strategy of a challenger from the position of a small market share. It presented itself as a potential partner, probably with Fianna Fáil, in a coalition government. The party put its leader at the centre of its short-term strategy in the 2007 election because it believed that his high recognition status and growing popularity would draw support to Sinn Féin candidates. Sinn Féin headquarters was confident that 2007 would see the election of several new younger TDs and allow the party to reposition itself as less dominated by politicians of 'the Troubles'. In the longer campaign, the party emphasised assiduous constituency service, especially in working class areas and marginal communities where political participation rates have been low. The party also targeted the youth vote, another under-mobilised group. This service-based approach always carries the danger of encroachment, so central to this longer marketing strategy has been building up Sinn Féin strength at local government level and being active in local issues.

Sinn Féin's aim was to be in government on both sides of the border and thereby position itself as the leader and as an all-Ireland party. Party strategists recognised the need to overcome the perception that Sinn Féin is a niche northern party – heavy on partition but light on prosperity. In 2007, the party misread the concerns of the Republic's voters and chose a strategy out of line with its market position. The Taoiseach rather than Gerry Adams picked up the electoral benefit of the progress in Northern Ireland and the associated media events in Belfast, London and the Boyne, all of which occurred during the final weeks of the 2007 campaign (see Chronology).

National campaigns 'on the ground'

All marketing strategies designed at corporate headquarters are tempered to varying degrees by local conditions where different issues, competitive priorities and communication styles reveal themselves. The limits of central headquarters strategy are particularly clear in the area of vote management and candidate selection. Political competition in individual constituencies can be as high between individuals from the same party as candidates of rival parties (see pp. 97–100 below). The number of candidates, their geographic spread and their profile as seen from Dublin may seem to dictate one strategy, but locally it cannot be delivered. Disappointed hopefuls regularly stand as Independents if not selected or the local organisation ignores central wishes and nominates the extra candidate (see chapter 4 for candidate selection).

The essence of the national–local tension is the understanding that the main campaign priority for each politician is that he or she is personally successful. To ensure success regardless of party strategy, a politician must have some basis of support among the electorate other than partisan allegiance. A reputation for service delivery at local levels provides this insurance. Apart from minor constituency services, some senior politicians are able to secure larger benefits. For example, Kerry South has benefited substantially from having John O'Donoghue, Minister for Arts, Sport and Tourism, as its representative. Even junior ministers highlight their 'pork barrel' power. Tim O'Malley, the PD Minister of State at the Department of Health and Children, openly claimed to have delivered a radiotherapies centre to Limerick East despite the advice of an expert group that it should be located elsewhere.

The importance of media representation is critical at all levels, and the 2007 campaign introduced some new and interesting dimensions. Web usage grew but was a largely static and uninspiring application, though we can anticipate a more interactive and sophisticated future. During the final weeks each party was, as usual, given time to state its case with free television broadcasts. The impact on the election outcome is difficult to measure because these generally slick and polished three-minute advertisements are viewed by a highly sensitised audience more open to having their judgements confirmed than challenged. Nevertheless, the broadcasts are an important part of the ritual of Irish elections and, for the smaller parties such as the Christian Solidarity Party, they afford an unparalleled advertising opportunity. Most of the parties stuck to the familiar formula of the leader talking to camera with cutaways to clichéd pictures of children, elderly people and workers in different roles. Fianna Fáil and the Greens, however, each produced an unusual film. The former presented a film montage of foreign leaders, including Tony Blair and Bill Clinton, praising Bertie Ahern, and the latter a piece in which only children appeared. Both received good media reviews.

The second half of the official campaign period was dominated by the contest between the alternative Taoisigh in what the media likened to an American presidential contest. The two party leaders' debate had been preceded the previous day by a television programme with a similar formula of individual statements followed by questions and answers between the leaders of the smaller parties. As a campaign device each party was keen to use the airtime to reinforce its central themes, highlight the debating strengths of its leader and avoid mistakes that might provide the basis of negative media comment the next day. Most viewers' minds were, no doubt, made up by the time of the debate, but the party that was notably negatively affected was Sinn Féin. Gerry Adams appeared ill at ease with the specifics of policy in the Republic and narrowly briefed on broader themes. The debate reinforced the sense that Sinn Féin was losing its sense of direction, an impression added to by its willingness to change its corporation tax policy during the final weeks. All the party leaders were interviewed individually on RTÉ's early evening news programme in the final weeks of campaigning, but again Adams's performance was perceived to be the least impressive.

The televised debate between the leaders of Fianna Fáil and Fine Gael emphasised the 'choice of Taoiseach' spin on the election. The question of Bertie Ahern's finances did briefly arise in the programme, but for the most part it was an occasion for the leaders to sound competent and well-briefed. In this head-to-head format, Bertie Ahern was particularly well-served by the course of events in Northern Ireland. Though the press reaction was ambivalent, polls suggested that the Taoiseach's grasp of detail and attack on the Fine Gael 'contract' impressed voters (see chapter 7 for fuller analysis of the poll evidence).

In the area of public communications, the party headquarters sought to varying degrees to impose a corporate template with prescribed colours, layouts and slogans on all election material. For Fianna Fáil in particular, 2007 saw an increase in uniformity compared to 2002 as candidates were more assured that the party's standing with the electorate was an asset. In general, billboard posters were distributed by commercial agents, sometimes in the wrong constituencies and with misspelling of candidates' names, while local activists attached smaller stiff versions to every available lamppost, road sign and other street furniture. As a localisation tactic, postering retains its place as the weapon of choice. Many posters featured the party leaders and were used in every constituency. Fianna Fáil and Fine Gael favoured these, while others had the candidate with the party leader, a Sinn Féin favourite. Fine Gael did attempt to use posters to project a negative impression of Fianna Fáil's record on quality-of-life issues such as commuting time and long working hours.[9] Headquarters staff proposed more extensive use of negative messages, but the party leader resisted. As noted above, Fine Gael did use posters to counter the impression reported from its focus groups that the party lacked policies. For the most part, however, parties eschew policy discourse, potentially divisive local issues and broad ideological statements. The picture of the candidate, accompanied by the briefest of slogans and the party logo, is given pride of place in all forms of publicity.

Each party's volunteers distributed very stylised leaflets, again featuring smiling candidates and little text, to as many houses as possible in the constituency. Few of the leaflets were persuasive, but some, especially the cartoons posted by the PDs, were amusing (some examples are included in the photo section of this book). In 2007, the pattern was the same as in previous elections though the range of promotional bric-a-brac was extended to pens, bottles of water and balloons.

In terms of an election campaign, critical local strategic decisions are, for the candidates of the larger parties in particular, constrained by 'orders' from headquarters. The purpose of these restrictions on candidates' freedom is to manage the vote (for vote management, see pp. 97–100 below). Candidates are asked to limit their canvassing to parts of their constituency, and encourage vote transfers to colleagues. The Fianna Fáil National Director of Elections, P. J. Mara, has a long record of success and in the 2002 election is credited with almost securing an overall majority for the party with just 41 per cent of the first preference vote. In 1997, under his strategic direction, the party secured an extra ten seats with 39 per cent of the vote, much the same as in the 1992 general election. The key tactic, with which Mara is closely associated, is maximising the return on the party's vote by running as few candidates as possible in any constituency. This demands strong leadership by the leader of the party and clear advice from the Director of Elections on the process of nomination in each constituency. In 2007, there were some instances where three candidates rather than two were permitted to run but overall the centre exercised firm control (see next chapter for fuller discussion).

An illustration of the constraints on competition within a party may be seen in Donegal North-East where, for various reasons, three sitting Fianna Fáil candidates were contesting a three-seat constituency. The 'solution' was a geographical divide – Niall Blaney canvassing in the Fanad Peninsula, Cecilia Keaveney in Inishowen and James McDaid in Letterkenny. A similar division of territory can be seen in Cork South-Central, though this is a more fraught tactic in the less easily differentiated urban setting. Here a five-seat constituency also had three Fianna Fáil candidates, two of whom were incumbents but only one of whom seemed certain of re-election. The party had gained three seats here in 2002. Thus, Minister Micheál Martin was asked not to canvass in the perceived bailiwick of Deputy John Dennehy. In all such cases competition between candidates is hard for headquarters to monitor and bitter rows between party colleagues about encroachment or failure to urge the transfer of votes are frequent. Occasionally, as in Kildare North, the only constituency with no sitting Fianna Fáil TD, the competition is between ideological wings of the same party. Michael Fitzpatrick was seen as representing former Minister for Finance Charlie McCreevy's right-wing element of Fianna Fáil against Áine Brady, associated with a far less ideological wing of the party. Though Fitzpatrick was a local councillor in Clane, no division of the constituency was agreed. Similarly, when selection reflects factors such as 'dynasty' candidates, as in Kerry North with Fianna Fáil's incumbent Tom McEllistrim and Norma Foley, a daughter of former TD Denis, both from Tralee, a straight fight for the party vote ensures undisguised intra-party competition despite pressure from party headquarters. In the Kerry North case, the Fine Gael candidate was the only one from the northern part of the constituency.

The permanent local campaign is usually about constituency service, visibility and accessibility. Some candidates, however, also seek to be associated with particular issues beyond the obvious constituency ones such as the inadequacy of local hospitals, which all candidates, whether government or opposition, seemed to home in on. Thus, for example, Fergus O'Dowd was *Magill* 'TD of the Year' in 2006 for his championing of the issue of poor nursing home care. This profile helped him counter the popularity of Máiréad McGuinness, a former TV presenter who got a huge vote for Fine Gael in the European elections in 2004 and could have run in several Dáil constituencies but chose Louth just before the close of nominations. Nevertheless, despite standing in the smallest county in the state, O'Dowd was also assiduous as a 'south Louth' candidate in order to target the non-Fine Gael transfers that helped elect him in 2002. Even high-profile national candidates such as the

Labour leader, Pat Rabbitte, raised the issue of immigration well before the final campaign, perhaps partly because of its salience in his own Dublin South-West constituency; Labour leaders have been locally vulnerable in the past.

Just as the poster photograph may afford the briefest opportunity to assess the candidate, the next most prized opportunity for individual candidates is the handshake. All candidates, from the most senior politicians to the rookies, attempted to meet as many voters as possible even though the contact may appear completely perfunctory. This form of canvassing involves either the candidate going to places where people gather, traditionally after Mass but now more assuredly at retail outlets, or a door-to-door meet-and-greet formula with politicians and their support team calling to voters' homes (see chapter 5 for candidates' campaigning techniques). The candidate's time must be maximised so activists will either visit a target area without the candidate or, more effectively, just ahead of the politician. Another handshake-generating occasion, especially for the two larger parties, is the visit of a party leader to the constituency. Again, the contact with individual voters is short, but local campaign managers as well as headquarters value the attention generated by a visit from Ahern or Kenny. For all the professionalisation of campaigning at HQ, 'Election campaigns are still fought "on the ground" by candidates pushing their own ambitions. This may sometimes be sub-optimal for the ambitions of the parties, but it is what voters expect, and they tend to respond well to candidates who demonstrate a strong local presence ...'[10]

Another important aspect of the Irish scene is the nature of the local press and broadcasting in the presentation of politicians and their policies, and of the sensitivity of politicians at all levels to those local media. There is an important gap between the national and local media, and ongoing attention to local interest remains critical to the image and standing of the politician. Both Fianna Fáil and Fine Gael headquarters courted local newspaper editors, made party leaders available for locally focused interviews and organised photo opportunities to facilitate publication deadlines. Local radio was also extensively targeted by politicians from the major parties seeking to avoid the more abrasive and sceptical tone of national broadcast journalists in RTÉ and elsewhere. Some candidates, such as Trish Forde-Brennan standing for the Greens in Limerick East, had become well-known through local radio campaigning on educational and health issues before entering the 2007 contest.

Conclusion

Despite the drama and heightened tension of the events of the final few weeks, it is not possible to understand the impact of marketing on the 2007 election without acknowledging the permanent campaign. For each party, strategy evolves over the long term while tactics are more immediate and more local. In this election, Fine Gael displayed the most adroit marketing approach starting soon after its debacle of 2002, reorganising effectively and retaining its leader focus and limited policy strategy throughout. For Fianna Fáil, the permanent campaign is central and, though in 2007 its final few weeks were unsettling, the attention to both new and traditional marketing techniques secured its position. In both the larger parties the tension between party headquarters' and local campaigners' understanding of the priorities was well-managed. Interestingly, for Fianna Fáil, local effort remained much more grounded than the central party.

Though 'events' can be unpredictable and crucial, choosing the correct marketing strategy is essential. The 2007 election demonstrated the wisdom of the Greens' independent and bold approach, and the difficulty for Labour in cooperative strategies. For Sinn Féin the expectation of being in government, and for the PDs actually being in government, proved their Achilles' heels. For the former, the analysis of their market position was faulty and for the latter there was no consistent or credible marketing analysis above the individual wish to survive. Ultimately, however, and for all parties, marketing strategies are only tools in a democratic process in which citizens as voters – rather than simply consumers – decide the outcome.

Notes

1. S. Blumenthal, *The Permanent Campaign: Inside the World of Elite Political Operatives* (Boston: Beacon, 1980).
2. Interview broadcast on 28 October 2006.
3. Fintan O'Toole, 'Spinning out of control', *Irish Times*, 5 May 2007.
4. For long-term trends see Michael Marsh, 'Parties and society', pp. 160–82 in John Coakley and Michael Gallagher (eds), *Politics in the Republic of Ireland*, 4th edn (Abingdon: Routledge and PSAI Press, 2005), at pp. 169–72.
5. Liam Reid, 'Fine Gael claims record membership of 34,000', *Irish Times*, 4 June 2005.
6. Paula Clancy, Ian Hughes and Teresa Brannick, *Public Perspectives on Democracy in Ireland* (Dublin: Tasc, 2005), p. 9.
7. 'Ahern says voters have "real choice" in election', *Irish Times*, 30 April 2007.
8. A long-running and widely-watched television programme that mixes light entertainment and serious discussion.
9. Paul Hughes, 'Hustings await', *Marketing*, January 2007.
10. Michael Marsh, 'Candidate centered but party wrapped: campaigning in Ireland under STV', pp. 114–30 in Shaun Bowler and Bernard Grofman (eds), *Elections in Australia, Ireland and Malta under the Single Transferable Vote* (Ann Arbor: University of Michigan Press, 2000), at pp. 129–30.

4
Candidate Selection: Democratic Centralism or Managed Democracy?

*Liam Weeks**

This chapter is concerned with the process by which the political parties picked their candidates for the general election. This encompasses a number of themes, including how the parties selected their candidates; how they decided on the number of candidates to run; who was selected; and the underlying tensions between the local and national party organisations in the pursuit of their separate strategies. This tension is often portrayed as the battle between the forces of democratisation and centralisation, and the media like to stir up the sense of internecine intra-party conflict. The grassroots of the party support democratisation because it affords them a greater role in the process, while the party executives are generally in favour of greater centralisation. This chapter assesses the extent to which there is really a battle between these forces; whether it is a 'phoney war'; or whether the two work together in peaceful coexistence.

The importance of candidate selection

Although this chapter is devoted to events that by and large took place a year or two before the election, the importance of candidate selection cannot be underestimated for a number of reasons:

1. It acts as a filter, reducing the number of potential candidates from the 3 million eligible citizens to approximately 350 party candidates. This has a significant effect on the choice available to the electorate on polling day, because 'the quality of candidates selected determines the quality of the deputies elected'.[1] Consequently, this can have an impact on the direction of future policy decisions,[2] and it is safe to say that decisions

made at selection conventions can be as important as those made at general elections.[3]

2. Selection conventions are the gateway to political office. The parties act like any recruitment agency, filtering the potential candidates according to the specific taste of the employers (the voters). Apart from the Independent route, to enter political life every aspirant must go down the route of the selection process, which is usually the most difficult hurdle to overcome.

3. It tells us where power lies within the party. Schattschneider observed that 'he who can make the nominations is the owner of the party'.[4] For example, a highly centralised process tells us that the party central executive is a very important player in the party.

Candidate selection: the rules

As in most countries, the parties are free to decide their own internal regulations for the selection of candidates. These rules are detailed in either the official rules and procedures or the constitutions of each of the parties. They have all adopted a similar format that can be described as 'local selection, but with national approval'. Candidates are generally chosen at local conventions organised on a constituency basis, but they must be ratified by the national executive, which reserves the right to deselect any candidate and add someone of its own liking to the party ticket. In recent years, a powerful central committee that oversees the selection procedure has evolved within each party, through which the centre exercises its power.

Key to understanding candidate selection strategy within Fianna Fáil is the party's Constituencies Committee. Its role is to seek out potential candidates, identify key marginal constituencies, and liaise with the local party organisations.[5] It also decides on how many candidates to run in each constituency and when the convention is to be called, and it can add or deselect candidates. Although the committee is answerable to the Ard Comhairle (the party national executive), the heavyweight nature of the committee's make-up (it included the party leader, deputy leader (Brian Cowen, the committee's chair), general secretary (Seán Dorgan), and director of elections (P. J. Mara)) helps to ensure that few of its recommendations are ever rejected. Exceptions to this rule were evident in constituencies where the party ran too many candidates (notably Dublin Central and Tipperary South).

Fianna Fáil is now the only party not using the one-member-one-vote system (OMOV) to select its candidates; under this system, each party member has the opportunity to vote in the candidate selection process. Candidates are instead chosen by delegates from the party's constituent branches, with votes counted under PR-STV rules (a system used by all the parties). Conventions usually take place on a constituency basis, except where a constituency encompasses two counties (such as Carlow–Kilkenny or Cavan–Monaghan), or where the

Constituencies Committee carves up the constituency on a geographical basis, and holds separate district conventions (as in Cork North-West, Longford–Westmeath, Mayo, and Roscommon–South Leitrim in 2007).

Fine Gael has also followed the path of centralisation with the establishment of a powerful Organisation of Candidate Selection Committee (OCSC). This is a ten-person body, chaired by the director of the national organisation, Phil Hogan. There was a separate Election Strategy Sub-Committee for Dublin, chaired by former TD Seán Barrett; its aim was to plan the party's recovery in the capital (where it had won only three out of 41 Dáil seats in 2002). To select its candidates, Fine Gael has used the OMOV system since 1996, and only members of at least one year's standing within the party are allowed to vote at conventions. Following claims that the system was abused in 2007 by the recruitment of 'ghost' members in some constituencies (Clare being one notable example), the minimum period of membership has since been extended to two years. Nominations, requiring the signatures of two party members, need to be submitted 14 days in advance to the OCSC, at which stage they can be rejected by the central executive, a power that is used sparingly.

The inclusion of rules related to candidate selection in Labour's constitution[6] is a relatively new development. While the party's central executive (the National Executive Council) is authorised with the task of organising the selection process, its constitution allocates power to an Organisation Sub-Committee (OSC) to recommend the number of candidates for selection at a convention. This marked a change since 2002, and was the first time the OSC had been given these specific powers. This committee, headed by the party's director of elections, James Wrynn, was responsible for overall candidate strategy in 2007. The party leader and chairperson can also add candidates to the ticket once the election has been called. This greater level of power afforded to Labour's central executive was counterbalanced by the introduction of the OMOV system in 2001; though it did not take effect until after the 2002 election, so 2007 was the first time it was used by Labour to select its candidates for a general election.

Unlike 2002, the PDs had written guidelines for candidate selection that were detailed in the party's constitution. The party leader, Michael McDowell, chaired an Election Committee, a post that neither the previous leader nor the leaders of the other parties occupied in 2007. It was indicative of the 'intense hands-on role'[7] McDowell took in the party's candidate selection strategy. The PD constitution stipulates that a convention must be held to select a candidate, but as in the other parties, this rule can be overridden by the national executive, which reserves the right to deselect or impose a candidate. Party rules stipulate that voting is usually by the OMOV system, but the national executive can also direct that it be delegate-based (for logistical reasons).

Reflecting their initial eschewal of traditional party structures, the Greens had no rules on candidate selection until the election of their first TD in 1989.[8] They prefer to leave the task of selecting election candidates to the local branches (again, using OMOV), which are usually given a free rein to decide when to call the convention and what candidates to select. However, the party has not escaped Michels' iron law of oligarchy (according to which power invariably rests at the top of any organisation), and since 2002 the centre has taken a more active role within the organisation. A new strategic plan was adopted in 2003, which included the establishment of an Electoral Task Force (ETF), a seven-person team that included the general secretary and party chair. Its main function is to centralise and coordinate the support given to the party's candidates, which had only been achieved at a very low-key level in 2002. All candidates must be ratified by the ETF, which has the power to deselect candidates it deems unsuitable.

As a consequence of the large number of elections it contests north and south of the border, Sinn Féin set up a permanent Election Department in 2004, which includes the party's director of elections for the whole island, Pat Doherty, and a separate director of elections for the Republic, Ken O'Connell. Like the Greens, Sinn Féin entrusts most of the matters concerning candidate selection to the local branches; the local convention decides on how many candidates to run, but at all times, the ultimate power over candidate selection rests with the Ard Comhairle. It forms a five-person committee to interview all prospective candidates before they are ratified, and reserves the right to deselect any candidate. Although voting at conventions usually operates according to the OMOV system, the Comhairle Ceantair can limit the vote to delegates, particularly where 'exact membership is hard to define'; that is, where the party suspects the possible infiltration of 'ghost' members. There were no instances warranting the exercise of this power in 2007. Although there is no charge put on membership of the party, to qualify for voting rights at a convention, members need to have sustained an 'acceptable level' of activity within their cumann.

Candidate selection: the practice

The widespread use of OMOV has had a positive effect on the attendance at selection conventions, which are now very inclusive practices. Over 2,000 members attended the Fine Gael convention in Clare, while approximately 1,500 were present in Carlow–Kilkenny, Cavan–Monaghan and Cork North-West. Using the delegate-based system, the numbers were slightly lower for Fianna Fáil, although there were still 1,500 in attendance in Laois–Offaly, and close to 1,000 in Cavan–Monaghan, Galway East and Mayo. While the lowest attended conventions for both these parties were in Dublin, the national average attendance for both was approximately 300. In general, fewer participated in the selection process for the smaller parties, with fewer than 100 present at the average Labour convention, approximately 60 for the PDs and 15 for the Greens. Given the large variation in attendances, these mean figures do not portray a very clear picture, especially for the minor parties. For example, while almost 600 Sinn Féin members attended a joint convention for the two constituencies in Donegal, as few as ten were present in Kerry South. Similarly, the PD conventions in both Galway East and Galway West witnessed a gathering of over 150 members, while close to 60 Green members participated in the conventions in Dublin North and Dublin South-East.

The informal rules of selection

The formal rules in operation for the selection of candidates tell only a part of the true story behind this process. By the night of the convention the crucial power struggles have often already taken place; the official selection 'is simply a formality which just puts the finishing touch on the work of the wire-pullers'.[9] The interaction between the different wire-pullers within the parties denotes the existence of the informal rules of candidate selection, which often paint a more realistic picture of the distribution of power. Because of their unwritten and private nature, it is difficult to outline what exactly these informal rules are; they can be understood only by an analysis of the interaction (and confrontations) between the central and local organs of the parties in their respective attempts to get their preferred candidates selected.

Working with the local organisations and through the use of private opinion polls, the Constituencies Committee in Fianna Fáil had a fair idea of the candidates it wanted selected in almost all the constituencies. In both Fianna Fáil and Fine Gael, candidate selection has now become a sophisticated, professionalised process; polling is one method the party executives use to both make and support their decisions because, in the words of one strategist, 'any corporation that doesn't understand its marketplace is wasting its time'. While most of Fine Gael's polling was carried out by their in-house psephologist (and director of elections) Frank Flannery, Seán Donnelly's company Public Opinion Ireland conducted all the polling for Fianna Fáil, to the extent that he was described by some as possibly the most important influence on the party's candidate selection strategy.

To 'assist' the selection of their preferred candidates, Fianna Fáil's Constituencies Committee employed a number of means: persuasive arguments, backed up by the support of the party leadership and the polling data; delaying the holding of conventions; and in some constituencies the committee cancelled selection conventions, instead conducting interviews with a number of prospective candidates. While this may portray an image of democratic centralism in action, it was not the case that the Fianna Fáil executive preached a message similar to the Henry Ford dictum on the choice of colours for his Model T car – that is, 'You can have any candidate you like, as long as it's ours.' Those favoured by central office were not simply unpopular carpetbaggers imposed on a disgruntled local organisation. The decision reached was based on information acquired from consultations within the constituency, and the executive sought to ensure that all candidates met with local approval; this is based on the logic that the support and assistance of the party's local councillors and members are necessary to engineer a successful election campaign.

The most colourful and dramatic clash between the centre and the periphery within Fianna Fáil occurred in Galway West. The local delegates favoured a four-candidate strategy, and were angry to be told on the night of the convention that the Constituencies Committee favoured the selection of just three candidates. Annoyed at what they described as 'another diktat from headquarters', delegates attempted a minor coup and temporarily seized the floor from the chair, Tony Killeen, who was left with little option but to declare a 'non-convention'.[10] The committee cancelled the convention, declared the two outgoing TDs (Éamon Ó Cuív and Frank Fahey) automatically reselected, and picked Michael Crowe, who had recently joined the party from the Independent ranks, as its third candidate following interviews with a number of aspirant councillors. A similar decree to select fewer candidates than favoured by delegates created some tension in Clare, where Senator Brendan Daly said the committee 'have certainly lost the plot on this one'; Tony Killeen TD, who was reselected, spoke of 'a lot of anger from what is seen by a lot of delegates as interference by Dublin in the business of the county in selecting people'.[11]

The cancelling of conventions was a generally new phenomenon in the selection process, and signalled the increasing centralisation within Fianna Fáil. Eight conventions were cancelled in total: Cork South-West, Donegal North-East, Dublin North-East, Dublin Mid-West, Dublin South-Central, Galway West, Meath East and Wicklow (where there was one district convention held, at which the incumbent TD Dick Roche was selected). In Dublin North-East, Senator Liam Fitzgerald, who had been expected to contest the convention, resigned from the party in protest. The local organisation was similarly vociferous in its frustration. It published a letter written to the Taoiseach, where it complained that 'by denying the party organisation in Dublin North-East the democratic process that is afforded by a convention, the party's democratic integrity has been seriously diminished'.[12] One consequence of the cancelled conventions was the opportunity for the Constituencies Committee to select a significant number of candidates. Nineteen were chosen in the constituencies where there were no conventions (including ten incumbent TDs), while a further eight candidates were added by the committee in constituencies where conventions had already taken place. While most of these were drawn from within the party ranks, all of the parties (with the possible exception of Sinn Féin) recruited some candidates from outside their respective organisations. These consisted of two types: Independent politicians and 'celebrity' candidates. The latter were well-known individuals with a 'profile', who are 'box-office potential' for a party because 'name identification is critical to getting your candidate selected'.

Fianna Fáil tended to approach Independents with a background in the party (known as 'gene pool' Independents). Along with Crowe, it recruited

Independent councillor Christy O'Sullivan in Cork South-West, while Independent Fianna Fáil TD Niall Blaney joined the party in July 2006. Former Dublin goalkeeper John O'Leary ran for the party in Dublin North, while it was also linked with Shane Byrne, a former rugby international, in Wicklow. Meanwhile, Fine Gael, following the addition of Independent TD Liam Twomey to its ranks in 2004, secured the services of Independent councillor (and former party activist) Molly Buckley in Laois–Offaly. Two prominent GAA celebrities, Graham Geraghty and John O'Mahony, ran for the party in Meath West and Mayo respectively. Brody Sweeney, founder of a successful sandwich bar chain, was selected in Dublin North-East.

Few celebrities were recruited by the main three left-wing parties (Labour, the Greens and Sinn Féin), but they were not averse to Independent councillors, such as Phil Prendergast in Tipperary South for Labour, and Vincent Martin in Cavan–Monaghan, Brian Scanlon in Sligo–North Leitrim, and Betty Doran in Longford–Westmeath for the Greens. Described by one internal strategist as the 'graveyard of celebrity candidates', the PDs have a history of recruiting such candidates, in large part a reflection of their weak grassroots organisation. Party headquarters talked with a number of Independent TDs, in particular Marian Harkin and Liam Twomey, while feelers were sent in the direction of Paudge Connolly and Paddy McHugh; none of these negotiations proved fruitful. Candidates with a pre-established profile (whether that can be termed 'celebrity' is another matter) were targeted in the Dublin commuter belt area, with negotiations proving successful in the cases of Jane Mullins (a local newspaper editor and former leader of Positive Action, a group representing the victims of the hepatitis C scandal) in Kildare South, Colm O'Gorman (founder of the One in Four organisation) in Wexford, and Frank McNamara (a composer and musician) in Dublin South-Central.

Like its equivalents in Fianna Fáil and the other parties, Fine Gael's OCSC had a good idea of who it wanted selected as the party's official candidates. Polling played a 'critical' role in this strategy, with over €150,000 spent on determining who were the suitable candidates, and on monitoring the progress of those selected. An example of the influence of polls occurred in Donegal South-West, where they indicated that the Fine Gael candidate, Terence Slowey, would struggle to win a seat. Consequently, the party executive persuaded Dinny McGinley, the sitting Fine Gael TD, to reverse his decision to retire in 2007. The committee also convinced Slowey to stand down, without having to exercise its formal powers of deselection. It was unclear at the time what form of persuasion was used to secure this decision, but an inside nomination (see p. 191) Slowey acquired in July for the Seanad election may not have been coincidental.

Unlike Fianna Fáil, Fine Gael's rules do not allow the OCSC to cancel a convention. Nevertheless, in several constituencies where the local organisation was weak, it was the OCSC that in effect selected the candidate, because it provided the nominees. The OCSC took an active role in recruiting candidates, persuading the aforementioned Dinny McGinley, and Galway West TD Pádraic McCormack, to reverse their decision not to contest the election. Along with the aforementioned 'celebrities', it also managed to coax former TDs Seán Barrett, Charles Flanagan and Alan Shatter out of semi-retirement. In total, the party executive added eight candidates to the ticket. Most of these did not cause too much tension, but a notable exception was Dublin North-East. Terence Flanagan was added after private polls indicated that Brody Sweeney, selected at the convention, was struggling because he was perceived as 'a parachute candidate who was not in tune with the people'. A public row between the two candidates that spilled over into the 'blogosphere' ensued, as Sweeney claimed that 'I wasn't parachuted in like our other candidate Terence Flanagan'.[13]

Working in parallel with the OSC, Labour established a committee in 2005, chaired by former party leader Dick Spring, to devise a potential candidate strategy. Also given the unenviable task of sounding out incumbents' plans to stand again, it recommended one-candidate tickets in most cases, with the exceptions being the seven constituencies where the party ultimately did run a second candidate. Labour fielded a candidate in every constituency for the first time since 1969. A similar strategy had been attempted in 2002, but had failed due to the lack of suitable candidates in some districts. Conventions were held in all constituencies bar Galway East and Limerick West, where there were no active branches of the party. None of the party's 18 TDs seeking re-election was challenged; one of its four Senators was, while in the other 17 constituencies, there were just six contests (all bar one of which were in Dublin).

It is difficult for the executives of small parties to exert as much centralised control over the selection process as their counterparts in the large parties can. This may be because small parties have access to fewer resources and patronage, rendering it more difficult to ruthlessly enforce their will. Party headquarters, however, tend to express more democratic reasons for their greater level of decentralisation; they claim to want to keep power resting mainly with the local branches, and say that were they to impose their own candidates, the party would have few members willing to provide manpower during the election campaigns. An example of this in Labour was the selection of Jim O'Brien in Kilkenny ahead of Eoin Pattison, nephew of the retiring TD. Although Pattison was a clear favourite of party headquarters, the OSC was content to leave the decision to the wisdom of the local members, even though it did not ultimately result in headquarters' preferred outcome, and observers predicted correctly that the candidates selected would not win a seat between them.

Two other conventions that were described as 'problematic' for Labour occurred in Dublin North and Dublin South. In the case of the latter, the OSC had initially decided to run just one candidate. Aidan Culhane beat Alex White in a lottery after the convention ended in a tie, but the OSC later added

White to the ticket, much to the annoyance of Culhane, whose response to the party leader, Pat Rabbitte, was 'are you having one yourself Pat?'[14] Along with White, five other candidates were imposed by the party executive (including the two in constituencies where no convention was held).

Following a poor local election performance in 2004 that yielded just 20 seats, the PDs had a limited pool of potential candidates to pick from in 2007; their choice was further restricted by the location of most of the party's councillors in constituencies where it already had Oireachtas representation. Thirty candidates ran in 26 constituencies, with selection conventions held in most cases. Since none of the nominations was challenged, there were no contests in 2007. The most contentious decision made at a convention was to run three candidates in Galway West, a strategy that had proved successful in 2002. While some inside the party questioned the wisdom of repeating this tactic, the strength of the local organisation (30 per cent of the party's councillors nationwide are in its ranks and 'it runs the TD') meant that the national executive was never going to veto this decision. Some in party headquarters favoured running a second candidate in the Longford–Westmeath constituency, because private polls indicated that the party's local TD, Mae Sexton, was struggling to make an impact beyond her electoral base of Longford. However, once she expressed her disapproval of the proposed addition of a Westmeath-based candidate the idea was quickly dropped, indicative of the power that the parliamentary party wields over head office within the PDs.

To give every voter an opportunity to vote for the Greens, the party ran a candidate in every constituency for the first time at a Dáil election. It was also keen to emphasise its evolution as an all-Ireland party, having joined forces with the Northern Ireland Greens some months earlier. Conventions were held in most constituencies, the exceptions being where there was no local group established or the local group could not find a suitable candidate. In such cases, the ETF proposed a nominee and afforded the local members an opportunity to register their disapproval of the executive's choice. This option was chosen because there was not sufficient time to organise a convention; in any case, no opposition to the ETF's choices materialised.

In view of their emphasis on decentralised power, it is somewhat surprising that the Greens were the only party whose central committee did not ratify some candidates selected at conventions. This occurred in two constituencies, and in both cases the ETF was motivated by concerns about the candidates' electability. These decisions were made after extensive negotiations with the two local groups concerned; rather than then imposing its own candidates, the ETF asked the respective groups to nominate more suitable individuals, which they duly did.

Sinn Féin fielded candidates in every constituency, with the exceptions of Cork North-West, Kildare South and Limerick West, where the local organisation was too weak on the ground. Most of the nominations were unopposed at conventions, and the main difficulty in a number of constituencies was not deciding which aspirant to nominate, but rather finding a suitable candidate. One factor that party strategists admitted had a negative effect on the numbers seeking a nomination is the internal rule that any elected office-holder takes just the equivalent of the average industrial wage (approximately €29,000 in 2007) from their salary, investing the remainder into the party organisation. The Election Department preferred not to intervene in the selection of candidates, because this would 'cause havoc' and 'bring more problems than it was worth'. There was little evident opposition within the party to the increasingly active role of the centre; if anything, the local organisations welcomed the establishment of the Election Department, because it provided more support and resources for the candidates.

Overall then, the pattern is of an increasingly centralised process. In all the parties, the national executive now has supreme control over the selection of candidates, but the extent to which it wields these powers varies a great deal; not surprisingly, the level of centralisation seems positively related to the size of the party. Although party strategists play down the increasing influence of the centre, its role very often took an interventionist nature. To this extent, one of the informal rules of the process is that not being favoured by party headquarters makes it extremely difficult to get selected. There were, of course, a number of exceptions to this rule in 2007, but when it was broken, the centre intervened again to add its own candidate to the ticket. Not including the reselection of ten incumbent TDs, the central committees of Fianna Fáil, Fine Gael, Labour and the PDs added 28 candidates in 2007, over 10 per cent of their combined total. At the same time, it needs to be emphasised that in most constituencies there was no conflict between the centre and local branches – for example, no incumbent was deselected by a local convention. The choice of candidate was obvious from the outset as there was either a sitting TD, senator or prominent councillor present. If we also include constituencies where there was no suitable candidate available and the central executive had to actively recruit a nominee, this leaves just a minority of constituencies where there was genuinely open competition. Because these constituencies tend to attract more attention, it often results in an exaggerated picture of omnipresent intra-party tension.

How many candidates to run

As shown in the previous section, deciding how many candidates to run can be a considerable source of tension within parties. Although not afforded the alchemic qualities of vote management, party strategists tend to place a great deal of importance in calculating the optimum number of candidates, which one former party organiser described as the second golden rule of candidate selection. The first golden rule is to pick the right candidates; if a party fails to abide by this, then it has to break the second golden rule by adding its preferred candidates to the ticket. The dominant reason for the increasing importance of this second golden rule is linked to the declining rate of intra-party transfer solidarity (see also chapter 6, pp. 93–4). When this rate exceeds 80 per cent (as it did for Fianna Fáil up until the 1970s), determining the optimum number of candidates to run is of less importance, because the great majority of votes stay within the party fold.

The main difference of opinion over the correct number of candidates tends to occur between the local branches and the respective party executives. In constituencies covering a relatively large territory, there are often many competing localities that want to have a candidate to represent their interests on the party ticket. Consequently, cases of overnomination can often be reasonably interpreted as evidence of where candidate selection has not become all-centralised, and where the local branches still retain a considerable level of independence.

Before Bertie Ahern became leader of Fianna Fáil in 1994, arguably the party did not have as controlled a candidate strategy and tended to run more candidates than it does since he took over. For example, Fianna Fáil ran 120 candidates in 1992 compared to 106 in both 2002 and 2007 (see also chapter 13). However, the party now subscribes to the mantra that candidates need to be in a winning position after the first count, which internal strategists term as being 'in the frame'. This requires a very tight candidate strategy, which has been an important factor in the increased level of influence the party executive takes in the candidate selection process. Before the votes were counted, there were just two cases of apparent over-nomination in 2007; ironically, one of these was the Taoiseach's own constituency of Dublin Central. Neither of these cases ultimately cost the party a seat.

In contrast to Fianna Fáil, Fine Gael did not have as tight a ticket, running a lot more candidates (91) than it expected to win. Before the election, the party was criticised for running four candidates in Clare, Galway East and Mayo; three candidates in Carlow–Kilkenny, Dun Laoghaire, Meath West, Sligo–North Leitrim and Waterford; and two in some cases where it had no sitting TD, in particular Dublin North-East, Kerry South and Kildare South. It was not the case that the central committee planned four-candidate strategies; this outcome occurred where party headquarters either 'screwed it up' or 'didn't get their man through', examples being Clare and Dun Laoghaire. Because the first golden rule of candidate selection was broken by the party's members, the executive had to break the second golden rule to add its preferred candidates.

The exceptions where Fine Gael headquarters claimed to stand firm was the running of a single candidate in constituencies where the party had won less than one quota-worth of votes in 2002. Most of the constituencies where the Organisation Committee enforced this policy were in Dublin; the others consisted of Kerry North, and the two Tipperary and two Donegal constituencies. Somewhat surprisingly, when the votes came in, over-nomination did not prove to be a major problem for Fine Gael, with the only possible cases being Sligo–Leitrim and Carlow–Kilkenny.

Because the other parties tend to run one candidate per constituency, the consequences of overnomination is an issue they rarely have to deal with. While Labour ran multiple candidates in seven constituencies, the PDs in three, the Greens in one, and Sinn Féin in one, the only contentious decisions occurred in the aforementioned cases of Dublin South for Labour and Galway West for the PDs.

What type of candidates were picked

The process of candidate selection has been described as the 'secret garden of politics',[15] because we know very little about what goes on at conventions, the values of the selectors, and the attributes they find desirable in potential candidates. Gallagher and Marsh's study of Fine Gael has shed some light on the values of party members,[16] but it is still difficult to determine why certain candidates are picked. In the absence of available data, one means of assessing what qualities are advantageous for aspirants to possess is by an analysis of the occupational and political backgrounds of those who successfully secured a nomination (see Table 4.1). Without similar data from all those who either desired or sought a nomination, this does not necessarily show evidence of the factors correlated with success, let alone provide the reason as to why these particular candidates were chosen. Nevertheless, it does provide an insight into the type of individuals who are ultimately selected as candidates.

Table 4.1 Occupational backgrounds of candidates, 2007

Occupation	Fianna Fáil	Fine Gael	Lab	PD	Grn	SF	Others	Total	%
Farmer	13	14	0	1	0	0	4	32	6.8
Commerce	33	26	6	6	10	6	20	107	22.7
Higher professional	21	18	10	7	11	2	10	79	16.8
Lower professional	18	19	10	0	6	1	10	64	13.6
Non-manual employee	17	7	10	7	6	10	11	68	14.4
Manual employee	2	0	7	0	0	10	14	33	7.0
Other	3	3	4	4	9	9	15	47	10.0
Unknown	0	4	3	5	2	3	24	41	8.7
Total	107	91	50	30	44	41	108	471	100.0

Note: The classification scheme employed is the same as in previous books in the *How Ireland Voted* series. 'Commerce' consists of businesspeople, predominantly the self-employed. 'Higher professional' includes doctors and lawyers, while 'lower professional' is comprised mainly of teachers and nurses.

In line with the findings of comparative studies on candidates' backgrounds, the middle classes are over-represented, accounting for almost 70 per cent of candidates (this includes those working in commercial, professional and salaried occupations). The different occupational backgrounds are not represented evenly amongst the parties. In keeping with previous elections, the vast majority (84 per cent) of farming candidates ran for either Fianna Fáil or Fine Gael. Teaching was the most common profession represented: 50 teachers in total were selected; 14 each by Fianna Fáil and Fine Gael, nine by Labour, five by the Greens, three by Sinn Féin, and none by the PDs. As at recent general elections, very few manual employees were selected by Fianna Fáil (2), Fine Gael (0) and the PDs (0).

Political experience was an important asset for aspirants seeking a party nomination (see Table 4.2): 60 per cent of candidates from the major parties were drawn from the Oireachtas, a comparable figure to previous elections (65 per cent in 2002 and 62 per cent in 1997). One in six candidates were 'electoral virgins', the bulk of whom (75 per cent) stood for the minor parties. Only 7 per cent of candidates from the three main parties were contesting their first election, reflecting (i) the larger pool of experienced candidates that the major parties have to pick from, (ii) the reluctance of parties to select someone who hasn't been tested on the electorate before, and (iii) the difficulty for new aspirants lacking an established network of support to get selected at local conventions. The central committees' awareness of the last of these factors explains why over half of these new candidates were those added to the ticket by the respective national executives.

Table 4.2   Political experience of candidates, 2007

Party	TD	Senator	Councillor	Previous electoral experience*	New**	Total
Fianna Fáil	68	8	19	6	6	107
Fine Gael	30	10	35	9	7	91
Labour	18	4	18	5	5	50
PDs	8	3	5	9	5	30
Greens	6	0	12	12	14	44
Sinn Féin	5	0	14	14	8	41
Others	12	1	19	41	35	108
Total	147	26	122	96	80	471

* 'Previous electoral experience' refers to candidates who were not public representatives when they were selected, but had previously run for election at either European, Dáil, Seanad or local government level.
** 'New' is defined as having no previous experience as a candidate in any public election.

Two other attributes worth noting are gender and kinship. Repeating a persistent trend, women were under-represented in 2007, comprising 17 per cent of candidates, a steady decline since 2002 (18 per cent) and 1997 (20 per cent). As at previous elections, Fianna Fáil selected the lowest proportion of female candidates (13 per cent), while approximately a quarter of candidates in the four smaller parties were female (see Table 4.3). Being related to a previous office-holder is a distinct advantage in Irish politics, because it brings immediate name recognition and evokes loyalty from party supporters. This appears a distinct advantage in Fianna Fáil, as almost one-third of its candidates were related to previous incumbents. The national average was 15 per cent, but the relatively new arrivals of the Greens and Sinn Féin onto the electoral scene explains the low proportions of their candidates with familial links. When assessing what factors help determine which candidates are selected, strategists within all the parties dismissed both gender and age, but stressed the importance of 'electability'. However, all of the parties do desire to have a 'reasonable' number (what this amounts to is a matter of interpretation) of women on their tickets – an aspiration which, although included in some of their constitutions, has not been yet made mandatory within any of the parties. To this end, some of the party strategists interviewed said that their respective national executives would have added women to the ticket if very few had been selected at conventions.

Table 4.3 Gender and family links of candidates, 2007

Party	Total	Women	%	Family link*	%
Fianna Fáil	107	14	13.1	35	32.7
Fine Gael	91	15	16.5	17	18.7
Labour	50	11	22.0	7	14.0
Progressive Democrats	30	7	23.3	4	13.3
Greens	44	11	25.0	2	4.6
Sinn Féin	41	10	24.4	0	0
Others	108	14	13.0	6	5.6
Total	471	82	17.0	71	15.1

* 'Family link' is defined as where a family relation has held office at either local or national level.

With regard to other possible influences on the process, the parties outside the established three of Fianna Fáil, Fine Gael and Labour did express a desire for candidates who shared their outlook on how society should be run, but in general political views had little effect on the selection process. One other factor that has not been mentioned is the importance of a candidate's geographical base. Given the strength of localism in the voting process, parties running multiple candidates within a constituency need to maintain a geographical balance to maximise their potential vote. They also need to ensure they have candidates from regions with a large catchment area. Parties cannot afford to ignore the importance of geography, because they will lose votes in a constituency if they do not run candidates from key population centres and from their traditional heartlands. For example, in the constituency of Mayo, both Fianna Fáil and Fine Gael selected candidates from the north, south and west of the county. However, while Fine Gael also ran a candidate in the county town of Castlebar, Fianna Fáil chose not to (a major factor in this decision was the presence of Independent (and former Fianna Fáil) TD Beverley Flynn). The result was that Flynn won a seat, while Fianna Fáil won only one of the five seats on offer, its worst ever electoral performance in the county. Along with electability, geography is one of the prime influences on the selection process. The strongest evidence of its significance occurs in constituencies incorporating two counties, where the parties often hold separate conventions within each county; examples include Carlow–Kilkenny, Cavan–Monaghan, Laois–Offaly and Longford–Westmeath.

Conclusion

In the key comparative work on candidate selection, Gallagher posed a number of questions that can be reasonably answered within the context of this chapter.[17] Do central agencies keep a keen eye on the affairs of their party across the country? Undoubtedly so. 'Managed democracy' was one term used by a Fine Gael strategist, although the level of management varies across the parties. Does it help or hinder an aspirant's chances of being selected if (s)he is regarded as a favourite of central office? This depends. Although being seen as a favourite of party headquarters did cause some tension amongst prospective rivals, this is a tacit acknowledgement of how valuable such backing can be. When conflict between local and national party organisations occurs, what is the outcome? This varies between parties, and is dependent on a number of factors, including the nature of the conflict. In any of the parties, the national organisation can exert its formal powers over the local branches on most issues, but this risks alienating the grassroots. Consequently, the centre tends to limit the forcing of its hand only to matters it deems vital, but yields to the local organisation on less significant issues.

The extent of centre–periphery infighting is somewhat exaggerated. 'There's an awful lot of yap spoke about that', claimed a Labour strategist, because in the majority of cases both the local and national organisations agree on who is the most suitable candidate. Tension occurs where party headquarters is portrayed as an absentee landlord who visits the locality once every five years to enforce his will against the wishes of the local grassroots. The reality is that the role of the centre is more akin to that of an arbiter, who evaluates which candidates have the best chance of winning seats for the party. One strategist said that this tension spills over into conflict where 'the grassroots don't always understand what the centre are doing', or where failed aspirants attempt to play the 'anti-Dublin card' to drum up support for their candidacy.

In *How Ireland Voted 2002*, the title of the chapter on candidate selection asked whether the process was 'more democratic or more centrally controlled?'[18] However, it is not the case that the wielding of power is a zero-sum game where increased centralisation implies less democratisation. If anything, it has been shown in this chapter that both tendencies were evident in 2007. Increased centralisation was apparent by the powers afforded to centrally-run election committees in all parties, especially in Fianna Fáil. The inclusive nature of the selection process, where all parties, with the exception of Fianna Fáil, use the one-member-one-vote system was evidence of democratisation. As one strategist said 'power is flowing in two ways'. Indeed, it could be argued that within the parties using OMOV, the candidate selection process has never been so democratic. Open conventions where hundreds of members get to vote freely on the candidates are far removed from the era of 'throat-cutting bloodbaths' that were controlled by local party barons. In general, the lower number of party dissidents running as Independents in 2007 (two in Fianna Fáil, and one each in Fine Gael and Labour), as compared to 2002, suggests a broad consensus reached between the centre and periphery.

Finally, while the degree of planning and coordination in all the parties' strategies was underlined, due heed must be paid to Gallagher's warning that academics are sometimes guilty of overemphasising the 'degree of care and rational calculation' employed by parties in selecting their candidates.[19] While the parties are increasingly professionalised in their activities, it was not the case that all policies were the product of a rational approach. Commenting on constituencies where they appeared to run too many candidates, one strategist remarked: 'we found it difficult to rationalise as well, but we just let them at it and hoped for the best'.

Notes

*   Much of the material in this chapter is based on interviews conducted with ten party strategists, one former strategist and six candidates. I am extremely grateful to them for their help.
1.   Michael Gallagher, 'Introduction', pp. 1–19 in Michael Gallagher and Michael Marsh (eds), *Candidate Selection in Comparative Perspective: The Secret Garden of Politics* (London: Sage, 1988), at p. 1.
2.   Crotty, quoted in Gallagher, 'Introduction', p. 2.
3.   Reuven Hazan, 'Candidate selection', pp. 108–27 in Lawrence LeDuc, Richard Niemi and Pippa Norris (eds), *Comparing Democracies 2: Elections and Voting in Global Perspective* (London: Sage, 2002), at p. 109.
4.   Quoted in Gallagher, 'Introduction', p. 3.
5.   David Farrell, 'Ireland: centralisation, professionalisation and competitive pressures', pp. 216–42 in Richard Katz and Peter Mair (eds), *How Parties Organize* (London: Sage, 1994), p. 228.
6.   www.labour.ie/party/constitution.
7.   All non-attributed quotes throughout this chapter are by party strategists.
8.   Farrell, 'Ireland: centralisation', pp. 227–8.

9. Ostrogorski, quoted in Gallagher, 'Introduction', p. 5.
10. Michelle McDonagh, 'FF Galway West convention abandoned in disarray', *Irish Times*, 30 January 2006.
11. Gordon Deegan, 'Senator warns Fianna Fáil after losing out', *Irish Times*, 5 April 2006.
12. Stephen Collins, 'FF Senator backs constituency call for selection convention', *Irish Times*, 22 March 2007.
13. John Drennan, 'Sandwich king may have to eat his words', *Sunday Independent*, 25 March 2007. See also Terence Flanagan's account in chapter 5.
14. Stephen Collins, 'Anger as Labour foists running mate on candidate', *Irish Times*, 12 July 2006.
15. Gallagher and Marsh, *Candidate Selection*.
16. Michael Gallagher and Michael Marsh, *Days of Blue Loyalty: The Politics of Membership of the Fine Gael Party* (Dublin: PSAI Press, 2002).
17. Gallagher, 'Introduction', p. 6.
18. Yvonne Galligan, 'Candidate selection: more democratic or more centrally controlled?', pp. 37–56 in Michael Gallagher, Michael Marsh and Paul Mitchell (eds), *How Ireland Voted 2002* (Basingstoke: Palgrave Macmillan, 2003).
19. Gallagher, 'Conclusion', pp. 236–83 in Gallagher and Marsh, *Candidate Selection*, p. 256.

5
The View from the Campaign Trail

Niall Collins (Fianna Fáil, Limerick West)

Niall Collins was standing for the first time in a general election. He had been elected to Limerick county council at the 2004 local elections. An accountant and former lecturer with Limerick Institute of Technology, he took leave of absence from the Shannon Regional Fisheries Board in order to work full-time as a public representative in the lead-up to the general election. His grandfather Jimmy was a TD for the constituency from 1948 until his death in 1967, and his uncles Gerry (1967–97) and Michael (1997–2007) followed him in representing the constituency in Dáil Éireann. Since 1948 Limerick West has been a three-seat constituency in which Fianna Fáil has won two seats on every occasion except 1997.

I faced a tough battle as I was competing against four outgoing Oireachtas members for three seats, but we in Fianna Fáil had two outgoing seats and I was one of only two candidates. I took leave of my job as assistant CEO with the Shannon Regional Fisheries Board to work full-time at politics in January 2006. This opportunity allowed me, through my work with my uncle Michael Collins TD, to concentrate fully on the constituency and the election. This helped level the playing pitch with the aforementioned Oireachtas members.

Overall I felt that if we maintained our share of the vote I would be elected. As a result of the redrawing of the constituency boundaries across the country, Limerick West was expanded to include a part of the East Limerick constituency. This area, we knew from tallies, had previously voted two to one in favour of Fianna Fáil over Fine Gael. I had recently got a good vote in the 2004 local elections where I polled 1,600 first preference votes in an area that has seven seats going with 19 candidates seeking election. Some local election candidates had the advantage that a seat was being vacated by an Oireachtas member, following the introduction of a ban on the dual mandate which meant that members of the Dáil or Seanad could not also belong to a local council. That was not the case in my local electoral area, though – I had to win a seat in my own right, and so the election was a good test for me. It was a very competitive election given the number of candidates and no one area was without a local candidate.

In May 2005 Michael Collins announced his intention to stand down from the Dáil at the next election. Our selection convention was held in July 2005 with only two names going to convention on the night: myself and outgoing TD John Cregan. In the run into the selection convention a third candidate was in the running, this being Councillor Kevin Sheahan, therefore up until the night of the convention there was a contest. Councillor Sheahan withdrew on the night and John Cregan and I were unanimously selected. Being selected very early was a huge help to me. Once you move outside your council area one has a lot of ground to make up on the more established TDs, so an early start was essential. In addition, the timing of the convention was coming off the back of a successful local election campaign in 2004.

No constituency divide between the Fianna Fáil candidates ever existed in Limerick West and not on this occasion either. The geographical spread of the constituency is vast with no one very large population centre – the largest is Newcastle West with a voter population of approximately 8,000. Traditionally there was never a divide arrangement in any party and it is my view that this will always be the case. In my view a three-seat constituency is always going to be a marginal, therefore all areas are open country for votes.

We used every available technique to try to attract votes: door-to-door canvassing, shopping centres, street canvass, public meetings, party meetings, canvassing Mass beforehand, radio interviews and print media, leaflet drops on local issues, SMS text messaging and voice messaging. Most effective was mass canvassing – there is no substitute for one-to-one person canvassing and asking a person for their support. I felt that nobody would stay around to meet a relatively unknown candidate after Mass, therefore meeting people on the way into Mass turned out to be a great technique. Also, people who go to Mass are more likely to vote. Many funny incidents occurred, most of which should not be put in print. One that can perhaps be related occurred when one person informed me that he could not vote for me, a Fianna Fáil candidate, as 'the government' would not license the medical drug for which he was a sales person on the Free Drugs scheme. When I enquired as to what the drug was for he duly informed me that it was for curing sexually transmitted diseases in teenage males.

I had many dealings with HQ in Dublin, and they provided a great back-up service to my campaign, for which I am very thankful. They took a positive proactive interest in helping my campaign, as did my wife and family and also the Fianna Fáil organisation in Limerick West. It was great to have the experience to call on through both Gerard Collins and Michael Collins, my uncles. Willie O'Dea (Minister for Defence and the poll-topper in the adjacent constituency of Limerick East) was also a great help to me in my campaign. The Fianna Fáil Press Office is now a very well-resourced service and provides a very good research function also. Being well-prepared and informed when making media appearances is very important.

There is no substitute for hard work well before and during the campaign by a great many people associated with my campaign. The Fianna Fáil organisation in the constituency recognised that we had a challenge and they rose to that challenge. A lot of motivated people delivered a decisive result. On a personal level I was naturally delighted with the result, I felt that my election was a very proud moment for my parents and in particular my father, whose own father, the late Jimmy Collins TD, had served the constituency of Limerick West from 1948 until his untimely death in 1967. As a new candidate a lot of people who never were previously involved in politics were involved in my campaign and hopefully they will be involved again the next time.

The lesson for the next campaign – well, the next campaign is already on, we now have a situation in this country where we have rolling campaigns between elections. One has to work hard at all times to keep in touch with constituents, keeping in touch is the key in my view.

Terence Flanagan (Fine Gael, Dublin North-East)

Terence Flanagan was elected as a TD for the Fine Gael party in 2007, the first time he stood at a general election. He is a qualified accountant who has worked in the banking sector for many years and is now a full-time politician. In 2003 he was co-opted onto Dublin City Council to replace Richard Bruton TD due to the ending of the dual mandate. He was elected in the 2004 local elections with an impressive 2,600 first preferences on his first outing. Fine Gael had not won a seat in the three-seat constituency of Dublin North-East in the 2002 election, when Fianna Fáil won two seats and Labour one.

My general election campaign began early in 2005 in the Dublin North-East constituency. Dublin North-East encompasses a vast suburban area stretching from Riverside, Clonshaugh, Priorswood, Darndale, Ayrfield, Edenmore and Donaghmede west of the DART railway line and Kilbarrack, Raheny, Baldoyle, Sutton and Howth to the east of the DART line. Historically, there has been a very low Fine Gael vote west of the railway line and my strategy was to concentrate on those areas initially. As a city councillor, I represented the

Artane ward which forms part of Dublin North-East and I was very familiar with the local issues affecting the people.

Dublin North-East is a three-seat constituency and competition was fierce during the 2007 election campaign. Fianna Fáil put forward its two incumbent TDs, Martin Brady and Dr Michael Woods, and likewise Labour ran Tommy Broughan TD. Sinn Féin put Larry O'Toole on the ticket and the Green Party selected David Healy. The national press predicted Fianna Fáil to lose a seat to Sinn Féin. At best, Fine Gael was predicted to win a seat through Brody Sweeney. I knew that with a two-candidate strategy in a three-seater Fine Gael could get one seat at best or split the vote. I was convinced that it would be either myself or Brody. Only the electorate would decide our fate!

I began my general election campaign very early, in the first months of 2005, by knocking on doors in the Artane ward and concentrating on dropping local leaflets to the other 70 per cent of the constituency where I was relatively unknown. I considered the strategy of meeting people in their homes outside an election period as crucial to building up my profile in the constituency. This gave me the time to meet people and to allow them to voice their opinions and grievances. It provided them with an opportunity to voice issues with me on a one-to-one basis in an informal setting, which would not be feasible during an election campaign where time is of the essence. In my initial meeting with the public, I furnished them with a leaflet outlining my aims and objectives. I noted all queries and forwarded them to the necessary channels and kept my constituents informed of all progress made. I then returned on numerous occasions to the area, providing constituents with newsletters outlining local issues of concern.

Before the Fine Gael party selection convention for the general election in November 2005, I was in the running as the lead candidate. However, with the introduction of Brody Sweeney to the constituency and with half of my new members disallowed to vote at the convention it became clear that Fine Gael headquarters fully supported Sweeney. I had no option then but to stand down at the convention and not challenge the party's strategy of running a high-profile celebrity candidate. Being a Fine Gael man at heart I made the difficult decision of asking my voters to vote for Sweeney at the selection convention to ensure his election as my leader had wanted. He would not have been selected on the night were it not for my supporters' votes as there were also two other credible candidates from the area challenging the convention.

After his win at the selection convention Sweeney took his foot off the gas. He felt he had defeated me and that a Dáil seat was his for the taking. The feedback I began to receive regularly was that he would not rate very highly with the local people as he had no political experience as a councillor or public representative and had no connection with the local people or the area. After all, he was from Dun Laoghaire and lived in Sandymount.[*]

---

[*] Eds: both on the south side of Dublin. For more on Fine Gael candidate selection in this constituency, see chapter 4, p. 55.

In March 2006 I spoke at the Fine Gael ard-fheis. In fact I was the only non-election candidate to speak on a motion and speculation was that it would only be a matter of time before Fine Gael party headquarters and the leadership would add me to the general election ticket.

Opinion polls were conducted by Fine Gael headquarters in May 2006 which included both myself and Sweeney and the results showed that I was the leading candidate. He clearly was not at the races according to political people and feedback from other political parties on a consistent basis around this time showed that Brody was just not cutting it. This was music to my ears but I was always aware that I was the underdog and that some people may have been telling me what I wanted to hear so as to get me to sit back. I continued to work and redoubled my efforts.

Brody began to inject huge sums of cash into a massive advertising campaign on a scale never seen before right across the constituency. Comparisons were made to a Kennedy campaign in America. He booked up every available advertising space in the constituency from bus stops to cigarette bins and had the front page of the *Northside People* newspaper almost every week at €1k a pop. Leaflets were being dropped into people's homes on a weekly basis by An Post. Despite all this, four months later he had not made any major headway with his campaign.

This period was a very difficult and challenging one for me as I was not allowed by Fine Gael head office to canvass or be in the most fertile Fine Gael areas of the constituency east of the railway line, which caused me much anguish. Also, I knew I could never compete with Brody financially. I had been canvassing the party national executive since the convention to be added to the ticket and knew that my chance of success was diminishing as time to the date of the general election was running out. I estimated that I needed at least two months to canvass the constituency once over. I also felt that if the election was called before Christmas Fine Gael would definitely not regain a seat and that there would be no chance of us being in government.

However, I remained focused on pounding the pavements whatever the weather, meeting people and addressing both their local and national issues and keeping them up to date. I produced, designed and, with a small dedicated team, helped deliver some black and white A4 newsletters. Being a local councillor I used my platform to raise queries and have them resolved satisfactorily on behalf of constituents.

By October 2006 party headquarters knew that the election strategy had to be changed as our chances of gaining a seat were diminishing every day so I was added to the ticket to boost Brody's vote. I continued canvassing vigorously, meeting as many constituents as I could on a daily basis as I felt I could take the seat.

Fine Gael headquarters divided up the Dublin North-East constituency for canvassing purposes. Candidates were allowed into certain areas only on allocated days. These areas were constantly rotated and I think that this tactic worked really well as both myself and Brody adhered to these guidelines and constituents were therefore not bombarded with visits from both the Fine Gael candidates on the same day or same week.

During the course of the election campaign, I wrote numerous articles in the local newspaper, the *Northside People*, and appeared on the local radio station, Near FM. During the week, in many areas people were out working during the day so it was unfeasible to begin canvassing until after teatime, which suited me as during this time I worked in my nine-to-five bank job but had a great campaign manager who took care of organising things each day.

When the Taoiseach eventually called the general election in late April for Thursday 24 May I could finally see an end to my two-year campaign. I stepped up my campaign as did other parties and began including after-Mass meetings. I rotated my attendance at all the local churches in my area, thus enabling me to meet a greater number of my constituents in the run-up to the election. I additionally visited schools, shopping centres and community centres. These outlets enabled me to meet a large number of people. The principal activity that I engaged in during the final month of the campaign was door-to-door canvassing. The loyal team of workers I had ensured that we met as many people as possible. I canvassed for as long as it was possible each day.

By the day of the election my tireless campaigning and getting things done for people had ensured that my name was well-known. I got many messages of thanks from constituents for jobs well done which made me feel positive about a good result.

The count was nerve-racking, especially after the previous weeks' intense campaigning by all parties, and Sweeney telling voters in a letter on Fine Gael-headed paper to vote number 2 for me as he was the lead candidate and the seat would be lost to Sinn Féin. Although I lost many votes by this, it may have backfired as I got 900 number twos from Sinn Féin when Larry O'Toole was eliminated. When the first tally was done at 10 a.m. I knew that I was the Fine Gael candidate in the running for the seat and that Sweeney would be eliminated early. However, it looked like Fianna Fáil were going to hold their two seats as Brady was at 22 per cent and Woods was at 20 per cent. In fact Dr Woods had appeared in the national media at lunchtime that day calling two seats for Fianna Fáil. By 7 p.m. that evening Sweeney's transfers were distributed which put me top of the poll by a few hundred votes. Flanagan, Brady, Woods and Broughan were all neck and neck on the final count in a three-seat race! It all depended on Sinn Féin's transfers – which normally go mainly to Labour and Fianna Fáil. At 9 p.m. I was told that I had taken a seat! I got 900 transfers from Sinn Féin which pushed me over the line in second place ahead of Dr Michael Woods (30 years in the Dáil), and Martin Brady (Fianna Fáil) had lost out.

I believe that my focus on micro-issues was paramount in my campaign. All the queries that I received, I dealt with in an efficient manner. I sent off letters to Dublin City and Fingal County Councils on every problem that was presented to me and then returned to the area with leaflets to remind voters that I had put the matter before the council. During the course of my campaign, the vast majority of people that I met were dissatisfied with the government's performance on local and national issues. The chief national issues of concern were health, crime and education. The people who voted for me voted for new blood in national politics and were looking for a change of government. In the end two out of the three seats in Dublin North-East went to the Alliance for Change. Unfortunately, Fine Gael did not gain enough seats nationally to form a government on this occasion. However, who knows what may happen come the next general election!

In conclusion, I wish to thank all those voters in Dublin North-East who supported Fine Gael in the general election, thus helping us reclaim our seat. I believe that I was successful in my election to the 30th Dáil because I was consistently working hard and to the best of my ability some years before the election was called. I had a highly dedicated and loyal team of workers who stuck with me through thick and thin.

For now, I look forward to serving the people of Dublin North-East to the best of my ability for many years to come.

Kathleen O'Meara (Labour, North Tipperary)

Kathleen O'Meara stood for Labour in the three-seat constituency of Tipperary North in 1997, following the retirement of the incumbent Labour TD John Ryan, and in 2002, winning over 10 per cent of the vote on each occasion but without securing election. She was formerly a journalist with RTÉ, and from 1994 to 1997 she was an advisor to a Labour Party minister of state. She was elected to the Seanad on the agricultural panel in 1997 and was re-elected in 2002, and was elected to Tipperary North Riding county council in 1999. After her defeat at the Dáil election in 2007, she decided not to seek a party nomination for the Seanad election.

This was the campaign to win and this time it would be done. This was my determined attitude for a long time before the general election was called, and when I say a long time I mean a long time. Sometimes it seemed as if I were living in the political Bermuda Triangle, a shadow world where time was suspended, waiting for Bertie to call the election.

So we started campaigning early, much earlier than ever before. When I think of this, my third election campaign as a candidate, what immediately comes to mind is the relentlessness and the duration of the canvassing.

I had been out and about long before the selection convention which was in December 2005, a full 18 months before the election. We also believed that intensive canvassing would have to have the effect of increasing my personal vote. And since we were very close to winning in 2002, our strategy was based on increasing that vote sufficiently to get over the line in this tight three-seater.

And the party nationally was up in the polls and with a good performance in the local elections of 2004 we believed we were well poised to gain a seat in North Tipperary in this, my third attempt to get to the Dáil.

So, in January 2006, as soon as Christmas was respectably out of the way, I headed for Thurles to meet our local councillor John Kenehan to start on his local patch, door to door, while we still had light. Gloves and a scarf and the warmest tights I had under strong leather boots were the order of the day. The election canvass had started.

From then on the Director of Elections arrived into my office every week with a detailed schedule of canvassing, based on prioritising each electoral area and allocating canvassing slots to each over a period of weeks.

We convened the Election Planning Group and held regular meetings. We raised funds and delivered localised targeted fliers, especially to towns and new estates. We launched a billboard campaign in March, expensive but high profile. By then the campaign was in full swing, with the party leader on tour, and the work rate of the constituency office, usually busy, beginning to hit the roof. We made a video and put it on YouTube, the first campaign locally to do so.

Local talk was, I was strong going into the campaign – well organised, with a high profile, good office and a track record of getting things done. My lead role in the campaign to defend services in Nenagh General Hospital and a strong identification with childcare, to name but two issues I had worked on, were considered to be strong pluses in my favour. Job losses in Procter & Gamble, the failure of the government to deliver on key local projects, the continuing threat to the future of A&E (Accident and Emergency) in Nenagh – these were all driven home strongly on the doorstep by the strongest-ever campaign team.

The little notebooks, the ones in which I recorded the canvass caseload, started to pile up on my desk in my office in Nenagh, with little sticky notes to let me know which estates it contained. I love canvassing, especially in new estates which were one of my priority areas, and always found that new families were delighted to meet their local politician, months out from the election. Often for the local person coming out with me, it was an opportunity for them to find who had moved into their area!

Our analysis of the constituency was that Michael Lowry's was the only secure seat. We knew he was strong but our canvass told us his vote would be up, from early on. We knew Fianna Fáil would take a seat and that Michael Smith must be vulnerable, but on the other hand the best thing to have said about you is that your seat is in danger, and from early on Smith ran a very strong campaign. We knew our biggest challenge was to get ahead of Noel Coonan (FG). We watched the Fine Gael poll rise with some concern but felt that, with Michael Lowry going well, Coonan would have his work cut out to increase his vote from the last election.

Finally, the election was called. That Sunday morning I was up early to do church-gate collections in Kilcommon and Rearcross, beautiful villages nestling in the hills above Silvermines when I heard the excited voice of Seán O'Rourke on RTÉ and knew straight away that Bertie had blown the whistle. At last! I was excited, ready for the off, delighted that we finally had a date!

We were ready and we were confident. We had started tentative postering a few days earlier but now there was no holding back. Our teams were ready for the road. And it was time for a change. Doorstep after doorstep confirmed this.

From early on it went well. Long-time canvassers reported a very positive response and as the campaign progressed, confidence grew. The other parties told us we were going down well on the doorstep. Fianna Fáil was worried. We were sure the result would be positive. Our media campaign went well locally and I performed well on the Tipp FM candidates' debate. Our canvass was extensive, particularly in Nenagh and Roscrea and with excellent organisation by the Director of Elections, we covered the ground. Of course we had our weak spots but we felt sure we could meet our target vote. My siblings, cousins and friends all turned up to canvass. We worked extremely hard, right up to when the polls closed.

Nationally, we were happy with our performance too. We believed Pat Rabbitte had a very good election, our media coverage was consistently good, there were no mistakes and we watched quite amazed at the drama surrounding Bertie and his finances.

There was certainly a mood for change and a lot of criticism of failures around schools, infrastructure and childcare. There was a high level of engagement on the doorstep, people were thinking carefully about their vote.

When the polls closed, we said we couldn't have done any more than we did, and we didn't see the result coming.

When the boxes were opened, our vote was down in virtually every one and it was clear from 10 a.m. that we would not win a seat. Our disappointment was massive.

So what happened? Why did we not win a seat?

The answer is both local and national.

Locally, Michael Lowry was stronger than ever, increasing his vote to 28 per cent – at the expense of everyone except Fine Gael and despite (or maybe because of) his non-stop complaint that his seat was under threat. His performance bucked the national trend which saw high-profile Independents such as Joe Higgins and Jerry Cowley bite the dust, but Lowry is quintessentially Tipperary and has a political machine of awesome proportions and put considerable resources into the campaign.

Fianna Fáil had a poor performance, its vote down eight points, its worst ever, taking the third seat under the quota. Fine Gael's vote was up and the Mullingar Accord ensured a very strong transfer from Labour, giving Noel Coonan the second seat. Nenagh town transfers from myself gave Máire Hoctor the Fianna Fáil seat, despite trailing Michael Smith from the first count.

And our own vote was very disappointing in North Tipperary. There was a drift to Fine Gael, enough to create a gap too big to make up. A bigger field of candidates hit us harder, especially in Nenagh, and a 10 per cent national vote left us with no bounce.

I am one of those who does believe that the leaders' debate on television and the presidential style of the campaign had an impact on the final result. In an era of growing political ignorance and complacency, to the vaguely political the leaders' debate was like the European Cup Final – it cut through the fog of general ignorance, confusion and disinterest to create the impression that there were two big parties and then there were the rest and that the real battle was between Bertie and Enda. Smaller parties were squeezed out, the second division, the also-rans.

Arguments about hospitals, childcare, commuting, traffic and crime took second place to the bigger issue about our economic health in the minds of those who ultimately swung the election. Those who wanted change, and they were many, saw Fine Gael as an equally legitimate choice, maybe even a better bet, than Labour, to achieve that change. We were right to give people a choice, but there is no doubt that it made Fine Gael more relevant to the electorate.

If I were to do it all over again, what would I do differently? It's hard to know. Ultimately we play a game called politics. We played a good game this time, but we didn't win. Time to study the video, revise the strategy and, above all, come out fighting!

Niall Ó Brolcháin (Green Party, Galway West)

Cllr Niall Ó Brolcháin is a former Mayor of Galway City (2006–07). He stood for election in the 2002 general election and was elected to Galway City Council in 2004. Niall organised three of the Green Party's most recent national conventions, including the first televised one in Galway in 2004. Niall lives with his wife and five children in Knocknarra in Galway City. He has worked in the computer industry for 15 years. He is a computer analyst by profession. He has also been involved in many

organisations and campaigns in the community and voluntary sector. He was one of the founder members of Galway City Community Forum. He had previously set up the Galway Environmental Alliance. Niall wrote a weekly newspaper column in the Galway City Tribune *for many years. He sprang to national prominence in the spring of 2007 as Mayor during the water crisis in Galway City.*

For a smaller party such as the Greens to successfully win a new Dáil seat in any constituency, a lot of things need to work in harmony with each other. For me in the general election of 2007 that did not happen and I was not elected.

I was hotly tipped to take a seat in the five-seater Galway West constituency. The bookmakers had me taking the third seat. The final constituency opinion poll before the election had me taking either the third or the fourth seat. To better understand why that did not happen it is perhaps necessary to put things in context.

During the election of 2007 I was Mayor of Galway City, having been first elected to the city council in 2004. I was the first and remain the only Green representative to be elected in Connacht at the time of writing.

I first ran for office in the general election of 2002 and performed well, finishing in seventh place. This had been the best result nationally in that election for a Green Party newcomer. The general election result was the basis of my success in taking a seat in the four-seat 'Ward of Death' (as Galway City South ward became known locally) in the 2004 local elections.

After I had declared as a candidate for the Galway City South ward, encompassing Salthill, Knocknacarra and the Claddagh, two sitting councillors from other wards (one for Labour and one for Fianna Fáil) decided to add their names to the South Ward ticket. I was of the view that this was a spoiling tactic to prevent the Greens from getting established in Galway.

In the end, I took the Fianna Fáil seat. This was the first time the party had failed to win a seat in any electoral area in Galway, and it lost three seats on the council in total. It was quite a blow to Fianna Fáil and I was seen as one of the principal architects of its misfortune.

While I have nothing against Fianna Fáil personally and get on well with many people in that party, I have great difficulties with their far too cosy relationships with certain property developers, certain public servants, certain members of the media and certain business people. The Fianna Fáil tent at the Galway Races for me symbolises a malaise in that once great party that I personally find difficult to tolerate.

As such, when I was asked that perennial media driven question as to whose seat I would take in the forthcoming election, I decided to be honest and say that I was after junior minister Frank Fahey's seat. While this didn't wash with most political commentators who believed Fahey to be unassailable, I was proved right in that Fahey just managed to hang on to take the last seat and has since been demoted to the back benches.

On the other hand there is perhaps wisdom in not answering that question honestly. To target a long standing and somewhat popular politician is not perceived as an endearing quality even if it is in all cases a reality even for candidates from the same party. If there is no vacancy you must of course knock somebody out in order to get a seat yourself.

The role of Mayor was certainly very good for my profile, Galway is a very vibrant city and the number of functions that I was invited to officiate at was unbelievable. I had more than 1,000 engagements during the year, often starting early in the morning and finishing late at night.

It was not good, however, in terms of allowing me to spend time planning for the general election. Too much time was necessarily spent doing a job that is very important in its own right. It cannot and should not be seen simply as a stepping stone into national politics. I always took the job of Mayor very seriously.

When an opinion poll came out in late March showing that I had the third highest vote at 11 per cent and would top the poll in Galway City, this was a red rag to all the other political parties in Galway West.

As Mayor, I was naturally being blamed for everything that went wrong in Galway City in the run-up to the election. That was only to be expected. However, this intensified when the opinion poll came out.

The 'water crisis' was in full flow, traffic was as bad as ever, health and education facilities have been suffering for years, all due to the unbalanced development of Galway City and the failure to develop infrastructure at the same rate as commercial and housing development.

The real worry that the conservative parties had with me was that they believed for some reason that I was anti-development. Galway is a very conservative and developer-friendly place despite all the spin to the contrary. Funnily enough, the parties of the left were worried that I was too conservative and not radical enough. The truth of course lies somewhere in the middle.

Then came the election. My chances were still rated very highly. I was one of the three great hopes for the Green wave or Green tide that never quite materialised. I was pictured in the *Sunday Times* on a surfboard alongside Mary White from Carlow–Kilkenny and Deirdre de Búrca from Wicklow as the great Green hopes.

I have always worked hard to get my message across in the media and otherwise, but in this case I failed to do so. This was summed up for me by an interesting piece in a local paper. Apparently some candidates complained after the election that I got far too much media coverage, more than my result warranted. The editor of that local paper clarified that this was because all political parties were repeatedly issuing statements about me except for the Greens.

Having said all that, the Galway Greens ran a very good campaign and built up an amazing team for the future. Door-to-door canvassing went very well. We did a good job with our posters. We put out perhaps too many leaflets and again our message was perhaps a bit scattered but that does not take away from the huge workrate of so many supporters.

Of the people involved many had not experienced a general election campaign before. However, we canvassed like people possessed. In South Connemara we had a great team and in the city we covered almost every blade of grass. We also did very well from a visibility point of view in many other parts of the constituency although not all.

Trevor Sargent, the Green Party leader, came down to visit us on as many as three occasions during the last weeks of the election campaign and we certainly had plenty of contact with head office in Dublin. We employed two party workers and set up a local office in Galway City for the duration of the campaign.

We were also fairly well-funded, having done most of our fundraising over the previous years – though, having said that, we were never going to match the spending of the bigger parties.

I am aware that spoiling tactics and unfounded rumours were being spread about me before during and after the election in a very orchestrated way. I am also well aware where these rumours were coming from. However, that is something it is difficult to react to and straight out of the underbelly of Irish politics. I would hate to see it becoming the norm. While these rumours did have an impact on the outcome of the election in Galway, they were only effective because of events elsewhere.

The fact that we did not get our message across adequately during the election campaign had some bearing on our failure to win a seat as did the efforts of other parties to undermine us. However, the biggest factor of all was the overall mood of the electorate on polling day that allowed the highly conservative nature of Galway to come to the fore and elect the same five TDs once again.

On the positive side we increased the Green Party vote in Galway West by a factor of 38 per cent. We also got a great election team together and ran a great campaign overall.

Despite all the hype, the electorate of Galway West was not ready for change and that appears to have been the case right across the country. It was a hugely conservative election, with the biggest irony being that my own party then decided to go into government helping to elect the same Taoiseach we had been so critical of a few weeks earlier.

A few weeks can be a very long time in politics. Politics never stands still. It is certainly going to be difficult for me to adjust to the new political landscape but I will adjust and I have no doubt that the future will present many new challenges.

6
The Earthquake that Never Happened: Analysis of the Results

Michael Gallagher

Those looking back on the 2007 election several decades hence may wonder why it was regarded at the time as such an exciting contest. Looking at the results, it seems that the electorate largely reiterated the verdict it delivered in 2002. The government to emerge was much the same as the outgoing one, and most parties came back with seat totals that showed little change from 2002. Fine Gael made substantial seat gains while Independents slipped back, but this could be seen more as a reversion to normality after the aberrant 2002 outcome than as an upheaval in its own right. Yet, as we saw in chapter 3 and will see in chapter 9, this was not what anyone expected during the campaign (see also the Chronology at the front of book). The theme of the 2007 results, then, is not just one of little change; it is one of little change in the context of widespread expectations of major changes. The story of the 2007 election outcome is primarily one of the dramatic changes that, in the event, simply did not happen. In chapter 7 Michael Marsh probes more deeply into just why the electorate drew back from the brink of setting the party system onto a different trajectory. In this chapter, we look at the performances of each party, at what transfer patterns tell us, and at intra-party competition and vote management.

The Irish constitution states that the ratio of TDs to population in each constituency 'shall, so far as it is practicable, be the same throughout the country' (Article 16.2.3). The constituencies on which the 2007 election were fought had been drawn up in 2004 on the basis of the 2002 census findings. A further census was conducted in 2006; the preliminary results were released in September 2006, but the final results, which were virtually identical, did not become available until 29 March 2007, a month before the election was called and thus too late to allow a fresh redrawing of the constituency configuration to take place. Two Independent TDs, Finian McGrath and Catherine Murphy, challenged the set of constituencies in place, arguing that it did not meet the constitutional requirement: far from there being the same ratio of population to TDs across the country, this ratio ranged from more than 30,000 to 1 in Dublin West and Dublin North to fewer than 23,000 to 1 in Dun Laoghaire and Cork NC. The judge's verdict was that the state had acted in accordance with the law and the constitution, in that it had had insufficient time before the election to rectify the undisputed anomaly, but he suggested that 'urgent consideration' should be given to amending the legislation so that in future the task of redrawing the constituencies (known as 'redistricting' in the US) could begin upon release of the preliminary census figures rather than having to wait for the final ones.[1]

Votes and candidates

The regulations on nomination of candidates had been changed before the 2002 election, allowing party candidates simply to demonstrate that they were endorsed by a registered political party while other candidates required the signatures of 30 'assentors' from the constituency, who had to present themselves at a designated local authority office within the constituency with proof of identity. This followed a decision by the High Court in 2001 that the existing rules requiring candidates to make a financial deposit, which was returned to those whose support exceeded a certain level, was unconstitutional. In November 2006 the Supreme Court ruled that while the requirement of 30 signatures was not itself unreasonable, the stipulation that they each had to travel to a particular office within the constituency was unduly burdensome, and so it declared the regulation unconstitutional. Accordingly, the rules were changed again, so that candidates not endorsed by a registered party could either be nominated by 30 assentors, who would have to complete statutory declarations, or lodge a deposit of €500. Despite these changing rules, the number of candidates has remained fairly stable: 484 in 1997, 463 in 2002, and 470 in 2007.

The statement that 'all politics is local' may have reached cliché status in Ireland, but this is partly because of the strong element of truth it contains. On average, each TD represents around 12,400 voters, but a much smaller number of votes pretty much guarantees election. Only three of the 82 candidates who received as many as 8,000 first preferences, and nine of the 120 to reach 7,000 first preferences, were not elected. With such a low number of votes to garner, we should not be surprised at the 'friends and neighbours' style of politics adopted by most successful politicians. Every candidate, bar one, who received fewer than 1,500 first preferences failed to qualify for reimbursement of election expenses (see note to Table 6.1). The shining exception was Cyprian Brady in Dublin Central, who received only 939 first preferences (0.14 quotas), the lowest of any Fianna Fáil candidate in the election, yet was elected due primarily to his receipt of the lion's share of

Bertie Ahern's transferred surplus, thus becoming the first candidate for 80 years to win election with fewer than 1,000 first preferences.[2] His election recalled to some observers' minds Conor Cruise O'Brien's suggestions in the early 1970s that Eugene Timmons, who was regularly elected in another Dublin northside constituency with the aid of large transfers from Charles Haughey's surplus, was Haughey's 'surplus in human form'; as Haughey's popularity waned, claimed O'Brien, Timmons was 'already beginning to flicker at the edges'. Receiving between 0.5 and 0.6 quotas gave a candidate about a 50–50 chance of being elected; only 2 per cent of those with fewer than this were elected, while 89 per cent of those with more succeeded.

Of the candidates outside the six main parties, 74 received fewer than 1,000 votes, and the great majority did not qualify for reimbursement of their (usually negligible) campaign expenses. Party candidates fared better, though the PDs, the Greens and Sinn Féin also ran many candidates who made little impact. As explained in appendix 5, parties have an incentive to

Table 6.1   Fate of candidates at the 2007 election

	Number	Average vote	Average Droop quotas	% elected	% not elected but qualifying for reimbursement of expenses	% not qualifying for reimbursement of expenses
All candidates	470	4,395	0.44	35	29	36
Fianna Fáil	106	8,100	0.81	73	27	0
Fine Gael	91	6,203	0.60	56	40	4
Labour	50	4,184	0.44	40	36	24
Green Party	44	2,204	0.23	14	27	59
Sinn Féin	41	3,498	0.35	10	49	41
Prog. Democrats	30	1,880	0.20	7	20	73
Others	108	1,268	0.13	5	16	80
Cabinet minister	15	11,299	1.20	93	7	0
Junior minister	15	8,824	0.88	87	13	0
Non-ministerial TD	116	7,197	0.72	77	22	1
Senator	27	5,698	0.55	52	30	19
MEP not in Oireachtas	2	4,190	0.47	0	100	0
County councillor	122	4,070	0.41	20	57	23
None of the above	173	1,563	0.16	6	17	77
Male	388	4,506	0.45	37	27	36
Female	82	3,872	0.40	27	40	33

Note: As explained in appendix 5, candidates qualify for some reimbursement of campaign expenses provided their vote total at some stage of the count reaches a quarter of the Droop quota (for explanation of the Droop quota, see appendix 4). Voting figures refer to first preference votes. 'County councillor' refers to those candidates who at the time of the election were members of a County or County Borough Council.

do this, since their total permitted campaign spending increases the more candidates they nominate.

Elective status, too, is strongly related to candidates' fates (see Table 6.1). Ministers had the strongest record of re-election: only three ministers lost their seats, all from the PDs (Michael McDowell from the cabinet plus junior ministers Tim O'Malley and Tom Parlon). TDs rarely fail to meet the threshold for reimbursement of expenses, and the exception this time was again a PD, Mae Sexton in Longford–Westmeath, who had been a surprise victor in 2002. Five senators – four from the PDs and one Independent – met the same fate. Candidates with at least some elective status fare significantly better than those with none. Among the latter, the great majority polled poorly (more than three-quarters received fewer than 0.2 Droop quotas), and only ten were elected, including a few with an electoral track record: three former Fine Gael TDs returning after defeat or retirement in 2002, and a Fianna Fáil candidate defeated in a 2005 by-election. Knowing a candidate's party label and elective status, then, goes a long way toward predicting their likely fate.

The proportion of female candidates was slightly lower than in 2002 (down from 18 to 17 per cent) and, as always, female candidates received fewer votes than men, though this is more realistically attributed to their party label and their elective status than to their gender. Although all parties pay lip service to the desirability of increasing the number of women TDs, women did not make up more than a quarter of any party's candidates, and the proportion among the two main parties' lists were especially low (13 per cent within Fianna Fáil and 16 per cent in Fine Gael).

Plus ça change

Before we look at the fate of the parties, we should mention that more attention than usual was focused on the level of turnout. According to official figures this had been declining steadily since the late 1960s, though some wondered whether this indicated a genuine decline or, rather, an increasingly inaccurate electoral register.[3] Although in most countries inaccuracy tends to refer to the non-inclusion of individuals who are entitled to vote, in the Irish context the criticism has been that the register contained a large number of names that should not have been there, so 'real' turnout was several percentage points higher than reported turnout, though it was still declining.[4] Between 2002 and 2007 there were highly publicised attempts to 'clean up' the register, so there was reason to expect an increase in turnout, especially given the perceived closeness of the contest this time.

That did indeed happen. Turnout (valid votes as a percentage of electorate) rose by over four percentage points from 2002 to 66 per cent, the highest figure (according to official data) since 1989. Compared with 2002, the total electorate rose by 109,000, while the number of valid votes rose by 208,000. Turnout rose in virtually every constituency, and the rise was greatest in

Dublin, where it was up by six percentage points, though turnout in Dublin is still lower than in the rest of the country (for full details see appendix 1). Dublin SE, one of only four constituencies where turnout declined, has the lowest turnout (53 per cent). Whether turnout as a proportion of the total number of eligible voters increased, and if so by how much, or whether the apparent rise is wholly or partly an artefact of the pruning from the electoral register of surplus names, requires further analysis.

Turning to the fates of the parties and candidates, the results of the election showed that only Fine Gael and Independents saw significant changes in their vote shares, and only these and the PDs registered significant seat changes (Table 6.2). The other parties' performances were remarkably close to those of 2002, although the changes were sufficient to bring about a change of government (see chapter 12). Table 6.2 also shows that the largest three parties gained from the electoral system, winning a combined total of 148 seats against their 'fair share' of just 136. We now turn to analysis of each party's performance.

Table 6.2   Result of the 2007 election, with changes since 2002

	% vote	Change since 2002	Seats	Change since 2002	% seats	'Fair' number of seats in proportion to first preference votes
Fianna Fáil	41.6	+0.1	77	−4	46.7	72
Fine Gael	27.3	+4.8	51	+20	30.9	47
Labour	10.1	−0.6	20	0	12.1	17
Green Party	4.7	+0.8	6	0	3.6	8
Sinn Féin	6.9	+0.4	4	−1	2.4	12
Progressive Democrats	2.7	−1.2	2	−6	1.2	5
Socialist Party	0.6	−0.2	0	−1	0.0	1
People before Profit/SWP	0.5	+0.3	0	0	0.0	1
Workers' Party	0.1	−0.1	0	0	0.0	0
Christian Solidarity Party	0.1	−0.2	0	0	0.0	0
Fathers' Rights	0.1	+0.1	0	0	0.0	0
Immigration Control	0.1	−0.0	0	0	0.0	0
Independents	5.2	−4.2	5	−8	3.0	2
Total	100.0	0	165	0	100.0	165

Note: For detailed results, see appendix 1. Table refers to contested seats; Fianna Fáil also won the one uncontested seat (automatic re-election of Ceann Comhairle), giving it 78 seats out of 166 in the 30th Dáil. Fathers' Rights and Immigration Control are not registered parties so their candidates were not officially listed as such. Last column represents allocation of seats by Sainte-Laguë method of proportional representation (generally seen as the 'fairest' since it does not systematically favour either larger or smaller parties) based on parties' national first preference vote totals; each Independent candidate is treated as a separate unit.

Fianna Fáil

The election, it was agreed after the votes were counted and the government formed, was a triumph for Bertie Ahern, who by becoming the first Taoiseach to win three consecutive terms since Eamon de Valera in 1944 had confirmed his unique bond with the Irish people. Fianna Fáil's dark days of the 1980s, when it was led by Charles Haughey, a man who failed to win an overall majority for Fianna Fáil in five attempts, were well and truly laid to rest. There was much discussion of the sources of Ahern's ability to broaden Fianna Fáil's appeal to sections of the Irish electorate that had shunned the party under Haughey.

Only those with a set of reference books by their side and, no doubt, an absence of generosity of spirit dared suggest that this version flew in the face of the facts. Ahern has now led the party into three elections, and the 41.6 per cent of the votes Fianna Fáil won in 2007 represents its high point under his leadership. In contrast, the *lowest* point that Fianna Fáil hit under Haughey was 44.1 per cent. Ahern has an excellent record of leading his party into government and is more politically adept at many things than Haughey was, but attracting first preference votes to Fianna Fáil is not one of them. In fact, Ahern's electoral record as Fianna Fáil leader is the second lowest of Fianna Fáil's six leaders; only Albert Reynolds, who was given just one chance to lead the party into an election, fared worse (see Table 6.3). While any previous leader who notched up an average support level of 41 per cent would have had Fianna Fáil TDs searching for a copy of the Corú (the mythical and virtually unobtainable party constitution) for the section on how to bring about internal party regime change, Ahern finds himself feted as a leader like no other.

Table 6.3 Fianna Fáil performance under six leaders, 1927–2007

	Elections	% votes	% seats
Eamon de Valera (1926–59)	12	43.6	47.0
Seán Lemass (1959–66)	2	45.8	49.7
Jack Lynch (1966–79)	3	47.5	52.1
Charles J. Haughey (1979–92)	5	45.2	47.4
Albert Reynolds (1992–94)	1	39.1	41.2
Bertie Ahern (1994–)	3	40.8	47.4
Total	26	43.4	47.0

This is partly because of the low expectations surrounding Fianna Fáil for much of the 2007 campaign (see Chronology). When early polls during the 1992 campaign had shown Fianna Fáil faring poorly, Albert Reynolds had famously declared that his strategy was to 'start low and finish high', but unfortunately he achieved only the first of these. In 2007, though, Ahern managed this perfectly, finishing higher than virtually anyone had expected.

Consequently the outcome was widely perceived as snatching victory from the jaws of defeat, whereas if Fianna Fáil had been expected during the campaign to achieve an overall majority the outcome would have prompted far more critical post mortems.

The other reason why the result was seen as a success for Ahern was, of course, that it meant the party would be returning to government. Since changing its stance on coalition in 1989,[5] Fianna Fáil has, exaggerating just a little, exchanged all of the power most of the time for most of the power all of the time, and Ahern's ability to build relations of trust with other parties has certainly played an important part in this. This is apparent in the process of building and maintaining governments (see chapters 1 and 12), but it also affects the way voters of other parties use their lower preference votes. In the pre-Ahern era supporters of virtually all other parties, from whatever part of the political spectrum, displayed an attitude of 'anyone but Fianna Fáil' when ranking candidates on the ballot paper, but under Ahern, Fianna Fáil, while not exactly acting as a magnet for transfers, does not repel transfers as it used to. There is now a greater range of parties than at most times in the past, and not all of their voters feel as antagonistic to Fianna Fáil as voters of Fine Gael and Labour did when the party system was, essentially, a competition between Fianna Fáil and the rest. The consequence is that although Ahern's record in terms of votes trails well behind that of the party's first four leaders, he has done better than any previous leader in converting votes into seats. In seat terms he is doing as well as Haughey and better than de Valera (Table 6.3).

Fianna Fáil's national vote share hardly altered compared with 2002, though this conceals some change in almost every constituency, with particularly large gains of over eight percentage points in Limerick E and Donegal SW and equally large losses in Mayo and Tipperary N. There were suggestions that it owed its success to the backing of voters in the commuter belt counties around Dublin (summed up in the cryptic neologism 'breakfast roll man'), who faced problems such as poor public transport and inadequate and expensive childcare provisions. Such voters had inflicted by-election defeats on Fianna Fáil in Kildare N and Meath in 2005, yet had backed the party in 2007, because, whatever the difficulty of travelling to their job, they saw Fianna Fáil as the party responsible for the fact that they had a job to travel to. The evidence is mixed: the party made above average gains, compared to 2002, in some of the constituencies doughnutting Dublin, such as Wicklow, Kildare S, and Meath, it is true, but it lost support in Kildare N and Louth. Overall the picture of gains and losses is shapeless, with no strong geographical patterns. Fianna Fáil lost five seats to Fine Gael, and most of its other gains and losses were due to redistricting: a reduction in the number of seats cost it one seat in both Cork NC and Dublin NC, while it picked up the newly created extra seats in Kildare N and Meath (see Table 6.4). The party remains over-represented by the electoral system due mainly to the small average number of TDs per constituency (only four, which is very low by the standards of proportional representation systems internationally), winning 47 per cent of the 165 contested seats with 42 per cent of the votes, but it was not so over-represented as in 2002. With a little luck it could have taken additional seats, as three of its candidates (Denis O'Donovan in Cork SW, Martin Brady in Dublin NE and Tom Fleming in Kerry S) missed out only narrowly, while only two of its TDs were equally narrow winners (Niall Blaney in Donegal NE and Martin Mansergh in Tipperary S).

Table 6.4 Party gains and losses, 2007

	FF	FG	Lab	SF	Grn	From PD	Soc	Ind	Redistricting	Total
Gains by										
FF	–							3	2	5
FG	5	–	2	1		6	1	5		20
Lab			–		1				1	2
SF				–						0
Grn		1			–					1
PD						–				0
Soc							–			0
Ind	1							–		1
Redistricting	2							1	–	3
Total	8	0	3	1	1	6	1	9	3	32

Fine Gael

Fine Gael's performance can be interpreted in two very different ways. Those who see a glass half full would hail it as one of the outstanding achievements in Irish political history. The party, which after the 2002 debacle some thought was bound for oblivion,[6] not only remained alive but gained 20 seats – a greater inter-election advance than any Irish party had ever made before. In the wake of the 2002 election some had predicted that by 2007 the new vigorous forces on the political scene would be dismembering what was left of Fine Gael's cadaver, but the party spectacularly defied these challenges and reasserted its status as the second largest party in the state, with more seats than all the smaller parties put together.

Others, though, see a glass half empty. The gain of 20 seats was based on a modest increase in votes; in 2002 its seat share dropped much more than its vote share, and this was simply reversed in 2007. If seats were allocated nationally according to first preference vote totals, Fine Gael's seat gain would have been far less dramatic, from 38 seats in 2002 to 47 in 2007. The 20 seats it gained, though impressive, is still a smaller number than the 23 it lost in 2002. Far from achieving any kind of breakthrough, Fine Gael has simply returned to the uninspiring level of support that has passed for normalcy since 1987. Indeed, its performance is virtually identical in both votes and seats to that of 1987, and its 1987 result was described in the relevant volume in this series in terms such as 'lowest vote share since 1957', 'unambiguously gloomy' and 'transported back to its feeble position of the late 1950s'.[7] Moreover, Fine Gael seems to be still almost irrelevant to government formation, with 51 seats bringing it no more power than 31 had in 2002.

Fine Gael made vote gains in all but eight constituencies, making 20 seat gains and sustaining no losses. The most spectacular gain was in Mayo, where the party's support rose by over 16 points as voters hoped they were playing their part in ensuring that the next Taoiseach would be a Mayo TD. Other notable gains were in Kerry South, where it won its first seat for 20 years; in Wicklow, where it won two seats for the first time since 1982; and in Clare, where it took two seats for the first time since 1989. Only Kildare S and three Dublin constituencies are now unrepresented by a Fine Gael TD, whereas there had been 13 such constituencies in 2002. Only two Fine Gael TDs lost their seats, in both cases to running mates. One defeated TD was Dr Liam Twomey, who was elected in Wexford in 2002 as an Independent[8] and joined Fine Gael in September 2004; while the other, Gerard Murphy, had unseated frontbencher Michael Creed in 2002 and now lost his seat to Creed. Most of its seat gains came from the government parties, with only two being made at the expense of its putative coalition allies, Labour and the Greens (Table 6.4). The party narrowly missed out on two further gains, as a swing of less than 1 per cent would have seen it take seats in Carlow–Kilkenny and Cork E. As against this, had its vote gains in Clare, Cork SW and Dublin NE been very slightly smaller it would not have gained seats in each of these constituencies.

Overall, given the despondency in the party after the 2002 result, Fine Gael is justified in emphasising the positives of its performance. Realistically, it could not have been expected to do any better than it did, and it might well have done worse. Entering office remains at least one more push away, but its 2007 result gives it a platform from which it can make credible claims to be a party of government after the next election.

Labour

Labour's result was much the same as at most previous elections of the past 30 years: up a bit here, down a bit there, much the same overall. Over the ten elections of the period 1977–2007, Labour's vote fell outside the band 9–12 per cent, and its seats outside the band 15–21, only twice: in 1987 when it plunged to 6 per cent after the uncomfortable experience of the 1982–87 coalition government, and in 1992 when the Spring tide raised it to 19 per cent of the votes. This remarkable stability, 1987 and 1992 apart, suggests a party that has found its level within the party system – or, some would say, is stuck in a rut. The incorporation of the bulk of the Workers' Party (which won 5 per cent of the vote in 1989) via Democratic Left and New Agenda has made no perceptible difference. While Labour, unlike some other parties that have flourished for a while, is not going to disappear, there is no sign that it is on course to achieve anything like the level of strength that the left in most of the rest of Europe has come to expect. Moreover, for as long as Fianna Fáil is able to command the kind of support it has received at the last three elections, Labour seems to have become almost as marginal in the government formation process as Fine Gael has.

The context in which we now evaluate Labour's performance (10 per cent of the votes, 20 seats) was expected to be very different. If the pre-election punditry had been correct, Labour would now be in a minority on the broad left, with Sinn Féin, the Socialists, the Greens and left-wing Independents having around 25 seats between them. Had that happened, analysts would have been quick to speculate on the displacement of Labour, the representative of the 'old left', by forces apparently more in tune with the twenty-first-century zeitgeist, and to suggest that Labour needs to move away from the centre if it is to broaden its appeal. Labour asserted its dominance of the left-hand side of the political equation by winning twice as many seats as Sinn Féin, the Greens and the Socialist Party combined – yet it did this despite winning 44,000 fewer votes than those parties did. Sinn Féin alone won more than two-thirds as many votes as Labour, an achievement obscured by its return of only four seats to Labour's 20; Labour would have been five seats behind the rest of the broad left, rather than ten seats ahead of it, had seats been awarded in proportion to national vote totals (Table 6.2). Labour's seats-to-votes ratio, calculated by dividing its share of the seats by its share of the votes, was, at 1.2, the highest ever. Clearly, there are many voters who are not attracted by the two main parties and whose inclinations are in some sense left of centre but who find other options more appealing than Labour.

Examining the entrails of Labour's 2007 result, we find that it slipped marginally in votes and fell back by one seat. It gained two seats, one at the expense of the Greens in Cork SC and the other by taking the new seat created in the Dublin Mid-West constituency. It lost three: the seats of retiring TDs in Carlow–Kilkenny and Dublin North were not held, and in Kerry South the incumbent Breeda Moynihan-Cronin, who was prevailed upon to stand again having earlier announced that she would be retiring, was defeated. Labour had been represented in Carlow–Kilkenny by father and son James and Séamus Pattison almost continuously since 1933, and another dynasty was ended when, for the first time since 1943, there was no Spring on the ticket in Kerry North, where Labour's vote dropped by over 11 per cent. At least, unlike in 2002, some new blood arrived in the Dáil group, with Joanna Tuffy in Dublin MW, Ciarán Lynch in Cork SC, and Seán Sherlock, who succeeded his father in Cork E, reducing the age profile somewhat (the 17 re-elected Labour TDs had an average age of 58 at the time of the election).

Although some in the party claimed after the election that a few hundred votes in a handful of constituencies could have made a significant difference, the evidence contradicts this. In only one constituency did Labour narrowly miss out on a seat (in Dublin SC Eric Byrne finished just 69 votes short of a seat), while in two (Cork E and Dublin W) it was Labour that clung on by its fingertips. Although the party leadership changed in the late summer, as it had within months of both the 1997 and 2002 elections, the new leader Éamon Gilmore, upon taking over, emphasised continuity of philosophy, improved organisation and better presentation of Labour's existing values and policies rather than a more fundamental reassessment. As at most elections over the last 30 years, Labour's performance was neither bad enough to prompt a root-and-branch self-examination nor good enough to lift it into the top division.

Sinn Féin

Sinn Féin confirmed its dominance over the SDLP in the Northern Ireland Assembly election of 7 March and confidently expected to continue its onward march in the Dáil election. It was to discover that the southern electorate needs wooing in a rather different way from northern nationalists. The party had been widely expected to win around 10–12 seats, and there were signs, such as Martin McGuinness's prediction that the other parties would be lining up to try to persuade it to join a coalition after the election, that it was coming to believe its own hype. The idea that it could actually slip in support compared with 2002 was never mooted, making its loss of one seat all the more of a shock and, quite apart from the details of its performance, the result punctured the myth of the party's unstoppable rise North and South.

Sinn Féin's national vote went up but it slipped back by two percentage points in Dublin, where it had been most confident of gains. It entered the election with two seats in Dublin and was regarded as virtually certain to add three more. In the event, one of its TDs lost his seat (Seán Crowe in Dublin SW), the other (Aengus Ó Snodaigh in Dublin SC) hung on by 69 votes, and none of the other three candidates seen as certainties to enter the 30th Dáil (Mary-Lou McDonald in Dublin Central, Larry O'Toole in Dublin NE and Dessie Ellis in Dublin NW) came close to taking a seat. Outside the capital its vote rose in all but a handful of constituencies, but only in Donegal, where it presumably picked up republican votes from the disbanded Blaneyite organisation (see 'Others' section below), did it really give the established parties a scare. For the most part it fell short on first preferences and compounded this by its continued inability to attract lower preferences at the same rate as most other parties.

On the basis of its national support it would have earned 12 seats on a proportional basis (Table 6.2), but it missed out on seats primarily because it did not have concentrated support in enough specific constituencies. The party won between 5 and 10 per cent of the votes in 11 constituencies, which added impressively to its national vote total but was nowhere near enough to win a seat in any one constituency. Only eight of its candidates won more than 0.6 Droop quotas, which as we saw earlier is the level above which a majority of candidates win election, and even four of these missed out on election due partly to their inability to attract transfers. In Donegal SW Pearse Doherty won the highest vote (0.85 quotas) of any unsuccessful candidate in the country. Only one other candidate had between 0.5 and 0.6 quotas; the other 32 started with less than half a quota, which spells almost certain defeat for any candidate, especially one with no running mate and no allied parties. Although it has slightly higher support than in 2002, its prospects look less bright than they did five years ago. After the 2002 election it was quite plausible to expect that one more heave in six to ten constituencies would bring a rich tranche of seats clattering into Sinn Féin's hands. After the 2007 election, in contrast, most of what seemed to be low-hanging fruit have retreated out of easy reach, and it remains to be seen whether 2007 is just a temporary setback to the party's inexorable progress or whether 2002 will come to be seen as Sinn Féin's high water mark.

Green Party

For the first time in its existence the Green Party entered government after the 2007 election, and that inevitably invests the party's electoral performance with the retrospective aura of success. When the votes were counted on 25 May, though, there did not seem to be very much to celebrate. The outstanding feature of the Greens' 2007 result, in fact, is how similar it was to its 2002 result. Usually, there is significant variation in a party's performance across the country, but the Green Party's 2007 vote level was within 2.5 per cent, either above or below, of its 2002 level in all but three constituencies: Cork SW, Cork NW, and Louth. Moreover, in the first two of those its growth was larger than the norm simply because it had not run a candidate in 2002, while in Louth its advance (3.4 per cent) scarcely represented a seismic shift in its appeal.

Its seat level remained unchanged, as it lost one seat and gained another. Its defeat came in Cork SC, where Dan Boyle, who had been seen as a likely minister if the party entered government, lost to Labour in one of the biggest surprises of the election. Because Boyle was seen as a virtual certainty to be re-elected, his campaign could not credibly send out the message that every vote was crucial. Irish politicians seeking election react to being described as 'safe' in the same way as Count Dracula reacts to garlic, and while their horror at the word sometimes seems to border on superstition, Boyle's defeat is a reminder that it is by no means irrational. Two other TDs came close to defeat. In Dublin SE John Gormley narrowly pipped Michael McDowell for the last seat, just as in 1997, and if McDowell had received a slightly more supportive transfer from Fianna Fáil on the last count then Gormley would have lost (see section on transfers below). In Dun Laoghaire, Ciarán Cuffe came within 110 votes of being eliminated after the eighth count. Indeed, of the six constituencies where the Greens won a seat in 2002, their vote dropped in four and remained unchanged in one; only Éamon Ryan in Dublin South showed any real increase in support. The party's three biggest vote losses came in constituencies where it had a TD, perhaps a sign that its voters had expected something from their Green TDs, either at national level or in terms of local activity, that they did not get. If it was the second half of the 'think globally, act locally' slogan that voters wanted more of, then the entry to ministerial positions of three of the party's six TDs may be electorally damaging rather than rewarding.

Its only seat gain saw the election of its deputy leader, Mary White, in Carlow–Kilkenny. This marked a number of firsts: White became the first female Green TD, the first woman ever elected from either Carlow or Kilkenny, and the first Green TD to represent a predominantly rural constituency. Even her vote fell back compared with 2002; her election in 2007 was due partly to there being an additional seat available in the constituency (one having been reserved for the Ceann Comhairle in 2002) and partly to poor vote management by Fine Gael (see later section). Other seat gains that had been predicted at the start of the campaign – Deirdre de Búrca in Wicklow, Niall Ó Brolcháin in Galway West (see chapter 5), and perhaps Mark Dearey in Louth or Tony McDermott in Dublin SC – did not come close to materialising, and no Green anywhere in the country was the runner-up in their constituency. While we do not yet know the constituency configuration on which the next election will be fought, at present there are more seats that the party is close to losing than it is close to winning, and the next election could be a challenging occasion for the Greens.

Progressive Democrats

Ever since the PDs were founded in the mid-1980s, and certainly from the 1989 election, the party has felt beset by unsympathetic critics predicting its imminent demise. On each occasion, sometimes only just, it was able to prove its detractors wrong – but in 2007 the prophecies of doom finally came true. The PDs' result represented something close to wipe-out. The party lost about a third of its votes and three-quarters of its eight seats, placing its continued existence in doubt. Those defeated included its leader, Michael McDowell, one of the first crop of PD TDs in 1987; its deputy leader Liz O'Donnell, a TD since 1992; its president Tom Parlon; Fiona O'Malley, a daughter of its first leader Des O'Malley; and Tim O'Malley, a cousin of Des O'Malley and the third in a line of O'Malleys who had held a seat in Limerick East continuously since 1954.

On a proportional basis its national vote total would have earned it five seats instead of the two it won (Table 6.2), but it has had lucky breaks in vote–seat conversion in the past and this time the pendulum swung the other way. Of its six defeated TDs, only Michael McDowell in Dublin SE and Tim O'Malley in Limerick E came close to holding their seats. In the other four cases the party's vote plunged to around half of its 2002 level, and, as mentioned above, one of its defeated TDs, Mae Sexton from Longford, was the only incumbent in the country who did not even qualify for reimbursement of expenses (Table 6.1).

Back in 1987 Fine Gael had been the main victim of the emergence of the PDs, and 20 years on it was Fine Gael that may have delivered the *coup de grâce* to the party, as five of its seat losses were definitely to Fine Gael and the sixth, that of Mae Sexton, while complicated by a rearrangement of constituencies in the north-west and midlands, is probably best seen that way as well. It was not just Fine Gael that bore responsibility for the PDs' virtual obliteration, though, for their coalition partner Fianna Fáil could have come to their aid through transfers. Instead, a weak terminal transfer from Fianna Fáil cost the PDs two seats (see later section), including that of their leader. It is as yet too early to be certain whether the PDs will remain in existence long enough to contest the next election. If they do decide to disband, we can confidently conclude that never before has a party that averaged just 5.6 per cent of the votes in the six elections that it contested made such an impact on government policy.

Others

Independent candidates took 13 seats in 2002, the highest number since 1951, and their ranks increased in 2005 when Catherine Murphy won the Kildare N by-election, but most of them came back down to earth with a bump in 2007. Only ten of these Independents contested the election under that label, along with an eleventh, Beverley Flynn (see next page). Two retired (Marian Harkin and Mildred Fox), and a further two joined parties. In Donegal NE Niall Blaney joined Fianna Fáil in July 2006, finally putting an end to the split that began in 1970 with the Arms Crisis, when his uncle Neil T. Blaney had been dismissed from government by Taoiseach Jack Lynch. Blaney had been a TD since 1948, and his father before him had represented Donegal from 1927. Neil T. Blaney was expelled from Fianna Fáil in 1972 and had styled himself and his organisation 'Independent Fianna Fáil', under which label he had been continuously re-elected until his death in 1995. He had been succeeded by his brother Harry, Niall's father. The durability of the Blaney dynasty in Donegal politics, and its strong roots in Fianna Fáil, gave Niall Blaney's incorporation into the party in 2006 something of the aura of the return of the prodigal son. The other Independent TD to join a party was Liam Twomey, who not only joined Fine Gael but became that party's spokesperson on health, but he then became one of only two Fine Gael TDs to lose a seat in 2007.

Of the 11 TDs who contested the election as Independents, five were re-elected, in most cases quite comfortably. Three had strong roots in parties – or, in Noel Whelan's now widely used phrase, came from a particular 'gene pool'. Michael Lowry, who headed the poll in Tipperary N, had been a Fine Gael TD and minister before parting company with the party in 1997 over his financial affairs. In Kerry S Jackie Healy-Rae, a one-time Fianna Fáil stalwart in the constituency, had won a seat as an Independent in 1997 and retained it ever since, being one of the 'gang of four' Independents who had supported the FF–PD minority government between 1997 and 2002. In Mayo Beverley Flynn, elected for Fianna Fáil in 1997 and 2002, was expelled from the party in May 2004 following the failure of a libel action she took against the national broadcaster RTÉ. Her father had been a Fianna Fáil TD and minister as well as a European Commissioner, and her 2007 campaign made clear her expectations of a return to the party fold: her advertisements used the phrase 'For Flynn', with the letters 'FF' highlighted. The other two, Tony Gregory and Finian McGrath, were left-wing Independents representing adjacent constituencies in Dublin. McGrath was a former member of the constituency organisation of Gregory, who, having been elected at all nine elections from February 1982 to 2007, has become the second most successful Independent TD in Irish political history, bettered only by Alfie Byrne, who was elected to 13 Dála and spent 31 years as a TD between 1922 and 1956.

The other six lost their seats. The only one elected prior to 2002, Séamus Healy, was a surprise and narrow loser to Fianna Fáil in Tipperary S. Catherine Murphy, like Healy a left-wing Independent, lost to Fianna Fáil in Kildare N. James Breen, a Fianna Fáil 'gene pool' Independent in Clare, lost narrowly to Fine Gael. The other three – Paudge Connolly in Cavan–Monaghan, Jerry Cowley in Mayo and Paddy McHugh in Galway E – lost around half of their 2002 support and came nowhere near retaining their seats.

Independents have followed an almost market-driven cyclical pattern at recent elections. After the 1997 election their scarcity, and the minority government's reliance on them, enabled them to make demands on behalf of their constituencies. As a result an Independent TD seemed to become a valuable commodity for a constituency, and in 2002 many more were elected – but now there was an over-supply, not to mention a majority government, and so they had much less value. This led to a drastic reduction in their numbers at the 2007 election, but those few found themselves in a position to secure benefits for their constituency in the government formation process (see chapter 12). On this basis, the next election might see a resurgence in Independents' fortunes.

Elsewhere in the 'others' category, the Socialist Party had been expected to return to the Dáil with two seats, but instead it lost the only one it had, when its leader Joe Higgins lost his Dublin West seat by around 400 votes. Higgins had possessed the rare capacity to unsettle the Taoiseach in parliamentary questioning, and (once he was safely defeated) even his political opponents agreed that, like the PD leader Michael McDowell at the opposite end of the political spectrum, he would be a major loss to parliamentary politics. The Socialists' other hope of a seat had lain in Clare Daly in Dublin North, where she had been the runner-up in 2002, but her vote slipped by nearly four percentage points. The Socialists were unfortunate in that their strongest two constituencies were also the two that suffered most from the failure of the

Dáil to redraw the constituencies in the light of the 2006 census (see above) – both Dublin North and Dublin West should have had an additional seat. However, the Socialist Party as a whole won only around 300 votes more than the Independent Michael Lowry. Further on the left, the People before Profit movement, largely a label for the Socialist Workers' Party, came close to winning a seat in the far from proletarian constituency of Dun Laoghaire, where its candidate Richard Boyd Barrett's 5,223 first preferences perhaps owed more to his local activism in defence of the area's amenities and heritage than to his views on international capitalism. Finally, the Christian Solidarity Party continued to fight the good fight against onrushing secularism in the face of an indifferent public; it ran eight candidates, but none of them managed to win even 1 per cent of the votes in their constituency.

Vote transfers

Under the PR-STV electoral system voters can rank candidates in order of their preference, and the transfer of votes from eliminated or elected candidates to continuing candidates as each constituency count progresses enables us to glean information about patterns in the preference orderings given by voters (see appendix 4 for a full explanation of PR-STV). Voters are free to rank candidates on any basis they wish, but for most voters the main criterion is party, with geography usually the second most important. Of course, we are unable to analyse all votes; the only ones available for analysis are those that were the subject of a distribution. Our ability to draw inferences about the preferences of supporters of different parties is reduced by the practice of multiple eliminations (the simultaneous elimination of candidates not all from the same party), making it impossible to tell how each candidate's votes transferred. Multiple eliminations save some time, but they reduce the transparency of the counting process.

If all voters were entirely party-oriented, we would expect all those awarding a first preference to a candidate of one party to give their second preference to another candidate of the same party. Analysis of intra-party transfers, shown in Table 6.5, shows that internal party solidarity is rather less than perfect.[9] In the case of Fianna Fáil and Fine Gael, around two-thirds of votes transfer to another candidate of the same party when one is available, while in Labour fewer than half of votes remained within the party fold. The figures are much the same as in 2002, and are well below those for the period from the 1920s to the 1980s, when Fianna Fáil's internal solidarity averaged over 80 per cent, Fine Gael's over 70 per cent and Labour's over 60 per cent. As in 2002, the main message in most candidates' election literature was 'Vote for Me', though in fairness 'And please give your next preference(s) to my running mate(s)' was usually to be found in small letters at the bottom of the page. As noted in both chapters 4 and 13, Fianna Fáil in particular has responded to this decline in straight party-ticket voting by running fewer candidates, thus ensuring that fewer votes 'leak away' on eliminations. In 1977 32 Fianna Fáil candidates across the country were eliminated at some stage of the count, but in 2007 there were only 14 Fianna Fáil eliminations. There was considerable variation across the country, with Fianna Fáil's solidarity ranging from only 45 per cent in Dublin MW to over 85 per cent in Cork NW and Donegal NE, and Fine Gael's from 48 per cent in Kerry S to over 80 per cent in Wexford.

Table 6.5   Transfer patterns at 2007 election (%)

From	Available	N	FF	FG	Lab	PD	SF	Grn
Internal solidarity:								
FF	FF	34	66.9					
FG	FG	29		64.4				
Lab	Lab	5			42.5			
Inter-party transfers:								
FF	PD	4				37.1		
PD	FF	9	49.0					
PD	FF, FG	9	49.0	27.9				
FG	FF, Lab	4	20.1		58.6			
FG	FF, SF	4	17.4				15.9	
Lab	FF, FG	10	19.9	45.9				
Lab	FG, Grn	3		33.9				36.8
Lab	FF, SF	2	15.1				10.7	
Grn	FF	17	11.0					
Grn	Lab	19			41.8			
Grn	FF, FG	17	11.0	28.7				
Grn	FF, Lab	16	10.0		39.9			
Grn	FG, Lab	19		26.4	41.8			
Grn	FF, FG, Lab	16	10.0	27.0	39.9			
SF	FF, FG	23	26.0	21.5				
SF	FF, Lab	20	23.6		26.8			

Note: The 'Available' column shows those parties that had candidates available in each case to receive transfers. 'Inter-party' transfers refer only to terminal transfers, in other words to cases where the party whose votes were being distributed had no candidates of its own left in the count.

The only seat that was lost to a party because of a weak internal transfer was in Carlow–Kilkenny, where upon the elimination of a Fine Gael candidate only about half of his votes went to the two remaining Fine Gael candidates while enough leaked to the Green candidate to ensure that she pipped the second Fine Gael candidate for the last seat. Geography played a large part here, as the eliminated Fine Gael candidate and the Green candidate were both from Carlow, while the other two Fine Gael candidates were from Kilkenny. The impact of geography was noticeable in many transfers around the country, perhaps most dramatically in the large constituency of Mayo, where on the last count 54 per cent of the votes of an eliminated Fine Gael candidate, Michelle Mulherin, passed to the other Fine Gael candidate, while the two remaining Fianna Fáil candidates received 26 per cent; the Fianna Fáil candidate from Mulherin's home town of Ballina received 1,924 of her transfers, while the Fianna Fáil candidate whose base was 40 kilometres away got just 89.

Turning to inter-party relationships, transfers between some pairs of parties were slightly stronger than at the 2002 election, which had been characterised by exceptionally low levels of inter-party solidarity. On the government side, transfers from the PDs to Fianna Fáil were up on 2002, though still ran at less than 50 per cent in situations where a Fianna Fáil candidate was available to receive terminal transfers from a PD candidate. On the opposition side, Labour voters preferred Fine Gael to Fianna Fáil, though despite the alliance between Fine Gael and Labour the pattern was not much stronger than in 2002, while Fine Gael voters were more strongly inclined to give preference to Labour over Fianna Fáil candidates (see photo section for examples from Cork SW and Dublin SE of advice to Fine Gael and Labour voters to give their next preference to the other party). These figures are a far cry from those of 1973, the high point of solidarity between Fine Gael and Labour, when more than 70 per cent of terminal transfers flowed from one of these parties to the other, a decline that reflects the wider range of acceptable alternatives now available and the less structured nature of political competition.

When, in the days after the election, the Greens were deciding whether to join Bertie Ahern's third coalition government, opponents claimed that Green voters had certainly not shown any sign that this was a government they had hoped for. Table 6.5 shows that Green terminal transfers were more than twice as likely to go to Fine Gael as to Fianna Fáil, and four times as likely to go to Labour rather than to Fianna Fáil, when this choice arose. When all three parties had candidates available to receive terminal Green transfers, the two opposition parties together received 67 per cent to Fianna Fáil's 10 per cent. This does not prove that the Green Party acted contrary to its mandate when it signed up to the Programme for Government, but it helps explain the cries of pain heard in some quarters. Sinn Féin terminal transfers did not display the mildly pro-Fianna Fáil leanings seen in 2002; this time, the party's votes were about equally likely to pass on to Fianna Fáil, Fine Gael or Labour. Sinn Féin itself continued to be unattractive to supporters of other parties. There are few cases available for analysis, but we can see from Table 6.5 that when supporters of Fine Gael or Labour had a straight choice between Fianna Fáil and Sinn Féin candidates to transfer to, they were even less likely to transfer to Sinn Féin than to Fianna Fáil.

In 2002 the two main opposition parties did not have a transfer pact, and as it turned out this cost them only one seat, in Tipperary North. The existence of such an agreement in 2007 brought them the modest dividend of two seats, Fine Gael benefiting in Cork SW and Tipperary N (see Table 6.6). Fianna Fáil did not gain a single seat due to inter-party transfers, while transfers among candidates of other parties cost the party five seats; had the party not suffered from this modest degree of solidarity among its opponents it would have won 83 seats and could have dispensed with some of its eventual coalition partners when forming a new government. The most striking of these transfers was in Dublin NC where the left-wing Independent Finian McGrath, over 1,800 behind Fianna Fáil's highly publicity-conscious incumbent Ivor Callely on first preferences, eventually finished more than 1,400 votes ahead of him, due primarily to receiving 70 per cent of the votes from the Green and Labour candidates upon their joint elimination, a level of transfer solidarity higher than we often see within parties these days, let alone between them. Table 6.6 also highlights the Green Party's appeal for voters across the board; transfers from the left took John Gormley into a seat ahead of the PD leader in Dublin SE, while transfers from the right enabled Ciarán Cuffe to overtake the People before Profit candidate in Dun Laoghaire. It also demonstrates the party's dependence on transfers; four of its six TDs were reliant on a favourable transfer from elsewhere to overtake a candidate of another party. Sinn Féin, in contrast, remained unattractive to supporters of other parties. This did not quite cost it any seats, though in Dublin SC it nearly did so as Eric Byrne of Labour, nearly 800 votes behind Sinn Féin's Aengus Ó Snodaigh on first preferences, narrowed the gap to 69 votes by the last count thanks mainly to transfers from the Green Party candidate.

Table 6.6 Constituencies where transfers affected the outcome

Constituency	Seat won by	At the expense of	Due to transfers from
Carlow–Kilkenny	Mary White Grn	John Paul Phelan FG	Lab, SF, FF
Cork SW	Jim O'Keeffe FG	Denis O'Donovan FF	Lab
Dublin MW	Joanna Tuffy Lab	Frances Fitzgerald FG	Ind, SF, FF
	Paul Gogarty Grn	Frances Fitzgerald FG	Ind, SF, FF
Dublin NC	Finian McGrath Ind	Ivor Callely FF	Lab, Grn, SF
Dublin NE	Tommy Broughan Lab	Martin Brady FF	SF
Dublin SE	John Gormley Grn	Michael McDowell PD	SF
Dun Laoghaire	Ciarán Cuffe Grn	Richard Boyd-Barrett PbP	PD, FG
Kerry S	Jackie Healy-Rae Ind	Tom Fleming FF	Lab, FG
Tipperary N	Noel Coonan FG	Michael Smith FF	Lab

As well as the seats that were swung by transfers, there were others that could have been but were not. In particular, weak terminal transfers from Fianna Fáil led to three seats going to candidates from the (then) opposition rather than to allies. Two of the defeated PD deputies, Michael McDowell in Dublin SE and Tim O'Malley in Limerick E, received an unimpressive share of the final Fianna Fáil transfer (43 per cent and 27 per cent respectively); each would have been elected had he received 50–60 per cent of these transfers. This rate of transferring was well below the levels seen in both 1997 and 2002 and perhaps indicates a cooling of enthusiasm among Fianna Fáil supporters towards the PDs under their new and more combative leader. The seats went instead to John Gormley (Green) and Kieran O'Donnell (FG). In Clare, 40 per cent of the final Fianna Fáil transfer went to the 'Fianna Fáil gene pool' Independent James Breen, which was not quite enough to give him, rather than Fine Gael's Joe Carey, the last seat. Had the PDs won four seats in total rather than two, and had one more well-disposed Independent been elected, then Fianna Fáil and the PDs would have had the numbers to form a minority government which, with one seat more than their 1997–2002 administration, would have been quite comfortable thanks to the support of friendly Independents.

Intra-party competition and vote management

Under PR-STV, candidates, especially in the two major parties, are in competition with their running mates as well as with candidates from other parties, and some of the most intense battles take place within the party fold. From the party's point of view, this competition can be beneficial; it gives each candidate an incentive to bring in as many votes as he/she can, both by active campaigning and by his/her work between elections, and thus contributes to maximising the party's overall vote total. At the same time, the party must try to ensure that intra-party competition does not get out of hand and disrupt its cohesion, leading to splits or the creation of bitterly opposed factions. In addition, candidates sense that concentrating their fire on a running mate rather than on the opposition does not impress the voters and, moreover, is likely to be looked askance upon by the party leadership and central organisation and may thus be costly when promotional opportunities (minister, frontbench spokesperson, parliamentary committee chair) arise. Consequently, parties try to maintain a public facade of unity, knowing that the media will prick up their ears if the fur starts flying in fights between its candidates.

Moreover, a party cannot simply leave its candidates to their own devices, because very often it feels that the number of seats it wins in a constituency could depend on how its votes are divided among the candidates. For example, suppose it expects to win about 32 per cent of the votes in a four-seat constituency, where the quota equals 20 per cent. If it runs two candidates, and these two split the party vote evenly between them, it has a much better chance of taking two seats than if one candidate has a quota or more on first preferences and the other is left behind on 12 per cent or less. In other words, parties often attempt to 'manage' their votes within each constituency with the aim of maximising their seat return. In most cases it is obvious retrospectively that the number of votes alone determined the outcome and that vote management could not have made any difference to the destination of the seats, but during the campaign itself this may not be apparent, and the head offices of both Fianna Fáil and Fine Gael, acting with and through constituency organisations, devise and try to implement vote management strategies in many constituencies. Parties are undoubtedly more aware of the benefits of vote management than they used to be, and with advances in communications the central election committees are able to monitor and if necessary intervene in any constituency on a daily basis. The constituency director of elections has responsibility for enforcing such schemes. In Mayo, for instance, local media reported 'a frank exchange of views' at a meeting where the four Fine Gael candidates, together with their agents, sat down with the director of elections to thrash out a new division of the constituency.[10] With the two incumbents secure, both non-incumbents sought to build a personal support base. One of the two non-incumbents, Michelle Mulherin, secured the backing of the party's elected representatives on Mayo County Council, while the other, John O'Mahony, the manager of the Mayo football team, was said to be mobilising the extensive GAA network in his support.[11]

Characteristically, vote management entails dividing the constituency geographically and, like handing out slices of a pie, awarding sections of it to individual candidates. In urban areas, an alternative approach that keeps candidates apart without formally dividing the territory involves allowing each candidate to canvass the whole constituency but making sure that only one candidate is in a particular area at a time (see Terence Flanagan's account in chapter 5). Candidates may be told which areas they are and are not permitted to canvass, and voters may be asked to vote in a particular way depending on which part of the constituency they live in. For example, in the Wexford constituency Fianna Fáil awarded each of its three candidates sole canvassing rights in their home area, while the Gorey area was divided among them down to the level of individual polling boxes. Within Fine Gael, the New Ross electoral area was open territory, and, moreover, each candidate was allowed to canvass one day a week in the other candidates' areas provided this was arranged in advance (see also the party's newspaper advertisement in the *Echo* newspapers, reproduced in the photo section).[12] Candidates will, of course, expect to be given the area around their home base, and so the borders of their respective bailiwicks, like a disputed frontier between states, are where trouble is most likely to flare. Matters can become particularly tense if one candidate is perceived as a front-runner, in which case vote management requires trying to siphon some of his or her support to the weaker member of the team. As well as provoking resistance from the front-runner, this tactic, if pushed too far, might have the unintended effect of leading to the election of the weaker candidate at the expense of the front-runner, thus costing the party one of its leading lights, as happened in Cork NW in 2002 when a Fine Gael vote management plan backfired and the front-bencher Michael Creed lost his seat as a result.[13]

When party support seems to be slipping candidates become edgy and the normal courtesies of intra-party conduct may be cast to the winds. In Cork E the two Fianna Fáil incumbents took their gloves off in the run-up to polling day. Michael Ahern, based in the south of the constituency, appealed for support from the northern area, the bailiwick of Ned O'Keeffe. Traditional boundaries, he said, meant nothing in this election: 'At the last election there was a boundary in place which he [O'Keeffe] broke lock, stock and barrel right up to my doorstep. This time there is no boundary so it is open territory.'[14] O'Keeffe, who had had to resign a junior ministerial position in 2001 and had then suffered the further pain of seeing Ahern appointed to the equivalent position in June 2002, said that if Ahern had performed competently in his ministerial post Fianna Fáil would have been pressing for three seats in the constituency instead of having to worry about holding on to two. Ahern rounded off the exchange by opining that some of O'Keeffe's comments amounted to slander, though he did not intend to take legal action. In the event, as at every election since November 1982, both Ahern and O'Keeffe were comfortably re-elected.

In Dublin Central vote management takes on a different meaning altogether. Fianna Fáil usually wins around 40 per cent of the votes here, making it competitive for two seats. Whereas the logic outlined above would suggest something like an even division of the votes between two candidates, the local constituency organisation, dominated by party leader Bertie Ahern, operates instead the tactic of trying to maximise Ahern's first preference support in the hope that enough votes will transfer from his surplus on to his running mate(s) to secure a second seat. Neutral observers believe that when Fianna Fáil has taken two seats in Dublin Central it has been despite rather than because of this singular approach, but, undaunted, the organisation repeated the tactic in 2007. Ahern received 12,734 first preferences, 83 per cent of the party total. On this occasion he had two running mates – reportedly this was simply because he had been unable to decide which one to drop from the ticket, and so let them both stand – and they were in effect competing for Ahern's second preferences, with the winner likely to take a seat. Although Mary Fitzpatrick received more first preferences than Cyprian Brady (1,725 compared with 939), Brady, a long-time member of Ahern's constituency organisation, received over 1,000 more of Ahern's second preferences than she did and went on to take the seat. It turned out that the party organisation had distributed 30,000 leaflets early in the morning of election day asking voters to vote 1–2–3 in that order for Ahern, Brady and Fitzpatrick (see photo section). While, Fitzpatrick said, 'I never thought they were the Legion of Mary', she had not expected the party to 'shaft' and 'undermine' her as it had.[15] However, one of Ahern's associates in the constituency, Chris Wall, explained that Fitzpatrick had brought her fate upon herself by firing the first shot: she had distributed campaign literature in some areas asking voters to give her their first preference. Wall said: 'She was asked not to do this sort of thing. Having then done it, she therefore effectively set in train a motion she wasn't going to be able to stop.'

In the event, Fianna Fáil's vote management schemes probably made little difference, because where they were applied it usually turned out that the party's level of support alone pretty much determined its level of support. There were three constituencies where a more even spread of support between its candidates could have brought an extra seat, most spectacularly in Limerick East, where its leading light Willie O'Dea won over 19,000 first preferences, 79 per cent of the party total, and it finished with only two seats in this five-seater despite winning 49 per cent of the votes. In Dublin Mid-West and Kerry South, too, a more even balance of support between its two candidates would have brought an extra seat. Fine Gael took seats in Laois–Offaly, Roscommon–Leitrim South and Wicklow that might have been forfeit had one of its candidates run too far ahead of the other, but let slip one to Mary White of the Greens in Carlow-Kilkenny by insufficient management. Labour rarely has enough votes to need to manage them, but in the one constituency where it had a real chance of taking two seats, Dublin SC, its front-runner was too far ahead of its second candidate, Eric Byrne (the victim of a five-vote defeat in 1992), who missed out on a seat by fewer than 100 votes in consequence.

The members of the 30th Dáil

Turnover, age and experience

The turnover in the composition of the Dáil was unusually high, though not quite as extensive as in 2002 when over a third of the membership had changed. In 2007, 19 TDs retired and 30 were defeated. Those retiring included three former cabinet ministers (Noel Davern, Síle de Valera and Joe Walsh), plus 'father of the house' and former Ceann Comhairle Séamus Pattison who stood down after almost 46 years' continuous membership, the sixth longest on record. The 49 departing TDs were replaced by 38 first-time TDs along with 11 former TDs who had departed from the Dáil in 2002 (ten were defeated and one retired) and were now reclaiming their place. These 11 returnees included the former deputy leader of Fianna Fáil, Mary O'Rourke, and the veteran Fine Gael campaigner from Cork SW, P. J. Sheehan, who has been contesting elections since the 1960s and at 74 may well be the oldest deputy ever to reclaim a seat.

The average age of the TDs in May 2007 was 51, and on average they had been aged 40 when first elected. These figures are a little higher than at some past elections, partly because several new TDs are not exactly youngsters: ten were in their fifties and two, Michael Fitzpatrick and Martin Mansergh, in their sixties. Among the party groups, Labour's average age is the highest at 55 while the Greens' is youngest (47). The median TD entered the Dáil in 1997, and 97 have known Dáil life only under a Fianna Fáil Taoiseach. Just seven TDs, including the leaders of the two major parties, entered the Dáil before 1981. Most TDs (97 out of 166) were elected the first time they stood, and only 11 succeeded after two or more defeats.

This was the first Dáil election to take place since the introduction of the prohibition of the 'dual mandate', meaning that TDs and senators can no longer simultaneously be members of a local authority. Some incumbents had expressed fears that as a result of being unable to participate in the work of their County or City Council, they would be more vulnerable than before to being unseated by running mates who could assiduously cultivate the grass roots that they were now prevented from attending to, but in the event there was nothing unusual about the pattern of turnover and certainly no sign that hungry young councillors were ousting deputies who were spending too much time for their constituents' liking on national parliamentary work. Of the 12 defeated Fianna Fáil TDs, only four were displaced by a running mate (three of these running mates were former TDs and the fourth was not a councillor), and while both defeated Fine Gael TDs were replaced by running mates, one of these was a former TD and the other the son of a former TD.

Routes to the Dáil

While there was no sign of councillors rising en masse to take the seats of incumbents, it remains the case that there is no better base for launching a Dáil career than being a councillor. Nearly 77 per cent of TDs were councillors before becoming Dáil deputies, and only 22 of the 166 TDs have never been councillors. The percentage of former councillors among the first-time TDs was, at 76 per cent, essentially the same as among TDs as a whole. Being a senator also helps: 14 members of the 30th Dáil moved across from the upper house. Fine Gael had picked its Seanad candidates in 2002 with the next Dáil election in mind,[16] and of its 15 Seanad members ten stood in the Dáil election and six of these won seats.

Rather than build a base from scratch, it is easier to take over one already built by a close relative. The Dáil continues to stand out in a comparative context for the very high number of its members (44 out of 166, or 27 per cent) who have been preceded by one or more relatives. On a subjective judgement, this was significant in the TD's initial election in all but six cases. The largest category consists of the 25 sons who followed their fathers into the house, and there are also five nephews, four daughters and three brothers.

Background of deputies

The Dáil has always been highly unrepresentative of the gender balance in Irish society, with the number of female TDs growing at a glacial pace. In 2007 even this slow advance ground to a halt, as only 22 women were elected to the 30th Dáil: the same number as in the 29th Dáil and one fewer than the number of outgoing female TDs.[17] Ireland, with women making up only 13 per cent of the Dáil, is now near the bottom of the parliamentary gender balance league. Women do not make up even 10 per cent of TDs of either Fianna Fáil or Fine Gael, so if change is to come it must entail a rethink by these parties of their candidate selection policies. In contrast, 35 per cent of Labour deputies are female, while the collapse of the PDs, whose Dáil group from 2002–07 was 50 per cent female, did not help matters.

Most TDs (54 per cent, the highest proportion ever) can be classified as having pursued a professional occupation before entering the Dáil, while very few have a background as manual workers. A significant proportion of TDs (22 per cent), as in earlier Dála, can be classified as having a 'commercial' background, characteristically being small business people such as auctioneers, shopkeepers or publicans. Only 9 per cent of TDs, the lowest percentage ever, are farmers – though as the proportion of full-time farmers shrinks while part-time farming grows, it is harder to draw a clear line between those who are farmers and those who are not. The rise in the proportion of professionals is mirrored by a rise in the level of educational qualifications – for the first time ever, a majority of TDs have a university degree.

Conclusion

The 2007 election produced a government that was little changed from its predecessor and much the same could be said about its impact on the composition of the Dáil. Fine Gael defied its obituary writers by recording a large seat gain, but, creditable as this was, it was the product of a modest gain in votes, merely restored it to its pre-2002 level of strength rather than representing any transformation of its position in the party system, and left it still stranded in opposition. Fianna Fáil, Labour, Sinn Féin and the Greens registered the same levels of support as in 2002 – Labour's result was expected but the predictions of significant gains and losses for the other three parties showed that in the right circumstances even a result of 'little real change' can make a dramatic story.

The next election will undoubtedly be fought on a different set of constituency boundaries, so the 2007 marginals may not be the key marginals during the next campaign. Whatever the boundaries, some constituencies are bound to prove very marginal: in 2007 there were two constituencies where a swing of fewer than 100 votes would have created a seat change and a further nine where fewer than 500 votes were needed. In general terms, several scenarios are plausible. Fine Gael, having made up so much ground in 2007, might be able to achieve the further advance that it needs in order to form the core of an alternative government, a task that would be facilitated were the PDs to disappear before the next election. However, Fine Gael's fortunes have waxed and waned consistently at recent elections – ever since February 1982, it has gained at one election and lost ground at the next one – and unless it can break this pattern Fianna Fáil will be very difficult to dislodge from office. The three main parties, having been reduced in 2002 to their lowest collective vote share since 1948, reasserted their dominance in 2007, invalidating predictions of the demise of the party system that has existed since 1932. The high proportion of marginal constituencies, together with the absence of uniform swing, makes it impossible to predict how many seats parties will win from a given level of national support. Despite this, and as we examine further in chapter 9, some people are willing to bet on the outcome, and at the time of writing, a Fine Gael–Labour government is favourite to emerge after the next election.

Notes

1. *Irish Times*, 8 June 2007.
2. Leaving aside the university constituencies, which returned TDs until 1933. The record was set by Brian O'Higgins in Clare in 1923, who was elected with only 114 first preferences in the face of a Droop quota (see appendix 4 for explanation of the Droop quota) of 6,575. Michael Gallagher (ed.), *Irish Elections 1922–44: Results and Analysis* (Dublin: PSAI Press, 1993), p. 26.
3. Pat Lyons and Richard Sinnott, 'Voter turnout in 2002 and beyond', pp. 143–58 in Michael Gallagher, Michael Marsh and Paul Mitchell (eds), *How Ireland Voted 2002* (Basingstoke: Palgrave Macmillan, 2003). The *Sunday Tribune* ran a campaign to get inaccuracies in the electoral register sorted out: see, for example, Odran Flynn, 'The flaws in the electoral register that threaten our democracy', *Sunday Tribune*, 19 June 2005; Shane Coleman, 'The 800,000 opportunities for voter fraud need to be sorted now', *Sunday Tribune*, 5 March 2006; Shane Coleman and Odran Flynn, 'Huge inconsistencies remain in electoral register', *Sunday Tribune*, 12 November 2006.
4. Eoin O'Malley, 'Apathy or error? Questioning the Irish register of electors', *Irish Political Studies* 16 (2001), pp. 215–24.
5. Peter Mair and Liam Weeks, 'The party system', pp. 135–59 in John Coakley and Michael Gallagher (eds), *Politics in the Republic of Ireland*, 4th edn (Abingdon: Routledge and PSAI Press, 2005), at pp. 149, 154.
6. Eoin O'Malley and Matthew Kerby, 'Chronicle of a death foretold? Understanding the decline of Fine Gael', *Irish Political Studies* 19:1 (2004), pp. 39–58, offered a downbeat assessment of the party's prospects.
7. Michael Laver, Peter Mair and Richard Sinnott (eds), *How Ireland Voted: The Irish General Election 1987* (Dublin: Poolbeg, 1987), p. 63.
8. See his account of this in Gallagher et al., *How Ireland Voted 2002*, pp. 83–7.
9. The analysis excludes transfers resulting from multiple eliminations, and the distribution of surpluses where the package of votes taking the elected candidate over the quota came from a candidate of a different party.
10. 'Fine Gael enter "vote equalisation" talks', *Connaught Telegraph*, 2 May 2007.
11. The GAA is the Gaelic Athletic Association. Even though O'Mahony's charges were beaten in the Connacht football championship by their closest rivals Galway just four days before the election, O'Mahony outpolled Mulherin and took the third Fine Gael seat.
12. 'Big two divide up electoral areas between candidates', *Wexford People*, 9 May 2007.
13. Michael Gallagher, 'Stability and turmoil: analysis of the results', pp. 88–118 in Gallagher et al., *How Ireland Voted 2002*, p. 110.

14. 'FF feud descends into open warfare', *Irish Examiner*, 23 May 2007.
15. Ronan McGreevy, 'Taoiseach's running mate accuses FF of "shafting" her', *Irish Times*, 31 May 2007.
16. Michael Gallagher and Liam Weeks, 'The subterranean election of the Seanad', pp. 197–213 in Gallagher et al., *How Ireland Voted 2002*, pp. 202, 208.
17. The number rose from 22 to 23 over the lifetime of the 29th Dáil following the success of Catherine Murphy in a by-election in 2005.

7
Explanations for Party Choice
*Michael Marsh**

There were marked similarities between the elections of 2002 and 2007. Each followed five years of Fianna Fáil–PD government; each followed a five-year period that saw considerable economic growth, but in which certain public services, notably health, seemed to be getting worse rather than better; each saw Bertie Ahern going into the election as the Fianna Fáil Taoiseach; and each saw Fianna Fáil winning just over 41 per cent of the vote and re-establishing a government with the PDs. Social scientists and historians are fond of counter-factuals: 'what if ...' questions. What would have happened in 2002 if Labour and Fine Gael had offered themselves as an alternative government rather than fighting the election independently; what if Michael Noonan had been a more popular leader of Fine Gael, and of an alternative coalition; what if the economy had been a little less strong, or if voters had been even more concerned with health; what if Mary Harney had not been leader of the PDs, and Labour had a more popular leader than Ruairí Quinn? The corresponding chapter to this one in *How Ireland Voted 2002* explored the impact of some of these factors and suggested that Fine Gael would have done better if health had been more important and Fine Gael's leader more popular, and Fianna Fáil would have done worse – although the former not very much better, and the latter not very much worse.[1] The 2007 election can be seen as another test of such 'what if ...' suppositions: Fine Gael and Labour ran as an alternative coalition government, Enda Kenny closed the gap on Bertie Ahern; more people were concerned about health and there was a greater degree of dissatisfaction with the government than at any time between 1997 and 2002. Fine Gael increased its vote share, but not at the expense of Fianna Fáil, which managed to sustain its vote and minimise seat losses. More change had been expected. Fianna Fáil was expected to lose votes and the party had done very poorly in the local and EP elections of 2004 (see chapters 1 and 9). The Greens and, even more so, Sinn Féin were also expected to make considerable gains. This was signalled in opinion polls and could be expected from the higher profile for climate change-related issues and the settlement in the North respectively. This chapter asks: how was Fianna Fáil able to sustain its vote, why did Fine Gael do better, and why did no other party make significant gains? We will start by assessing the case that conditions were much less favourable for Fianna Fáil in 2007.

The electoral battleground

The record of the government

The economy is often seen as a significant driver of government satisfaction. While events such as scandals and policy successes may cause fluctuations in satisfaction, the state of the economy provides an equilibrium position to which support will continually return.[2] It is evident that the economy in the 2002–07 period was less remarkable than in 1997–2002. Figure 7.1 shows the record of growth, probably the best single indicator of economic well-being. The pace of growth was generally lower, particularly in the early part of the period, although in the last year or so there was little difference. There were also reports in the media questioning the underlying strength of the economy, and some signs of a fall in the property market, but unemployment was still below 5 per cent and numbers at work still growing, while inflation was no greater than in 1997–2002.

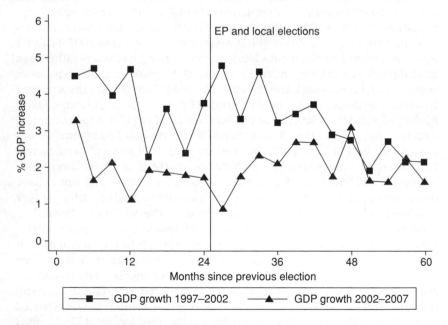

Figure 7.1   GDP quarterly growth rates during the 1997–02 and 2002–07 governments (four quarter moving average)

Source: OECD *Economic Outlook* No. 81, Volume 2007 Issue 1, Annual and Quarterly data.

Between 1997 and 2002, an average of 57 per cent expressed themselves as satisfied with the government. Only twice did popularity drop below 50 per cent for two consecutive polls, and this was around mid-term in the electoral cycle. In contrast, the 2002–07 government averaged 41 per cent in the satisfaction ratings, and indeed popularity was below 30 per cent at one point and at no time did it reach its mean rating for 1997–2002. Figure 7.2 shows the pattern, with both sets of popularity figures graphed on the same scale for comparison. In each case the final pre-election poll is the end point. If a 57 per cent rating brought 41 per cent of the vote, it would have been expected that a 41 per cent rating would have brought significantly fewer electoral returns. Voters were very slow to forgive the post-election cutbacks that had been concealed from the electorate in the 2002 campaign (see p. 3 above), yet popularity was rising almost throughout, was above average over the last 18 months, and the two series were very close six months out from their respective elections. Certainly the gap had narrowed significantly for the general election from where it stood for the mid-term local and EP elections.

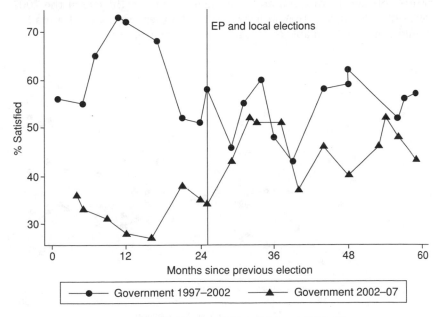

Figure 7.2 Satisfaction with government, 1997–2002 and 2002–07

Source: TNS mrbi/*Irish Times* polls.

So while the record of 2002–07 as a whole might suffer in comparison with 1997–2002, the differences over the last year were not pronounced. Reinforcing this is the evidence from monthly consumer confidence surveys, both those carried out by the market research company Behaviour and Attitudes and those by ESRI/IIB.[3] These seem to indicate that consumer confidence was not very different in May 2007 from what it had been in May 2002, but that there was a lot of difference between the overall record across 2002–07 and 1997–2002. Certainly the great days of the Celtic Tiger were well in the past by 2007, but the economic circumstances were certainly not unfavourable.

The party leaders

The picture is a comparable one as far as the leaders were concerned. Ahern's popularity always lagged far behind the levels that he enjoyed as part of the previous regime, typically by about ten percentage points. Kenny began the period with little obvious popularity. Though few found him unsatisfactory, many simply knew little about him. His popularity levels caught up with those obtained by John Bruton (who was leader until 2001) after the EP elections, but over the last 12 months far outstripped those obtained by Noonan, his immediate predecessor. (See Figure 7.3.) On the eve of the election the gap between Kenny and Ahern was only 12 points compared with almost 40 points between Fianna Fáil and Fine Gael leaders on the eve of the 2002 election. This suggests that, at least to the extent leaders matter, Fianna Fáil should not have been able to repeat its 2002 performance.

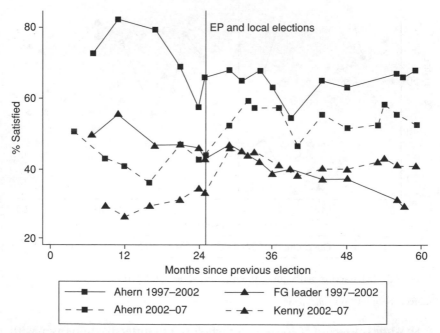

Figure 7.3   Satisfaction with Fianna Fáil and Fine Gael leaders, 1997–2002 and 2002–07

Source: TNS mrbi/*Irish Times* polls.

However, these survey measures of leaders, and of government satisfaction, are individual evaluations, not comparative ones. Just because people are dissatisfied with a government does not mean they will prefer the alternative, and there is no comparable question on the opposition or the alternative government. The evaluations of leaders are of each leader in turn. They do not indicate which leader is preferred, and by how much, although the closer the satisfaction ratings, the closer we might expect the rankings to be. Analysis of the final TNS mrbi poll of the campaign indicates that a majority (58 per cent) were satisfied with one of these two leaders and not satisfied with the other. There were some satisfied with both (24 per cent), and others with neither (18 per cent). In the same poll voters were asked whom they preferred as Taoiseach. Ahern won out clearly by 58 to 29. Even among those satisfied with Kenny, but not with Ahern, Kenny wins out by only by 51–37. Hence many of those unhappy with Ahern as Taoiseach and happy with Kenny as Fine Gael leader nevertheless preferred Ahern as Taoiseach.[4] Even so, the gap narrowed significantly from 2002. In the exit poll in 2007 Ahern was preferred as Taoiseach by 52–34. The comparable figures in 2002 were 64–23. What these leader ratings do indicate, however, is that there was a basis for uncertainty amongst voters. There was no huge majority satisfied only with Ahern.

The choice

A third apparent difference in 2007 was that Fine Gael and Labour had established an agreed alternative to the existing government. In 2002, there was a clear perception there was no alternative to a Fianna Fáil-led government, a perception that many saw as benefiting both the PDs – who could portray themselves as the electorate's watchdog – and Independents, who would at least fight to extract local benefits from the new government. In 2007 there was a choice. The presentation of Fine Gael + Labour as a real option could only be credible if the constituent parties were doing well enough in the polls to make it so, and this proved to be the case, with several polls in the run-up to the election putting the alternative government ahead of the incumbents. The voter going to the ballot box this time could see him/herself as choosing a government and, informed by the polls, this was how the media tended to portray the 2007 election (see chapters 10 and 12 for more details). Table 7.1 shows the preferences for government in the 2002 and 2007 exit polls. In one respect it is evident that the alternative was preferred over the incumbent government in 2007. Some 30 per cent opted for Fine Gael + Labour, while only 18 per cent wanted Fianna Fáil + PDs, a very significant drop on the 28 per cent who did so last time. While Fianna Fáil + PDs might be only the first choice of 18 per cent, that is not to say that a majority would prefer Fine Gael + Labour to Fianna Fáil + PD if that were the only choice. Indeed, when given just that choice in several polls, the balance was much closer.

Table 7.1   Preference for government, 2002 and 2007 (%)

	2002	2007
FG + Labour	19	30
FG + Labour + Greens	12	13
FF	15	15
FF + PD	28	18
FF + Labour	9	8
FF + Greens	4	4
FF + SF	6	7
FF + Independents	7	5
None of them	1	1
Total	100	100

Source: analysis of RTÉ/Lansdowne exit poll 2007.

The issues

Issues in Irish elections tend to be those of competence, although there have been instances where parties took clearly different positions on issues, or where a party emphasised an issue that others neglected (see chapter 2). While there were differences in terms of election promises during the campaign, such as on tax rates or pensions, and differences with respect to the means of addressing some issues – such as co-location as a means of addressing the shortage in hospital beds – in general the issue agenda in 2007 looked much as it did in 2002. The exit poll asked people to name the issues that had affected their vote. Reservations are in order as to how far this sort of information can actually explain why people voted as they did. People cannot always report on their reasons for behaviour in such simple terms and while a long interview might be able to elicit people's reasoning, a single question has little chance of doing so. Nor should it be assumed that all voters decided 'on the issues': indeed, there is much evidence to the contrary.[5] However, what this question can tell us is how people saw the political agenda.[6]

Table 7.2 shows the responses in the exit poll. The lists of issues and frequency with which each was mentioned by voters in 2002 and 2007 look remarkably similar. Health, crime and the economy respectively top the list of concerns in each year. With the media focus on Ahern's finances, the choice of Taoiseach seems to have been more salient, but then 'honesty' – other than mention of Ahern's finances specifically – was less so, perhaps in consequence. A few things are very notable by their relative absence: Northern Ireland, stamp duty on property purchases, and unemployment – which topped the agenda throughout the 1980s and 1990s.

This similarity may conceal some real changes since 2002 in how people viewed the economy, crime and health and the capacity of different parties to deal with the issues being raised. There is evidence to suggest that voters

Table 7.2 Issues mentioned as influencing vote, 2002 and 2007 (%)

	2007 Exit poll	2002 Exit poll
Health	45	39
Crime	24	33
Economy	23	22
Cost of living	18	13
Choice of Taoiseach	15*	8
Environment	13	8
Honesty	11	18
Housing	11	9
Specific local issue	10	10
Education	8	8
Drugs	8	8
Public transport	7	5
Stable government	7	5
Pensions/elderly	5	5
Roads	4	6
Govt. spending	4	6
Taxation	4	6
Northern Ireland	4	4
Stamp duty	4	0
Unemployment	3	6
Immigration	2	0

* Choice of Taoiseach in 2007 includes 8 per cent who gave this reason and a further 7 per cent who mentioned the Taoiseach's finances.

Notes: Question asked was 'What were the issues or problems that most influenced your decision as to which party to vote for? (PROBE) What other issues influenced you?' (RECORD UP TO THREE MENTIONS IN ORDER MENTIONED).' In this table we report on 'any mention'. So, 45 per cent of respondents in 2007 mentioned health either first, second or third. By extension 55 per cent did not mention health at all.

Source: analysis of RTÉ/Lansdowne exit polls 2007 and 2002.

viewed each of these three areas with more concern than in 2002. A panel survey of voters in 2002, 2003, 2004 and 2006, carried out as part of the 2002 Irish election study, suggests that fewer people were giving positive answers in 2003–06 than were giving them in 2002 when asked whether or not each had changed for the better in the lifetime of the government. Very few at all thought the situation as regards crime or the health services was improving, but a majority saw the economy, after a precipitate fall in 2003, as continuing to improve.[7] Similar questions were posed in several newspaper polls during the 2007 campaign. A Millward Brown IMS poll conducted in April asked whether the health service had got better or worse over the last five years – 61 per cent said worse, and only 16 per cent said better.

The same poll asked about the government's handling of the economy, and while 51 per cent were satisfied with that, 44 per cent were dissatisfied.

The same respondents were also asked which issues they thought would most influence their vote choice. This poll thus also provides us with some information about how they evaluate the government's performance on the issues they say are important to them. In all, 72 per cent mentioned health as an important issue. Of those who thought the service was improving, 66 per cent said health was an important influence as against 77 per cent of those who thought the health service was getting worse.[8] On the economy, there was no difference in the salience of the issue of economic management between those who were satisfied and those dissatisfied with the government's handling of the issue.

Indecision

After five years of government, and a campaign that seemed to have gone on for much of the previous year, it might be expected that voters would have made up their minds well before the election was called, the Dáil was dissolved and the official campaign finally got under way. Yet this ignores the fact that for many voters, party politics is of very little salience. Much of what constitutes the basic diet of political journalists and party activists is no part of the everyday consumption of ordinary voters. Only when the campaign proper gets under way do such voters pay attention. Even then, many have what is in effect a strong tendency to vote a particular way. Respondents in the exit poll were asked *when* they made up their mind who to vote for. This is a difficult question to answer, certainly for those who do not always vote the same way, but the overall distribution of responses is significant. In 2007, 28 per cent reported that they decided in the last week and 44 per cent before the campaign started. This suggests that, on average, voters made up their minds a little later than in 2002, when 25 per cent decided in the last week and 43 per cent before the campaign started. This difference is more striking since 9 per cent could not remember in 2007, while only 3 per cent could not remember in 2002. If we set these aside, 31 per cent decided in the last week as against 26 per cent in 2002.

In general, we might expect that supporters of Fianna Fáil would make up their minds more quickly. They are disproportionately older and have a stronger attachment to their party, characteristics associated with an earlier decision. In 2002, 48 per cent of those who made up their mind before the election voted Fianna Fáil, as did 46 per cent of those who said they always voted that way. Fianna Fáil's share of those who decided in the last week was just 32 per cent. In 2007, however, Fianna Fáil's share of late deciders was 39 per cent, close to its overall vote share of 42 per cent, and no greater than its share of those who decided before the campaign.[9] In contrast, Fine Gael's share varied little by time of decision, either in 2002 or 2007. At the very least this suggests that Fianna Fáil's supporters were a little less certain of their allegiance than in previous years.[10] This interpretation gets added support from an analysis of the reported previous voting behaviour of those questioned in the exit poll. Some 71 per cent of those voting Fianna Fáil in 2007 reported also doing so in 2002. This is almost the same figure as was obtained by asking Fianna Fáil voters in 2002 about their 1997 behaviour: 70 per cent. Of those who reportedly voted Fianna Fáil in 2002 and voted in 2007, 89 per cent stayed with the party, but even so, 20 per cent of them reported that they decided to vote for Fianna Fáil only in the last week. Thus the campaign in general, and particular the campaign in the last week or so, does seem to have had a significant impact.

It was suggested at the start of this chapter that 2007 might be seen as a re-run of 2002 under conditions less favourable to Fianna Fáil and more favourable to Fine Gael. This section has sought to ascertain how accurate that depiction might be. It is clear that the government was less popular than its predecessor, although differences are much more obvious when we set 1997–99 against 2002–04 than when 1999–2002 and 2004–07 are contrasted. The satisfaction ratings of alternatives for Taoiseach also appeared smaller, although Ahern still maintained a clear lead in a straight choice between himself and Kenny. If the election were to be fought on whether health was more important than the economy to voters, then that also appeared to favour Fine Gael, as the health service issue appeared to be much more salient than the economy, particularly in the early part of the campaign. Again, though, a qualification must be introduced: the link between how voters evaluated the health service over the last five years and its importance as an issue for them was not as striking as we might have expected. Perhaps as a consequence of the changed situation, Fianna Fáil-inclined voters seem to have been more indecisive than is typical of them.

Of course all this assumes that the economy, leaders, government satisfaction, the existence of choice and concerns about specific issues actually matter in Irish elections. While there is clear evidence, not least in earlier volumes of this series, that these matter to some degree, it could be that they do not matter much and that voters are much more concerned about their local TD and his or her attention to the constituency, or even a part of it, than they are about who forms the government. Some general support for this perspective, that voters are interested in candidates rather than parties, comes from the commonly asked poll question: 'Which of these was most important to you in making up your mind how to vote in this election?' The options are: choosing who will be Taoiseach; choosing the set of ministers who will form the government; choosing between the policies as set out by the parties; and choosing a candidate to look after the needs of the constituency. The last of these is always the most frequently selected option, taken by around 40 per cent of respondents in 2007. Ministers (23 per cent), a Taoiseach (12 per cent) and policies (25 per cent) are very much each minority concerns it seems, although it could be argued that a majority are picking a party-related reason. Typically, and 2007 is not an exception, Fianna Fáil voters are less likely to select the candidate option, but were more likely to mention ministers and choosing a Taoiseach. Green, Labour and Fine Gael voters were more likely to mention policy. There has always been some scepticism about the apparent weight of the candidate factor, and recent extensive research into this question bears out much of that doubt. It is clear that candidate factors do not preclude party loyalties, and the number really driven fundamentally by candidate attractiveness may be very much smaller than this figure of 40 per cent suggests.[11] This is not the place to pursue this line of enquiry as the data available from campaign polls are inadequate to do so. However, it should be admitted that while there is a group of voters for whom government formation is relatively unimportant, this number is not so large as to mean that election results cannot be interpreted as significantly dependent on the performance of the government on national issues and the credibility of an alternative government to do better.

One final point concerns Fianna Fáil's performance in 2002. It is important to look at Irish elections in a manner that allows for a complex competition between parties. In the US, the focus of much of the work on elections, the contest is generally a simple one where one party's loss is the other party's gain. If conditions are bad for one party, we expect the other to take advantage. In multi-party systems there are many more options for the voter. Moreover, we know that most voters are attracted to more than one party. Different voters will also have different 'tipping points', at which one party is chosen over another. A recent analysis of the impact of the economy on party choice across Europe which tries to account for the apparent variability in economic effects argues that the impact of an improvement or worsening of economic circumstance on support for a government – even a government of one party – will depend on how close many voters are to evaluating equally the government party and one from the opposition. If the gap is large, it will take a big deterioration to remove the government from office; if it is small, a minor change in circumstance will suffice.[12] In 2002, Fianna Fáil stood very high in popular esteem. Analysis of data from the 2002 Irish election study suggests that its supporters were generally very sure in their support. On the basis of a widely employed battery of questions identifying how people view the different party options, Fianna Fáil voters can be shown to have preferred their party to any other to a much greater degree than did those who voted for other parties.[13] The implication of this is that Fianna Fáil had a good cushion: in the minds of its individual voters it was well ahead. It could afford to lose a degree of support if conditions were somewhat less favourable without necessarily losing votes.

In the next section we examine the relationship between the factors outlined and party choice, asking, for instance: how important was a concern about health for the Fine Gael vote, and how important was the economy for those choosing Fianna Fáil? It must be said at this point that while there is a lot of evidence scattered across the various polls carried out in 2007, these polls are generally designed for media consumption rather than academic

Table 7.3 Party preferences of various social groups

	FF	PDs	FG	Lab	Grn	SF	Others	Total	N
Total	41.6	2.6	26.2	10.0	4.8	7.3	7.5	100	3,206
Men	41.7	2.4	27.2	9.8	4.4	8.4	6.2	100	1,611
Women	41.6	2.8	25.3	10.1	5.3	6.1	8.8	100	1,595
18–24 years	35.3	2.4	24.1	12.4	7.6	10.7	7.4	100	381
25–34 years	38.8	3.1	23.2	9.3	8.0	9.9	7.7	100	667
35–49 years	40.1	2.7	25.4	10.4	5.0	7.9	8.4	100	1,016
50–64 years	45.2	2.3	28.5	8.8	2.2	5.6	7.5	100	784
65+ years	48.8	2.2	31.1	9.9	1.7	1.5	4.7	100	358
AB (middle class)	37.2	4.4	29.5	12.4	8.2	3.5	4.9	100	562
C1 (lower middle class)	40.8	2.8	23.5	11.0	6.9	5.6	9.4	100	1,033
C2 (skilled working class)	42.7	2.6	21.7	9.2	4.5	8.7	10.5	100	804
DE (unskilled working class)	43.9	1.9	23.2	9.7	2.0	13.3	6.1	100	661
Farmers	43.9	0.7	44.4	5.5	0.0	3.5	2.1	100	146

Source: analysis of RTÉ/Lansdowne exit poll 2007.

analysis. Explanations are generally sought by asking voters why they did things, in contrast to the dominant method of academic electoral analysis that seeks to test explanations by seeking patterns in the data. Moreover, while each poll contains useful items, no poll carries anything like the full range of questions required for a more definitive analysis, which could properly assess the balance of long- and short-term forces and the extent to which each voter cares more about local personalities than national parties. The 2007 election study, the final wave of a panel running since 2002, will permit a much deeper analysis, but that data will not be available before 2008. In its absence, therefore, we turn back to the evidence of the polls on why people voted as they did.

Party choice

We start by looking at who voted for each party. The catch-all nature of the appeals made by most Irish parties and the subsequent absence of the distinct demographic patterns found in party choice in many other countries has been the subject of much discussion by those exploring Irish electoral behaviour. Hence it is not a surprise to see a weak demographic basis of party support in 2007. Table 7.3 shows party choice by gender, age and social class. Gender differences in party choice are small and generally not statistically significant, although it is evident that women have a slight tendency to support the smaller parties, or Independents. The tendency of women not to support Sinn Féin, despite the presence of some women candidates with a very high profile, is an exception in this respect, and one of long standing. There is more variation in party support by age. Support for both Fine Gael and Fianna Fáil appears to increase with age, with those aged 65 or more 30–40 per cent more likely than those under 25 to vote for these parties. On the other hand, the Greens and Sinn Féin do very much better in the younger groups. Those under 25 are six times as likely to vote Sinn Féin as those over 65, and for Greens the corresponding figure is more than four times. Such patterns have typified all recent elections. For the other parties there is no significant pattern. This reflects the newness of Sinn Féin and the Greens in particular, as against the much more established position of the two big parties, whose supporters have been growing into the habit of supporting them for many years. We might have expected younger voters to be attracted to Independents for that reason – many are quite new candidates – but it may be that the message and image of most such candidates is not so youthful.

Finally, the class profile of the parties: Fianna Fáil is a little weaker in the AB (middle class) category, where Fine Gael is significantly stronger. Generally though, apart from the relative strength of Fine Gael in the diminishing group of farmers, the more distinctive profiles are again those of the smaller parties. The Greens are four times as attractive to AB voters as they are to those in the DE (semi- and unskilled working class and dependants) category, while

Sinn Féin provides almost the mirror image of the Green profile. PD support, small as it is, is twice as high among AB voters as it is among DE voters. Confirming the picture given by most recent studies, Labour tends to do a little better as you go up the social scale, but the differences are very small compared with those within Sinn Féin and the Greens. All this is remarkably similar to 2002, and to 1997.

Table 7.4 shows the patterns for Fianna Fáil, Fine Gael and Labour in each of the last three elections. These figures suggest that the profile of Fianna Fáil support has been pretty much unchanged in the last ten years, barring a significant upsurge in support in the C1 category in 2002. Fine Gael support has fluctuated, as we know. It won back support more successfully in the AB group (and among farmers) than in other social strata in 2007, but the gap between it and Fianna Fáil among C1 (lower middle class) voters has not narrowed as much as might have been expected. Fine Gael won 28 per cent of votes in both these groups in 1997, compared to the Fianna Fáil share of 35–36 per cent, but Fine Gael's share of AB support now is seven points higher than its share of C1 support, while Fianna Fáil's share of AB support is four points less than its share of the C1 vote. These are small changes, but the C1 group is very large, comprising a third of all voters in this survey, so losses there have a big impact.

Table 7.4 Party supporters in different social classes, 1997–2007 (%)

		AB *middle* *class*	*C1* *lower* *middle* *class*	*C2* *skilled* *working* *class*	*DE* *semi- and* *unskilled* *working class*	*Farmers*
Fianna Fáil	1997	36	35	43	42	49
	2002	37	40	43	45	51
	2007	37	41	43	44	49
Fine Gael	1997	28	28	23	18	38
	2002	23	19	18	19	32
	2007	30	23	22	23	42
Labour	1997	11	12	12	15	4
	2002	12	15	12	12	4
	2007	12	11	9	10	6

Sources: analysis of RTÉ/Lansdowne exit polls 1997, 2002, 2007.

A key factor in vote choice is that for many people it is hardly a decision at all: they tend to vote for the same party independent of circumstances. They are party loyalists. Each party has a core of supporters on whom it relies, and who play a major role in providing the stability of electoral outcomes that we have seen over the years. Such loyalty seems in decline, with loyalists estimated at no more than a quarter of all voters in 2002 compared with more than a half of all voters in the 1970s.[14] The exit poll asked voters whether or not they felt 'close' to any particular party, and 43 per cent reported that they did. The heightened feeling of attachment may be due to the context of the survey. Voters were leaving the polls after a very hard-fought campaign, when the evidence is that support for parties in general always rises. It might also indicate that the downward trend has been reversed. More evidence is needed before we can judge that. However, this does give us a measure of the longer-term loyalties of voters. Fianna Fáil, Fine Gael and Sinn Féin all succeeded in getting the support of between 80 and 90 per cent of their more committed voters, but the smaller parties are less successful at this. Only 60 per cent of those close to Labour voted Labour with their first preference, 63 per cent of Greens voted Green and 54 per cent of PDs (when the PDs ran a candidate) supported their party. As Table 7.5 shows, those without an affiliation break down much more evenly between Fianna Fáil and Fine Gael than do those who are close to a party. The respective standings are 37 and 26 as opposed to 48 and 26. Greens, PDs, Labour and, naturally, Independents all do relatively well amongst the unaffiliated. It is the existence of enduring loyalties that gives Fianna Fáil an extra edge.

Table 7.5   Closeness to a party and party choice (%)

	FF	FG	Lab	PD	Grn	SF	Others	Total
Not close	37.0	26.2	10.7	3.0	5.7	7.2	9.4	100
Close	48.2	26.5	8.8	2.0	3.6	7.4	3.6	100
Total	41.6	26.3	9.9	2.6	4.8	7.3	7.0	100

Source: analysis of RTÉ/Lansdowne exit polls 2007.

The issue agenda was much the same as it had been in 2002. One of the notable features of the 2002 election was that while Fianna Fáil suffered because of the health issue, Fine Gael seemed to get very little benefit from it.[15] Did health help Fine Gael this time? More importantly, did it hurt Fianna Fáil? Table 7.6 shows the party choices made by those who cited each of the 11 issues most frequently cited as important. The analysis suggests health again damaged Fianna Fáil, but that this time Fine Gael was the main beneficiary. Crime too seems to have been a vote-winner for Fine Gael at the expense of Fianna Fáil. Even so, the advantages gained are quite small, Fine Gael winning only eight percentage points more votes among those concerned with health than it did among voters who did not cite that as an issue.[16] On the economy, or at least on the issue of economic management, Fianna Fáil did very well, winning 57 per cent among those mentioning this as an issue and only 37 per cent among those who did not. Fine Gael did not do well on that issue, winning 21 per cent of the vote among voters who cited that as an issue as against 27 per cent among those who did not – although the latter figure is only one percentage point above the party's support in the exit poll. Most of these relationships are weak. In contrast, the importance of the environment for the Green Party is very clear: 23 per cent of those citing this as an issue voted Green, compared with only 2 per cent of those who did not! There is little sign otherwise that any of the smaller parties and groups made much political capital out of particular issues, in a way that Independents, for instance, did last time on health. Where they did disproportionately well, as did Sinn Féin on housing, the overall impact of the issue on that party's vote is still very small, as relatively few cited housing as an issue.

Table 7.6 Relationship between party choice and issue salience (%)

	FF	PD	FG	Lab	Grn	SF	Ind	All	No.
Health	33	3	31	11	5	9	8	100	1,452
Crime	36	3	33	9	3	8	8	100	800
Economic management	57	3	21	8	3	4	5	100	743
Inflation	44	3	27	9	5	7	7	100	568
Education	39	3	27	10	5	7	7	100	491
Government experience	75	2	7	5	5	7	7	100	442
Environment	28	2	21	14	23	3	7	100	414
Honesty	21	3	41	13	6	5	11	100	352
Housing	35	2	19	15	7	10	11	100	330
Local issue	43	3	24	10	4	8	6	100	319
All	42	3	26	10	5	7	7	100	3,206

Source: analysis of RTÉ/Lansdowne exit poll 2007.

While it is tempting to see these relationships as causal, it may be that those who support a party will justify their choice by citing issues prominent in a party's campaign. Another possibility is that one party is widely seen as being more competent at dealing with a particular issue, either because of a specific policy proposal, because it gives an issue a higher priority, or because of the previous record of the respective parties. It is not possible to decide between these interpretations on the basis of the evidence in Table 7.6. In particular, Table 7.6 and the question on which it is based, does not throw direct light on which party is seen as being more competent to deal with a particular issue. However, judgements offered by interviewees in the final TNS mrbi poll (18 May) suggest that there were clear differences in perceived competencies. Respondents were asked to identify the leader (choosing between Ahern and Kenny) best able to deal with the issues of the economy, health and crime. Ahern led Kenny by 55–25 per cent on the economy, but lagged by ten percentage points on health (32–42). Ahern also led Kenny by two percentage points on crime. An earlier Millward Brown IMS survey conducted on 9–10 May indicated the same relationships with respect to capabilities of the two party leaders on the economy and health: Ahern won by 48–35 per cent on the former, but Kenny won by 45–34 per cent on the latter. Putting this information together with that in Table 7.6 does support the view that the link between the health issue and opposition voting, and the economy and Fianna Fáil voting, does have firm roots in perceptions of who could deal with each issue best. In addition, this data on perceived competence suggests significant changes in perceptions during the second half of the campaign. It is always problematic to compare answers across different polls to different questions, but it is very noticeable that while the health assessment did not change significantly between these two polls, taken just over a week apart, the gap on the economy widened appreciably, increasing from 13 points to 30 points.

There have been suggestions that the TV debate between the leaders just a week before the election was critical in Fianna Fáil's eventual victory, in particular by emphasising the difference between the leaders on their ability to manage the economy well. The past evidence from other countries on the effects of such debates has been mixed,[17] but there were some important features of this particular debate. First, a higher proportion of voters than watched either of the previous two debates viewed it. Second, it was held a week before the election, allowing for the impact, if any, to be fully felt (but not so early as to be forgotten). Third, voters thought Ahern won the debate, in contrast to 1997 and 2002. Finally, there is evidence of growing support for Fianna Fáil in the later part of the campaign, and the timing of this event fits in with that (see chapter 8). The comparative details of debate evaluations are shown in Table 7.7 and these are consistent with the media perception that this time at least the debate influenced the outcome in a significant way. It is also the case that those deciding in the last week were more likely than the early deciders to have watched the debate: 35 per cent as against 27 per cent. It is extremely difficult to assess the impact of one such event as this with the aid merely of surveys after the event, in part because even significant effects may be small, but also because effects may be both direct – on watchers – and indirect, impacting on people who read about the debate or who talk to others about it.[18] However, much of the other evidence in the exit poll is not consistent with the argument that it was the debate that won it for Bertie. Those who did *not* watch the debate were more likely to vote Fianna Fáil than those who did, and this is true regardless of when the decision was (reportedly) made. Fianna Fáil voters are typically less likely to watch such debates. This year was just like 1997 and 2002 in this respect but, even allowing for that, there was no greater tendency for late deciders who watched the debate to vote Fianna Fáil than there was for early deciders to do so, relative to those whose TV watching was directed elsewhere or who simply did not watch the TV at all. A total of 41 per cent of those who decided in the last week and who did not see the debate voted Fianna Fáil, as against 35 per cent of those who did see it; earlier deciders voted 47 per cent Fianna Fáil among non-viewers and 38 per cent among viewers. Certainly, the voters did not feel it was important: only 3 per cent of them offered it as an explanation for their vote, and the bias towards Fianna Fáil in that group could have been worth at most 0.5 per cent to that party's final vote share.

Table 7.7 Voters' assessment of the TV debates, 1997–2007

	1997	*2002*	*2007*
Did not watch debate	43	37	32
FG candidate won	27	30	12
FF candidate won	15	15	36
Neither won	12	16	17
Don't know	2	3	3
Total	100	100	100

Source: analysis of RTÉ/Lansdowne exit polls 1997, 2002, 2007.

Whatever the importance of the debate itself, the simple link between the preferred Taoiseach and vote is always a strong one, and it is equally so in 2007. The data on which we might be able to make an assessment of how important leaders were this time is not yet available.[19] Analysis of the 'preferred Taoiseach' question does show a strong link with party choice: 70 per cent of those who prefer Ahern voted Fianna Fáil, as against 11 per cent who did not prefer Ahern; while 58 per cent of those who preferred Kenny voted Fine Gael, as opposed to 10 per cent who did not prefer Kenny. Those preferring Ahern, but who did not support Fianna Fáil, were spread evenly across the other parties. This illustrates the extent to which Ahern's appeal stretches across the political spectrum. In contrast, Kenny supporters who did not vote for Fine Gael tended to support Labour (15 per cent) or Fianna Fáil (10 per cent). This certainly overestimates the impact of the leader on the vote, not least because those asked to choose between rival parties' candidates will hardly disregard which party they would like to see in government, and the question does not even ask them to do so. The more particular question about leaders in 2007 is: did 'Bertiegate' have much impact on the election? Obviously, unless leaders matter in the first place, doubts about a particular leader's honesty, or sympathy with him in the face of an unjustified media witch-hunt, is unlikely to matter much. One answer is given by the exit poll, which asked people this question directly. Subject to the caveats already made about such questions, it is worth pointing out that 6 per cent said it led them to vote for Fianna Fáil, while 16 per cent said it led them to vote against Fianna Fáil. If we take this at face value, this suggests Fianna Fáil lost 10 per cent through 'Bertiegate', which sounds extremely unlikely. In fact, only 46 per cent of those who said it made no difference voted Fianna Fáil, but it still seems very unlikely that the affair cost the party even five percentage points. A different perspective is given if we look at the behaviour of those who did *not* voluntarily mention the Taoiseach's finances as an issue – 43 per cent voted Fianna Fáil, implying that the issue cost the party at most just over one percentage point.[20]

If it is difficult to separate party and Taoiseach, it is also difficult to separate party and the make-up of government. As we have seen, the Fine Gael + Labour option was more attractive this time, and the Fianna Fáil + PD option less attractive. How did this influence voting behaviour? While we might expect that people's vote will be determined by their government preference, this could be a simplistic view, or even completely wrong. Certainly people could vote sincerely, expressing a preference for their preferred party in government, but strategic considerations might well intervene. Should someone who wants a Fianna Fáil + PD government vote just PD, or Fianna Fáil + PD, running the risk of a single party government, or vote PD + FF, opening up the same risk?[21] Many voters also deny that this is uppermost in their minds, choosing to place constituency representation above the question of government. Even if people do vote in a manner that is consistent with a government preference, this hardly explains why they vote as they do, since the preference for a particular government may be a consequence, rather than a cause, of their vote. However, as Table 7.8 indicates, there is a very clear relationship between first preference voting and the government voters say they would most like to see. Some 81 per cent of those who wanted a Fine Gael + Labour coalition voted for one or other of those parties, and 76 per cent of those who wanted the larger Fine Gael + Labour + Green coalition voted accordingly. Between 80 and 90 per cent voted in accordance with their declared preference for a Fianna Fáil-led coalition, including the 89 per cent of those who wanted a single party Fianna Fáil government who voted Fianna Fáil. So 83 per cent do then vote in a way that is consistent with the government they would like to see. There is a little less consistency in voting for the Fine Gael-led government than for the Fianna Fáil-led ones: 79 per cent as opposed to 88 per cent. A minority of those who would like to have seen a change of government nonetheless voted first for Fianna Fáil, or for an Independent candidate. It might be thought these were people who opted primarily for a good local candidate, but in fact the Fianna Fáil voters who preferred a Fine Gael-led government were actually less inclined to say they voted 'locally' than other Fianna Fáil voters. It might also be an indication of the sort of inconsistent result commonly found in survey data and usually put down to errors in understanding questions or recording answers.

People may have used lower preferences to bring about the desired governmental outcome, and even those whose first preference was apparently inconsistent may have given an appropriate number 2 vote. The exit poll gives some information on this, although since people are asked only to indicate which other parties they voted for, it is not possible to separate those who gave a Fianna Fáil candidate a second preference from those who placed that

Table 7.8   Party preferences by preference for government (%)

	FF	PD	FG	Lab	Grn	SF	Ind	Total	Consistent
FG+Labour	9.8	0.8	63.1	17.5	0.8	3.5	4.6	100	80.7
FG+Labour+Greens	8.3	1.1	41.7	15.2	18.8	4.3	10.6	100	75.8
FF	88.7	0.2	3.3	2.4	0.0	1.3	4.2	100	88.7
FF+PD	79.0	11.8	2.5	1.1	0.6	0.5	4.6	100	90.7
FF+Labour	64.3	0.4	4.6	19.3	2.3	2.7	6.3	100	83.6
FF+Greens	40.4	0.0	3.8	5.3	41.6	2.9	6.0	100	82.1
FF+SF	21.2	0.4	1.6	2.9	1.2	67.1	5.6	100	88.4
FF+Independents	45.6	1.1	5.1	4.5	2.2	2.0	39.6	100	85.2
Total	41.6	2.6	26.2	10.0	4.8	7.3	7.5	100	83.0

Source: analysis of RTÉ/Lansdowne exit poll 2007. Twenty-five respondents who said 'none of the above' are excluded.

party's candidates 11, 12 and 13 out of 13. However, since voters typically support only two to three parties and very few fill in the entire ballot, it is worthwhile looking at which other parties were 'supported'.[22] The analysis is not shown here, but what is clear is that while lower party choices are less consistent with government preferences than are first preferences, people's lower preferences do tend to correlate with their government preferences. One illustration is the behaviour of Green Party voters. Of those who would like a Green + FF government, 43 per cent also voted for Fianna Fáil as against 17 per cent of other Green voters who did so. Of those who would like a Green + FG/Labour government, 53 per cent also voted for Fine Gael as against 22 per cent of Green voters who did not choose a Green + FG/Labour option. In each case the government preference involving Fianna Fáil or Fine Gael with Greens more than doubles the chance of a lower vote for Fianna Fáil or Fine Gael respectively. Labour voters responded even more strongly. While they were more likely to report also having voted for Fine Gael than for Fianna Fáil, they were three times more likely to support Fine Gael or Fianna Fáil when their preferred government option involved that party than they were when it did not. This is really quite clear evidence that voters were motivated by the choice of a government as well as a party in 2007.

A model of party choice in 2007

The above analysis of a number of factors treats each separately. This has the advantage of being straightforward, but that comes at the cost of ignoring any possible relationships between the factors, such as how far those concerned about health are also concerned about crime, and so on. We have also focused on the party choice in 2007 without regard to the previous behaviour of the voters. As we have seen, some consider themselves close to parties, others report that they usually vote for a particular party, and most 2007 voters would have cast a vote in 2002. In assessing the impact of their individual issue concerns, we argued that it was difficult to separate whether respondents voiced a concern with an issue because of their party's focus on that issue, or because a concern with that issue led them to a party. In this section we try to take some account of the importance of more enduring loyalties as well as the interrelationships between many of the other factors considered here.

This is done using a multivariate method of analysis, which identifies the unique relationship between party choice and each of the various factors associated with it. The model we present is still very simplistic. It assesses the relationship between each factor and party choice holding all others factors constant. It does not allow for the fact that there may be a path of influence through which one factor influences another and in turn both influence a third, a process described by one highly influential analysis of voting as a 'funnel of causality'.[23] For that reason, we have left out any mention of choice of government or Taoiseach, except where these were given as reasons by respondents. They would obviously show up as important, but would obscure the influence of other factors that would have had an impact on the voter's judgement about which government was best or which potential Taoiseach was preferred.

The data used here come from the 2007 exit poll. We include three sets of factors. The first set is demographics, including urban/rural residence and church attendance patterns as well as the gender, class and age variables discussed separately above. The second set includes reported vote in 2002 and being close to a party. These are limited here just to Fianna Fáil and Fine Gael, as those parties are of most concern in this analysis. Together, they give a measure of party loyalties. Finally, the third set includes the more frequently mentioned issue concerns, also discussed above. Table 7.9 shows the impact of each factor on party choice. This impact is shown as a ratio of the odds of voting for a party (say Fine Gael) and the odds of voting Fianna Fáil, dependent on the respondent's having a particular characteristic. Numbers above 1.0 indicate the odds are positive and that the characteristic increases the likelihood of a vote for the non-Fianna Fáil party. A number below 1.0 indicates that the odds are negative, and so the characteristic decreases the chances of a non-Fianna Fáil vote; that is, it increases the likelihood of a vote for Fianna Fáil. While the upper bound is infinite, the lower bound is zero, so we should see the number 0.5 as the negative equivalent of 2.0, and 0.25 as the negative equivalent of 4.0, and so on. The number 1.0 indicates there is no relationship. The stronger relationships are indicated by a number of stars, with three stars denoting a relationship that is so far from 1.0 that it can be seen as likely to have arisen by chance only 1/1,000 times. Two stars indicate the chance is no more than 1/100 and one star 1/20. All other coefficients can be seen as not significantly different from 1.0 and so indicate that there is no significant relationship. As explained, each column shows the choice between Fianna Fáil and one other party. In order to assess the choice between, say, Fine Gael and Labour, the reader should compare the coefficients in the Fine Gael/FF and Labour/FF columns.

Table 7.9   A multivariate model of party choice

	FG/FF odds ratio	Lab/FF odds ratio	PD/FF odds ratio	Grn/FF odds ratio	SF/FF odds ratio	Ind/FF odds ratio
Demographics:						
Female	1.02	0.91	1.11	0.96	0.67**	1.31*
Middle class	1.31*	1.16	1.87**	1.52*	0.41***	0.58**
Older	0.99	1.00	0.97	0.95	0.85***	0.94*
Rural	1.25*	0.48***	0.70	0.67*	0.93	0.46***
Weekly churchgoer	1.11	0.92	1.30	0.77	0.90	1.28
Loyalties:						
2002 vote FF	0.27***	0.10***	0.27***	0.16***	0.12***	0.15***
2002 vote FG	5.76***	0.78	0.63	0.73	0.15***	0.68
Close to FF	0.13***	0.09***	0.16***	0.21***	0.10***	0.16***
Close to FG	4.31***	0.63	1.41	0	0.24**	0.66
Issue concerns:						
Health	1.97***	1.58***	1.28	1.80***	1.53***	1.27
Crime	1.49***	1.17	1.19	0.89	1.17	1.40*
Econ. management	0.76*	0.75	0.90	0.55**	0.41***	0.63**
Environment	1.28	1.93***	1.08	12.70***	0.57*	1.23
Inflation	0.91	0.75	0.77	0.71	0.62**	0.90
Education	1.03	0.98	0.88	1.26	0.69*	1.11
Honesty	3.61***	3.25***	2.14**	2.33***	1.63*	3.82***
Housing	1.17	1.86***	1.03	1.74*	1.37	1.78**
Local issue	1.29	1.25	1.31	1.08	1.18	1.01
Choosing Taoiseach	0.71	0.35***	0.35*	0.14*	0.37**	0.61
Bertiegate	3.30***	2.56***	1.24	1.82	1.63	1.65

Notes: Coefficients estimated using multinomial logit. Fianna Fáil is the reference group. ***indicates coefficient is significant at .001 level, **at .01 level and *at .05 level. Log-Likelihood intercept only is –5118.760: Log-Likelihood full model is –3833.190. A constant term is included, but not shown.

Source: analysis of RTÉ/Lansdowne exit poll 2007.

For instance, take the coefficient 1.31 in the first column of the second row. This shows the relationship between voting Fianna Fáil or FG and being middle class (as opposed to not being middle class). The 1.31 means that the chances of a Fine Gael, rather than a Fianna Fáil, vote are 31 percent higher when the voter is middle class than when the voter is not, all other things (measured in Table 7.9) being equal. The single star indicates that the difference in the chances is relatively modest. Moving to the other end of the row, the coefficient is 0.58. This indicates that the chances of a voter supporting an Independent rather than Fianna Fáil are much less if she is middle class than they are if she is not, with an Independent vote (rather than a Fianna Fáil one) by a middle-class voter almost half as likely as it would be if the voter was not middle class. This time two stars indicate that this is a stronger relationship. Comparing across the row we see that a much stronger relationship would be the contrast between Fine Gael – more middle class than Fianna Fáil – and Independents, who are less middle class.

As far as demographic factors are concerned, most differences are small, but Sinn Féin stands out as relatively unattractive to female voters. Most parties are more middle class in their appeal than Fianna Fáil, the exception being Sinn Féin and Independents – just as in 2002. Again, the differences are quite small, except in the case of Sinn Féin, but the differences between Sinn Féin and Fine Gael, or Sinn Féin and Labour, are very striking. Younger voters are also attracted relatively more than older ones to Sinn Féin. Urban voters are disproportionately attracted to the smaller parties over both of the larger ones, with Fine Gael the most successful (relatively) in rural areas. There are no significant differences with respect to religious observance.

Not surprisingly, the variables measuring past behaviour and party attachment show very strong relationships with Fianna Fáil and Fine Gael choice. Of most interest is the contrast between a past vote for Fianna Fáil and a past vote for Fine Gael in predicting 2007 vote choice. The figure of 0.27 for the former is analogous to one of 3.7 for the latter, but in fact the latter is close to 6. This means that a Fine Gael vote in 2002 is a better indicator of current Fine Gael/Fianna Fáil vote than a past Fianna Fáil vote is an indicator of support for Fianna Fáil/Fine Gael in 2007. In other words, Fine Gael did better among past Fianna Fáil voters than vice versa, probably because it was the hard core that stuck with Fine Gael last time. However, closeness to the party seems to have exerted a stronger impetus towards a Fianna Fáil vote than a Fine Gael one.

The issue variables suggest a number of concerns that did make a difference between parties although hardly any relationship is very strong. The Green/FF odds ratio for the environment is 12.7, by far the biggest effect in the whole table. The most potent reasons to vote Fine Gael seem to have been honesty and 'Bertiegate', but neither was a widespread concern. Among the big issues, health and crime both helped Fine Gael over Fianna Fáil. Significantly, given Fine Gael's very strong emphasis on health, the party did not dominate this issue: all opposition groups except Independents won votes from the government on health to much the same degree, whereas last time the health issue was a significant impetus only in the swing to Independents.[24] The party certainly capitalised much better on this issue than it had done last time: the impact of the health issue on the Fine Gael vote was significant. Those concerned with health are ten percentage points more likely to vote Fine Gael. Corresponding numbers are: for crime, six points; honesty, 16 points; and 'Bertiegate', 20 points, but the latter were very much minority concerns so the net effect of all these on the Fine Gael vote was small. Substituting crime for housing, Labour's profile is similar, although like all the smaller parties, Labour voters were less likely to mention choosing a Taoiseach. Green support is marked by the environment in particular, but also by honesty; Sinn Féin's also by health and honesty, and Independent voting by honesty and housing. The only significant positive influence on the PD vote was honesty – reflecting the party's 2002 role as Fianna Fáil watchdog perhaps. The only widespread positive influence on Fianna Fáil support is the economy, but that is not very significant for the most part. Overall, those mentioning the economy were 8 per cent more likely to vote Fianna Fáil. It is easier to see why people did not vote for Fianna Fáil than why they did vote for them. This is in part because most reasons correlating positively with a Fianna Fáil vote were mentioned by fewer people: things such as stable government and experience in government were mentioned almost solely by Fianna Fáil voters, and even then not by most of them. What this suggests is two things. The first is clear: that even on the issues that might have hurt the party badly, like health and crime, Fianna Fáil kept the damage within bounds. Many saw the party as competent to deal with that issue and no other party was able to place its own stamp on the issue and corner the market. The second is more uncertain, but it seems as if Fianna Fáil's support was perhaps less than wholehearted, and for many was based less on a reason to vote for Fianna Fáil and more on the absence of a good reason to support the opposition.

Further analysis on perceptions of competence is possible using the last pre-election TNS mrbi poll, carried out just a week before the election. As stated already, this showed Ahern with a clear lead over Kenny with respect to the economy, Kenny leading on the health issue and the two closely matched on crime. If these are taken as predictors of preferred government, which proves most effective? It is not possible to control here for previous vote, or for party loyalties, as these variables are not available in that survey. However, the three factors can be looked at simultaneously. This is done in Table 7.10. It is very clear that the economic judgements are more important. Indeed, the impact of rating Ahern rather than Kenny as most competent on the economy is to increase the likelihood of choosing a Fianna Fáil-led government by 58 percentage points, as compared with 38 on the economy and 25 on crime.[25] If vote rather than choice of coalition is made the object of analysis, the relative weights are if anything stronger. This provides a significant qualification to the suggestion from the exit poll that the economy was overshadowed by health, and perhaps fits better with the eventual outcome.[26]

In an additional analysis not shown here we explored the impact of the TV debate, adding variables tapping who won the debate, when the decision was made and a further variable measuring the combination of the two into the model estimated in Table 10.9. While those who thought Ahern won were significantly more likely to vote Fianna Fáil, this can simply be put down to the fact that the debate confirmed and reinforced what people already believed rather than changing minds. More importantly, there was no evidence that those *who made up their mind in the last week* and thought Ahern had won were more likely to support Fianna Fáil.[27]

Table 7.10   Impact of perceived leader competence on choice of government

	Fianna Fáil vs Fine Gael-led government odds ratio
Ahern most competent on the economy	3.72***
Ahern most competent on health	2.22***
Ahern most competent on crime	1.66***

Notes: coefficients are estimated with logit. *** indicates coefficient is significant at .001 level. Log-Likelihood intercept only is –578.092; Log-Likelihood intercept Full Model is –341.849.

Source: analysis of final TNS mrbi/*Irish Times* poll, 18 May.

Conclusion

The main question in this chapter is: why did the Fianna Fáil vote hold up so well? The conditions seemed less favourable than in 2002, with the government and leader less popular, the economic record less impressive and the existence of an apparently better organised and more credible alternative. A number of answers have been suggested here. The first is that conditions were still favourable: the government was on balance popular, Ahern remained ahead of his rivals, and voters were reasonably confident about the future. While the ratings of government and leader had dropped, the rankings remained similar, with Fianna Fáil still preferred to the rest. A second point is that even if things had been worse, Fianna Fáil's voters in 2002 preferred that party to any other by a big margin. Even if circumstances had become less favourable, support could easily be retained. We have seen that Fianna Fáil voters were much less certain than they had been last time, reinforcing the argument that circumstances narrowed the gap in their minds between Fianna Fáil and some alternative, but in the end they still plumped for Fianna Fáil. A third point is that while the existence of a stronger alternative helped Fine Gael, helping to answer a second question in this chapter, it might also have helped Fianna Fáil. This time, the election was more clearly about the formation of government and that could have sustained Fianna Fáil at the expense of smaller parties. It is clear that voters supported parties in a manner consistent with their governmental preference. A fourth point is that while the issues appeared to favour the alternative, and Fine Gael in particular used this to better advantage, it was still unable to dominate the government on any issue and therefore could not make the necessary gains to depose Fianna Fáil from office. It seems likely that the data available in the exit poll survey underestimate the impact of the economy. Our analysis of the more appropriate data in the TNS mrbi poll does indicate that the economy mattered much more than health or crime, and that the economy worked to the advantage of Fianna Fáil.

Notes

* The author is grateful to Des Byrne of Behaviour and Attitudes Ltd for providing his reports on consumer confidence, Paul Moran of Millward Brown IMS and Richard Colwell of RED C for providing their data and information about their methodologies, the Irish Social Survey Data Archive for providing me with the 2007 exit poll and TNS mrbi survey data, and to Independent Newspapers Ltd, the *Irish Times*, the *Sunday Business Post* and RTÉ for permission to use the data they paid to collect. None of them is responsible for the use I have made of that data or the interpretations that I have placed on the analysis.

1. John Garry, Fiachra Kennedy, Michael Marsh and Richard Sinnott, 'What decided the election?', pp. 119–42 in Michael Gallagher, Michael Marsh and Paul Mitchell (eds), *How Ireland Voted 2002* (Basingstoke: Palgrave Macmillan, 2003).

2. Michael Harrison and Michael Marsh, 'A re-examination of an Irish popularity function', *Public Choice* 94 (1998), pp. 367–83.

3. See *Consumer Confidence: Impact on the General Election* (Dublin: Behaviour and Attitudes, 2007) and the monthly Consumer Confidence Index published by the Economic and Social Research Institute (ESRI) and Irish Investment Bank (IISBank): www.esri.ie/irish_economy/consumer_sentiment/latest_consumer_sentiment/?

4. Ahern, of course, is evaluated as Taoiseach while Kenny is evaluated only as Fine Gael leader. The standards are different.

5. Michael Marsh, 'Candidates or parties? Objects of electoral choice in Ireland', *Party Politics* 13:2 (2007), pp. 500–27. See also Garry et al., 'What decided the election?', p. 125.

6. A Millward Brown IMS/*Sunday Independent* poll carried out on 16 April reported that 22 per cent thought the stamp duty issue would have a lot of influence on the way they voted, with a further 27 per cent saying it would have some influence. But in the previous question in this poll, just 7 per cent mentioned this issue unprompted as a possible influence on their vote.

7. Michael Marsh and James Tilley, 'Golden halos and forked tails: the attribution of credit and blame to governments and its impact on vote choice', table 3. Paper delivered at the Annual Meeting of the American Political Science Association, Philadelphia, 31 August–3 September 2007.

8. Admittedly the difference is greater among the 35 per cent who gave health as the *most* important issue: 23 per cent of those who saw the service as improving saw the issue as important but 43 per cent of those thought it was getting worse.

9. In 1997, 35 per cent of those deciding in the last week chose Fianna Fáil, compared with 45 per cent of those deciding before the campaign.

10. This data could be used to assert that particular parties gained or lost ground during the campaign. While this may well be true, this interpretation entails treating those who had not finally made up their mind as 'undecided' in opinion poll terms. This is quite unrealistic as 'undecideds' are typically well under 20 per cent, and are much more likely than those who do voice a party preference not to vote at all (see Gail McElroy and Michael Marsh, 'Why the opinion polls got it wrong in 2002', pp. 159–76 in Gallagher et al., *How Ireland Voted 2002*, p. 165; see also chapter 8 in this volume). The exit poll consists only of voters. In practice,

people may 'decide' for a poll, but then change their mind later, perhaps more than once, so this would be an unrealistic assumption.

11. For notes of scepticism see Peter Mair, *The Changing Irish Party System: Organisation, Ideology and Electoral Competition* (London: Frances Pinter, 1987), p. 92, and Richard Sinnott, *Irish Voters Decide* (Manchester: Manchester University Press, 1995), pp. 168–72. This theme of candidate or party runs through Michael Marsh, Richard Sinnott, John Garry and Fiachra Kennedy, *The Irish Voter: The Nature of Electoral Competition in the Republic of Ireland* (Manchester: Manchester University Press, 2008). See also Marsh, 'Candidates or parties?', passim.

12. Wouter van der Brug, Cees van der Eijk and Mark N. Franklin, *The Economy and the Vote: Economic Conditions and Elections in Fifteen Countries* (Cambridge: Cambridge University Press, 2007), especially pp. 31–53.

13. For a full explanation of these measures, see Michael Marsh, 'Stability and change in the structure of electoral competition 1989–2002', pp. 94–111 in John Garry, Niamh Hardiman and Diane Payne (eds), *Irish Social and Political Attitudes* (Liverpool: Liverpool University Press, 2006).

14. Michael Marsh, 'Party identification in Ireland: an insecure anchor for a floating party system', *Electoral Studies* 25:3 (2006), pp. 489–508.

15. Garry et al., 'What decided the election?', pp. 133–4; Marsh et al., *The Irish Voter*, chapter 5.

16. Given that 22.6 per cent of those *not* citing health as a major influence voted Fine Gael, and that overall (in the exit poll) 26.3 per cent of respondents voted for that party, this indicates that the health issue could have boosted the Fine Gael vote by less than four percentage points. However, health cost Fianna Fáil eight percentage points. This simple method of estimating these effects, of course, assumes that nothing else correlated with health also has an impact on vote choice, an assumption taken up below.

17. Most research has concluded that such debates served only to confirm prior beliefs, but other research has taken a more positive view, suggesting that they may be important, even crucial events: see, for example, André Blais and M. Martin Boyer, 'Assessing the impact of televised debates: the case of the 1988 Canadian election', *British Journal of Political Science* 26:2 (1996), pp. 143–64, and Peter R. Schrott, 'The political consequences of winning televised campaign debates', *Public Opinion Quarterly* 54:4 (1990), pp. 567–85.

18. The media reaction to the debate was that nobody won a clear victory, so any indirect effects in this case would be more likely have come from face-to-face contacts.

19. For an extensive analysis of the impact of party leaders on the 2002 vote, see Marsh et al., *The Irish Voter*, chapter 6. That analysis makes use of a set of evaluations about each of the leaders and of their parties in an effort to estimate the separate impact of leader and party. It concludes that leaders make only a modest contribution to party choice.

20. It was also argued in some quarters that the media's attention on the issue galvanised the party's activists, who worked even harder to get out the vote (see p. 36 above). If so, and there is no evidence available to support this view at present, 'Bertiegate' may have actually helped Fianna Fáil.

21. See Michael Laver, 'STV and the politics of coalition', pp. 131–52 in Shaun Bowler and Bernard Grofman (eds), *Elections in Australia, Ireland and Malta under the Single Transferable Vote: Reflections on an Embedded Institution* (Ann Arbor: Michigan University Press, 2000).

22. Michael Laver, 'Analysing structures of party preference in electronic voting data', *Party Politics* 10:5 (2004), pp. 521–41; Marsh, 'Candidates or parties?'

23. A. Campbell, P. Converse, W. Miller and D. Stokes, *The American Voter* (New York: Wiley and Sons, 1960).

24. This was the conclusion of a similar analysis carried out of the same questions in the 2002 exit poll: Garry et al., 'What decided the election?', p. 136.

25. This poll was carried out just after the TV debates. A similar analysis carried out on the earlier Millward Brown IMS/*Sunday Independent* poll discussed above – carried out the previous week – suggests the economy and health were then of equal weight. This may further indicate the growing importance of the economy as the campaign unfolded.

26. The TNS mrbi/*Irish Times* poll also contained assessments on four other matters: representing Ireland abroad, improving public services, keeping taxes down, and providing affordable childcare. When all are included in the same model, the economy remains the most important, followed by representing Ireland well, improving public services, affordable childcare, and then health and crime. Economic assessments have twice the impact of health and three times that of crime.

27. Nor was the timing of the decision significant, except with respect to FF/SF and FF/Independents, where in each case late deciders were more likely to vote Fianna Fáil – regardless of who they thought won the debate.

8
The Polls: A Clear Improvement

*Gail McElroy and Michael Marsh**

All one has to do is use a properly drawn sample of the electorate large enough to minimise random sampling error, get honest answers from everyone, do the questioning close enough to the time of voting to minimise changes in voting intentions, anticipate how the undecided will vote, and, finally, distinguish between voters and non-voters in the electorate.[1]

In the aftermath of the 2002 general election it was widely held that many of the media commissioned opinion polls had performed poorly.[2] Fianna Fáil's vote had been consistently overestimated at the national level and industry standards were frequently abandoned at the constituency level. This provided ammunition for those who had argued for a ban on opinion polls during the campaign period, something that the government had tried to introduce a year previously. In this chapter we address the performance of both national and local polls in the 2007 election to see what, if any, lessons were learned in the intervening five years. We examine how the polling companies reacted to the disappointments of 2002 and the predictive accuracy of the 2007 polls.

Irish voters were awash in polling data this time. Nine national polls were conducted over the course of the official 25-day campaign, and there was one exit poll. Three additional polls were conducted in the two weeks immediately prior to the calling of the election and many others in the year-long build-up to the vote. The fashion for local polling that had emerged in 2002 continued, with 16 of the 43 constituencies being polled (some more than once).[3] In addition, there was a major new entrant into the market in the form of RED C Market Research, which conducted a series of 22 polls for the *Sunday Business Post* in the months leading up to the election, publicly documenting the oscillations of party support. RED C was also the first major polling company in Ireland to commit to interviewing respondents for newspaper polls by telephone rather than face to face, a practice now standard elsewhere. There were two other significant changes from 2002. The first is that TNS mrbi and Millward Brown IMS each eschewed the use of the simulated ballots employed in their respective national polls last time and returned to the use of traditional vote intention questions. The second is that both companies adjusted their estimates to counter what they expected would otherwise be a pro-Fianna Fáil bias. We discuss this in more detail below.

Did the polls get it right?

It is to be expected that poll findings and election results will not match. The issues are whether the mismatches are larger than we would expect, given statistical considerations, and whether the differences are systematically biased in favour of certain parties. Polls capture opinion on a given day, often well in advance of the election. Opinion may change; indeed, this change is what polls are designed to capture. In order to assess the accuracy of any individual poll fully we would need some 'true' measure of public opinion on the particular day the poll was conducted but, with the exception of exit polls, this does not exist. Thus, when we compare opinion polls with election outcomes we cannot be certain of the extent to which the variation we witness between each poll's estimates and the actual election result stems from real movement in public opinion or from simple survey error, and in the latter case, whether this arises from acceptable sampling error or from some other factor.

Irish polling companies claim that reported results have a margin of error of at least plus or minus 3 per cent.[4] This figure of 3 per cent derives from probability theory and is based on the assumption of a pure random sample with roughly 1,000 respondents. However, pure random sampling is prohibitively expensive and is not used in Irish media polls. Usually, interviews take place in about 100 locations drawn at random and companies employ quota techniques to ensure representative samples drawn from homes round these sites, normally in terms of social class, age and gender. For phone polls, random sampling is merely of phone numbers with quota controls introduced at pre-interview stage. These deviations from a simple random sample will increase the margin of error. Local opinion polls, with their smaller samples of around 500 respondents and correspondingly fewer locations, have a margin of error of at least plus or minus 4 per cent. Such large margins of error can make a huge difference to the perceived viability of smaller parties and individual candidates.

With these caveats in mind, we start by assessing the accuracy of the opinion polls vis-à-vis the final results and also examine whether there were systematic biases in the polls. Two widely used measures are employed in the following analysis.[5] The first computes the mean error in the poll, averaging the deviations in percentage points between predicted and observed results for each party. The second calculates the absolute value of the difference between the margin separating the two leading parties (in this case, Fianna Fáil and

Fine Gael) in the poll and the difference in this margin in the actual vote. We also use a third, more recently developed, measure of poll accuracy (A). This again concentrates just on the two leading parties. A is zero when there is perfect agreement between a poll and the election result. A negative sign on the accuracy statistic indicates, in the Irish context, that a poll is biased in a Fine Gael direction, while a positive sign indicates a pro-Fianna Fáil bias. A is small because it is the natural log of a larger number and particular attention should be given to the sign.[6]

National polls

Table 8.1 gives the results of the major opinion polls conducted by each company during the election campaign and for each poll displays its performance on each of these three measures. We also consider sampling error. Where figures are in italics it indicates that the election outcome was outside the normal margin of error associated with a random sample of that size.[7] It is interesting to look at all of these polls, not just at the last ones. If nothing much changed during the campaign then there would be no reason to expect later polls to be more accurate. If there were trends, then the later polls would be better placed to reflect them, although the vagaries of sampling error might still mean an earlier poll was more accurate. In fact, the final TNS mrbi poll came very close to the actual result. Its errors were small and only the estimate for Sinn Féin was outside the normal margin of error. Overall, the degree of 'error' was generally smaller than in 2002.

Taking our first measure, the average score of the last poll by each company in 2002 was 1.9 as against 1.5 this time. The large party error, measure two, was 3.2 in 2002 as against 2.1 this time. The final TNS mrbi and RED C polls were closer than those of Millward Brown IMS and Lansdowne, but only the former were taken in the last week of the campaign. Earlier polls all tended to underestimate Fianna Fáil support significantly, and most polls overestimated support for Sinn Féin. Labour's support was also overestimated in some early polls. The last survey carried out by each of the companies proved more accurate than those carried out by the same company earlier in the campaign, although the size of the error dropped markedly only in the final two polls. However, all companies got closer to the final Fianna Fáil vote share figure in their last polls, and also closer to the final Sinn Féin and Labour figures. Fine Gael estimates were changeable, with Millward Brown IMS and RED C each further away in its final poll than in at least one of its earlier polls. No poll shows a Fianna Fáil bias (in terms of the Fianna Fáil/Fine Gael vote share measure, A). This runs counter to the pattern, dating back to 1987, of final polls overestimating the Fianna Fáil vote. As will be discussed below, the reasons for this may lie with the way in which final figures are now adjusted, but it may also be that the Fianna Fáil support was increasing in the later part of the campaign, a trend that led inevitably to an apparent bias against the

Table 8.1 Accuracy of campaign polls in predicting final outcome

Polling company Date survey conducted	Lansdowne 1–2 May	RED C 7–9 May	TNS mrbi 8–9 May	IMS 9 May	IMS 14–15 May	RED C 17 May	TNS mrbi 18–19 May	RED C 20–21 May	Election result May 24
Fianna Fáil (%)	37	35	36	35	37	36	41	38	41.6
Fine Gael (%)	26	29	28	26	25	27	27	26	27.3
Greens (%)	6	6	5	5	5	8	6	6	4.7
Labour (%)	*13*	12	*13*	*13*	12	11	10	11	10.1
PDs (%)	2	3	2	3	3	2	2	3	2.7
Sinn Féin (%)	8	7	*10*	*10*	9	*10*	9	9	6.9
Independents/others (%)	9	8	6	8	9	6	5	7	6.6
N	1,006	1,263	1,000	1,082	1,107	1,201	1,060	1,019	
Average error	2.0	2.0	2.0	2.3	2.0	2.1	1.0	1.4	
Winner – runner-up	3.3	8.3	6.3	5.3	2.3	5.3	0.3	2.3	
Predictive accuracy (A)	–0.06	–0.24	–0.16	–0.12	–0.03	–0.13	0.0	–0.04	

Note: Numbers in italics significantly lower or higher than election outcome.

Sources: *Irish Times* and TNS mrbi; RED C and *Sunday Business Post*; Lansdowne Marketing and RTÉ and the *Irish Examiner*, *Sunday Independent* and Millward Brown IMS.

party in the polls as a whole. Fine Gael support was underestimated in two of the last three polls, but this pattern is typical.

We should also consider the record of the polls in a more comprehensive way. This is important if we are to assess the record of the campaign polls throughout the campaign as a whole and not just of the final ones before the election. Again it should be borne in mind that polls may vary from one another, and from the actual result, simply because of sampling error. We carried out a 'poll of polls', using all the original poll data and allowing for two sorts of differences between each poll. First, there may have been differences between companies, sometimes called 'house effects', the possible roots of which will be explored below. Second, differences may stem from opinion change over the course of the campaign. This is hinted at in the pattern of errors in Table 8.1, with later polls being more accurate. If on election day we had taken all the campaign polling data into account without assuming any poll was better than any other (but had allowed for trends), what would our best guess have been about election day? Table 8.2 shows the expectations.[8]

Table 8.2   Expectations from a poll of polls

	Expected percentage	Margin of error	Actual percentage	Absolute error
Fianna Fáil	38.7	36.5–40.8	41.6	2.9
Fine Gael	26.0	24.1–28.0	27.3	1.3
Greens	5.5	4.5–6.5	4.7	0.8
Labour	10.8	9.4–12.1	10.1	0.7
PDs	3.2	2.3–4.0	2.7	0.5
Sinn Féin	9.5	8.2–10.9	6.9	2.6
Independents/others	6.4	5.3–7.5	6.7	0.3

Source: authors' analysis using all campaign polls except Lansdowne's 1 May survey for the *Irish Examiner*; see also note 8.

The results demonstrate that Fianna Fáil's vote was underestimated by the campaign polls, even allowing for the margin of error of the polls.[9] The actual Fianna Fáil vote falls just outside the expected level of support.[10] Fine Gael support was also underestimated, although the outcome was within the margin of error. Support for each of the other parties was overestimated, but only Sinn Féin's significantly so. This pattern reinforces that found in Table 8.1, showing it was characteristic of the polls as a whole and not just the final ones. Two other findings from this exercise are important. The first is that there were house effects. TNS mrbi tended to have a higher estimate for Fianna Fáil support; IMS had a higher PD and lower Green support; and RED C had a much higher Green and lower PD support. There was also a significant upward trend in support for Fianna Fáil, whose expected vote rose by almost 3.5 per cent between the first poll of the campaign, taken on 1 May, and the last, taken on 21 May. Reasons for the overall improvement as well as remaining sources of such error are discussed below, but before that, we turn to the record of the local polls.

Local polls

Local polls were conducted in 16 constituencies in the nine months before the election.[11] The major methodological difference between the national polls and the local polls is that for the latter, respondents are provided with mock ballots to complete.[12] The use of such ballots may make the local polls more 'realistic',[13] but it may also directly influence the outcome by affecting the way parties campaign and even whom they choose to nominate. This is a well-known problem, and not one confined only to polling. The observation of something may result in a change in what is observed, a factor that makes it more problematic to assess accuracy when there is such a big time gap between the initial observation, the survey, and the election itself. A candidate's perception of their chance of winning (or their party's perception of the candidate's chance) is presumably a factor in choosing to run or in getting a nomination, and the local opinion polls, often conducted well in advance of the election, may play some part in this (see examples in chapter 4, and the account of Terence Flanagan in chapter 5).

The smaller sample sizes for these polls, typically 500, leads to expectations that there will be bigger differences between the estimates of support in the polls and the final outcome than was the case for the national campaign polls discussed above. In addition, given the longer timeframe, the list of candidates running in a constituency was frequently unknown at the time of polling. Thus it was not unusual for the mock ballot and final ballot to have rather different slates of candidates. Given that the number of candidates running varied from constituency to constituency, direct comparison of the average absolute error may be misleading (although this measure is reported in Table 8.3) and we concentrate on the two remaining measures. The rankings produced by these two measures are also roughly consistent.[14]

Table 8.3 Results of constituency polls

	Average absolute error	Difference in FF–FG	Predictive accuracy	N
All	2.9	6.0	0.01	23
RED C	2.6	5.1	–0.03	13
TNS mrbi	3.4	7.6	0.08	9

Source: see note 11. The total of 23 includes one Millward Brown/IMS poll.

As Table 8.3 makes clear, there are differences between polling companies, with RED C polls being more 'accurate' than those carried out by TNS mrbi, although this difference is statistically significant only for the measure in the final column. RED C also gets a little closer to the actual gap between the two largest parties. The average error here is larger than it is for the national polls, as would be expected given the smaller samples. In the 2002 election there was a slight bias towards Fine Gael at constituency level.[15] This time there is evidence of a pro-Fianna Fáil bias, indicated by the positive sign on the summary figure of 0.01. TNS mrbi shows a significant bias to Fianna Fáil. This difference may reflect the fact that TNS mrbi does not adjust its local constituency results, whereas RED C does. Surprisingly perhaps, further analysis (not shown) does not indicate that the poll results get closer to the actual result the nearer the poll was taken to election day.[16]

The impact and nature of such adjustments are detailed in the next section, but before that we look at the local polls in more detail to see how well they predict the final share of votes for each party's candidates. Media outlets frequently speculate about who will take the seats come election time on the basis of a local poll, but this type of 'accuracy' is difficult to achieve. First, as already stated, parties and candidates respond to poll figures. We might expect, for instance, that less well-known candidates might improve their standing over the course of time. Second, parties often try to manage party support so that their vote is shared fairly evenly between their candidates so as to maximise the number of seats they win (see the section in chapter 6 on vote management, and examples in the photo section at the front of the book).

We have calculated the vote ratio of the first to second candidate (or second to third where parties nominated three candidates) in each of the constituencies in which opinion polls were undertaken.[17] For instance, if the first Fianna Fáil candidate got 25 per cent of the vote and the second got 10 per cent, the ratio reported is 2.5. We expect that the vote ratio will be lower in the election than in the last local opinion poll. Figure 8.1 shows the relationship between the shares in the poll and in the election. If there was no change in candidates' relative shares, all the points would lie on the straight line that runs at 45 degrees to the horizontal axis. In fact, in almost all cases the vote ratio is lower in the election than the corresponding opinion poll, so most points fall below that line. In other words, the polls overstate the differences between candidates of the same party. In addition, where there were several surveys in a constituency, the exaggeration was reduced in the later polls. How far this is a consequence of vote management and how far it is simply because the profile of the 'weaker' candidate is raised during the campaign would require a lot more analysis than there is space for here. What is clear though is that the local polls are poor guides to final candidate performance.

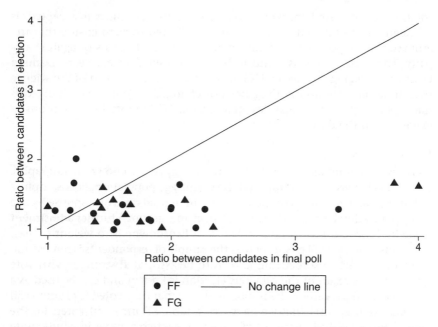

Figure 8.1 Ratio between candidates of same party in the final local poll and the election: Fianna Fáil and Fine Gael only

Note: ratios are for first to second party candidate in polls and election, regardless of which party candidates are in these positions. Thus ratio does not reflect changes in individual candidate rankings. Where three candidates nominated, the ratio is calculated for vote ratio of second to third party candidate.

Source: Authors' calculations based on polls listed in note 11.

The adjustment game

While in principle the task facing polling companies seems uncomplicated, in reality they face a number of formidable problems, as the opening quote in this chapter reminds us. Even with a perfectly drawn sample of the electorate, polling companies must determine, amongst other things, how to allocate undecided voters and what to do about the fact that some respondents will vote while others will abstain on election day. The raw figures that emerge from interviews typically require a significant adjustment.

The first problem, though, is that survey samples now turn up more Fianna Fáil voters than they should do, resulting in an overestimate of Fianna Fáil's support. It could be that Fianna Fáil voters are more available to respond to pollsters, whatever method is used. Alternatively, it could be that those with no firm views are more likely to respond 'Fianna Fáil' when asked their vote intention, as this is the best-known party.[18] One solution to this problem, whichever of these two accounts is accepted, is to weight the sample after data has been collected so as to ensure that the estimates of support then calculated are not biased towards or against any party. The need to do this seems to have increased in recent years. Damien Loscher, managing director of TNS mrbi, explained that 'Much of the science that underpins opinion polling has not changed ... What has changed is how opinion polling companies view the reliability of voting intentions as expressed on the doorstep.'[19]

Past vote

Pollsters have long used such techniques to adjust for known demographic differences between the sample and the voting age population. Post-sampling weighting can be used to compensate for differential rates of response by age group, education level or, where relevant, ethnic group. A further adjustment made by Millward Brown IMS, RED C and Lansdowne is to weight by past vote. This is one way of ensuring that the sample of respondents is representative with respect to something known to be associated strongly with vote intention. The result of the previous election is known and can be used as a yardstick. If 50 per cent of the respondents say that they voted for Fianna Fáil in 2002, we may infer that we have oversampled Fianna Fáil voters (as the party achieved only 41 per cent of the vote). No two companies apply quite the same adjustment for past voting and these differences in methodology will lead to different estimates. For instance, RED C compares the reported past vote to the actual result of the last general election and weights to the mid-point of the two, while Millward Brown IMS and Lansdowne simply adjust to the result of the last election. This brings down the estimate of the Fianna Fáil vote share. Table 8.4 shows the impact of adjustment in the last

Table 8.4   Raw and adjusted vote shares in final IMS and RED C polls (%)

	Millward Brown IMS 14–15 May		RED C 21 May		Result 24 May
	Raw vote shares	Adjusted vote shares	Raw vote shares	Adjusted vote shares	
Fianna Fáil	43.1	37.5	39.2	39.1	41.6
Fine Gael	23.6	24.6	24.3	24.8	27.3
Greens	3.9	5.4	7.1	6.4	4.7
Labour	11.1	11.6	10.9	10.2	10.1
PDs	2.1	3.2	2.8	3.1	2.7
Sinn Féin	9.8	9.0	8.5	9.2	6.9
Independents/others	6.5	8.7	7.1	7.2	6.7

Note: Adjustment is for past vote. Millward Brown IMS basic figures are already adjusted for demographic representation. RED C's adjustments for likely turnout are not shown here.

Source: Authors' analysis of original data.

RED C and Millward Brown IMS polls. In the case of Millward Brown IMS, adjustment reduces the estimate of the Fianna Fáil vote share from 43.1 per cent to 37.5 per cent, with consequent small increases for most of the other parties. The adjusted distributions come closer to the actual gap between the two big parties although the average error after adjustment is actually larger. Adjustment has only a marginal effect on RED C's estimates. However, the net result is again to provide slightly more accurate estimates by the criteria used previously.

RED C's *unadjusted* estimates of Fianna Fáil support are much lower than those of Millward Brown IMS (and TNS mrbi, as we see below). This probably reflects the different survey methodologies described above: RED C polls are done by phone while the others are face to face. However, it is not clear why telephone polls should turn up fewer Fianna Fáil sympathisers, particularly when weighted for demographic accuracy.

Turnout

A second basis for adjustment relates to voter turnout. About a third of the eligible population will not vote in a national election, but this population – those who will vote – is unknown at the time of the survey. Different techniques have been developed, but no global standard has been discovered that will deal with this vexing and increasingly important issue.[20] RED C asks respondents to attach a probability to their likelihood of voting, using a 10-point scale. It then excludes all respondents who claim their probability of voting is 4 or less on this scale. RED C's research has found that 80 per cent of respondents report their probability of voting at 5 or higher. All these respondents are retained in the sample, even though turnout in Irish elections has not approached such a level for many decades.[21] This further adjustment increases the estimate of Fine Gael support by 1 per cent at the expense of Independents.

Since 1997 TNS mrbi has recalibrated its raw data on party support with the aid of surveys conducted on the day of the election. (This recalibration was not done on 2002 campaign polls, because it was assumed, probably incorrectly, that the use of mock ballots would make any adjustment unnecessary.) The company conducts surveys on the day of an election among those who have yet to vote and those who have already voted and they use this information to try to identify the difference between intended and actual voters. This is then used as a basis on which to adjust the raw data on party support. The adjustment has a marked impact on the figures presented. Table 8.5 shows that the TNS mrbi adjustment reduces Fianna Fáil support from 46 per cent to 41 per cent and increases that of Fine Gael and Labour, with each change moving the estimate for each party closer to the election outcome. The set of estimates for all parties is more accurate in terms of each of the criteria used above, although adjusted figures are less accurate for the Greens, Sinn Féin and for others.

Table 8.5   Raw and adjusted vote shares in final TNS mrbi poll (%)

	TNS mrbi 18 May		
	Raw vote shares	*Adjusted vote shares*	*Result 24 May*
Fianna Fáil	46	41	41.6
Fine Gael	25	27	27.3
Greens	5	6	4.7
Labour	9	10	10.1
PDs	2	2	2.7
Sinn Féin	8	9	6.9
Independent/others	5	5	6.7

Note: Adjustment is for likelihood of turnout. Raw figures already controlled for demographic representation.

Source: *Irish Times*, 21 May, p. 8.

'Undecideds'

The final puzzle, concerning 'undecideds', has confounded pollsters for decades. Some respondents are genuinely undecided when questioned by pollsters and others may simply refuse to reveal how they intend to vote (a separate problem from refusal to participate in the survey at all). Millward Brown IMS and Lansdowne press 'undecided' respondents for an answer by asking them if they are 'leaning' towards a party. This may overcome part of the problem, but it does not eliminate it. The simplest solution is to allocate undecided respondents to parties in the same proportion as declared voters are distributed. Lansdowne, Millward Brown IMS and TNS mrbi do this. Another popular option is to allocate by some other information about the respondent, such as party identification, attitudes to issue items, or previous voting history. RED C ascribes a 50 per cent probability to the party that the undecided voted for previously (if the respondent has provided this information) and allocates the remainder proportionally.

The undecideds (and we include the small group who refused to answer or said they would not vote here) typically constituted about 15 per cent of poll samples during the campaign period, with no obvious trend until the last week, when three of the last four polls recorded figures below 13 per cent, with the final RED C poll recording only 8 per cent. The final TNS mrbi poll is an exception with 15 per cent undecided – a fairly consistent figure in the TNS mrbi campaign polls. Is there any evidence that such voters leaned in any disproportional way towards (positive) or against (negative) a particular party? The short answer here is no. While there are patterns of association in the unadjusted data, they do not appear after the adjustments have been made, implying that the adjustment process already discussed itself takes care of any problems in the potential preferences of undecideds.

A late swing?

While this discussion of the various ways in which each company makes adjustments to its basic findings explains how each arrives at its estimates, it cannot explain why the polls as a whole got it wrong, at least by a little bit: underestimating Fianna Fáil in particular and overestimating some of the smaller parties. There was a trend towards Fianna Fáil. We have seen that each polling company reported a higher estimate for that party in polls coming later in the campaign than in its earlier polls. (See chapter 7 for evidence that, on average, Fianna Fáil's voters made up their minds to support that party later in the campaign than is normal.) It may be that this movement towards Fianna Fáil became more pronounced in the last days. The best evidence of such a change would be obtained from a pre- and post-election panel survey in which the same people were contacted before and after the election.

Fortunately, RED C contacted those whom it first interviewed for its final poll and asked them how they actually voted. The results are shown in Table 8.6. This compares the vote reported *after* the election with the vote intention declared a few days *before* the election. Of course, neither can be validated, but taking each at face value we can explore whether patterns of change are in accord with the hypothesis of 'late swing', or some other explanation for change between polls and election results. Unfortunately, we are looking for evidence of very small changes of around one or two per cent. The number of cases here is only 486, and because the margin of error will exceed any change we find, these results must be seen as suggestive rather than conclusive. The most important result is that the two larger parties hung on to their support better than did the rest, losing fewer supporters either to other parties or to abstention. This combination of late swing and differential abstention boosted the support of Fine Gael and Fianna Fáil at the expense of the rest.[22] The small parties claimed in the aftermath of the election that they had been 'squeezed' by the larger parties. This evidence suggests that the last few days did help the larger parties at the expense of the smaller ones, but only when it comes to those who expressed pre-election voting intentions. The second result is that while the slight movement from the smaller parties to larger ones was very much a movement to Fianna Fáil rather than to Fine Gael, Fianna Fáil lost more voters to Fine Gael than it gained from that party, meaning that the hypothesis of an overall net late swing to Fianna Fáil (rather than to Fine Gael) cannot be sustained on the basis of this data. The third result concerns those who were undecided or unlikely to turn out. Most of these did not vote at all, which goes some way to justify the proportional allocation used by pollsters, but those who did vote favoured the smaller parties disproportionately. Of course, the numbers are very small in this case (only 29 reported a vote) and we might be sceptical that so many unlikely voters did actually turn out on the day. More research is necessary on this point.

Table 8.6   Differences between vote intention and reported vote in final RED C poll (%)

Reported vote 5–12 June	Fianna Fáil	Vote intention 21 May Fine Gael	Others	Will not vote etc.
Fianna Fáil	82	4	13	7
Fine Gael	7	82	3	11
Others	5	8	69	21
Did not vote etc.	7	7	15	61
Total	100	100	100	100
N	166	103	151	66

Source: Authors' analysis of RED C pre- and post-election panel study.

Conclusion

Perhaps too much is expected of the pre-election media polls. Many voters decide at the last moment how to cast their ballot and many others change their minds between parties over the last couple of days; campaign polls are bound to miss these movements and there is nothing that can be done methodologically to correct for this. Nonetheless, the performance of the polls in the 2002 election led to considerable introspection on the part of the Irish polling industry and major changes were made to the manner in which the raw figures that polls throw up are adjusted. TNS mrbi dropped the use of mock ballots and returned to its idiosyncratic method of adjusting its estimates of party support. Millward Brown IMS also dropped the mock ballot, and introduced what is a more standard method of weighting vote intention by reported past vote. Lansdowne followed suit. RED C, the new player, followed the methods that proved most successful in 2002 when employed by ICM – polling by telephone and then weighting by past vote and likelihood of turnout.

In general, this contributed to a better performance. Average error was down, and there was less bias in the estimated vote of the two biggest parties. However, 2007 was unusual for the fact that the polls as a whole underestimated Fianna Fáil support, probably because Fianna Fáil's support was increasing through the campaign proper, an increase captured by all polls. Only the final TNS mrbi poll appeared to get it right, but to accept that this is so requires us to assume that Fianna Fáil's support stopped rising when that poll was taken, several days before the day of the election and, given the trend across all the polls, this would seem to be an unjustifiable claim. It is still clear that face-to-face surveys, unlike phone polls, overstate Fianna Fáil support significantly and that some adjustment is therefore necessary. Almost any method that succeeds in giving a smaller estimate for Fianna Fáil seems to work. We remain a little sceptical that the problem is essentially one of differential turnout, since panel studies around both the 2002 and 2007 elections suggest those with a Fianna Fáil vote intention are not less but more likely to turn out, although such studies give us only reported and not actual turnout.

The record of the local polls was much the same, although thankfully there was less evidence of the use by the media of mythical polls. Their accuracy is in any case much harder to judge, taken as they are over a very long period of time in which party fortunes may ebb and flow. Some early ones look very accurate indeed, while later ones may look skewed. The smaller sample size of such polls naturally gives rise to larger absolute error for party support than we see with national polls, but more important is the great change shown in the distribution of candidate support within parties. The effect of the campaign itself as well as deliberate efforts at vote management make such polls a poor guide to eventual candidate outcomes, however accurate they may be at the time.

More than 30 countries have banned the publication of polls in the week (and in some cases up to three weeks) prior to election day, arguing that they have a negative influence on the democratic process. This argument has much greater weight in cases where the polls themselves have a very poor record of accuracy. This at least was not the case this time.

Notes

*   The authors are grateful to Paul Moran of Millward Brown IMS and Richard Colwell of RED C for providing data and information about their methodologies and to the Irish Social Data Archive for providing us with the 2007 exit poll and several TNS mrbi surveys, and to Independent Newspapers Ltd, the *Irish Times*, the *Sunday Business Post* and RTÉ for permission to use the raw data they paid to collect. None of them is responsible for the use we have made of that data or the interpretations placed on the analysis.

1. Paul Perry, 'Certain problems in election survey methodology', *Public Opinion Quarterly* 43:3 (1979), pp. 312–35, at p. 312.

2. For a review see Gail McElroy and Michael Marsh, 'Why the opinion polls got it wrong in 2002', pp. 159–76 in Michael Gallagher, Michael Marsh and Paul Mitchell (eds), *How Ireland Voted 2002* (Basingstoke: Palgrave Macmillan, 2003).

3. This figure does not include the *Evening Herald* poll of all of the Dublin constituencies and the many private polls conducted by parties that were frequently covered by the media.

4. It is almost 3.0 per cent, plus or minus, for the typical 40 per cent won by Fianna Fáil. It is smaller for Fine Gael, more like 2.5 per cent, because it wins only around 25 per cent, and smaller again for tiny parties. For the PDs, at around 3 per cent of the vote, it is just under 1.0 per cent. It is expected that the 'real' figure will fall outside these margins of error one time in twenty.

5. These come initially from F. Mosteller, 'Measuring the error', pp. 54–80 in F. Mosteller, H. Hyman, P. J. McCarty, E. S. Marks and D. B. Truman (eds), *The Pre-Election Polls of 1948: Report to the Committee on Analysis and Pre-election Polls and Forecast* (New York: Social Science Research Council, 1949). See also I. Crespi, *Pre-*

Election Polling: Sources of Accuracy and Error (New York: Russell Sage, 1988); Warren J. Mitofsky, 'Review: was 1996 a worse year for polls than 1948?', *Public Opinion Quarterly* 62:2 (1998), pp. 230–49; N. Panagakis, 'Response to "Was 1996 a worse year for polls than 1948?"', *Public Opinion Quarterly* 63:2 (1999), pp. 278–81.

6. This measure of predictive accuracy (*A*) computes the natural logarithm of the odds ratio between the two largest parties in a poll and in the outcome of the election. See Elizabeth Martin, Michael Traugott and Courtney Kennedy, 'A review and proposal for a new measure of poll accuracy', *Public Opinion Quarterly* 69:3 (2005), pp. 342–69.

7. We have taken the published figures here, which are rounded to a whole number. It is possible that the unrounded number would be more (or less) accurate, but not by much.

8. This was accomplished by regressing vote choice on the time of poll and the company carrying it out. Estimation was done using multinomial logit. The over time change modelled here is essentially linear. Expectations are generated using prvalue command in Stata 9, setting time to election day and company to mean values.

9. This is by the polls as a whole. If we take simply TNS mrbi, its polls could be said to overestimate Fianna Fáil's final support, assuming the trend evident in the polls continued up to 24 May.

10. Note that the confidence intervals here are smaller than the typical ±3 percent reported in opinion polls. Not only is the sample size much larger than in an individual poll, but also margins of errors in polls are calculated slightly differently from those in linear regression, though the two are related.

11. The following is a list of local polls analysed here, giving constituency, date of poll, who the poll was carried out for and who carried it out: Carlow–Kilkenny, 19–25 February, *Carlow Nationalist*, RED C; Clare, 18 September–2 October, RTÉ/Nuacht, TNS mrbi; Cork North Central, 7–15 April, *Evening Echo*, RED C; Cork North West, 26 March–17 April, Radio Na G, TNS mrbi; Cork South Central, 14–22 April, *Evening Echo*, RED C; Donegal South-West, 2–18 April, Radio Na G, TNS mrbi; Galway West, 2–14 October, RTE/Nuacht, TNS mrbi; Galway West, 5–16 March, Radio Na G, TNS mrbi; Kerry South, 2–14 November, TG4, TNS mrbi; Kerry South, 27 March–1 April, *The Kingdom*, RED C; Kildare South, 7–12 March, *Kildare Nationalist*, RED C; Laois–Offaly, 26 March–1 April, Laois Nationalist, RED C; Louth, January 2007, *Drogheda Independent*, RED C; Louth, 23–29 April, *The Argus/Drogheda Independent*, RED C; Mayo, 28 August–6 Sept 2006, RTE/Nuacht, TNS mrbi; Mayo, 5–11 March, *Western People*, RED C; Mayo, 10–14 April 2007, *Mayo News*, Millward Brown IMS; Roscommon–South Leitrim, 2–8 April, *Roscommon Herald*, RED C; Sligo Leitrim, November 15–24, RTÉ/Nuacht, TNS mrbi; Sligo–North Leitrim, 12–18 March, *Sligo Weekender*, RED C; Waterford, 19–26 March, *News and Star*, RED C; Wexford, 19–30 October, RTÉ/Nuacht, TNS mrbi; Wexford, 26 February–4 March 2007, *Wexford Echo*, RED C.

12. Given the use of mock ballots in constituency polls, RED C conducts these polls by the traditional face-to-face method.

13. Garret FitzGerald, *Irish Times*, 7 May 2007.

14. The correlation between these two measures is .86, despite using quite distinct scales.

15. McElroy and Marsh, 'Why the opinion polls got it wrong in 2002', p. 169.

16. This is in contrast to 2002: ibid., p. 169.

17. These vote ratios are not attached to particular candidates, but simply reflect the ratio of the vote between first and second candidates (or second and third where relevant) regardless of identity. In many instances, the first candidate in the poll is not the first candidate at election time. For instance, Michael Ring topped each of the three opinion polls in Mayo, with Enda Kenny ranked second, but this ordering was reversed at the election.

18. This latter interpretation is supported by evidence from the Irish election panel study 2002–06. Respondents questioned in 2006 as to their vote choice in 2002 – a choice they initially reported in 2002 – were disproportionately apt to recall voting Fianna Fáil when they had not done so. Calculations by the authors.

19. *Irish Times*, 27 April 2007.

20. Michael W. Traugott and Paul. J. Lavrakas, *The Voter's Guide to Election Polls*, 2nd edn (New York: Chatham House, 2004).

21. This inflated figure reflects in part the reluctance of respondents to admit they will not vote, but also reflects the fact that those who are sampled in surveys are more likely to vote than the population at large. The 2002 Irish Election Study used marked registers to check how many of the sample voted. With weighting just for demographic characteristics, it was estimated that 81 per cent of the sample claimed to have voted but that only 71 per cent actually did so. Official turnout data record that only 63 per cent voted. This is in line with the findings of surveys elsewhere. Those reporting a vote for Fianna Fáil were slightly more likely than those reporting any other preference to misreport having voted, a result in line with TNS mrbi's adjustment strategy: see Michael Marsh, Richard Sinnott, John Garry and Fiachra Kennedy, *The Irish Voter* (Manchester: Manchester University Press, 2008), appendix II, for further details.

22. This pattern of differential turnout also appeared in 2002; see McElroy and Marsh, 'Why the opinion polls got it wrong in 2002', p. 164.

9
The Election as Horse Race: Betting and the Election

*Michael Gallagher**

Betting is generally associated with sporting events such as horse races or football matches rather than the political process, but the 2007 election campaign was notable for the prominent coverage given to the way in which bookmakers and punters were viewing it. Expert commentary on the national picture and individual constituency contests sometimes drew on trends in the betting markets as an indicator of what was going on – as well as potentially influencing those markets.

For many, following the election via (or directly participating in) the betting markets gave extra interest to the campaign, and in this chapter we will examine the way the markets reacted to campaign developments. Over and beyond the entertainment value supplied by betting possibilities, there is a respectable body of literature that argues that betting markets are actually the most accurate guides to likely election outcomes, outperforming both pundits and opinion polls.[1] As we will see, the record of the markets on this occasion was mixed.

Prediction markets and political betting

Betting on elections has a long history – it was recorded at the time of George Washington's election, for example. There was an organised market for all US presidential elections in the late nineteenth and early twentieth centuries, peaking in 1916 when the volume of money wagered was twice the total amount spent by the parties on their campaigns.[2] Betting on Irish elections, at least in any large-scale way, seems to be a much more recent phenomenon. Although there have been markets on one-off events such as party leadership contests,[3] presidential elections and referendums, the 2002 election was the first at which there was a wide choice of markets. Most bookmakers no doubt made a profit from the contest, but one, luvbet.com, collapsed later in 2002 due, it is thought, to huge losses on the election.[4] Betting in 2007 was on a vastly different scale – for example, one bookmaker, Paddy Power, took over €1 million in bets compared with just €75,000 in 2002. Paddy Power is regularly the most publicity-conscious and hence most cited bookmaker operating in Ireland, but the relative newcomer Celtic was probably more prominent in media coverage of the election because its managing director, Ivan Yates, is a former Fine Gael TD[5] and minister who often appears in the media as a pundit and, to some extent, as a 'front man' for the political betting industry as a whole.

Betting on political events is now very much a part of the business–entertainment world; it also has a respectable place in the calculations of those who want to estimate the likelihood of developments in politics, business or science. Prediction markets exist on the likelihood of a vaccine being developed for SARS, the cloning of a human being by 2020, the estimated box office receipts of a film, whether US petrol prices will reach a certain level by the end of the year, or the level of a company's sales over the next 12 months. The Foresight Exchange Prediction market (which does not involve real money) offers odds on the likelihood of George W. Bush resigning as US President, of an American attack on Iran, on who will emerge as the Democrat and Republican candidates at the next US presidential election, on a female Vice-President of the US before 2013, and so on.[6] The rationale of establishing such markets, some of which involve only 'play money' rather than large sums, is that the market aggregates knowledgeable opinion and proves a more reliable guide to the future than any other prediction method. Some of the events around which markets develop are important for governments, firms or ordinary citizens, and if the markets deliver accurate predictions their value is obvious.

Of course, there are normative objections to such markets, and in particular to betting on election outcomes. Those already concerned about the media's tendency to concentrate on the 'horse race' aspects of elections (who's going to win?) rather than to inform the public in depth about the substantive policy issues see the development of serious betting as a deplorable if logical extension of the trivialisation of election coverage. Betting on some events seems inherently distasteful – though, in effect, the life insurance industry is based on calculations about people's likely lifespan.[7] Ethical concerns were one reason for the decline of betting on US presidential elections after the 1930s.

Relying on betting markets rather than on opinion polls as a guide to what is likely to happen on election day has several things to commend it. First, we are tapping into a pool of what we hope is relative expertise. The market aggregates the judgements of those who inform themselves about all the relevant factors and delivers their collective assessment. Whereas respondents to opinion polls may give a casual, weakly held and easily changed answer to a question about their voting intention, those betting on an election outcome are putting their money where their mouth is. They have a strong incentive to inform themselves about the factors that could affect the result, and moreover they are explicitly trying to predict the outcome, whereas survey respondents are merely reporting how they would have voted on the day of the survey. A poll, as pollsters repeatedly remind us, offers only a snapshot of attitudes on the day of the poll, not a prediction of the result, but prediction is expressly what a betting market is about. The incentive for punters to get it right is usually financial, though it can also be reputational or be based on the psychological gratification of 'beating the bookie', because markets based on symbolic sums or play money prove as accurate as real betting markets.

Second, it is cheap – in fact, it is free. Why would an observer who wants a reliable steer as to the outcome of the next election pay a polling company money to conduct a survey, with all the costs and complications, when he or she can simply peek at the state of the market?

Third, it reacts instantly to events. A dramatic political development, a gaffe or a scandal can be reflected almost immediately in a change in the odds, whereas a poll takes a few days to organise – and by the time the poll's findings appear, something else may have happened that leaves everyone unsure as to whether the picture it paints is still accurate.

Fourth, it has a proven track record. In the US, where as we have already mentioned there is a long history of betting on elections, the market correctly predicted the winner on 11 of the 12 occasions when there was a clear favourite during the 1884–1940 period, in the pre-opinion poll era.[8] More recently, the Iowa Electronic Markets (IEM) have run a market on US presidential elections since 1988, with a smaller error in their predictions of the candidates' votes than the polls have displayed.[9] In the run-up to Tony Blair's sweeping election victory in 1997, the spread betting markets predicted the Labour vote more accurately than either the pollsters or the pundits, and they also, so it is claimed, outperformed the polls in 2005.[10] A political stock market was much more accurate than opinion polls in predicting the outcome of the 1994 Swedish referendum on EU membership.[11] In Australia, too, the betting market did better than the polls, both at national level and in individual constituencies, in 2001 and 2004.[12] Closer to home, the bookmakers' predictions for the seats that the parties would win in the Northern Ireland Assembly elections of March 2007 proved extremely accurate.

However, the betting market cannot be assumed to be a perfect source of information as to what will happen. One reservation is that bettors, particularly if small amounts are involved, may bet with their heart rather than with their head, whether on an election or on a football match involving their team, so if partisans of one party are wealthier or more likely than others to wager on an election, as has been suggested for Ireland,[13] the market may overstate that party's chances. It has become a standard photo-opportunity for party leaders to place bets in a bookies' shop on a successful outcome for their party as a sign of their faith, even though better odds might be available on the internet.[14] Against this, the odds are initially set by the bookmaker on the basis of expert advice, though it is true that they are adjusted in response to the volume of bets on the different options.

A second objection to relying on a betting market rather than on polls is that bettors in a market may be distinguished from the rest of the population not by their greater expertise but simply by their greater propensity to gamble.

Third, a concern about any market is the possibility of market manipulation, which in this context could occur if supporters of one outcome back it heavily in order to demotivate its opponents. In the leadership race for the British Liberal Democrats in 2006 there was suspicion that supporters of one candidate, Chris Huhne, were backing him down to favouritism in order to generate publicity for him and enhance his credibility.[15] At an Irish election, this could be a rational strategy in an intra-party contest at constituency level, where heavy betting on one candidate of a party could be designed to shorten his or her odds and lengthen those of the running mate, creating a 'buzz' about the former and making the latter seem unelectable. Pundits could have an incentive to talk down the chances of a likely winner in the hope of lengthening the odds and enabling them to make a killing in the market, but fortunately Irish electoral pundits are universally of such high ethical standing that this possibility can safely be dismissed.

Fourth, while betting on Irish elections is relatively new, its record is mixed. In March 2002 the market confidently predicted a Yes vote (the final odds were around 1–5) in a referendum on abortion, but the outcome was a No, albeit very marginally.[16] At the May 2002 election it correctly pointed to a Fianna Fáil seat total in the low 80s, but it overestimated Fine Gael; it dropped its prediction over the course of the campaign, but even its final figure, in the low 40s, was out of line with the 31 seats the party won. Its prediction for the PDs was just two seats, compared with the actual eight. Of course, the opinion polls also performed poorly in 2002.[17]

A fifth reservation is that while the market may get it right at the death, a market that is open for several months yet points to the correct outcome only in the last few moments cannot really be claimed to have delivered an accurate prediction. Those who back the favourite at an earlier stage simply because it is the favourite, believing the market must have 'got it right', may end up losing. Defenders of markets would acknowledge that a herd instinct can develop but argue that although markets can get it wrong, especially in the early stages of a campaign, they usually end up right.

Although the bookmaker is popularly portrayed as being in an inherently competitive relationship with an undifferentiated mass of punters, an alternative perspective sees the bookmaker as essentially a conduit for the systematic transfer of money from ill-informed outsiders, or 'mug punters', to shrewd operators, while taking his own commission. In order to attract the knowledgeable insiders to the market, the odds offered on the plausible options, especially on the favourite, must closely reflect the real probabilities. The revenue to pay them and still make a profit is generated by the bookmaker's overpricing the low-probability options, secure in the knowledge that the mug punters, aiming for a lottery-style big win, will not realise or perhaps not even care that the odds on their 20–1 selection should rightly be more like 200–1. This helps explain the 'favourite–longshot bias' noticed in a number of betting markets.[18]

The question of where the political betting market is assumed to get its information from is an open one. While some models see opinion polls and the market as completely independent, this seems unrealistic. Bettors draw on polls as one source of information, and another source, no doubt, are the predictions of supposed experts, or 'pundits'. Anecdotal evidence suggests strongly that some pundits in Ireland not only draw on opinion polls to shape their predictions but also are very likely to back their judgement with the bookmakers. In addition, the prices offered by the market are shaped in the first place by the advice of other presumed experts. The betting market, then, is undoubtedly affected by both polls and pundits, and cannot realistically be seen as operating independently as if insulated from other monitors of developments.

The overround on a betting market is much studied by economists and by the more aware bettors. It refers to the bookmakers' margin, the extent to which bettors over-pay on their bets compared with the market-predicted probabilities implied by the odds offered. For example, in a two-horse race the favourite might be at 1–2 and the outsider at 6–4. The favourite is, therefore, given a two-thirds chance (0.667) and the other horse a four-tenths chance (0.4), giving a total of 1.067; that is, an overround of 6.7 per cent. On a football match there are three options (home win, draw, or away win) and the overround is typically of the order of 11–12 per cent. The overround could be determined by three factors. One is the sheer uncertainty of the outcome: the higher the number of possibilities, the higher the overround tends to be.[19] A second is what the market will bear; punters with less awareness might continue to bet in a market with a high overround at which professionals would turn up their nose. A third is the bogeyman of anyone trying to set a market, namely the fear of insider trading by those in possession of information not factored into the market price. The greater the fear, the higher the overround needed to protect the bookmaker from inside traders swooping on what turn out to be generous odds.

Finally, if a market is working efficiently, the 'law of one price' operates. In a betting market, the odds offered by different bookmakers may not be identical, but they should be very close. If they are not, this gives alert bettors the chance to spot arbitrage opportunities; that is, a bettor can, by cherrypicking the best odds from different bookmakers, place bets in such a way as to guarantee a profit. In the rare eventuality of an arbitrage opportunity emerging, there is in effect a market with a 'negative overround', in which the sum of probabilities is less than 1. In such a situation the market is not conveying clear information about the event it is covering and, in effect, has little predictive value.[20]

Election betting markets in 2007

As with football matches, the number of aspects of elections on which punters may bet has expanded greatly. Because Ireland has a multi-party system, with government formation expected to be a complex business that would get under way in earnest only once the election results were known, the simple choices that might face bettors on a US presidential election – who will win, and by how much? – are not directly applicable.

Most firms offered betting on the composition of the next government. A market on the next Taoiseach was also nearly universal; here, although the two main party leaders dominated the betting, the strong presence of Fianna Fáil's deputy leader Brian Cowen, at around 5–1 or 6–1 in the last fortnight of the campaign,[21] reflected speculation that Ahern might have to stand down if anything else emerged about his personal finances. Most bookmakers allowed betting on party strengths in the Dáil, in the form of bands of seats that the party might win; for Fianna Fáil in the first week of the campaign, for example, the bands were 63 or fewer, 64–67, 68–71, and 72 or more.[22] The odds on the lower bands shortened, and those on the higher bands lengthened, as the campaign progressed and Fianna Fáil support seemed to be slipping. Only SportsSpread (and later Sporting Index) offered spread betting on seat totals, and on voting strength as well.[23]

Markets on which TDs would be elected in individual constituencies were widespread and, after a slow start, all 43 constituencies were covered, making it possible to place a bet on any of the 470 candidates. To set these markets bookmakers sought expert opinion, cultivating a range of contacts within each of the parties – the markets are adjusted during the campaign in response both to the developing judgements of these contacts and to the weight of money for the different options. Markets were also offered on the next Tánaiste. Even this does not exhaust the range of markets available. Paddy Power in particular has always been enterprising at developing publicity-generating markets, and on this occasion it duly offered a book on the televised leaders' debate between Ahern and Kenny: punters could bet on what colour tie each leader might wear (for each man a cravat was a 50–1 outsider) and on which of a list of clichés (for example, 'I didn't interrupt you') would be uttered first. Although a market on which opinion poll would prove closest to the final result was introduced on 14 May, representing an interesting case of interaction between polls and bookmakers, it had disappeared by the next day.

As already mentioned, the market was quite sizeable by Irish standards. As well as the €1 million or more bet with Paddy Power, Celtic took over

€0.5 million, and bets placed with William Hill amounted to over €700,000. The availability of internet gambling opened up the market to bettors all over the world, and William Hill said that almost €300,000 of the money wagered with it came from outside Ireland.[24] Unlike the other firms, Celtic did not offer internet betting and its odds were not even posted on the internet. This ensured strong protection against the risk of being outsmarted by inside traders, while exasperating some punters – in market terms, it meant that it was much more difficult for shrewd, price-sensitive punters to find, take, influence or make efficient Celtic's odds than those of other firms. A new development in 2007 was the arrival of betting exchanges, the best known of which is Betfair, which allow punters either to back (that is, bet on) or to lay (that is, bet against) an option. Rather than backing their selected option with a bookmaker, they can back it with another punter if they believe it is being offered at good odds or, if they prefer, take a bet from another punter if there is a punter willing to take what they regard as poor odds. Each punter is now betting against other punters, which not only provides richer betting opportunities but also potentially captures market sentiment more accurately than the bookmaker-set odds do.[25] Betting exchanges also make it clear how much money may be wagered at a given price, whereas punters sometimes suspect that bookmakers, perennially wary if not paranoid about the risk of inside traders, may accept only small bets at the prices they advertise.

Paddy Power reported that its largest market was on the next Taoiseach (approximately €400,000), followed by the composition of the next government (€200,000), with 43 individual constituency markets together weighing in at around €300,000 (i.e. an average of €7,000 per constituency).[26] Betfair's breakdown was even more strongly concentrated on the next Taoiseach market: on election day, €186,000 was riding on this, with €22,000 on the composition of the government and less than €3,700 each on the number of seats each party would win and the next Tánaiste. Individual constituency markets averaged only around €750 each, with just three attracting more than €1,500. To place these figures in context, over €9 million was matched on Betfair on the outcome of the Champions League final played in Athens the previous day. Interestingly, something like three-quarters of Betfair's total betting activity took place after the polls closed, with lively trading on 25 and 26 May, as the votes were being counted, on the number of seats parties would win. The markets on the next Taoiseach and government grew apace after election day; the former had reached around €520,000, and the latter around €70,000, by 14 June when the government was formed. Altogether, Betfair's Irish election market attracted 705 punters from 32 countries, though most were based in Ireland or the UK.[27]

Examining some of these markets in more detail, prediction of the next government is much more complicated in a multi-party system than in a two-party system. This is reflected in the plethora of options on offer, as illustrated in Table 9.1.[28] This implies that, for the voters, the 'identifiability' of the possible options (in other words, the voters' ability to identify the government options on offer and choose between them) was very low, and that while voters could choose a party they could not choose a government. Proportional electoral systems frequently score low on this criterion, whereas under non-PR systems, or in presidential elections, the voters usually know that they have a choice between two alternative administrations.[29] In 2007 the market confirms that the voters could not tell what was likely to happen. This was a particular problem for Labour voters who wanted Fianna Fáil to be ejected from government since, despite the party's repeatedly stated aversion to a coalition with Fianna Fáil, a Labour voter could not be sure whether or not their party would, as in 1993, go into coalition with that party having roundly criticised it during the campaign. Much the same uncertainty was felt by Green voters, while Fianna Fáil voters could not be certain whether their party, if it remained in government, would do so with the right in the form of the PDs or the left in the shape of Labour or the Greens or even Sinn Féin.[30] The table also illustrates the strong position of Fianna Fáil, which was seen by the market on election day as having a 78 per cent chance of being in government after the election, compared with 47 per cent for Labour, 43 per cent for the Greens, 27 per cent for Fine Gael, 26 for the PDs, and 7 per cent for Sinn Féin. The strategic weakness of Fine Gael, in relation to its size, within the Irish party system is highlighted by the market: the party is not strong enough to form the core of a non-Fianna Fáil government but is too strong to be a conceivable partner for Fianna Fáil (see chapter 12 for fuller discussion).

Table 9.1 Expected composition of next government, election day

	Odds	Implied probability
FF + Labour	9–4	0.21
FG + Labour + Greens	10–3	0.16
FF + Greens	10–3	0.16
FF + PDs	10–3	0.16
FF + PDs + Greens	8–1	0.08
FF + SF	9–1	0.07
FG + Labour	14–1	0.05
FF + FG	16–1	0.04
FF alone	20–1	0.03
FF + Labour + Greens	25–1	0.03
FG + Labour + PDs	40–1	0.02
Total		1.00

Note: The terms and conditions made it clear that parties had to have cabinet positions to count as part of the government. For the calculation of 'implied probabilities', see note 28.

Source: www.paddypower.com, 24 May 2007.

The volatility in this market shows how expectations changed over the 17 months before the election and, as Table 9.2 shows, even over the five months leading up to election day on 24 May.[31] The incumbent FF–PD combination was the favourite for the first few months of 2006, but during the summer the alternative Fine Gael–Labour–Greens option narrowly took pole position. After the positive opinion poll findings following the discussion of Bertie Ahern's finances in autumn 2006, the government's odds shortened dramatically to 5–4, and it remained favourite until early April 2007. During April, though, it slid from 9–4 to 7–1, and it had drifted to a no-hope 10–1 by mid-May before coming back to 10–3 by election day. Like a number of markets, 'next government' seems to have been strongly affected by the TNS mrbi poll published on 21 May that showed a five-point leap in Fianna Fáil support. The FG–Labour–Greens option remained as first or second favourite the whole time, the best price being 10–3 in April 2006 and on election day. By the day the election was called it was 5–4 favourite, and though it moved out to 7–4 in the second week of the campaign, it subsequently shortened to evens by 15 May, before drifting in the last few days of the campaign. A consistent third favourite was a revival of the 1993–94 coalition between Fianna Fáil and Labour, which was never available at more than 9–2 from January 2006 and which during the second and third weeks of the campaign was a mere 9–4 despite Labour's evident lack of enthusiasm. Even more strikingly, the FF–SF option came in to 11–2 in the second week of the campaign, indicating some scepticism about Fianna Fáil's repeated and emphatic ruling out of this option. The other option to attract serious money was Fianna Fáil and the Greens, which came in to 9–2 joint favourite during April but which lengthened to 11–1 during the campaign as both parties slipped in the polls before shortening dramatically as election day approached. The eventual outcome was never shorter than 8–1.

Table 9.2   Shortest and longest odds about government options, 1 January–24 May 2007

	Shortest odds	Date	Longest odds	Date
FG + Lab + Grn	1–1	15 May	10–3	24 May
FF + PDs	5–4	16 Jan	10–1	15 May
FF + Lab	2–1	3 May	9–2	14 Apr
FF + Grn	3–1	23 May	11–1	17 May
FF + SF	11–2	8 May	16–1	16 Jan
FG + Lab	6–1	27 Apr	14–1	22 May
FF + PD + Grn	8–1	24 May	14–1	16 Jan
FF on own	8–1	27 Feb	25–1	17 May

Note: When the odds about an option were the same on more than one day, the date recorded here is the earliest.

Source: www.paddypower.com.

In a similar fashion, the odds on the next Taoiseach showed Ahern starting the campaign as favourite before gradually being overhauled by Kenny, who was 4–5 favourite, with Ahern at 5–4, by 18 May. Once again, the final *Irish Times*/TNS mrbi poll brought about a major shift in expectations; Ahern shortened to 8–15 on the day the poll was published and reached 1–4 by election day, with Kenny languishing at 11–4.

The spread betting on the number of seats to be won by each of the parties also reflected declining expectations for Fianna Fáil over the first three weeks of the campaign followed by a surge in the last four days.[32] Fianna Fáil's predicted seats declined gently to a mere 63 by 18 May before rising to 69 by election day. This apart, the spread bet market did not register any significant changes over the course of the campaign. Betting on this market continued on Friday 25 May, the spreads shifting continuously as news came in from the counts.

Betting on which individuals will win seats in the constituencies illustrates the personal nature of Irish elections. An example of these constituency odds is shown in Table 9.3.[33] At first sight the odds look surprising, with several candidates being odds-on; the explanation, of course, is that four of these candidates will be elected. The odds reflect the inter-party and intra-party contests under way. Two candidates seemed fairly certain of election, according to the market, with Daly also strongly favoured. After that, four candidates were in close contention for the remaining seat. It was unclear whether Fianna Fáil could be expected to take two seats or just one, and

Table 9.3 Betting on winners in Dublin North constituency

Candidate	Party	Odds	Implied probability
Trevor Sargent	Green	1–50	0.81
James Reilly	FG	1–7	0.72
Clare Daly	Socialist	4–9	0.57
Michael Kennedy	FF	10–11	0.43
Brendan Ryan	Labour	10–11	0.43
Darragh O'Brien	FF	11–10	0.39
John O'Leary	FF	6–4	0.33
Joe Corr	Green	13–2	0.11
David O'Connor	Ind	7–1	0.10
Tom Morrissey	PD	20–1	0.04
Matt McCormack	SF	25–1	0.03
John Donnelly	Ind	66–1	0.01
Cathal Loftus	CSP	66–1	0.01
Total			4.00

Note: Four candidates would be elected. See note 33 for a caveat concerning the implied probabilities.

Source: www.paddypower.com, 24 May 2007.

which of their candidates was the strongest. Those candidates priced at 13–2 or above were real outsiders. The table also illustrates the difficulty in post hoc evaluation of the market's accuracy because it is hard to be certain what the market is predicting. Suppose, for example, that Kennedy, instead of being 10–11, had been marginally longer at evens. Then a simplistic interpretation would have been that the market was predicting the success of the four shortest-priced candidates: Sargent, Reilly, Daly and Ryan. Yet this outcome would have left Fianna Fáil without any seats even though the sum of implied probabilities for its three candidates was 1.15, and no one ever suggested that the party could fail to take at least one seat here. (The eventual winners in this constituency were Sargent, Reilly, Kennedy and O'Brien.)

Overrounds on all markets were substantial (see Table 9.4). One of the most popular markets, on the next government, had the highest overround: bettors would need to wager €145 here to be sure of getting €100 back.[34] Only in the individual constituency market was the overround less than 20 per cent; the potential vulnerability to insider trading was presumably offset by the low activity levels. There was considerable variation across constituencies: from 1.12 to 1.26 in the case of Paddy Power and from 1.04 to 1.24 for Celtic. Celtic offered odds for all constituencies, though in 34 of the 43 constituencies there was at least one candidate for whom no odds were available as he or she was regarded as pretty much certain of election (though in fact two such candidates, Seán Crowe and Denis O'Donovan, failed to be elected). These overrounds can be compared to the lower figures reported for a range of sporting markets, from 2 per cent in baseball to 11 per cent in football, though they are comparable to those for greyhound and horse racing.[35] Unless the bookmakers misread the political scene when setting their prices, they stood to make a healthy profit from these markets.

Table 9.4   Overrounds in election betting markets

Market	Bookmaker	Date	Sum of probabilities
Composition of govt	Paddy Power	24 May	1.45
Next Taoiseach	Paddy Power	24 May	1.22
FF seats	Paddy Power	24 May	1.25
FG seats	Paddy Power	24 May	1.24
Labour seats	Paddy Power	24 May	1.29
Green seats	Paddy Power	24 May	1.23
PD seats	Paddy Power	24 May	1.28
SF seats	Paddy Power	24 May	1.24
Constituency contests	Paddy Power	24 May	1.19*
Constituency contests	Celtic	17 May	1.14**

*   Average figure per seat across all 43 constituency contests.
**   In cases of candidates where no odds were offered, such candidates have been treated as contributing 1 to the sum of probabilities.

In 2007 the law of one price did operate, more or less, for the larger markets such as the next Taoiseach or the next government, but the market did not deliver consistent information in other areas such as the number of seats parties would win, where arbitrage opportunities sometimes appeared (for example, during the first week of the campaign on Labour's seat total). In the betting on individual constituencies different firms, not surprisingly, usually had much the same set of candidates as favourites to take seats, but there were sometimes significant divergences. In Donegal South-West in particular the two most high-profile bookmakers, Paddy Power and Celtic, took a very different view of the likely outcome. Both agreed that Fianna Fáil would take two seats, but while Paddy Power regarded Dinny McGinley (FG) as strong favourite to take the other seat, quoting him at 1–3, Celtic rated him a 2–1 chance and instead saw the Sinn Féin candidate as being 1–8 to take a seat.[36] A clear arbitrage opportunity existed here, with bettors needing to put down only 91 units to be certain of receiving 100 back whatever the outcome. In short, in these markets the law of one price did not fully operate, which was a boon for punters looking to cherrypick the odds but a problem for those hoping that the betting market would provide an unambiguous pointer as to what would happen.

The market as a predictor

How accurate were the betting markets? The largest market, as we have seen, was that on the next Taoiseach, and by election day this was pointing strongly to Bertie Ahern. Ahern and Kenny had been virtually neck and neck until the last few days of the campaign, but following the TNS mrbi poll findings released on 21 May showing a jump in support for Fianna Fáil, money poured in for Ahern, pushing him in the space of a few days from 5–4 second favourite to 1–4 favourite. Once the final seat totals for the parties were known, it was apparent that there was indeed very little chance of anyone other than Ahern becoming Taoiseach, so the market can claim this as a success.

Regarding the composition of the next government – which entails predicting both how the seats will be distributed among the parties and then what deals will be done among those parties – the market, to be blunt, got it wrong. The eventual outcome, Fianna Fáil plus the Greens plus the PDs,[37] was introduced as an option in January 2007 and remained in the 10–1 to 14–1 band up until the day before voting, when it shortened to 9–1. On election day it was 8–1, which made it fifth favourite. Once the distribution of seats was known it shortened only a little further, to 13–2, before dramatically becoming favourite at 1–5 once serious discussions between Fianna Fáil and the Greens got going on 3 June (see chapter 12 for these). Even then, it bounced back out to 2–1 on 11 June, when those talks seemed to have faltered, with the incumbent FF–PD coalition now favourite at 2–5. Those who had backed any of the five options that had dominated the market since 2002 – Fianna Fáil and the PDs, Fianna Fáil and Labour, Fianna Fáil and the Greens, Fine Gael and Labour, or Fine Gael, Labour and the Greens – lost their money, and the faith of those who imagined that the market was conveying reliably that one of these five options would take office after the 2007 election proved misplaced.

The spread betting markets, too, did not perform well. Of the eight markets listed in Table 9.5, the spread setters got only one (Fine Gael's vote) right. In every other case the outcome was outside, often well outside, the spread entirely, offering rich pickings for the cognoscenti. Fianna Fáil's vote and seats were both greatly underestimated, Labour was also underestimated, and the smaller parties were overestimated. This market did at least pick up the late growth in Fianna Fáil support (a week from election day its seats had been predicted at 63.25 and its vote at 34.38 per cent), but, with the final spread on Fianna Fáil's seats at 68 to 69.5, anyone with an upbeat assessment of the party's likely actual total could have made a significant profit by 'buying' its seats at 69.5.[38] The best one can say is that the market here made the same mistakes as the pundits (see the Chronology at the front of the book for these).

Table 9.5   Predictions of spread betting markets, election day

	Spread	Mid-point of spread	Result
FF seats	68–69.5	68.75	78
FG seats	48.5–50	49.25	51
Lab seats	17–18	17.50	20
PD seats	3–3.6	3.30	2
Green seats	8.8–9.5	9.15	6
SF seats	9.7–10.5	10.10	5
Other seats	*	7.95	5
FF % vote	36.60–37.35	36.98	41.56
FG % vote	27.00–27.75	27.38	27.32

* There was no actual market on this; mid-point inferred from sum of mid-points of other groups' spreads.

Source: www.sportsspread.com, 24 May 2007.

The regular betting markets, too, offered an imperfect guide to the seat totals the parties were likely to achieve. Paddy Power offered four bands for each party. For Fianna Fáil, the outsider of the four on polling day was 76 or more at 9–2; this proved the eventual winner. Surprisingly given the TNS mrbi poll, this market recorded a slippage in Fianna Fáil support during the last three days of the campaign; 72–75 seats had been the 7–4 favourite at the start of the final week, with 76 or more seats available at 9–4. Not only was the level of support inaccurately assessed, but the direction of change was wrongly identified. The 'favourite' in this market by election day was 68–71, priced at 6–4. This firm overestimated Sinn Féin strength, with the lowest band, 8 or fewer, being correct at 5–2. In the case of the other parties the actual outcome did at least fall within the shortest-priced band, with the market for the PDs being particularly accurate: 1–2 seats was a short-priced evens favourite.

The record of success of individual constituency markets was also mixed – though, as we have noted, this is difficult to evaluate precisely. Most of the shortest-priced candidates were of course elected, but a surprising number were not. In all, 20 candidates priced at 1–3 or shorter were defeated.[39] The shortest priced losers were Dan Boyle (Green, Cork SC) at 1–33, Seán Crowe (SF, Dublin SW) at 1–20, Máiréad McGuinness (FG, Louth) at 1–10, Mary Lou McDonald (SF, Dublin Central) at 1–8, and Martin Brady (FF, Dublin NE), Dessie Ellis (SF, Dublin NW) and Catherine Murphy (Ind, Kildare N), all at 1–7. The market on the three-seat Dublin NE constituency was particularly inaccurate, with the candidates ranked third, fifth and sixth in the betting being the eventual winners (see chapter 5 for the account of one of these winners). That is not to suggest that long-priced outsiders achieved much success: in only 13 of 43 constituencies did a candidate priced at odds against win, and only three priced at 2–1 or more won (Ciarán Lynch at 5–2 and Terence Flanagan and Michael Woods at 9–4). Any punter backing longshots would thus have sustained heavy losses. Undoubtedly, most pundits would have made the same mistakes as the markets in these cases (see the Chronology for a summary of pundits' predictions).

Sometimes a market can at least reflect a trend; a flurry of support for a horse in a field of newcomers, for example, may indicate that 'somebody knows something'. Here too the record was mixed. In Cavan–Monaghan, the market, having initially predicted the election of Joe O'Reilly (FG, 1–6) and the defeat of Margaret Conlon (FF, 7–4), recorded a dramatic turnaround so that by election day Conlon was 1–5 and O'Reilly 5–4; in this case the market read the trends correctly, Conlon being elected and O'Reilly defeated.[40] M.J. Nolan (FF), Niall Blaney (FF), Dinny McGinley (FG), Joe Higgins (Soc), Niall Ó Brolcháin (Green), Breeda Moynihan-Cronin (Labour) and Beverley Flynn (Ind) were others whose odds changed significantly during the campaign in what proved to be the right direction. Others, though, moved in the wrong direction. For example, Dessie Ellis (SF) shortened from 4–9 to 1–7, and Séamus Cosai Fitzgerald (FG) from 7–2 to 8–11, yet neither was elected, while some successful candidates drifted in the market, such as Terence Flanagan (FG) from 6–4 to 9–4 and Noel Grealish (PD) from 4–5 to 6–4.[41] Finally, the one real 'surprise' candidate of the election, Richard Boyd Barrett in Dun Laoghaire, who did not register on any pundit's radar but who finished as runner-up in the constituency, was not picked up by the market, starting and finishing as the second longest-priced candidate in a field of 11. Here, too, the market cannot claim success.

Treatment of the Louth constituency enables a direct comparison between different methods of prediction. On 9 May the *Drogheda Independent* predicted, on the basis of a poll with a sample size of 500, that Fine Gael would gain a seat from Fianna Fáil in this four-seater. The four candidates elected would be, in order, Dermot Ahern of Fianna Fáil, Arthur Morgan of Sinn Féin, Fergus O'Dowd of Fine Gael and Máiréad McGuinness of Fine Gael, with incumbent Séamus Kirk of Fianna Fáil the narrow runner-up. On 11 May a national newspaper did a constituency profile of Louth and, while stating that 'it would be easier to predict the winner of the Grand National than the outcome of this constituency', predicted that Ahern, Morgan and O'Dowd would take the first three seats but that the fourth would be taken by Mark Dearey of the Green Party.[42] Like most media constituency profiles, the article drew on the local opinion poll but did not mention the betting market as a possible guide to what would happen. On 10 May the market suggested that the race in Louth was in effect over: Ahern was at 1–66 to be elected, O'Dowd and McGuinness were each at 1–10, and Morgan was at 1–7. There was a large gap to Kirk at evens, followed by Dearey at 7–4. None of these proved correct, but the opinion poll was closest: Ahern, O'Dowd and Morgan were elected, as everyone expected, but the other successful candidate, Kirk, headed the poll, while McGuinness was quite a distant runner-up and Dearey was even further behind.

The number of markets available to bettors makes it difficult to come to a single judgement as to whether the market 'got it right'. In some areas, such as the identity of the next Taoiseach, it did; in others, such as the number of seats and the vote shares to be won by individual parties, it did not, partly because the small size of the market meant that it was not drawing upon a large pool of expertise. The accuracy of its predictions of the outcomes of individual constituencies varied. Generally speaking, the greater the amount of money wagered on a market, the better its predictions. The main reason for the market's failure to deliver more accurate predictions was, as far as we can tell, simply a shortage of expertise – those who placed bets exhibited, not coincidentally, the same misjudgements as the pundits.

Conclusion

Betting on the outcome, a sideshow at previous elections, moved closer to the centre of the election discourse in 2007. In a campaign that, like most recent Irish elections, did not feature much disagreement among the main parties over policy, horse race aspects again loomed large in media coverage (see chapter 10), and for the first time betting was sometimes quoted as an indication of the likelihood of various scenarios. The amount of money wagered was vastly greater than that placed on any previous Irish election.

A growing literature on political betting suggests that the market is at least as reliable an indicator of what is happening as conventional methods of assessing trends such as analysing opinion poll findings or consuming the opinions of pundits. The more hyperbolic claims made for political betting markets were not really borne out by the 2007 election. Where reliable opinion polls existed, the markets faithfully reflected the trends they portrayed, but where they were largely left to their own devices, as with individual constituency outcomes, their record was mixed, partly because these markets were too small to be credibly regarded as a distillation of a wide range of informed opinion. The markets did not establish themselves as a repository of wisdom that was unavailable anywhere else, but they did enough to suggest that at future elections they should be examined by anyone wanting an additional pointer to the likely outcome.

Appendix: bookmaker expressions of probability

In Ireland and the UK, odds are conventionally expressed as 'x to y', where x and y are both integers. y represents the stake and x the profit (not the total return, which equals $x + y$). Thus a price of 6–1 indicates that for a stake of 1 unit a winning bettor will receive a total of 7 from the bookmaker. If $x > y$ the option is 'odds against', and the potential profit is greater than the stake; for example, a winning wager of 10 units on odds of 5–2 produces a return of 35 (the stake of 10 plus 25 profit). If $y > x$ the option is 'odds on', and the potential profit is less than the stake; for example, a price of 2–7 indicates that staking 7 delivers a return of 9 (2 + 7) if the bet wins. If $x = y$ the price is 1–1, referred to as 'evens'.

Notes

* Thanks to Raj Chari, Eoin O'Malley, Feizal Rahman and Leighton Vaughan Williams, and especially to Paddy Waldron, for supplying information and/or comments on an earlier draft.
1. For a review of this literature, see Leighton Vaughan Williams (ed.), *Information Efficiency in Financial and Betting Markets* (Cambridge: Cambridge University Press, 2005), especially chapters 2, 3, 7 and 18.
2. Paul W. Rhode and Koleman S. Strumpf, 'Historical presidential betting markets', *Journal of Economic Perspectives* 18:2 (2004), pp. 127–42, at p. 128.
3. In November 1982 a Labour TD saw an opportunity to clear the debt of his constituency organisation by placing £100 at 10–1 on Dick Spring to become his party's leader, though when he attempted to place a bet the bookmaker claimed the book was closed. Ruairí Quinn, *Straight Left: A Journey in Politics* (Castleknock: Hodder Headline Ireland, 2005), pp. 180–1.
4. Paddy Waldron, 'Online gambling', *The Investor* 3:9 (2005). For an overview of the Irish betting industry, see this article and the same author's 'Place your bets: a review of the Irish gambling market', *The Investor* 3:8 (2005), pp. 46–9.

5. In this capacity he contributed an account of his campaign to an earlier book in this series: 'On the campaign trail', pp. 48–52 in Michael Gallagher and Richard Sinnott (eds), *How Ireland Voted 1989* (Galway: PSAI Press, 1990).

6. The Foresight site is at www.ideosphere.com, while the 'Long Bets Foundation' has a site (www.longbets.org) which is described as 'an arena for competitive, accountable predictions', and as 'a way to foster better long-term thinking'. On prediction markets generally, see Georgios Tziralis and Ilias Tatsiopoulos, 'Prediction markets: an extended literature review', *Journal of Prediction Markets* 1:1 (2007), pp. 75–91; Justin Wolfers and Eric Zitzewitz, 'Prediction markets in theory and practice', in Lawrence E. Blume and Steven N. Durlauf (eds), *New Palgrave Dictionary of Economics*, 2nd edn (London: Palgrave Macmillan, forthcoming 2008).

7. Geoffrey Clark, *Betting on Lives: The Culture of Life Insurance in England 1695–1775* (Manchester: Manchester University Press, 1999).

8. Rhode and Strumpf, 'Historical presidential betting markets', p. 129. Generally, see S. G. Kou and Michael E. Sobel, 'Forecasting the vote: a theoretical comparison of election markets and public opinion polls', *Political Analysis* 12:3 (2004), pp. 277–95.

9. See www.biz.uiowa.edu for information on the history of the IEM and for current markets. Also Ray C. Fair, *Interpreting the Predictive Uncertainty of Presidential Elections*, Discussion paper 1579 (New Haven, CT: Cowles Foundation for Research in Economics, Yale University, 2006). Even critics of the IEM acknowledge this, while claiming that, properly interpreted, the polls can be the basis of a more accurate forecast than that provided by the markets. See Robert S. Erikson and Christopher Wlezien, 'Are political markets really superior to polls as election predictors?', *Public Opinion Quarterly*, forthcoming.

10. Martin Rosenbaum, 'Betting and the 1997 British general election', *Politics* 19:1 (1999), pp. 9–14, at p. 13; Leighton Vaughan Williams, 'The betting markets', *Significance* 2:2 (2005), pp. 50–3.

11. Peter Bohm and Joakim Sonnegard, 'Political stock markets and unreliable polls', *Scandinavian Journal of Economics* 101:2 (1999), pp. 205–22.

12. Justin Wolfers and Andrew Leigh, *Three Tools for Forecasting Federal Elections: lessons from 2001*, Research paper 1723 (Stanford CA: Graduate School of Business, Stanford University, 2001); Andrew Leigh and Justin Wolfers, *Competing Approaches to Forecasting Elections: Economic Models, Opinion Polling and Prediction Markets*, Discussion Paper 502 (Canberra: Centre for Economic Policy Research, Australian National University, 2005).

13. According to Ivan Yates, 'normally FF supporters are the heaviest betters'. Ivan Yates, 'Election bookie', *Sunday Tribune*, 6 May 2007.

14. For example, in 2002 Mary Harney placed a bet that the PDs would win eight seats, more than all pundits predicted – and the PDs ensured that photographers were on hand to record the event and to witness her collecting her winnings after the election. See Michael Gallagher, Michael Marsh and Paul Mitchell (eds), *How Ireland Voted 2002* (Basingstoke: Palgrave Macmillan, 2003), p. xxix. The link between bookmakers' shops and campaigning featured even more prominently in media images of the 2007 campaign – see the photo section at the front of book, and front cover.

15. Mike Smithson, *The Political Punter: How to Make Money Betting on Politics* (Petersfield, Hampshire: Harriman House, 2007), pp. 106–8, 130.

16. See the appendix to this chapter for an explanation of the odds.

17. Gail McElroy and Michael Marsh, 'Why the opinion polls got it wrong in 2002', pp. 159–76 in Gallagher et al., *How Ireland Voted 2002*.

18. Michael Cain, David Law and David Peel, 'The favourite–longshot bias: bookmaker margins and insider trading in a variety of betting markets', *Bulletin of Economic Research* 55:3 (2003), pp. 263–73; Bruno Deschamps and Olivier Gergaud, 'Efficiency in betting markets: evidence from English football', *Journal of Prediction Markets* 1:1 (2007), pp. 61–73; Vaughan Williams, *Information Efficiency in Financial and Betting Markets*, passim.

19. Hyun Song Shin, 'Measuring the incidence of insider trading in a market for state-contingent claims', *Economic Journal* 103:420 (1993), pp. 1141–53.

20. In an efficient market, an arbitrage is valuable to observers because it is virtually guaranteed to generate trade, but if, for some reason, potential traders are disinclined or unable to take advantage, as was the case in some 2007 election markets, observers cannot be sure what the market is saying.

21. For explanation of these odds, see the appendix to this chapter.

22. Odds from www.paddypower.com.

23. In spread betting a punter backs their judgement as to how far above or below the bookmaker's offered 'spread' of seats or votes the outcome will be. The extent of the wins or losses depends on how far from the spread the outcome is.

24. Conor McMorrow, 'Fianna Fáil staff pocket a pretty penny by keeping the faith', *Sunday Tribune*, 27 May 2007.

25. On betting exchanges and politics, see Smithson, *The Political Punter*, pp. 38–46.

26. Spokesman for Paddy Power, quoted in McMorrow, 'Fianna Fáil staff'; Tom Rowe, 'Betting on Bertie', *Village*, 7 June 2007.

27. Information provided by Feizal Rahman of Betfair.

28. 'Implied probability' means the underlying probability implied by these odds; the sum of the implied probabilities is by definition 1. Implied probability is calculated by dividing the perceived probability of each possibility by the sum of probabilities, thus correcting for the overround. For example, the perceived probability of an FF–Labour government was 4/13, or 0.31. Adding together the perceived probabilities of all the options produces a sum of 1.45. Thus the implied probability equals 0.31 divided by 1.45, or 0.21. This calculation ignores the 'favourite–longshot bias', which characterises some (though not all) markets; if it operates here, the true probability of the short-priced options would be somewhat greater, and of the long-priced options somewhat less, than the figures here suggest. Using the approach outlined in Hyun Song Shin, 'Optimal betting odds against insider traders', *Economic Journal* 101:5 (1991), pp. 1179–85, the differences in Table 9.1 would be very slight. FF + Labour, for example, would be 0.24 rather than 0.21 and the next three options 0.17 rather than 0.16 – thanks to Paddy Waldron for these calculations.

29. G. Bingham Powell Jr, *Elections as Instruments of Democracy: Majoritarian and Proportional Visions* (New Haven and London: Yale University Press, 2000), pp. 69–88.

30. According to the penultimate Millward Brown IMS poll (9 May), 55 per cent of Labour supporters believed Pat Rabbitte's commitment not to serve in an FF–Labour government while 35 per cent did not, and 39 per cent of Green voters believed that Trevor Sargent would not lead his party into coalition with Fianna Fáil while 38 per cent did not. Moreover, in the previous IMS poll of 16–17 April, only 55 per cent of Fianna Fáil supporters believed Bertie Ahern when he said he would

not go into government with Sinn Féin, and only 28 per cent of Sinn Féin voters believed him. Thanks to Michael Marsh for this information.

31. All odds from Paddy Power unless otherwise stated.

32. Market from SportsSpread.com.

33. See caveat in note 28 about the favourite–longshot bias, which if taken into account would affect the implied probabilities more than in Table 9.1. The odds of 1–50 for Sargent certainly reflect a significantly higher expected probability than 0.81, something close to 1, that he would be elected.

34. Strictly speaking, they could not be sure of winning even if they backed every option, since the combinations on offer did not exhaust the theoretical possibilities.

35. Cain et al., 'The favourite–longshot bias', p. 268.

36. These were the odds on 18 May; they did not change significantly over the remaining six days of the campaign.

37. Although the eventual government was backed by some Independent TDs, they were not deemed part of the government given that they received no cabinet positions.

38. As, it is said, a number of staff at Fianna Fáil's campaign headquarters did, making around €42,000: Pat Leahy, 'Fianna Fáil pulls off a coup with bookies', *Sunday Business Post*, 3 June 2007; McMorrow, 'Fianna Fáil staff'.

39. Discussion based on final odds offered by Paddy Power, 23 and 24 May. All other bookmakers also had very short-priced losers.

40. This discussion refers to Paddy Power's odds; Celtic took the same initial position as Paddy Power but did not change during the campaign.

41. Other examples of a market movement in what proved to be the wrong direction include Frances Fitzgerald (FG), Ivor Callely (FF), Larry O'Toole (SF), Seán Crowe (SF), Tom Fleming (FF), Tom Sheahan (FG), Catherine Murphy (Ind), Dara Calleary (FF) and Deirdre de Búrca (Grn).

42. Marie O'Halloran, 'FG's high-risk strategy in Louth', *Irish Times*, 11 May 2007.

10
The Media and the Campaign

*Heinz Brandenburg and Zbyszek Zalinski**

While the 2007 election may look like a tighter re-run of the 2002 campaign, from a media perspective this campaign differed markedly from its predecessor. The 2002 campaign had been a rather frustrating experience, run too smoothly by the Fianna Fáil spin machine,[1] but this time around the media's role was much more proactive, even controversial.

'Bertiegate' – the story that put the Taoiseach's private finances in the spotlight for the first days of the campaign – is what sets 2007 apart from previous elections (for more details, see chapter 1 and the Chronology). Repeatedly, and most openly in an interview with the *Irish Independent* on 20 May, four days ahead of polling, Ahern complained bitterly about what was, in his view, an invasive media inquisition: 'There were large sections of the media for the first 10 days that were just totally unbalanced.'[2] The media appeared to run their own campaign – and from Ahern's point of view a negative, anti-Fianna Fáil one, while journalists themselves reflected frequently on their own role and ethics in this episode. We will investigate here the extent to which media coverage was dominated by 'Bertiegate', and the impact that this confrontation between the Taoiseach and the mass media had on the balance and traditionally claimed impartiality of Irish news coverage.

We will start by providing an overview of the Irish media landscape in 2007, taking into account recent changes, especially the emerging world of online media, which have already come to play a crucial role in US campaigns and are starting to make an imprint on political communication in Ireland. We will then present data that allows us to compare media attention in 2007 with that in previous campaigns, evaluating the particularities of 2007's media agenda, and investigating the balance of partisan reporting.

The media markets

Although traditional media markets – that is, press, television and radio – may have undergone massive changes in the 1990s, we are now in a period of relative stability. RTÉ remains dominant in the television and radio market, certainly with regard to information programming. Latest listenership figures show, however, that RTÉ's radio market share slipped in 2006, while its commercial competitors gained listeners. The number of daily newspapers and, by and large, their readership figures, have remained consistent.

The press

As reported in Table 10.1, the *Irish Independent* remains the paper with the largest estimated readership. Irish readers differ markedly from their British counterparts – at least insofar as considerably more of them read broadsheet newspapers. Whereas in Britain, tabloids (red tops in particular) outsell broadsheets by massive margins, the combined readership of the three Irish broadsheets (*Times, Independent* and *Examiner*) just about matches that of the four main tabloids (*Star, Mirror, Sun* and *Herald*).

Table 10.1   Readership of Irish national newspapers, 2006

Newspaper	Readership
Irish Independent	535,000
The Irish Times	336,000
Irish Examiner	249,000
Irish Daily Star	401,000
Irish Daily Mirror	176,000
Irish Sun	251,000
Evening Herald	299,000

Source: National Newspapers of Ireland (www.nni.ie/readfigs9.htm).

While newspaper readership in Ireland is generally said to be stagnating, and the overall distribution of readership[3] has remained relatively stable since 2002, some sizeable changes have occurred since the last election: the *Irish Times* and *Irish Examiner* have gained between 8 and 10 per cent, while the *Irish Independent*, the *Daily Star* and the *Evening Herald* have lost each over 10 per cent of the readers they had five years ago.[4]

As is traditionally the case, Irish newspapers refrained from endorsing any of the parties, or prospective coalitions. However, the *Irish Independent* provided a noteworthy intervention by urging the *Irish Times* to be honest with its readers and to admit that it had actively campaigned against Fianna Fáil and Bertie Ahern, and hence to come out in favour of a Fine Gael–Labour coalition:

> What we don't need is a denial that the *Irish Times* has a preference. If it does support a prospective government, it should spell it out. There is nothing shameful in expressing an honestly held opinion.[5]

Referring to its own decision to support the Fianna Fáil–PD coalition in 1997 (which was a major departure from the usual Irish newspaper impartiality), its editorial stated that if a newspaper's editorial board believes that one particular prospective coalition at the time provides the better alternative for the country, 'they will be abdicating their responsibility if they don't tell their readers so'. Apart from attacking its colleagues at the *Irish Times* quite harshly, and denouncing them as hypocritical for their 'conspiracy theories' about the *Independent*'s 1997 endorsement of Fianna Fáil, this editorial is a unique document in the modern Irish context insofar as it advocates party political endorsements on principle. Albeit far from suggesting that Irish papers should adopt the British or US approach of regularly, if not habitually, taking sides in elections, the editorial does question the equally rigorous tradition in which Irish newspapers refrain from endorsing parties, as if this were the only way of keeping true to journalistic codes of impartiality and objectivity.

The issue of party endorsements featured quite often during the 2007 general election campaign. Not only was there a war of words between the *Irish Independent* and the *Irish Times*, but it was also suggested that the *Sunday Independent* – the best-selling Sunday newspaper in Ireland – stopped criticising Bertie Ahern and his party after a meeting between the deputy leader of Fianna Fáil, Brian Cowen, and the owner of Independent News & Media, Anthony O'Reilly.[6] This was denied by the newspaper, which said that it changed its stance because of Bertie Ahern's change of policy regarding stamp duty.[7]

Television

RTÉ is the dominant TV station in Ireland and provided the most extensive election coverage during 2007. All the usual current affairs programmes, such as *Prime Time, The Week in Politics* and *Questions and Answers* were devoted to the campaign. In addition, several programmes were prepared especially for the general election: *Prime Time Late Debate, So You Want to be Taoiseach,* and *Frank Opinion*. The latter brought to Ireland an American pollster, Frank Luntz, who conducted televised focus groups, providing what was supposed to be an in-depth exploration of attitudes towards parties and their leaders that would go beyond the simple numbers given in conventional polls. They certainly had an impact in media terms, but these programmes were not to everyone's taste. Luntz himself is a controversial figure. He was behind the Republican party's 1994 'Contract for America' campaign platform and he is a partisan Republican.[8] More importantly, his methodology has been criticised and he was reprimanded by the American Association for Public Opinion Research in 1997 for refusing to release documentation in support of his comments. The inclusion of Luntz in RTÉ's election coverage was criticised in Ireland too, with mainstream commentators, such as Terry Prone, and political bloggers highlighting his mistakes and lack of experience of Irish politics.[9] The commercial TV station TV3 also incorporated special election programming into its May schedule. This was less extensive than that offered by RTÉ and was notably lighter in tone. Its flagship programme was *Polls Apart*, presented by Today FM radio presenter Matt Cooper and media personality Eddie Hobbs, the latter being well-known for his series of TV programmes entitled *Rip-Off Republic*. This programme was 30 minutes long and featured interviews with some of the main candidates. TV3 also offered its usual weekly, half-hour programme – *The Political Party*. The election themes were also incorporated into the morning programme *Ireland AM*. The focus was, however, less on policies and more on entertainment-like information, such as which candidate has the best poster, who is the best dressed or who's styling whom.

The pièce de résistance of the TV coverage was undoubtedly the leaders' debate between Bertie Ahern and Enda Kenny. Aired on Thursday 17 May on RTÉ1 and moderated by Miriam O'Callaghan, it had an average audience of 941,000 – a national audience share of 63.3 per cent. It had a reach of 1.4 million viewers through the course of the programme. The debate between Ahern and Michael Noonan in 2002 had an average audience of only 835,000 – a national audience share of 58.8 per cent. The debate between the other party leaders, which was shown on Wednesday 16 May, attracted 581,000 viewers, a 38.4 per cent share of the total TV audience.[10] In view of this it is not surprising that 68 per cent of the respondents in RTÉ's exit poll said that they had watched the debate. The corresponding figure in 1997 was 57 per cent, and it was 63 per cent in 2002.[11]

As the national broadcaster, RTÉ also showed the party political broadcasts. There were 16 in total, watched by on average almost 500,000 per broadcast. Fianna Fáil's six broadcasts were watched by an average of 423,000 viewers, Fine Gael's four by 456,000, Labour's two by 550,000, the Greens' single broadcast by 667,000, Sinn Féin's by 556,000, the PDs' by 564,000 and Christian Solidarity's by 562,000 viewers.[12] These were also available on the RTÉ website. This highlights the trend of media convergence that was a visible characteristic of the 2007 campaign. A variety of media content was available through a range of different media channels. Viewers could watch many of the RTÉ TV election programmes online, even after they were broadcast. This provided an opportunity for those who missed them on traditional TV and also created a convenient and readily available online archive. Another example of media convergence was the availability of an SMS text alerts service, provided by RTÉ, with all the latest news about the campaign delivered to mobile phones.

Radio

Each weekday, an impressive 2.84 million (85 per cent of the adult population in Ireland) tune into radio (Joint National Listenership Survey January 2006–December 2006).[13] Once again the national broadcaster takes the lion's share of the market. RTÉ is by far the most listened-to radio station in Ireland. It also has nine of the ten most popular radio programmes. Of the time that adults aged 15 and over spend listening to the radio each weekday between 7 a.m. and 7 p.m., 21 per cent is spent listening to RTÉ Radio 1; 13 per cent goes to RTÉ 2 and 12 per cent is taken by a commercial competitor, Today FM. RTÉ experienced a slight loss of market share, whereas Today FM gained a little compared with 2002.

RTÉ Radio 1 provided campaign coverage to match and complement its TV branch. Before the start of the campaign, *The Constituency* – a programme hosted by Rachael English – covered all the constituencies in Ireland and the issues most important for each of them. There were special editions of *Morning Ireland* focusing on key election issues, produced in different parts of Ireland. These included broadcasts on crime, quality of life and the economy. Party leaders answered listeners' questions on *Today with Pat Kenny*. Parties' manifestos and hot election issues were presented, analysed and discussed by a variety of journalists across different RTÉ radio programmes. *News at One* on Radio 1 with Seán O'Rourke also focused heavily on the election campaign. Vincent Browne examined the issues of the day again in his daily night time programme.

Commercial broadcasters also offered a lot of campaign coverage. Programmes such as *The Last Word* with Matt Cooper on Today FM, or the *The Right Hook* with George Hook on Newstalk 106 FM, also offered interviews with the main candidates and the leaders, discussions on the key election issues and day-to-day commentary on the campaign.

Almost all of these programmes mentioned above were available to download via the internet as podcasts and so were accessible to the listeners even after the original broadcast time and also offered an instant reference library. This again illustrates the emerging trend of media convergence and the growing prominence of the internet in the election campaigns.

Internet

The 2007 campaign was the first time in Irish politics when the internet and the new media played such an important role both for the media and for the parties and the candidates. Once again RTÉ, as the biggest media organisation in the country, provided the biggest online campaign coverage, parallel to and interconnected with the traditional media outlets, such as radio and TV. The corporation launched an entire news portal devoted to the elections at www. rte.ie/election, with everything from guides for first-time voters to audio and video content. There were also exclusive web events, such as the first-ever web debate, held on 9 May between Noel Dempsey, Minister for Communications, Tommy Broughan and Eamon Ryan, respectively the Labour and Green Party spokespersons on communications. RTÉ's website experienced a boost in numbers of visitors due to its extensive campaign coverage. For example, on the day of the leaders' debate it received 1,504,597 hits.[14]

Parties and candidates also used the internet in their election campaigns. Websites have become a staple of any campaign, but this election saw a growing interest in Web 2.0 applications. These put an emphasis on user-generated content and social networking. We could see clips related to the campaign on video-sharing website YouTube and become 'friends' with some of the candidates via such social networking websites as Bebo, MySpace or Facebook. Some politicians and parties prepared their own election broadcasts and uploaded them to YouTube. One such video – prepared by the PDs and showing Mary Harney talking about healthcare reform – was viewed 4,156 times (up to 23 July 2007). Ciarán Cuffe, the Green candidate for Dun Laoghaire, was one of the most prominent and extensive users of the new technologies. Not only does he have his own regularly updated blog, he also used YouTube to distribute video messages to potential voters. The Greens also decided to première their party political broadcast on the internet, following the example of US presidential hopeful Hillary Clinton. Their clip was watched 13,219 times (up until 23 July 2007). There were also innovative ideas from citizen bloggers. For example, VoteTube.org sought to bring together all the video clips related to the election campaign. Such blogs as those at irishelection.com and politics.ie provided election coverage with a twist, as they are not part of any big media organisation, but are run by politically engaged citizens.

Media attention to the campaign

One would expect that media interest in an election is to some extent driven by closeness of the race. However, if we compare the figures in Table 10.2 with those from five years ago, we find that this campaign, even though much closer than the 2002 race, did not generate any more media attention. On the contrary, the attention of broadsheet newspapers was unchanged, while the tabloids were even less interested in following political matters than they were last time around.

The *Irish Sun*, the *Irish Daily Star* and the *Evening Herald* devoted hardly any front page headlines to the campaign, and gave no mention at all to the election on their front pages on more than half of the days of the campaign. On the other hand, the three broadsheets, the *Irish Independent*, the *Irish Times* and the *Irish Examiner*, almost invariably mentioned the campaign on front pages, as they did in 2002, and more often than not allocated their main header to the campaign – the *Examiner* less regularly so than the *Times* and the *Independent*, who only on rare occasions, for example the Paisley/McGuinness inauguration, led with anything but the campaign.

Compared with 2002 then, attention levels remained constant for broadsheets, but were considerably down for tabloids, despite the more competitive election. Broadsheets tend to treat an election campaign as a generically important event while tabloids appear to become ever more non-political (or even anti-political) over time. In particular the *Irish Daily Star*

Table 10.2   Prominence of campaign coverage in the Irish press

	Issues published between 30 April and 24 May	Campaign on front page	Front page main header on campaign	Mean inside pages with campaign coverage	Std. dev. inside pages with campaign coverage
Irish Independent	22	21 (95%)	18 (82%)	11.9[*]	2.5
Irish Times	22	22 (100%)	19 (86%)	4.7	1.1
Irish Examiner	22	21 (95%)	13 (59%)	3.8	0.7
Irish Daily Star	22	11 (50%)	3 (14%)	2.8	0.9
Irish Daily Mirror	22	10[**] (63%)	5[**] (31%)	2.1[**]	0.3
Irish Daily Mail	22	17 (77%)	15 (68%)	4.2	1.4
Irish Sun	22	9 (41%)	1 (5%)	2	0.3
Evening Herald	22	7 (32%)	2 (9%)	2.9	0.9
Total	176	108 (64%)	71 (42%)		

[*] Averages are based on the tabloid version of the *Irish Independent*.
[**] Six issues missing (11, 12, 14, 15, 17, 19 May). Percentages and averages in this row and in 'Total' row based on coded issues only.

confirmed this judgement by demoting almost all campaign coverage to the inside pages two days into the race, at best providing readers with headlines unaccompanied by text which read, for example, 'McDowell is a big girl's blouse: see page 12'.

With regard to TV coverage, we find that attention was highest during the first week or so of the campaign, when even TV3 devoted regularly more than half of its main evening news bulletin to the campaign (see Figure 10.1). Attention dropped dramatically thereafter and resumed prominence only briefly during the beginning of the final week of the campaign. This could be interpreted as a commercial television station paying its dues to the media ritual that is the coverage of a national election campaign before losing interest and thereafter applying the criterion of newsworthiness to decide how much time to devote. Alternatively, given that the amount of attention given by TV3 to the campaign co-varies strongly with the limited half-life of the 'Bertiegate' story, it could be that commercial television deemed the political event newsworthy only as long as sleaze remained at the top of the campaign agenda. Neither issue debates nor even polls were anything like as newsworthy.

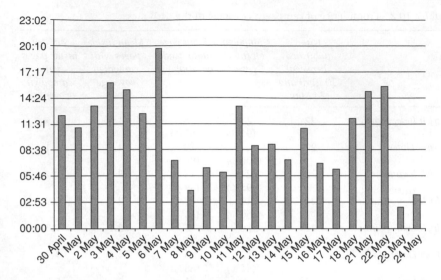

Figure 10.1   TV3's 5:30 News election coverage

Notes: Minutes devoted to election campaign coverage. Total time of coded news: 10:44:00, without commercial breaks: 09:13:30, total election coverage 03:58:01 (43%).

The media agenda: stories and issues of the campaign

In terms of pure issue content, the biggest story was health. For this analysis we used Factiva Insight™ from Dow Jones. Factiva Insight/Media Intelligence uses a text-mining/database search technology, which enables the coding of thousands of stories from a variety of sources.[15] According to the Factiva Insight data reported in Figure 10.2, 23 per cent of the stories scanned for the campaign period were concerned primarily with the health service, more than twice as many as were concerned with any of the other issues.[16]

Interestingly, as can be seen from Figure 10.3, there was little change in the issue agenda over the campaign. The three top priorities, health, tax and housing, moved largely in parallel. It seems as if the campaign priorities remained stable over time while only the amount of total issue coverage oscillated. The economy was demoted to quite a low, fifth place on the newspapers' agenda. This was very different in 2002 when economic and welfare issues dominated the media agenda.[17]

This phenomenon of a consistent media agenda that is subject to variation only in terms of overall attention to policy may be taken as one of the indicators of a media approach to the 2007 campaign that was much less party – and media management – driven than in 2002. A more detailed look at the dynamics in 2007 reveals that, while the media agenda was essentially a convenient platform for shrewd campaigners in 2002,[18] this time around

Issue volume analysis

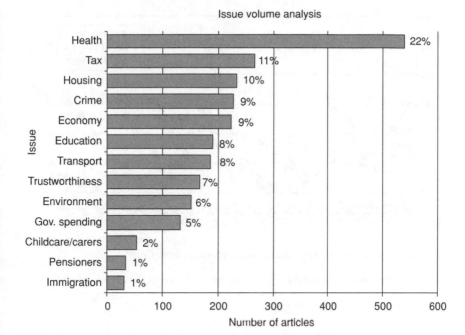

Figure 10.2   Newspaper issue agenda, 30 April–24 May

Notes: Article counts from *Irish Independent, Irish Times, Irish Examiner, Evening Herald, Sunday Independent, Sunday Business Post* and *Sunday Tribune*. Total: 2,349.

Source: Factiva Insight™ from Dow Jones.

it was fed from four different sources of varying influence: real-world events, statistics (that is, polls), the party campaigns, and the media's own logic and interests.

Politicising events

Election campaigns are highly attractive for parts of the mass media, particularly television, radio and broadsheets, because they provide a source of story material of political, social and economic significance over a prolonged period. While tabloids tend to apply their sensationalist concept of newsworthiness, and report (apart from the start and the end of the campaign) only, if irregularly, on the conflict, sleaze or the human interest sides of an election, the 'serious' media rarely get distracted from allocating prominence to the campaign. However, some real-world events have the capacity to demote an ongoing election campaign to second-rate status. For example, the British election campaign in 2005 took about a week to take its usual place in terms of media appreciation, because first the papers and television had to pay

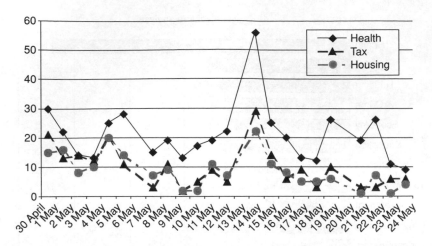

Figure 10.3   Coverage of three main campaign issues over time

Notes: Article counts from *Irish Independent, Irish Times, Irish Examiner* and *Evening Herald.*

Source: Factiva Insight™ from Dow Jones.

their tribute to a royal wedding, a Pope's funeral and the following papal election.

The Irish campaign in 2007 was overshadowed repeatedly by domestic and international events, although some of these events turned into campaign-related stories. The most politically significant was the restoration of devolved government in Stormont on 8 May. Most of the papers devoted their main front page story to this event, and the *Irish Independent* and the *Irish Examiner* their entire front pages. In the following days it was turned into a campaign event because it gave the Taoiseach, Bertie Ahern, a platform to exploit his role in the peace process, and this was further enhanced by his appearance addressing both houses of the British parliament. However, the events did not raise the issue of Irish unity in any of the editorials or opinion pieces.

Two other events did serve to raise issues to a more prominent status on the agenda than one of them might otherwise have gained. That surprise issue was abortion, while the other issue, which would always have been important, was health. The events that highlighted these issues were, on the one hand, the nurses' strike (which may have contributed to the prominence of the health issue in the Factiva analysis), and, on the other hand, the high court challenge by 'Miss D', a 17-year-old who was pregnant with a foetus suffering from a brain condition and an expected life expectancy of three days after birth.

The 'Miss D' story first appeared on the front pages on 1 May and rose to increasing prominence throughout the first week of the campaign. Front page coverage, in the *Irish Times* and elsewhere, including most of the tabloids, refrained from making connections with the campaign, but editorials and political commentaries in the broadsheets increasingly questioned the reluctance of all parties and party leaders to promise new legislation on abortion. An editorial in the *Irish Independent* on 1 May, for example, stated that 'Decades-long political cowardice has spawned an alphabet soup of distressed women – mostly minors – who have fought the Government in national and international courts for safe and legal access to abortion services at home and abroad.' The case itself was first and foremost a human interest story that inescapably generated much media interest, in broadsheets as much as tabloids, but because of the nature of the underlying issue and the history of repeated abortion-related referendums, the story pushed a matter onto the media agenda that was neither promoted nor wanted by any of the campaigning parties.

The industrial dispute between unions and health management over pay and working hours of nurses entered a critical phase with short strikes during the third week of campaigning, and it generated coverage of a similar pattern to that of the abortion case. We find very few references to the ongoing election campaign in front page stories about the strike, but editorials and opinion pages make this connection quite clearly:

> The proportion of voters who make [health] the top issue has risen from 36pc to 43pc since April. This was to be expected in view of the nurses' strike, the Government's difficulties with the consultants and the confrontation over 'co-location' of private hospitals. It is now more certain than ever that it will damage both parties in the governing coalition.[19]

Health is now a common battleground in election campaigns, but policy news and commentary generated from a real-world event allows the mass media to allocate their issue attention independently from the party campaigns, and both these issues highlight the deliberate attempts by the mass media not to repeat the largely party-driven campaign of 2002.

Crunching numbers

Treatment of individual poll results during the campaign is quite ritualistic. The broadsheets and the *Irish Daily Mail* led simultaneously with poll results on three occasions: they all proclaimed a bounce for Fianna Fáil on 11 May; a severe slump, or even 'nosedive',[20] for them on 15 May, and a last-minute recovery on 21 May. The *Irish Daily Mail*, for example, saw the poll on 11 May as spelling 'doom for Enda' and the one on 15 May as leaving 'Ahern rocked by poll slump', despite virtually identical figures for both parties in each of those polls.[21]

Beyond the ritualism and over-interpretation of minute changes, the significance of polls before and during the campaign lay in the fact that they indicated a closeness that had not been experienced in 2002, and that they provided the media with evocative frames to interpret leader behaviour and to speculate about bargaining clout and strategies.

During his announcement of the general election, the Taoiseach stated that 'No one knows what the outcome of this election will be. The people have a real choice and two very different alternatives before them.' An editorial in the *Irish Independent* on 30 April saw this to be evidence that 'possibly for the first time in the history of this State, Mr Ahern made a major concession to his opponents at the Fianna Fáil launch of the campaign yesterday'. The *Irish Daily Mail* labelled the calling of the election 'the biggest gamble of his political career',[22] while the *Irish Examiner* understood it as 'the equivalent of a dawn raid on his political rivals'.[23] While almost all newspapers made connections between the calling of the election and Ahern's financial affairs and the Mahon tribunal, which is partly why they used terms like 'gamble' and 'raid', the opening of the campaign was also marked by uncertainty about the likely outcome and an appreciation that, because of the coalition pact between Fine Gael and Labour, the voters were provided with two clearly identifiable alternatives this time around. From the start, the papers understood this election to be both interesting, because uncertain, and meaningful, because of the clear opposing camps. That was, on both counts, a significant departure from the overall atmosphere of the 2002 election, where the only open question was who would join Fianna Fáil in coalition, the PDs or Labour. That, in the view of the media, made for a lack of drama and also for a lack of choice, which is why most commentators entered the 2007 campaign with somewhat heightened enthusiasm:

> In any election, a straight fight and a clear choice are desirable. This time, up to a point – but only up to a point – the straight fight and clear choice are available. We enter the campaign with the outgoing coalition of Fianna Fáil and Progressive Democrats confronting a Fine Gael–Labour alliance.[24]

Party promises and squabbling

All political parties appear, on the surface, to have been ineffective when it came to setting the media agenda. There were no repeats of Michael Noonan's stunt appearance in an unopened hospital wing in 2002, with which he managed to monopolise front page coverage and to highlight health policy as an issue. And neither was the Fianna Fáil campaign machine as potent as it had been in 2002. Indeed, the main photo from the Fianna Fáil manifesto launch that was published in all three broadsheets on 4 May showed Bertie Ahern grasping his lectern, slumped over with closed eyes, as his manifesto launch was, as reported throughout, 'hijacked' by Vincent Browne, the RTÉ radio host, who confronted the Taoiseach with 'a barrage of forensic questions ... regarding payments to Celia Larkin'.[25] The press highlighted the inability of Fianna Fáil to dominate proceedings throughout the first week of campaigning, as well as the apparent inability of Bertie Ahern to switch into his campaign mode. The *Irish Times* spoke of 'Fianna Fáil's efforts to regain the political initiative ... after five days of desultory campaigning',[26] while the *Irish Daily Mail* described Ahern as looking 'haunted and flustered on the campaign trail'.[27] And at the beginning of the second week, the *Irish Independent* judged Ahern to have turned from an asset to his party to a liability: 'The dissembling and bumbling figure we have seen of late does not measure up to the one who was his party's principal asset in both 1997 and 2002.'[28]

Neither front pages nor editorials show signs that any of the parties managed systematically to set the media agenda. The exception to the rule was the issue of stamp duty on property purchases that was placed on the agenda first by the opposition parties and then, during the first week of electioneering, by Fianna Fáil, which copied the campaign promises of its opponents. It briefly replaced the 'Bertiegate' story on the front pages of all broadsheets on either 3 or 4 May, and made half a dozen further appearances throughout the campaign in different outlets. Housing was one of the big issues of the 2007 campaign. In this case, the explicit competition between all of the parties ensured that the housing question was inescapably newsworthy.

Other than that, only about 15 per cent of campaign-related lead stories on the broadsheets' front pages carried obvious policy content. And more of these were event-induced (such as by the nurses' strike) than were generated by the parties' campaigns. A comprehensive analysis of campaign effects on media coverage is beyond the scope of this chapter, but parties appeared rather more responsive, defensive and at best adaptive in their media relations than had been the case in 2002.

Apart from the housing/stamp duty issue, only in the last few days, mostly as a result of statements in the leader debates, did we see issues that can partly be traced back to party statements again enter media discourse. These were not policy matters, but rather questions of coalition bargaining. The Labour Party and its leader, Pat Rabbitte, got considerable coverage on whether they would enter a coalition with Fianna Fáil in order to prevent Sinn Féin from playing any part in a future government. Again, this was not a matter emanating from deliberate party initiatives, but rather clarification demanded by the media. It certainly does not equal the success of the Progressive Democrats' last-gasp initiative in 2002 when they warned the public of the possible dangers of single party government and the need to keep them in coalition with Fianna Fáil to ensure some control over that party in government.[29]

Pack journalism

As mentioned in the beginning, the outstanding media aspect of this election was that the journalists themselves appeared to run a campaign. In the US context, the term 'pack journalism' is used to describe the manner in which reporters who jointly cover an institution or a campaign feed off one another, reinforcing their joint focus on a particular issue or aspect of a story, and conjointly creating a hunt-like dynamic.[30] Certainly the 'Bertiegate' story was pushed relentlessly by much of the media. The *Irish Independent* was most open to allowing Ahern the space to vent his anger at the media and to restate his criticism. This is not to say that the *Independent* took Ahern's side – it did run just as many front page stories about the matter, and provided just as many critical editorials about his financial shenanigans. The *Sunday Independent* was less critical. On 13 May it carried an interview with Ahern, a statement by him, a summary of the interview and two opinion pieces relating to his arguments. A week later, in a scathing criticism of RTÉ and its 'editorial edge, aimed almost exclusively at Ahern', it prided itself in having conclusively disposed of the 'Bertiegate' issue:

> The media cannot argue with public interest. If the story had public importance, it would still be alive today. But the *Sunday Independent* killed it stone dead last Sunday and so far it has defied all RTÉ News's attempts at resuscitation.

Ahern himself blamed Associated Press and its outlet, the *Irish Daily Mail*, as the main perpetrator of the media frenzy, which he considered intruded into his private life.[31] No election coverage relating to anything else but 'Bertiegate' made it to front pages in the *Irish Daily Mail* for the first nine days of the campaign and, considering that on eight of the first nine days, the election, or at least 'Bertiegate', provided the lead story, a certain obsession with the matter is evident. It was also one of the very few campaign matters that had enough sensationalist value to make it onto front pages in the tabloids, most notably the *Irish Sun*. Altogether, the application of the term 'pack journalism' to this episode appears validated by the fact that all daily newspapers (with the notable exception of the *Daily Star*) pursued the story consistently during the first nine days of campaigning, and returned briefly to it again together on the Monday (14 May) after Bertie Ahern had issued a lengthy statement on the matter.

Ultimately, the story, and Ahern's complaints about media bias that accompanied it, became controversial enough for the media to devote time to self-reflection. Essentially, one of the biggest stories of the 2007 campaign became the media themselves. In that sense, this Irish election campaign provides us with an ideal-typical example of a phenomenon that communication scholars in Europe and the US have paid increasing attention to in recent years: the paradox of expecting commercial news media to act in the public interest.[32] It is paradoxical primarily because this expectation is not just raised by academics or other voices outside the mass media, but is ingrained in codes of journalistic ethics and the credo of individual journalists.[33] Irish journalists, certainly those working for broadsheets, do not differ from their American, British or continental European counterparts, and their overwhelming concern with the 'Bertiegate' story during the early part of the campaign seemed to force them either to find normative justifications for doing so, or reluctantly to admit their true 'pack journalism' nature and castigate themselves for pushing 'the real issues' into the background.

The self-reflecting approach was taken by the *Irish Times*, which published a column by Noel Whelan musing how 'the media may get bored' with this particular matter 'and move on to other issues'.[34] In contrast, the *Sunday Independent* chose to lay the blame elsewhere and distance itself from the media frenzy over Bertiegate. In a feature article entitled 'A proud day for Ireland but not for the begrudgers in Montrose', the unnamed author described what he regarded as an episode of RTÉ-led pack journalism as if neither he nor his newspaper had been remotely associated with it: 'For the past three weeks, RTÉ News – tamely tailed by most of the print media – followed a tedious trail about Ahern's finances, first laid down by Frank Connolly in the *Irish Daily Mail*, which finally disappeared in the wood of public apathy.'[35] This quote is an example of what Russell Frank described as occasions 'when pack journalists bash pack journalism'.[36]

Journalists and political commentators remained ambiguous about their own role in pushing the issue to the fore. The *Sunday Independent*, for example, published in its edition of 13 May a comment entitled 'issues and not personalities should decide the election', in which Colum Kenny complained that: 'Bertie's finances [...] have so far overshadowed this general election campaign [and] made it harder than ever to sustain serious debate about a range of important matters.' In the same issue, Gene Kerrigan advanced the contrary argument that:

> it's our job to ... procure and analyse that information ... without worrying about the public's boredom threshold or the political fortunes of any individual or party. It would be bizarre indeed to ignore the arrival in Mr Ahern's custody of six big lumps of cash .... During an election campaign, politicians use the media to carry their propaganda and must therefore come out from behind their minders. This opens them to questions. Not to ask relevant questions would be to sink to the level of the opposition leaders – running from their duty, for fear of adverse reaction.

Bertie Ahern not only complained about media interference in his private matters, but also accused the media of biased reporting. The final section below will investigate the extent to which media obsession with Ahern's finances did actually lead to unbalanced coverage.

Bias in the Irish media?

The Irish media have a reputation for relatively balanced and impartial reporting (partly because of their refusal to endorse parties openly), but systematic bias was found in 2002, with not so much the tone but the amount of reporting favouring the government parties.[37]

The Factiva data seem to suggest some different patterns in 2007. Looking at the article count from four of the daily national newspapers (Figure 10.4), it is obvious that Fianna Fáil received less coverage than a 'stopwatch' approach based on either the size of its parliamentary representation or its current opinion poll standings would have warranted. Fine Gael received around 25 per cent of the coverage, which reflects its strength quite accurately, but Fianna Fáil was given considerably less than 30 per cent of the coverage. The PDs were systematically over-represented (with around 13 per cent of coverage) as they were in 2002, while Sinn Féin remained the most marginalised party in the Irish media (4 per cent). In the print media, Labour barely rated above the PDs. Arguably, however, the prominence of the PDs in the election coverage can be explained by the nature of news associated with them (stability of the coalition, 'Bertiegate', health (Mary Harney) and crime (Michael McDowell)) rather than something stemming from their own efforts at self-promotion. Figure 10.5 shows that both Fianna Fáil and Fine Gael were under-represented on RTÉ radio and television during the election campaign, receiving 33 per cent and 20 per cent of airtime respectively. The smaller parties were over-represented.

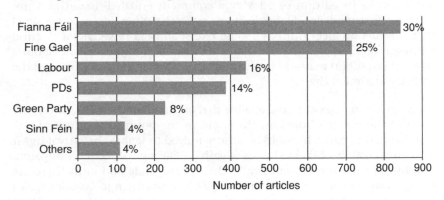

Figure 10.4   Party coverage in national newspapers

Note: Article counts from *Irish Independent, Irish Times, Irish Examiner* and *Evening Herald*.

Source: Factiva Insight™ from Dow Jones.

While party treatment appears only slightly skewed, a detailed look at the treatment of party leaders produces more skewed results. We coded all the headlines from the front pages of all the daily newspapers published during the campaign. Out of all the campaign headlines on the front pages of the three broadsheet newspapers, 68 per cent were devoted to party leaders. Bertie Ahern was mentioned in 70 per cent of those, Enda Kenny in only

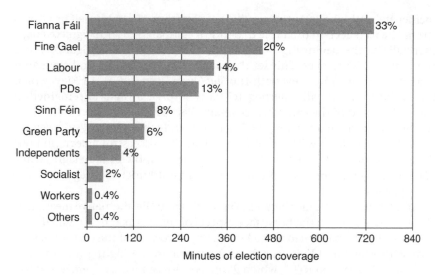

Figure 10.5   Party time allocation on RTÉ radio and TV election coverage

Notes: Period covered is between 29 April 2007 and 22 May 2007. Total of election coverage on all the RTÉ radio and TV programmes: 2,294.5 minutes.

Source: RTÉ data.

9 per cent and Michael McDowell in 15 per cent. Tabloid newspapers did not devote as many front page stories to the campaign as broadsheets, but of all campaign stories on their front pages, 72 per cent mentioned Ahern, 11 per cent Kenny, 11 per cent Cowen and 6 per cent McDowell. Of course, this intense concentration on Ahern might be seen by both Ahern and Fianna Fáil as unwelcome and indicating a bias against them.

Both the broadsheet newspapers and the tabloids devoted the same amount of campaign headlines to 'Bertiegate'. It was mentioned in 22 per cent of all campaign headlines on the front pages of the newspapers. Bertie Ahern was also the most visible in the photos of party leaders printed on the front pages of the newspapers during the campaign. He was in 46 per cent of all the photos in the broadsheets showing one or more leaders, Enda Kenny was in 20 per cent and Michael McDowell in 14 per cent. The tabloids showed Bertie Ahern even more often: there were 28 photos (69 per cent of all the photos coded) of him on the front pages of all the tabloids. There were only six photos of Enda Kenny (15 per cent), two of Michael McDowell and only one of Pat Rabbitte.

Conclusion

The most remarkable thing about the media during the general election campaign in 2007 is the fact that the media became the story. The focus on

'Bertiegate' and subsequent accusations of bias from Ahern himself prompted the media to reflect on their role in political campaigns. Campaign coverage, especially at the beginning, was overshadowed by the investigations into the Taoiseach's finances. This set the tone for the campaign, and even after Ahern's exclusive interview with the *Sunday Independent* on 13 May, which purported to 'reveal all', 'Bertiegate' refused to go away and remained in the background of the campaign coverage. Parties found it more difficult to set the media agenda than in 2007 and the old techniques did not seem to work. Michael McDowell's attempt to recreate his successful 'telegraph pole' PR stunt from 2002 ended in the fiasco of the 'Rumble in Ranelagh', while Fianna Fáil's communications machine could not knock 'Bertiegate' off the front pages for days.

The closeness of the race between Fianna Fáil and the alternative meant that the media focused on the horse race aspects of the campaign. It seemed that, at times, the campaign had turned into a 'light' version of the US presidential race, with Ahern and Kenny as the main candidates. A highlight of this was the leaders' debate on RTÉ1, which garnered a lot of media coverage and was watched by a record number of people. This was also the first big political campaign in Ireland in which the internet could be said to have offered an alternative to the mainstream election coverage.

The 2007 general election campaign might turn out to be significant for Irish politics. It marked a failure for the parties' communications machines, which sought to dictate the news agenda. The media found it increasingly difficult to navigate the stormy waters of conflicting interests of commercial endeavours, public interest and impartiality. The internet offered a new public space, a new 'town square',[38] and with the Web 2.0 emphasis on user-generated content, it might grow to offer a truly alternative, citizen-oriented election coverage. In many respects the coverage of the 2007 election was still quite traditional. A chapter reflecting on the media and the campaign in *How Ireland Voted 2012* might read very differently.

Notes

* The authors would like to thank RTÉ's reference library for its help with this chapter.
1. Heinz Brandenburg and Jacqueline Hayden, 'The media and the campaign', pp. 177–96 in Michael Gallagher, Michael Marsh and Paul Mitchell (eds), *How Ireland Voted 2002* (Basingstoke: Palgrave Macmillan, 2003), p. 193.
2. 'Media tried to topple me, says Ahern', *Irish Independent*, 21 May.
3. Readership is measured by means of the Joint National Readership Survey, carried out by the Institute of Advertising Practitioners of Ireland (IAPI). No readership figures are available for the *Irish Daily Mail*, which had a circulation of 57,397 in 2006. The readership survey found that newspapers have between 2.3 (*Irish Sun*) and 4.4 (*Irish Times*) readers per copy (www.finfacts.ie/finfactsblog/2007/03/irish-newspaper-readership-2007.html).

4. The comparable figures for 2002 can be found in Brandenburg and Hayden, 'The media and the campaign'.

5. *Irish Independent*, editorial, 19 May.

6. 'FF met O'Reilly before election – Cowen', *Irish Times*, 22 May 2007.

7. Eoghan Harris during a live debate with Fintan O'Toole on *The Last Word with Matt Cooper* on Today FM, 26 May (www.todayfm.com/goout.asp?u=http://audio. todayfm.com/files/HARRIS-1.wma).

8. 'PBS Using Discredited GOP Pollster to Provide Analysis of Democratic Forum?', Media Matters for America (http://mediamatters.org/items/200706250002).

9. 'Frankly Crap', Irish Politics Blog, 15 April (www.irishelection.com/04/frankly-crap/). Terry Prone, 'Luntz seems unable to grasp that our capacity to be outraged is limited', *Irish Examiner*, 16 April.

10. 'Massive audience watched the leaders' debate on RTÉ Prime Time', RTÉ Press Releases, 18 May 2007 (www.rte.ie/about/pressreleases/2007/0518//leadersde-batemay07.html).

11. For an analysis of the impact of the debate, see chapter 7.

12. Data provided by RTÉ. Fianna Fáil's broadcasts attracted between 194,000 and 546,000 viewers, Fine Gael's between 367,000 and 588,000 and Labour's between 494,000 and 608,000. Audience share averaged 35 per cent, but it fluctuated a lot, from 25 per cent for one Fianna Fáil broadcast to the 47 per cent who watched the Green Party's programme (which immediately preceded the leaders' debate on 17 May). The scheduling was almost certainly a factor in this variation, as perhaps was length: Christian Solidarity's message was only one minute long, and was shown just before something very popular.

13. TNS mrbi, *Joint National Radio Listenership Survey* (www.tnsmrbi.ie/cms/uploads/press_release_jnlr_apr_06_to_mar_07.pdf).

14. 'Spectacular figures for RTÉ election coverage', RTÉ Press Releases, 29 May 2007 (www.rte.ie/about/pressreleases/2007/0529//electionfiguresmay07.html).

15. Factiva Insight™ from Dow Jones enables users to track and monitor changes in the levels of media coverage of chosen variables. It was customised for the use during the 2007 Irish general election by Dow Jones for Radio Telefís Éireann. It used text mining and database search technology to code thousands of stories, which appeared in a variety of different media. These included published content from Irish newspapers (*Irish Times, Irish Examiner, Irish Independent, Evening Herald, Sunday Independent, Sunday Tribune, Sunday Business Post*) as well as websites, blogs and boards. The chosen variables were: parties, parties' spokespeople, issues (economy, health, education, environment, crime, immigration, tax, trustwor-thiness, government spending, housing, transport, childcare/carers, pensioners), regions. Factiva Insight enables customised reporting, which was used in this chapter. This made it possible to include only relevant sources and examine the period between 30 April 2007 and 24 May 2007.

16. Of course, one has to take into account that the Factiva software was programmed only to search for a limited number of issues, as identified in note 15. These did not include any non-policy matters apart from trustworthiness.

17. Heinz Brandenburg, 'Political bias in the Irish media: a quantitative study of campaign coverage during the 2002 general election', *Irish Political Studies* 20:3 (2005), pp. 297–322, at pp. 305ff.

18. Brandenburg, 'Political bias in the Irish media', p. 304.

19. *Irish Independent*, 15 May. Hospital co-location in Ireland refers to the building of private hospitals, by private businesses, on the grounds of public hospitals. It was

proposed by the outgoing government as a cheap and quick way to free up beds in public hospitals currently used by private patients, as it would entail moving such patients to the new private hospitals. Those opposed to the policy claimed it would mean subsidising private healthcare with public resources as the land on which the private hospitals would be built would be leased from the state, and there would be tax breaks on the capitals costs involved.

20. *Irish Independent*, 15 May.
21. For details of all campaign polls, see chapter 8, Table 8.1.
22. *Irish Daily Mail*, Monday 30 April.
23. *Irish Examiner*, 30 April.
24. *Irish Independent*, editorial, 30 April.
25. *Irish Examiner*, 4 May. Celia Larkin was the Taoiseach's partner in the mid-1990s when the payments behind 'Bertiegate' were made.
26. *Irish Times*, editorial, 5 May.
27. *Irish Daily Mail*, 1 May.
28. *Irish Independent*, editorial, 7 May.
29. Brandenburg and Hayden, 'The media and the campaign', pp. 190ff. See also the image on the front cover of Gallagher et al., *How Ireland Voted 2002*.
30. See Michael Schudson, 'The news media as political institutions', *Annual Review of Political Science* 5 (2002), pp. 249–69, at pp. 256ff. The term 'pack journalism' was originally introduced by Timothy Crouse, who studied the behaviour of journalists on the presidential campaign trail in 1972; see Timothy Crouse, *Boys on the Bus* (New York: Ballantine, 1973).
31. Bertie Ahern, in the *Sunday Independent*, 13 May 2007.
32. See, for example, Leo Bogart, *Commercial Culture: The Media System and the Public Interest* (New York: Oxford University Press, 1995); David Croteau and William Hoynes, *The Business of Media: Corporate Media and the Public Interest*, 2nd edn (Thousand Oaks, CA: Sage, 2006); Jean Seaton, 'Broadcasting in the age of market ideology: is it possible to underestimate the public taste?', *Political Quarterly* 65:1 (1994), pp. 29–38.
33. Jeremy Iggers, *Good News, Bad News: Journalism Ethics and the Public Interest* (Boulder, CO: Westview Press, 1996).
34. Noel Whelan, *Irish Times*, 5 May 2007.
35. *Sunday Independent*, 20 May 2007.
36. Russell Frank, 'These crowded circumstances: when pack journalists bash pack journalism', *Journalism* 4:4 (2003), pp. 441–58.
37. Brandenburg, 'Political bias in the Irish media'; Brandenburg and Hayden, 'The media and the campaign', p. 189.
38. Olof Peterson, Monika Djerf-Pierre, Soren Holmberg, Jesper Stromback and Lennart Weibull, *Report from the Democratic Audit of Sweden 2006. Media and Elections in Sweden* (Stockholm: SNS Forlag, 2006), p. 150.

11
The Seanad Election

*Theresa Reidy**

Elections to Seanad Éireann take place within 90 days of the dissolution of Dáil Éireann. The Seanad is the upper house of parliament and its members are elected in a complex process by a very small electorate. Consequently, the elections attract little public attention, taking place outside the public domain. This point was reinforced in 2007 with a public disagreement between RTÉ and Seanad candidates. RTÉ notified a candidate that 'it would not be providing coverage for the elections to the Seanad because the vast majority of its audience has no say in who is elected'.[1] A recurrent feature of every Seanad election campaign is a discussion on the democratic credentials of the elections.

Seanad Éireann

The Seanad consists of 60 members, 11 of whom are appointed by the Taoiseach. Six members are elected by university graduates and the remaining 43 are elected from panels of candidates, representing specific vocational interests. The electorate for the 43 vocational seats consists of 1,096 voters: members of the incoming Dáil, the outgoing Seanad and members of County and City Councils. The electorate is in effect made up of practising politicians. Voters for the six university seats are split into two groups; graduates of the University of Dublin (Trinity College) and graduates of the National University of Ireland (NUI). Each group of graduates elects three senators.

The composition of, and the electoral process for, the Seanad set it apart from the upper houses of parliament in many other European countries. The norm for members of upper houses is either direct election or indirect appointment. The vocational panel dimension found in Seanad Éireann is quite unusual.[2]

In most countries, the upper house of parliament is politically subordinate and this is especially true of Seanad Éireann. The Seanad has limited powers to revise or delay legislation. It does have a number of important, though seldom invoked, constitutional functions.[3] Yet, defenders of Seanad Éireann rarely speak of its specific powers, but instead argue that its main strength is that it provides a forum for political debate in a calmer, less politically charged, arena than the Dáil.

The structure of the Seanad was set down in the 1937 constitution (Bunreacht na hÉireann) and much of the law governing the detail of Seanad elections comes from the Seanad Electoral Act of 1947. The largest group of senators in the Seanad are elected from the vocational panels. The idea of vocational interests in the Seanad stems from the ideas of corporatism and vocational representation that were prominent in Catholic social thinking in the 1930s. In reality, the vocational dimension plays little or no role. As senators are voted in by sitting politicians, the process of election is very much a party political event with the large political parties playing a controlling role.

The 43 senators are elected from panels of candidates expected to have specific knowledge or practical experience from one of the following five areas:

1. Culture and education
2. Agriculture
3. Labour
4. Industry and commerce
5. Administration

The electoral process

The process by which senators are elected differs from all other electoral contests in the Republic of Ireland. In the first instance, there is a very restricted franchise. Candidates wishing to run for office must secure nominations in a particularly complex manner, and 11 senators are appointed directly by the Taoiseach. There are few restrictions on candidates, but they must be citizens of Ireland, aged 21 or over, and no one can be a member of both houses of the Oireachtas at the same time. Candidates contesting the Seanad election are covered by the terms of the 1997 Electoral Act, and the Standards in Public Office Commission issues general guidelines for candidates. As at local elections, no spending limits apply and the main thrust of the guidelines relate to recording and returning details of political donations.

The electorate of the vocational panel seats is made up entirely of elected representatives. As each member of the electorate is either affiliated to a political party or is an independent public representative, it is possible to calculate with some certainty the potential vote any group can expect.[4] Although transfers play a very important role, a strong party vote and associated transfer pattern is assumed by campaign strategists. This allows the parties to develop precise vote management strategies and, to some extent, the election has more to do with determining which candidates are elected from each party rather than the numbers elected from each party, which can be predicted with some accuracy in advance. The strength of the parties is set out in Table 11.1.

Table 11.1   Composition of the Seanad electorate

	FF	*FG*	*Lab*	*PDs*	*Grn*	*SF*	*Others*	*Total*
TDs	78	51	20	2	6	4	5	166
Senators	25	9	4	4	0	0	8	50
Councillors	302	293	98	19	18	54	96	880
Total votes	405	353	122	25	24	58	109	1,096
% vote share 2007	37.0	32.2	11.1	2.3	2.2	5.3	9.9	100.0
% vote share 2002	44.6	30.0	9.0	3.0	1.0	2.4	10.0	100.0

Sources: Calculated from figures provided by the political party headquarters and the Houses of the Oireachtas.

It is worth noting that the abolition of the dual mandate (see p. 101 above) increased the electorate of the vocational panels by 126, taking it to its highest level.[5] Following successful local elections in 2004 and a good performance in the 2007 Dáil election, Fine Gael increased its share of the electorate by over 2 per cent. Sinn Féin, Labour and the Greens also entered the Seanad campaign with a higher potential vote share than in 2002. Arising from a poor local election and reduced Dáil numbers, both Fianna Fáil and the PDs had a lower percentage share. As in 2002, just over 90 per cent of the electorate had a party affiliation.

There are two ways in which a candidate may secure a nomination to contest a vocational panel seat. The first route is to receive a nomination from a designated nominating body. The Clerk of the Seanad maintains a register of nominating bodies who may nominate a candidate to the panel of candidates. To register as a nominating body, organisations must be involved with, or be a representative of, the interests of one of the panels. An organisation can be registered as a nominating body for only one panel. The register is revised annually and in 2007 it contained 103 organisations. The role of nominating bodies in the electoral process is frequently criticised, as many of the organisations are small and some are particularly obscure.

Once nominations open, candidates have two options. They may seek a nomination from a nominating body, or those confident of securing a nomination from their political party can wait until the Oireachtas nominations are announced.[6] The majority of the candidates seeking a nomination are affiliated to one of the political parties. A variety of different selection criteria and processes are applied by the nominating bodies. In some cases, organisations nominate one of their own leading members. This was particularly true of the culture and education bodies in the past. However, in 2007 a number of organisations indicated that they opted for party-affiliated candidates, acknowledging that their own members rarely achieved much success. Most nominating bodies operate an open submissions policy and any candidate can make an application to be considered for the nomination, although a few bodies, such as the Association of Secondary Teachers in Ireland (ASTI), will consider applications only from members of their organisation. The final nominee is usually selected by the national council or executive of the organisation.

Organisations have different motivations in making their selection but most are interested in having their policy priorities or interests raised and supported at national level. This helps explain why many nominating bodies consider the electability of the candidate to be as important as his or her ability to reflect their views. For large organisations with clear policy objectives, such as the unions, agriculture bodies and the vintners, the opportunity to have political influence within the system is very appealing. Smaller organisations tend to view their involvement in the Seanad campaign as a means of raising their profile amongst the political classes and focusing interest on their area.

Candidates seeking a nomination for the Seanad are by law required to have specific knowledge of the area on whose panel they are running. In 2002, the returning officer initially queried the qualifications of Kathy Sinnott, a high-profile Independent, to run on a panel. This step was unusual and the requirement for specific knowledge is loose at best.[7] Nominating bodies differ in how they apply this requirement, with some issuing open invitations to candidates to present their credentials, while more formal membership requirements are operated by other organisations.

Party political candidates balance a variety of factors when seeking a nomination. Their main priority, obviously, is ensuring that they receive a nomination. Some effort is made to have a link to the vocational nature of the panel. Candidates can choose an active body with a wide network of members such as the teaching organisations, or they may seek a nomination from a smaller organisation with which they share common policy objectives. Some candidates secure multiple nominations at each election. This can be seen on a number of panels, with one candidate on the culture and education panel securing nominations from four bodies. Multiple nominations can broaden the potential networks that a candidate can appeal to, as well as reducing the number of bodies from which fellow competitors can seek a nomination. In 2007, nominations from nominating bodies closed on 15 June. Table 11.2 provides summary details on the candidates put forward on the nominating bodies sub-panel.

The second means of securing a nomination is from four members of the Oireachtas: incoming TDs and/or outgoing senators. Since Oireachtas nominations close a week after nominating bodies, the political parties have a clear advantage in the nominating process. They are able to assess the candidates who have already been selected and consider strategic additions to their party ticket. This second route to nomination through the political parties undermines the vocational dimension to the Seanad. Furthermore, candidates themselves describe nominations from Oireachtas members as 'inside' nominations while 'outside' nominations come from a nominating body. This code, in itself, reflects the way candidates view the process. They contend that a nomination from a political party confers an electoral edge, making it easier to attract votes from party members outside their direct circle. An 'inside' nomination is viewed as a direct endorsement by the party. In reality, the electoral law of the Seanad requires that a minimum number of candidates are selected from each nominating sub-panel, ensuring that the nominating bodies retain their role in the process.

Table 11.2 Candidates put forward by nominating bodies at the 2007 Seanad election

Panel	Culture & education	Agriculture	Labour	Industry & commerce	Administration
Senators to be elected	5	11	11	9	7
Number of registered nominating bodies	33	11	2	43	14
Number of bodies that made nominations	15	11	2	32	13
Number of nominations each body can make	1	2	7	1	1
Number of candidates nominated by nominating bodies	12	19	14	29	9
Minimum to be elected from each sub-panel	2	4	4	3	3

Sources: Calculated from *Iris Oifigiuil*, no. 24, 23 March 2007, and *Iris Oifigiuil*, no. 52B, 29 June 2007.

The number of candidates that a party can nominate is determined by its numerical strength in the recently elected Dáil and the outgoing Seanad. This gives a dominant position to the two large political parties, which are in a position to make the greatest number of nominations and they can draw on a large base of affiliated councillors to support their candidates. The nomination process is carefully choreographed, although it is by no means infallible. In 2007, Fianna Fáil TD Ned O'Keeffe went against his party's instructions by helping to nominate outgoing Fianna Fáil senator Don Lydon. Lydon had not secured an outside nomination and, for various reasons, had not been included on Fianna Fáil's 'inside' list.

Smaller parties tend to make strategic nominations to panels where they may have individual interests. Sinn Féin used its Oireachtas members to nominate Pearse Doherty to the agriculture panel. Independent Oireachtas members used their strength to nominate former TD Paudge Connolly. The Labour Party nominated two candidates to the labour panel, Phil Prendergast and Eric Byrne, and one to the others. The PDs helped Fianna Fáil to maximise the number of nominations it could make.

Not all members of the Oireachtas make a nomination, and in 2007, three panels did not receive the legal minimum number of candidates required to be nominated by Oireachtas members. In order to ensure a competitive election, each sub-panel must have two nominations more than the maximum number of senators that could be elected from it. Four candidates were nominated by the Taoiseach to fill the required spaces (see Table 11.3).

Table 11.3   Candidates put forward by Oireachtas members at the 2007 Seanad election

Panel	Culture & education	Agriculture	Labour	Industry & commerce	Administration
Legal minimum number required	5	9	9	8	6
Nominated by Oireachtas members	4	7	11	7	7
Nominated by an Taoiseach	1	2	0	1	0
Nominated on Oireachtas sub-panel	5	9	11	8	7
Total nominated on both sub-panels	17	28	25	37	16

Source: Calculated from *Iris Oifigiuil*, no. 52B, 29 June 2007.

Political parties vary little in the way they make their selection decisions. They use their nominations strategically with future electoral contests carrying considerable weight in the decision-making process. Candidates in a good position to contest the next Dáil election are often given priority, and parties use a Seanad term as an effective means of grooming individuals for higher political office. These are known as launchpad candidates. A second category of politicians are those that failed to achieve re-election to the Dáil. Some will be considered for a term in the Seanad if they seem to have a reasonable prospect of election at the next Dáil election. A smaller number are offered a Seanad nomination as a consolation prize. This practice has given rise to the 'retirement home' perception of the Seanad. The final category are career senators, candidates who do not intend pursuing election to the Dáil and who may already have spent a number of terms in the Seanad.

An interesting pattern evident in Seanad elections over the last decade is the increase in the first category of candidates, the launchpad group. Candidates with future potential are increasing in number, often at the expense of retirees to the Seanad and career senators. The Fine Gael selection strategy in 2002 was probably the best evidence of this trend, although all parties pursue the policy.[8]

There are a variety of internal processes within the parties to decide the candidates that are nominated. Labour has the most straightforward process with the national executive committee selecting the candidate(s) nominated to each panel. The national executive is made up of party members (with representatives from various sections including Labour Youth and Labour Women) as well as the party leader and a number of other elected representatives. The party leader does not have any additional powers. Candidates are invited to put themselves forward for the nomination and the final decision is made by the executive. Though no formal guidelines exist, potential candidates for the nomination emphasise their electoral potential in their submissions to the executive. The capacity to gain a seat at the next Dáil election was considered an overriding priority in 2007. Due to a vote pact with Sinn Féin (discussed in more detail later) Labour put forward six candidates, two more than in 2002. (See Table 11.4.)

Table 11.4 Candidates put forward by affiliation, 2007 Seanad election

		FF	FG	Lab	SF	Others
All Panels	N	37	32	1	0	13
	O	17	15	6	1	1
Total		54	47	7	1	14

Note: N denotes nominating body candidates, O denotes candidates nominated by Oireachtas members. The four candidates nominated by the Taoiseach are included in the Fianna Fáil figure. Cllr Tom Kelly is a member of the Green Party but was not an official candidate for the Green Party and is included in the Others category. Cllr Tom Costello is a member of the Labour Party but was not an official candidate for the Labour Party, so he too is included among Others.

Outgoing Labour senator Michael McCarthy sought an outside nomination. His decision to go outside the party route was informed by a sense that a party nomination would not be forthcoming. It is unusual for Labour Party candidates to seek an outside nomination as the party carefully manages the Seanad elections to ensure a favourable outcome. With a finite electorate, all parties try to control the process but smaller political parties, in particular, minimise the number of renegade party candidates seeking an outside nomination. This is a deliberate strategy to ensure that the party vote is not diluted among too many candidates, raising the possibility that no party candidate might succeed. The ultimate success of the candidates has more to do with the party's strength in the electorate than their individual appeal or ability.

Sinn Féin nominated one candidate to the agricultural panel, Pearse Doherty. Nominations from the branches go to an election committee which makes a recommendation to the Ard Comhairle, the party's main decision-making body.

The Fianna Fáil Ard Comhairle manages its selection process. Candidates apply to their local (or in some instances neighbouring) constituency executive for inclusion in the party nominations. Each constituency executive can nominate one person. Former TDs, not re-elected in the most recent Dáil election, are entitled to nominate themselves for inclusion in the candidate selection process. The number of candidates to be selected and the overall electoral strategy is decided by the Ard Comhairle. It holds an internal election to select the candidates that will go forward. TDs, MEPs and senators are entitled to vote. Once the successful candidates are identified, the Ard Comhairle reviews the outcome and is empowered to add candidates. Most of the candidates tend to be outgoing members of the Seanad. A number of defeated Dáil deputies, including Ivor Callely and Cecilia Keaveney, put themselves forward. A smaller group comprises candidates seeking a route into national politics. This differentiates the Fianna Fáil approach somewhat from that of the other parties, where aspirant national politicians make up the largest cohort challenging for a Seanad nomination.

Fine Gael is an obvious example of the aspiring Dáil politician strategy. Its approach to the selection process prioritises candidates with future potential in national elections. The party has a Seanad Electoral Commission with responsibility for picking Seanad nominees. Each constituency executive can make a nomination, along with the executive council, Young Fine Gael, and the parliamentary party, each of whom can nominate a limited number of candidates. A shortlist is drawn up by the commission and ratified by the national executive. The commission considers a number of criteria when selecting candidates: constituencies with no Fine Gael representatives are prioritised, followed by constituencies that may be on the target list for gains at the next general election. Successions were considered important in 2007, and constituencies where high-profile party members would be retiring were given some consideration for Seanad seats. Following a successful strategy in 2002, many of Fine Gael's career senators had been phased out with only three proving successful in 2007.

Selecting candidates to contest the next election was an important criterion for all of the parties in the Seanad election. With 14 senators having successfully contested the general election in May, a term in the Seanad can reasonably be seen to improve a candidate's chance of election.

The electoral process for the university seats is slightly different. Candidates wishing to run for election on the university panels must secure nominations from two registered voters of the university, and a further eight must assent to the nomination. Candidates do not need to be graduates of the university or connected to it in any way. Nominations for the university panels closed on 1 June and ballot papers were issued on 9 July. The poll closed on 23 July.[9]

As with other elections in Ireland, the gender breakdown of candidates is not inspiring. In total, 23 women contested the vocational panels out of 123 candidates. Seven of the 24 candidates on the NUI panel were women, and two of the 11 candidates on the University of Dublin panel were female. Women were more likely to receive an outside nomination, with just nine of the 23 securing an inside nomination from Oireachtas members.

The campaign trail

Campaigns for the Seanad take place below the public radar and 2007 was not significantly different, though a number of issues managed to break into the public arena. The start of the campaign was dominated by a dispute amongst Green Party councillors regarding the possibility that their ballot papers might be inspected by the party leadership to ensure they were voting for Fianna Fáil candidates, in accordance with an agreement between the two parties. In the first instance, this would have been illegal, a point that the Green Party leadership took some time to realise. A somewhat embarrassing public dispute was played out in the newspapers. In contrast, Progressive Democrat support for Fianna Fáil candidates was agreed and carried out quietly. Speculation mounted on the possibility of a government minority in the Seanad before the election. Informed by the poor performance of Fianna Fáil at the local elections and the uncertainty around the support of Green Party councillors for Fianna Fáil candidates, commentators speculated that the government might not achieve a majority in the Seanad.[10]

The recurrent theme of every Seanad campaign is Seanad reform. A queue of candidates and commentators lined up to list the faults of the Seanad and outline their remedies. This year they were joined in their concerns by the newly appointed Minister for the Environment, John Gormley, who gave a commitment to further the case of Seanad reform by creating an action plan. With 12 reports over the last 50 years, many would agree that more planning for reform is not required. Former senator Mary O'Rourke became a champion of Seanad reform in the midst of the campaign. Her 2004 all-party report on Seanad Éireann was held up as a blueprint for the changes required.[11] Despite an implementation commitment from the Taoiseach on its publication in 2004, no change has been made.

Voting pacts were the order of the day for many of the political parties with Labour entering an agreement with Sinn Féin. This received some discussion and was decried most vociferously by Fine Gael, which ended up as the only party without a voting partner. The Labour and Sinn Féin pact was clearly a pragmatic and ultimately successful approach to the election. Sinn Féin with 58 votes had more than half of a quota but would have failed to elect a senator on any of the panels. Labour with 122 votes was short of a quota on at least one of the panels. Forming a vote pact allowed both parties to maximise their potential seat gains. The structure of the vocational panels in many ways encourages voting alliances among smaller parties. The pact was negotiated and administered by Joe Costello TD on the Labour side with Aengus Ó Snodaigh TD and Joan O'Connor (Sinn Féin Election Department) handling the pact for Sinn Féin. Both parties declared themselves very satisfied with the outcome of the pact, although Labour was quick to state that it was not an indication of a new alignment in Irish politics, citing a previous pact between the PDs and Democratic Left in 1993 as evidence that Seanad voting pacts are simply a numbers game.

Fianna Fáil received support from its partners in government, the Green Party and the Progressive Democrats. This arrangement had been negotiated during the coalition talks. Green and PD votes were promised to Fianna Fáil candidates in return for two senators for each of the parties in the Taoiseach's 11 nominees to the Seanad. The voting arrangements are noteworthy in that they are evidence of a fluidity in Irish politics and provide an indication of new patterns of political transaction.

The private face of the Seanad campaign sets it apart from all other Irish elections. It is a unique experience for any politician seeking election. It is a five- to six-week campaign during which candidates travel to all 26 counties seeking out votes. Victory celebrations for newly elected TDs, council meetings and public meetings are assiduously attended by would-be senators. Most politicians and commentators agree that the Seanad campaign is the toughest and most gruelling that any politician will endure. With an electorate of professional politicians, candidates often face unrelenting questioning, which must be carefully considered and responded to in the hope of securing a preference. As the outcome of the election is frequently very tight, with only a small number of votes separating the candidates, every preference is worth negotiating. Direct observation of this process reveals that the main focus of discussion is most often the candidate's likelihood of being a candidate at a future Dáil election. Pragmatism is the order of the day amongst all of the political parties. Surely, in no other election do candidates receive votes to be elected to one house of parliament based on their potential to successfully challenge for election to another house of parliament. Candidates face a difficult electorate, entirely different from local or Dáil elections. During an interview, one candidate somewhat bitterly compared the experience to campaigning in local elections 'where you meet ordinary liars, in the Seanad campaign, you are dealing with professional liars'.

The approach to campaigning varies across candidates with some seeking a high preference, ideally a number 1, and others, knowing that this would be over-optimistic, asking for at least a lower preference. With so many voting pacts in operation, candidates who once had to visit only members of their own parties found themselves canvassing a new group of voters from a different party. Even with voting pacts in place, personal contact is considered essential in the Seanad campaign unless a voter advises a candidate that a visit is not necessary. Non-party or Independent voters make up a sizeable portion of the electorate and special attention is paid to their 'swing' votes. With only a small number of non-party candidates contesting the Seanad campaign, many of these votes were available. Despite this, many candidates indicated in interviews that they considered geography and personal relationships to have been the major determining factors for independent voters.

There are many distinctive features to the campaigning techniques that are adopted by candidates in Seanad elections. Election lore suggests that some voters are offered inducements in the course of the campaign. This was highlighted with particular effect by a councillor in Roscommon who was posted a voucher for a hotel break by one of the candidates. After he had brought it to public attention on national radio, the story was subsequently pursued by the press. In the end, the candidate received only six votes. On the university panels, votes were offered for sale on eBay for the first time. The vote listed with a starting price of €1.62 but was quickly removed once it was discovered that it is illegal to sell votes.

Candidates receive very little assistance from their respective political parties during Seanad campaigns. Financial assistance is not forthcoming from any of the parties. Some offer to help with printing or give practical assistance in locating councillors. Labour writes to all of its electorate drawing attention to the official candidates in the race, while Fine Gael reminds its voters of the candidates nominated on the 'inside' panel. All things considered, though the election is dominated by the political parties, individual party headquarters tend to be far removed from the contest. For the most part, this is because parties view the Seanad election as an intra-party contest.

Candidates on the university panels do not face the same punishing trek throughout the country to meet their electors. Contact is mostly through the postal system. An Post reported that over 3 million pieces of literature were delivered during the campaign. The use of the postal system does pose some difficulty, as many voters first registered upon graduation and limited resources are put into updating the addresses of voters. Voters are personally responsible for supplying up-to-date contact information and countless voters still receive literature at their family home addresses, but for many, literature goes undelivered. This is a particular problem in the case of the ballot papers that are delivered by registered post. Many people are not at home to sign for the ballot papers and An Post reported that more than 20,000 ballot papers were returned. Concerns were also raised about the accuracy of the registers and this prompted a number of candidates to seek a meeting with the Minister for the Environment, John Gormley. Linda O'Shea Farren, a candidate on the NUI panel, argued that the registered electorate of 103,000 was grossly inaccurate and that close to 250,000 voters should in fact be registered. Disquiet about the state of the register of electors has been a feature of many Seanad elections.

These problems aside, many voters received an array of glossy election material. The literature outlined careers, achievements and included endorsements from graduates, academics and political personalities. The one feature that appeared on much of the literature was candidates' intention to seek immediate reform of the Seanad. Interestingly, incumbents were the least likely to dwell on Seanad reform. Incumbents have a considerable advantage in Seanad elections. They can exploit their existing profile and use the secretarial and research assistance that has been at their disposal over the preceding five years to create a detailed database of would-be voters.

Results

Panel seats

Counting in the Seanad election takes place in Leinster House, and in 2007 took four days. It was closely monitored by political insiders, though it received little media or public interest. The results included a number of surprises and provided confirmation that the voting pacts between the parties held up. Fianna Fáil lost two seats but had been expected to lose more. Table 11.1 compares the percentage vote share of the parties with their position in 2002. It shows Fianna Fáil and its government partners entering the election with a 6 per cent lower share of the vote than they had in 2002. Despite predictions, which we mentioned earlier, that the government might fail to secure an overall Seanad majority, Fianna Fáil secured 22 seats, indicating that votes from the Green Party and the PDs did materialise as promised. The Labour and Sinn Féin pact was a success, with Labour picking up two extra seats over 2002 and Sinn Féin's Pearse Doherty taking the party's first seat in the Seanad. Fine Gael was the surprise loser, dropping one seat despite an increase in Dáil representatives and in councillors from the 2004 local elections.

Of the 1,096 electors for the vocational panels, 1,086 returned ballot papers, a turnout rate of over 99 per cent. Despite this being an electorate of professional politicians, a small number of voters managed to spoil their votes, bringing down the total valid poll. On the culture and education panel, of the 1,086 ballot papers returned, 14 were rejected as spoiled, four voters did not include a preference and the remaining ten did not contain the required declarations of identity and witness documents. The counting process begins with the verification of each vote and the separation of ballots into the appropriate panel. Culture and education is the first panel to be counted, followed by agriculture, labour, industry and commerce and administration.

Table 11.5 outlines the results of the election. Uncertainty about whether the voting pacts amongst the parties would materialise on the ground made the outcome more difficult to predict. The growth of Sinn Féin at the local elections in 2004 left it short of a quota on any of the panels but put it in a good negotiating position for a voting deal. Its pact with Labour saw it secure a Seanad seat, and Labour also increased its representation by two. The table demonstrates the careful vote management conducted by the parties, clearly visible in the precise vote split between Sinn Féin and Labour on the agriculture panel.

Table 11.5   Results of the panel elections

	FF	FG	Lab	SF	Others	Total	Quota
Core party electors	405	353	122	58	158	1,096	–
Number of candidates	54	47	7	1	14	123	–
Culture & education	509(3)	354(1)	198(1)	–(0)	11	1,072 (5)	178.66
Agriculture	490(5)	361(4)	96(1)	103(1)	22	1,072 (11)	89.33
Labour	490(5)	366(4)	172(2)	–(0)	48	1,076 (11)	89.66
Industry & commerce	535(5)	361(3)	109(1)	–(0)	62	1,067 (9)	106.70
Administration	556(4)	385(2)	129(1)	–(0)	–(0)	1,070 (7)	133.75
Total votes (no.)	2,580	1,827	704	103	143	5,357 (43)	
Total votes (%)	48.2	34.1	13.1	1.9	2.7		
Total seats (no.)	22	14	6	1	0	43	
Total seats (%)	51.2	32.6	13.9	2.3	0	100	

Notes: Figures in parentheses show the number of seats. The Others figure for party electors includes the votes of the 25 PDs and the 24 Green Party votes.

Sources: Results calculated from data provided by the Clerk of the Seanad. The Green Party and the Progressive Democrats are included with Others as no official party candidates contested the panel elections.

On the culture and education panel Labour made a direct gain at the expense of Fine Gael, with Alex White, who had been backed by the party centre for a Dáil candidacy but had missed out on election (see pp. 55–6 above), becoming the first person elected to the 23rd Seanad. The Labour gain materialised from the voting pact with Sinn Féin but Fine Gael candidates indicated that a strategy miscalculation on their party's part resulted in two strong candidates contesting the inside panel slot. Liam Twomey was elected first for Fine Gael and ultimately Terence Slowey lost out to Ann Ormonde of Fianna Fáil when the rules requiring the election of a minimum number of candidates from the outside panel were invoked.

Fine Gael had been targeting an additional seat on the administration panel but this did not materialise and the balance remained the same. Labour made a gain on the labour panel and outgoing senator Michael McCarthy was joined by Phil Prendergast. Fianna Fáil stemmed any potential losses with robust voting pacts with its government partners, and additionally its candidates seem to have proved attractive to many of the non-party voters.

Party allegiances were very strong, and Table 11.5 displays this clearly. The core vote of each party came through on each panel with only small amounts of variation outside of the voting pacts. This view is further reinforced by examination of the transfer patterns, where party coherence was maintained at a very high level. The numbers also provide evidence of the voting pacts on different panels.

The balance between 'inside' and 'outside' nominations has shifted slightly, with 22 candidates being elected from the nominating bodies sub-panel and 21 from the Oireachtas members' sub-panel.[12] As with previous contests, Fianna Fáil candidates proved most successful on the nominating bodies sub-panel taking 50 per cent and upwards of all of the seats won on each of the nominating bodies sub-panel. Labour secured one seat on the 'outside' panel with Michael McCarthy. This was not considered a success by Labour as McCarthy had displaced the inside nominated candidate Eric Byrne, who was the party's choice for the seat. McCarthy's success does provide evidence that occasionally individuals can thwart their party's intentions in the Seanad.

On balance, all of the parties, apart from Fine Gael, were satisfied with their performance. Labour and Sinn Féin increased their representation. Fianna Fáil minimised its losses to two following careful vote management. Fine Gael lost one seat despite the increase in its core vote, leaving it the victim of the evolving voting arrangements of other parties. The election improved the gender balance in the Oireachtas and the 23rd Seanad includes 13 women – 21 per cent of the Seanad. This is the highest level of female representation ever achieved in the Seanad and it is well ahead of the level in the Dáil (see pp. 101–2 above).

University seats

The university seats are criticised as the most elitist aspect of Seanad Éireann. Six senators are elected by graduates on two panels. Moreover, the graduates of only a small number of institutions – the constituent institutions of the NUI and the University of Dublin – have a vote. Graduates from other universities in the state have no right to vote in Seanad elections, despite a constitutional referendum passed in 1979, which facilitated extending the range of institutions involved in the Seanad elections. This absence of activity in itself provides further evidence of the lack of interest in Seanad reform.

There are arguments presented in favour of university representation. Perhaps one of the most vocal defenders is senator David Norris, who frequently argues that while the university seats may have a restricted electorate, their electorate is many multiples of the electorate for the vocational panel seats. In 2007, 103,085 graduates were registered to vote on the NUI panel with a further 48,880 graduates registered for the University of Dublin panel. In addition, supporters of the university seats have argued that these have always been the only area where political parties have not taken control and independent voices have emerged.

Incumbents on the university panels have a sizeable advantage over challenger candidates and university seats are not known for throwing up surprises. Consequently, the defeat of Brendan Ryan (Labour) on the NUI panel by Ronan Mullen, a barrister and newspaper columnist, caught many commentators unaware. The NUI panel itself was more attention-grabbing than usual. Mullen had established a profile as a columnist and commentator and had at various points been president of the Students' Union at NUI Galway and a spokesman for the Dublin Archdiocese. He is associated with a conservative Catholic platform and has been involved in pro-life campaigns, among other things. Despite being a first-time candidate, he received the second highest vote on the panel, outpolling two incumbents, Brendan Ryan and Feargal Quinn. Joe O'Toole topped the poll and was first elected. He was followed by Quinn, with Ronan Mullen third.

Although the Labour Party lost a seat on the NUI panel, the victory of Ivana Bacik on the Dublin University panel goes some way to balancing the loss of Ryan. Bacik is a high-profile academic and campaigner who ran in the European elections for Labour in 2004, although she stated that she would not be taking the Labour whip in the Seanad. The retirement of Senator Mary Henry from the Seanad and her endorsement of Bacik created an opening through which Ivana Bacik was able to successfully build on her previous vote in the Seanad campaign in 2002. She was elected on the eighth count. Both incumbents, Shane Ross and David Norris, were elected comfortably on the first count, both exceeding the quota of 4,230.

The university seats are striking in the contrast that they provide to the vocational panel elections. The university graduates have elected a cohort of interesting candidates, several of whom can be identified with specific ideological positions. Shane Ross is a well known neo-liberal, Feargal Quinn is an entrepreneur and business-oriented representative, Ivana Bacik is a long-term campaigner for women's rights and liberal advocate, while Ronan Mullen argues a consistent conservative line in policy debates. The ease with which candidates can be identified with specific issues and clear ideology differentiates them strongly from the party political senators elected in the vocational panels. Although the university panels are frequently criticised as elitist, in reality they bring the only independent dimension to the Seanad.

Turnout in the university panels is quite low relative to other elections, being below 40 per cent for both university panels. In a final indictment of the electoral process, close to 1,000 voters, all university graduates, returned invalid votes. Most of the ballots were rejected because the declarations of identity had not been included, or had been completed incorrectly.

Taoiseach's nominees

The Taoiseach appoints 11 of the 60 senators, a provision designed to ensure that the government has a majority in the Seanad. With the government bloc reduced to 22 in the panel elections, party political nominations were the order of the day. Although there had been much speculation about the possible candidates, when the nominees were announced on 3 August there were a couple of surprise inclusions. Under a deal struck as part of the coalition talks, the Taoiseach included two Greens and two PDs in his 11. In each party the Seanad nominees were selected by an internal committee convened to make recommendations to the leader. Dan Boyle, a defeated Dáil deputy, and Deirdre de Búrca, an unsuccessful Dáil candidate, were nominated on behalf of the Green Party, while Fiona O'Malley, also a defeated TD, and Ciarán Cannon, also an unsuccessful Dáil challenger, were the PD nominees.

The Taoiseach has a record of appointing one non-political member to the Seanad, and Eoghan Harris, a journalist with the *Sunday Independent*, received the nomination this time. The appointment was not without controversy, as Harris had made a spirited defence of Bertie Ahern on a *Late Late Show* appearance in the last week of the general election (see the Chronology at the front of the book). The remaining six candidates were taken from Fianna Fáil and included a number of defeated Dáil deputies. Again not without controversy, John Ellis and Ivor Callely, both of whom had been involved in political scandals at various points, were included in the 11.[13] In an almost direct swap with his constituency colleague, Donie Cassidy was appointed by the Taoiseach as the successor to Mary O'Rourke as the Leader of the Seanad.

As usually happens when the nominees are announced, discussion arose on the secretive nature of the selection process, followed by calls to abolish the Seanad.[14] With the Taoiseach's nominations producing six additional Fianna Fáil senators and four from its government partners, the government ended the Seanad election with a slim majority, 32 of the 60 seats. The overall composition of the Seanad is set out in Table 11.6.

Table 11.6   Composition of 23rd Seanad

	Panels	University seats	Taoiseach's nominees	Total
Affiliation:				
Fianna Fáil	22	0	6	28
Fine Gael	14	0	0	14
Labour	6	0	0	6
Sinn Féin	1	0	0	1
PDs	0	0	2	2
Green Party	0	0	2	2
Independents	0	6	1	7
Gender:				
Male	35	5	7	47
Female	8	1	4	13
Total	43	6	11	60

Note: Ivana Bacik, a member of the Labour Party, is included as an Independent as she will not be taking the Labour Party whip in the Seanad.

Conclusion

The Seanad election carries very little suspense. The only open vote occurs in the university seats and here the incumbents have a major advantage. The 23rd Seanad is a more politically diverse institution than most of its predecessors, with representatives from Sinn Féin and the Green Party taking up seats there for the first time. Indeed, the campaign strategy pursued by Labour and Sinn Féin is also a new departure. Against the odds, the government maintained its majority, with Fianna Fáil securing a stronger vote than had been anticipated during the campaign, a trend that mirrored that of the general election. In many ways, Fine Gael was the underperformer in the election, securing fewer seats than its political strength should have generated. It alone remained outside the voting pacts pursued by all of the other parties.

Notes

* Background research for this chapter comes from interviews with successful and unsuccessful candidates, party officials, personnel from nominating bodies, staff in the Seanad and personal observation of the canvassing process.
1. Quoted in Jerome Reilly, 'Senators irked as RTE ignores their elections', *Sunday Independent*, 17 June 2007.
2. For further discussion, see John Coakley and Maurice Manning, 'The Senate elections', pp. 195–214 in Michael Marsh and Paul Mitchell (eds), *How Ireland Voted 1997* (Boulder, CO: Westview and PSAI Press, 1999).
3. These functions and potential reforms are discussed in detail in the 2004 *Report on Seanad Reform*, completed by the Seanad Éireann Committee on Procedure and Privileges.
4. This feature was clearly demonstrated in Coakley and Manning, 'The Senate elections'.
5. Prior to 2004, Oireachtas members holding a County or City Council seat were doubly qualified to vote, although each person could vote only once.
6. Candidates unsure of their chances of receiving an Oireachtas nomination may initially enter the competition for a nomination from a nominating body only to turn it down once they are certain of an 'inside' nomination.
7. Michael Gallagher and Liam Weeks, 'The subterranean election of the Seanad', pp. 197–211 in Michael Gallagher, Michael Marsh and Paul Mitchell (eds), *How Ireland Voted 2002* (Basingstoke: Palgrave Macmillan, 2003), p. 203.
8. Fine Gael's strategy in 2002 is discussed in ibid., pp. 202, 208.
9. Postal voting is used in Seanad elections. The ballot is secret but voting must be witnessed by a designated person, from a list that includes the county manager, county registrar or a garda superintendent for the vocational panels. Similarly, graduate voters must have their secret ballot witnessed, although they are not restricted to the designated list of witnesses.
10. See Mark Hennessy, 'Greens to vote for FF Senators', *Irish Times*, 10 July 2007.
11. *Report on Seanad Reform* (2004).
12. More detailed consideration of this point is included in Gallagher and Weeks, 'The subterranean election of the Seanad'.

13. Discussion on the nominees appeared in all newspapers. All the main points are covered in Stephen Collins, 'Taoiseach does it his own way', *Irish Times*, 4 August 2007.
14. See Fergus Finlay, 'The Seanad is a waste of taxpayers millions and should be abolished', *Irish Examiner*, 7 August 2007.

12
Government Formation in 2007

*Eoin O'Malley**

Background

The 2007 election pitted alternative governments against each other: the incumbent government of Fianna Fáil and the Progressive Democrats against the self-styled 'Alliance for Change' of Fine Gael and Labour. The politics of coalition formation is important not only once the election has revealed the numbers that determine the possible government options, but also before the election, because voters may make their choices on the basis of possible governments, and if certain governments are perceived as unviable this may affect a party's level of support. This may help to explain Fine Gael's disastrous performance in 2002.[1] It is also important because the electoral system, PR-STV, allows voters to rank order candidates and by implication parties. Voters can ensure that if their vote is transferred it passes to their party's indicated preferred coalition partner.[2]

In 2002 Fine Gael and Labour had contested the election as independent parties, despite the best efforts of the former. Labour, under Ruairí Quinn, refused to agree a transfer pact, fearing that the larger party might bring the smaller party down with it or that Fine Gael would be boosted at Labour's expense.[3] That said, in 2002 Labour had indicated that the Rainbow government was its preferred option.

In 2007 Fine Gael and Labour, under new leaders Enda Kenny and Pat Rabbitte, presented an alterative to a Fianna Fáil-led government at the election. With both Fianna Fáil and the PDs indicating that their preferred option was a continuation of their government, the election could be viewed as offering voters a clear choice and this gave a focus to media interest in the campaign. The possible governments that could be formed and the likelihood of these possibilities were the centre of much speculation in the long run-up to the election. This gave the campaign a 'horse race' quality, following the varying fortunes of the two stated governments on offer, as well as the parties as individual entities (see Table 12.1).

Table 12.1   Vote intention for alternative coalition governments

	May 2006	October 2006	December 2006	February 2007	April 2007	11 May 2007	22 May 2007	Result
Fianna Fáil and PDs	34	43	43	38	37	38	43	44
Fine Gael and Labour	43	37	38	38	41	41	37	37

Source: TNS mrbi/*Irish Times* polls.

However, in December 2006 an estimated 57 per cent of the electorate believed that the incumbent government would be returned, whereas just 17 per cent thought the alternative coalition was possible, even with the support of the Green Party.[4] That said, opinion polls registering party support levels through much of 2006 suggested that the Fianna Fáil–PD government was not going to be returned, but that Fine Gael's recovery was not sufficient to allow it to provide the basis for any new coalition, even with Green Party support.[5] If neither government won a majority then the likely alternative would be led by Fianna Fáil in a repeat of the 'any government as long as it's Fianna Fáil' pattern that has emerged since 1989.[6] It was assumed that Fianna Fáil would lose seats and in that case only Labour might be big enough to form a government with Fianna Fáil. In this context attention focused on the Labour Party which, it was thought, might be pivotal to any government formation, with the media trying unsuccessfully to force the Labour leader to admit that he would lead Labour into office with Fianna Fáil if a Fine Gael–Labour coalition was unviable.

Post-election options

Though much was made prior to the election of the chances of the various possible governments (as outlined in chapters 1 and 9), it is only after an election takes place and the size of the various parties is established that we know which possibilities are feasible. For instance, few, if any, would have predicted a Fianna Fáil–PD coalition before the 1989 election. The fact that the two parties' Dáil strengths combined to give them together a bare majority changed each party's outlook.

The requirement for a formal vote of investiture means that a Taoiseach needs the support of 83 of the 166 TDs in order to be elected, assuming no one abstains. The election of the Ceann Comhairle, who chairs the sessions,[7] takes place before the nominations for Taoiseach, so there are 165 voting members in those votes. Electing a Ceann Comhairle from the other side of the house therefore reduces one's target by neutralising a vote against. This has occurred on a number of occasions.[8]

Table 12.2 Party seat strengths in the 166-member 30th Dáil

	Seats
Fianna Fáil	78
Fine Gael	51
Labour	20
Green Party	6
Sinn Féin	4
PDs	2
Independents	5*

* Of which two were FF 'gene pool', two left-leaning and one FG 'gene pool'.

The results of the 2007 election meant that neither of the two alternative governments presented to the electorate, the incumbent Fianna Fáil–PD coalition or Fine Gael plus Labour (even with the Greens), could form a majority government (see Table 12.2). The outgoing government, with 80 seats, could probably still have re-formed with the help of three Independents. Though a repeat of the 1997–2002 government between these two parties would have been possible, it would have been much less secure. In 1997, the combination of Fianna Fáil, the PDs and the 'gene pool' Independents[9] constituted 84 votes; in 2007, that combination could be assured of only 82 votes, so one additional Independent was necessary (see Table 12.3). There were also some serious question marks about the reliability of some TDs' support. Beverley Flynn at the time was under threat of being declared

Table 12.3 Some post-election coalition options

	Dáil votes
Pre-election government options:	
FG/Labour/Greens	77
FF + PDs	80
Some minority government options:	
FF + 'gene pool'	80
FG/Labour/Greens/FG 'gene pool' + left Independents + Flynn	81
Some majority government options:	
FF/PDs + 'gene pool' + one other Independent	83
FF/Greens	84
FF/PDs/Greens	86
FF/PDs/Greens + 'gene pool' Independents	88
FF/Labour	98

bankrupt, which would have resulted in her ceasing to be eligible to remain a TD, arising out of her unsuccessful libel action against RTÉ; there were concerns over the health of Jackie Healy-Rae; newly elected Fianna Fáil TD Mattie McGrath was being charged with assault and, had he been convicted, may not have been in a position to vote in the Dáil and would certainly have had to be expelled from the party; and Dr Jim McDaid was seen as 'unreliable' following friction with the leadership around his selection as a candidate. A repeat of the 1997–2002 government was just one of the 1,040 mathematically possible winning coalitions, but given Fianna Fáil's size and the disparity among the other parties, it was a near certainty that any government to actually achieve office would be led by Fianna Fáil.

Enda Kenny declared repeatedly that he was not giving up on the possibility of putting a government together. He may have retained some hope that his alternative government could achieve power, or perhaps he wanted to put the other parties under pressure in government formation. For a combination not involving Fianna Fáil to have had a reasonable chance of success would, however, have required a coalition of Labour, Greens, the PDs, Fine Gael, three Independents (two left-wing and one Fine Gael gene pool), as well as relying on Beverley Flynn to make good on an earlier suggestion that she would support Kenny for Taoiseach.[10] This could have given Kenny 84 votes. Such a government of 'everyone but Fianna Fáil' had been formed in 1948, but it seemed unlikely that the policy differences between the parties could be bridged. He made contact with all relevant groups within days of the election and he attempted to put it together, indicating to the PDs in the weeks between the election and the first meeting of the new Dáil that retention of certain controversial policies such as co-located hospitals would not be a barrier. Though doubtless not very keen on the idea anyway, the PDs, under their acting leader Mary Harney, decided that such a coalition was not achievable because the Green Party had already opened negotiations with Fianna Fáil. Even had the PDs been willing, their inclusion would have been unacceptable to Labour if they had demanded the health portfolio and the retention of their health policies as the price of their participation. The Green Party felt that Kenny was never serious in seeking to become Taoiseach; if he were serious he should have spoken to Sinn Féin, but this was never likely to happen because Sinn Féin would have been unacceptable coalition partners to many in Fine Gael and Labour – as much for its violent history and, some would assert, current activities, as for its economic policies, which would have been unacceptable to many in Fine Gael. That said, it could be argued that the gap that Fine Gael and Clann na Poblachta bridged in 1948 was as wide.

The plausible government formation options put Fianna Fáil, and Bertie Ahern as its leader, in the strongest negotiating position.[11] Given that it had a number of realistic options – a deal with Labour, the Greens or the PDs plus Independents, or some combination of these – it could use this to play off the parties against one another. For the parties involved, each might have seen an agreement as useful to its long-term interests. The Independents could demand projects or investment in their constituencies, helping to ensure their re-election. The PDs were at the point of collapse and had few resources to sustain the party out of government. The Green Party could conceivably demand certain policies on environmental issues, get two cabinet posts, a number of senate seats, and rid itself of its image as a party of protest. Given the age of Labour Party TDs (all except its newly elected TDs were in their fifties or sixties), many senior people in the Labour Party may have wanted to form a government with Fianna Fáil if only because it would be their last chance to achieve office.

Ahern claims to have 'retained the possibility of a Fianna Fáil–Labour deal, but that was killed off' a week before the election.[12] This is disingenuous as Labour could not have accepted such overtures a week before the election. Nor was Ahern serious about an agreement with Labour in the aftermath of the election – at least not while other options were open. As early as 27 May, the day after the election results were known, the Independents were approached by Ahern's programme manager, Gerry Hickey. Over the following week, the Greens and PDs were also approached and Ahern let it be known that his preferred government was an oversized coalition with the Greens, the PDs and some Independents. Such a government would have a parliamentary base of at least 89 seats. This choice may have seemed surprising as Ahern had considered Green economic policies 'to be a bit wobbly and scary... if we were going to go into coalition with them they would have to temper some of their more extreme policies', although at the same time he had highlighted what he saw as Fianna Fáil's green credentials.[13] Retaining the support of the PDs and Independents gave Ahern a guarantee against Green Party threats, and minimised any one group's bargaining power. An agreement with Labour would have given the minor party an effective veto, as would a government of Fianna Fáil and the Green Party on their own. Bringing in Labour would also have been more 'expensive' in terms of cabinet places as it could reasonably have expected four seats and might have demanded five. The Fianna Fáil–Green–PD plus Independents government also gave the impression of novelty and change. Yet, although this was Ahern's preferred government, it was still some way from being achieved.

The formation process and Programme for Government

In the run-up to the election the Green Party leader spoke of Bertie Ahern as a political 'dead man walking' and said that no party could consider serving in a government led by him because of uncertainty about his personal finances.[14] Fine Gael tried to put the Greens under pressure by raising the issue again on 28 May, and a few days later Green TD Ciarán Cuffe wrote in his blog that a 'deal with Fianna Fáil would be a deal with the devil'. The negotiations to elect a Taoiseach on 14 June, the day the new Dáil was due to meet, could have taken place under the cloud of suspicion raised by the opening statement of the Mahon tribunal's Quarryvale module into issues related to certain planning issues. In particular, it was to investigate the allegations that Bertie Ahern had received money in relation to the re-zoning of lands. This issue was sidelined as the negotiating parties said they would wait for the report of the tribunal to be published. The Green Party at its conference in 2007[15] and in its manifesto spoke consistently about achieving office, and the leadership knew that the only way to realise this was an agreement with Ahern.

Negotiations

On 1 June Gerry Hickey, the Taoiseach's programme manager, opened contact with the Greens and in turn the Greens sent a document outlining their core policy proposals, which included a carbon tax and an end to corporate donations. Negotiating teams were chosen and policy documents exchanged. The teams comprised Fianna Fáil ministers Brian Cowen, Séamus Brennan and Noel Dempsey, and Green TD John Gormley, defeated TD and economic spokesperson Dan Boyle, and the party's general secretary, Dónal Geoghegan. On Sunday 3 June the two sides met for a few hours' 'cordial and constructive' discussions. The Green Party set a week for the negotiations and fixed the following weekend for a meeting of its party members who, under the party's rules, had to ratify any agreement by a two-thirds majority. Talks continued, but according to sources in the Green Party '[n]othing happened in the first five days of negotiations. Nothing.' Apparently the meetings raised issues and identified common ground, but when it came to an area of disagreement, the issue was parked and they moved on to another policy. This was described by a Fianna Fáil source as 'normal practice for negotiations'. Though there was some disquiet among the Greens about the apparent inclusion of the PDs, the negotiations continued with a deadline for Thursday, and then Friday. Given that the PD and Fianna Fáil manifestos were largely compatible, the PDs were kept informed of the negotiations with the Green Party at advisor and programme manager level. The PDs' acting leader was aware of the weak negotiating position of her party and allowed Ahern to construct the government as long as he kept her informed. Talks with the Greens broke down late on Friday night, 8 June, and though many in the media assumed at the weekend that the possibility of a deal was lost, John Gormley said he was 'very disappointed' at the breakdown and Fianna Fáil made contact again on the Sunday. There was speculation that the breakdown was tactical, or that the party leader, Trevor Sargent, or the party's 'reference group', which included the party leader, the party's national coordinator and the chairperson of the national council, had overruled Gormley and Boyle, who wanted a deal, but this is denied. It is claimed that Fianna Fáil was just not offering any concessions to the Green Party.

In the meantime, a number of Independent TDs had agreed deals with Bertie Ahern through his programme manager. The number of agreements was unclear: Ahern said three, but four TDs were said to have one – the last, Beverley Flynn, claimed she had made a verbal agreement with the Taoiseach.[16] The written deals mainly concerned the provision of resources to local amenities in those TDs' constituencies, though one also included wider issues. One TD read parts of his agreement into the Dáil record. This was four pages long, with 12 sections, and it caused some controversy as it could be alleged that this was buying parliamentary support at the taxpayers' expense. Ahern told the Dáil that,

> ... as leader of Fianna Fáil I entered into political arrangements with Deputies Lowry, Healy-Rae and Finian McGrath. I have no arrangement with Deputy Flynn ... The issues discussed, as is normal and appropriate, are covered in the national development plan, Transport 21 and the multi-annual capital programmes for public expenditure ... The projects are not outside planned current or capital expenditure in the years ahead ... Several times I have tried to bring forward initiatives more quickly and efficiently and I intend to honour these political commitments to the three Deputies ... With regard to contact, the Members concerned will have direct contact with the Whip's office, as has been the case for the past decade.[17]

The agreements are with Bertie Ahern as leader of Fianna Fáil and were not seen or agreed by his party or the other parties in government. Within Fianna Fáil it is claimed that these are non-deals, merely offering Independents the opportunity to put their names to projects that were already going ahead. The Independents could say, however, that while many projects are promised, they can ensure that theirs are implemented.

The breakdown in talks instigated by the Greens, tactical or not, may have concentrated Fianna Fáil minds. The talks continued and reached agreement on the night of 12 June when the two party leaders met to discuss government formation; that is, ministerial posts. The Greens had looked for an end to new road-building and a stop to the controversial M3 road which would run past the historic Tara site in County Meath. They also wanted a carbon tax in the lifetime of the government, a moratorium on new co-located hospitals, a ban on corporate donations, and an end to the use of Shannon airport by US troops for 'extraordinary rendition'. Some of these the Greens certainly did not achieve: the M3 would go ahead and corporate donations would continue. Whether they achieved any of these was debatable and the subject of some controversy. Yet the Greens held their member conference and, despite protests outside from groups once close to the Green Party, such as the anti-war movement (see photo section at the front of the book), the special conference passed the Programme for Government easily, supported by 87 per cent of delegates – a result that 'shocked' the party leadership. Rather honourably, the party leader, Trevor Sargent, referring to his earlier commitment that he would not lead his party into government with Fianna

Fáil, resigned his leadership and said he would not seek a place at cabinet. The Green Party's internal decision-making contrasted sharply with that of Fianna Fáil. Fianna Fáil's negotiators referred only to Ahern and, almost as an afterthought, a meeting of the parliamentary party was arranged at which Ahern's candidature for Taoiseach was ratified unanimously following a one-and-a-half-hour meeting. The agreement was distributed only after one TD complained that Green Party members had access to it. Though some, particularly those representing rural constituencies, had expressed reservations about coalition with the Greens, few were in a position to oppose the party leadership, especially on the back of a third electoral victory.

The following day, 14 June, Bertie Ahern was elected Taoiseach for the third time in a row with 89 votes. As well as 77 Fianna Fáil TDs (one had been elected Ceann Comhairle earlier in the day), support came from the six Green Party TDs, both PDs, and four Independents. The Green Party was taunted in the chamber by Fine Gael and Labour, though some in Labour acknowledge that this was inspired by jealousy as much as anger. Many of these taunts related to the Programme for Government, with the Green Party accused of selling out too cheaply.

The Programme for Government

During the debate on the nomination of the government, Enda Kenny accused the Green Party of 'naively' wandering into a Programme for Government with Fianna Fáil written all over it.[18] Labour's leader, Pat Rabbitte, told the Dáil that the Programme for Government was 'from the Greens' point of view, a policy-free zone'.[19] When pressed as to what the major concessions to the Greens were, the Taoiseach cited the Commission for Taxation – which is an advisory group rather than a concrete policy. Even Dan Boyle, one of the Greens' negotiators, claimed that the Programme for Government was 'not an ideal document. It's not even a good document, but there are good elements.'[20]

The 2007 Programme for Government was much longer than previous ones – 33,000 words compared to 14,000 in 2002 and 7,500 in 1997. The longer programme would seem to suggest that the Greens and Fianna Fáil were suspicious of each other. The document locks each into specific policies by putting more in writing and thereby minimising the areas for potential future disagreement. Parties that are ideologically similar, by contrast, may have no need of such a long agreement.[21]

The programme is taken largely from the Fianna Fáil manifesto. Using a computer program to measure the similarity of texts for detecting plagiarism among students (turnitin.com) we get a score on a 'similarity index' between the Fianna Fáil manifesto and the new Programme for Government. According to this analysis 76 per cent of the programme came directly from the Fianna Fáil manifesto, with only 'the Government' substituted for 'Fianna Fáil' in places.[22] While some of the Fianna Fáil manifesto did not make it into the Programme for Government, most of what was removed consisted of section introductions outlining the apparent achievements of the previous government. This could be interpreted as a capitulation by the Green Party. However, given that the Green Party constitutes about 7 per cent of the government's parliamentary support, the contribution of a quarter to the Programme for Government would be an impact significantly greater than its size might justify. Much of what is added does have Green fingerprints on it. Nevertheless, a problem for the Green Party is that many of the commitments or additions that the party achieved are so vague that they are not commitments at all. In the programme, the word 'review' appears 49 times, and 'examine' 23 times. Typical of this is the commitment to 'mandate the HSE to publish a comprehensive report on the fluoridation of water'.[23] This certainly does not achieve the Greens' desired objective of an end to water fluoridation and leaves ample opportunity to block any such move. The Greens claim that there are areas with concrete commitments and that the Programme for Government was not of great importance to them per se. Rather more important was securing the ability to implement those policies through the control of key ministries. While it will certainly be difficult to block the Green Party ministers in their efforts to achieve some of the policies on which there are commitments in the programme, any further policies and any legislation will need to be agreed in cabinet. Given their lack of ministerial experience, the Greens might find they are unable to achieve much in the way of significant changes in policy.

Cabinet selection

Whereas most European prime ministers can select as ministers individuals not in parliament, the Taoiseach is constitutionally restricted to members of the Dáil or Seanad, with at most two belonging to the Seanad. Within this restriction, the Taoiseach has few constraints as to whom he can choose for his cabinet. Politically, however, the Taoiseach knows that he is restricted by the need to form and maintain a government. The Green Party had exerted pressure to have Mary Harney moved from Health and Children, though she was never offered a move to Foreign Affairs, and she would have refused. The Green Party thought that two cabinet seats were necessary if the party were to be a full player in the government, and it had three portfolios in mind – Transport, Energy and Environment. In the event it obtained two full cabinet posts: one being Environment, Heritage and Local Government, and the other Communications, Energy and Natural Resources. These are senior ministries, one of which (Environment) also enables ministers to be associated with many popular infrastructural projects. The ministries will put them in position to achieve some of the more vague promises of the Programme for Government. Because Sargent ruled himself out of cabinet, two other TDs were to be chosen. John Gormley, as the next most senior TD, the head of the negotiating team and the 'official party candidate' for leader (he was later elected as leader), was an obvious choice and he went to Environment. The second Green TD in cabinet was Éamon Ryan. He was considered a hardworking and competent performer in the Dáil committee on his new portfolio of Energy, and had been considered of sufficient quality that Pat Rabbitte had suggested that Labour could support his bid for the Irish presidency in 2004.

For the 12 Fianna Fáil posts, Bertie Ahern was as cautious as he had been in the past. He brought in only one new minister, Brian Lenihan, who had sat at cabinet as a 'super-junior' since December 2005. As an extra seat (compared with 2002–07) was needed for coalition partners, this meant that two Fianna Fáil cabinet ministers were not reappointed. One, John O'Donoghue, was made Ceann Comhairle, having previously been demoted in 2002. It was suggested that he was punished for failing to achieve two seats for Fianna Fáil in South Kerry, though this is hardly plausible, as he had not achieved this in 2002 either. The other minister, Dick Roche, returned to a post outside the cabinet as Minister of State responsible for European Affairs, which he had occupied from 2002 to 2004. He had attracted much media and opposition criticism, but so had Martin Cullen in Transport. Some in the media argued that Cullen was safe because there were no other ministers in his region, the south-east. The extent to which ministerial selection is ever made on the basis of geography, however, is debatable.[24] Of the outgoing cabinet, nine (including the Taoiseach) retained their existing portfolios. The lack of turnover means the cabinet is ageing somewhat. The average age is 51 and the youngest member, at 42, is hardly new, having spent 20 years in the Dáil. The cabinet also has more Dublin-based ministers than any cabinet since 1973 – seven of the 15 represent Dublin constituencies.

One of the problems for Ahern in building coalitions is that he is forced to give up some of the prizes most cherished by his own party, government ministries. Furthermore, his conservatism in building cabinets increases impatience among backbench TDs wishing to advance their careers. Though he denies it, it was probably in order to maintain backbench loyalty that Ahern announced he would increase the number of junior ministries from 17 to 20. Trevor Sargent became minister for food, and the other posts went to Fianna Fáil TDs, some of whom had been critics of Ahern in the previous Dáil. This led some TDs to complain that their loyalty had not been rewarded. There was further unhappiness at the suggestion that Beverley Flynn might expect a ministerial post if she returned to Fianna Fáil.[25] However, Ahern's promise of a mid-term reshuffle, expected in 2009, will probably concentrate the minds of those in posts and keep aspiring TDs loyal.

Conclusion: the new government's prospects

The 2007 government formation was not simply more interesting than might have been predicted, it was also ground-breaking. In going into government the Green Party followed the example of a number of other Green parties in Europe. This brought Green politics to the fore in Ireland and involved Fianna Fáil in its first three-party coalition. Ahern also said that he intended this government to last five years. He has already presided over the two longest peace-time governments, both going to as near their legal limit as made no difference. However, this government might be a less secure prospect. The relationship between the PDs and the Green Party is potentially fraught with problems. Throughout the negotiations there were no tripartite talks, and the agreements were individual ones with Fianna Fáil rather than with each other. That the Greens are unwilling to acknowledge that it is a three-party coalition is not a good start – though they could be forgiven for thinking this as the participation of the PDs seems to owe more to Ahern's relationship with Mary Harney as an individual than it does to the PDs as a party. These parties are likely to be opposed ideologically on a number of issues – though they may be mutually supportive on others, such as the break-up of the ESB, local government reform, and social issues. Much will depend on them developing personal relationships in the first months of office.

Internally the Green Party may face difficulties. Within weeks of the election it had already had to swallow hard on certain issues, such as hospital co-location, as the opposition put down motions on issues that it hoped would embarrass the party when forced to support the government. It did not attempt to use its place in cabinet to influence decisions on the stamp duty payable on property purchases. The decision to go into government was a risky one for the party. It could suffer at the polls if it fails to deliver some major policies for its own electorate. Its choice of departments, Energy in particular, might be regretted, as climate change is hardly something that Ireland can do anything about on its own or one where visible benefits can be presented to the electorate. If one were able to present real improvements to people's lives through the provision of improved public transport one might be better able to argue for its decision to enter government. It feels its behaviour in government will be more important, and accused other small parties of behaving in an arrogant manner that turned off their voters.

For Fianna Fáil a third successive term is proof of that party's dominance. In an earlier edition of this book series Peter Mair predicted that Fianna Fáil's decision to accept coalition could lead it to govern indefinitely.[26] The formation of this government supports Mair's analysis, and we might continue to wonder how Fianna Fáil might be removed from office without a major realignment of the Irish party system.

Notes

*   This chapter is partially based on interviews with representatives from the three government parties who were close to the negotiations and with one Independent TD.

1. See Eoin O'Malley and Matthew Kerby, 'Chronicle of a death foretold? Understanding the decline of Fine Gael', *Irish Political Studies* 19:1 (2004), pp. 39–58.
2. Some research suggests that voters follow their preferred party's advice on these matters; see Fiachra Kennedy, 'Elite level co-ordination of party supporters: an analysis of the Irish aggregate data, 1987–1997', *Representation* 38:3 (2001), pp. 284–94; see also pp. 93–7, this volume.
3. Ruairí Quinn, *Straight Left: A Journey in Politics* (Castleknock: Hodder Headline Ireland, 2005), pp. 398–9. The party's deputy leader, Brendan Howlin, claimed that 'analysis over a long period of time [showed] that the best option for Labour is not to exclude options, but to present an independent position as a radical party': *Irish Times*, 26 October 2004. Indeed Fine Gael tends to do better when it has such a pact: see O'Malley and Kerby, 'Chronicle of a death'.
4. Stephen Collins, 'Widespread perception opposition cannot win', *Irish Times*, 1 December 2006. Despite this, the cumulative figures for the two parties suggested it was in fact a real possibility.
5. Fine Gael's support remained around the mid-20s for most of that Dáil, well below the 39 per cent it achieved in 1982 when it last formed a government from an election. Fianna Fáil, meanwhile, varied from the low to high 30s. See also Figure 1.1, p. 16 above.
6. Paul Mitchell, 'Government formation in 2002: "you can have any kind of government as long as it's Fianna Fáil" ', pp. 214–29 in Michael Gallagher, Michael Marsh and Paul Mitchell (eds), *How Ireland Voted 2002* (Basingstoke: Palgrave Macmillan, 2003).
7. The Clerk of the Dáil chairs proceedings until a Ceann Comhairle is elected (Standing Order 6.1).
8. Frank Fahy in 1948; Patrick Hogan in 1951, 1961 and 1965; John O'Connell in 1981; Seán Treacy in 1987 and 1989; and Séamus Pattison in 1997. Fahy was a Fianna Fáil TD retained by the inter-party government. Hogan was a Labour TD. Both O'Connell and Treacy were Independents who had previously been Labour TDs. The position is very attractive because the Ceann Comhairle is returned unopposed at the following election.
9. 'Gene pool' Independents are those Independent TDs who have strong ties to a particular party. Many failed to secure the nomination of the party to which they belonged and went on to win a seat as an Independent. These TDs often vote with the party they have ties to and usually support that party's nominee for Taoiseach.
10. Beverley Flynn had been elected as a Fianna Fáil TD in 2002, but was expelled in 2004 following the loss of a libel action against RTÉ. As a TD from Mayo, she indicated that she would support Enda Kenny, as a Mayo man, for Taoiseach if that were a realistic prospect.
11. Interestingly two 'power' indices used in political science, the Shapley–Shubik and the Banzhaf indices, each gave Fianna Fáil significantly more bargaining power than Fine Gael – .58 and .63 for Fianna Fáil as against .10 and .08 for Fine Gael out of a possible 1.00. Fine Gael's bargaining power was equal to that of the Greens (source: Kenneth Benoit, TCD).
12. Senan Moloney, 'Labour spurned coalition advances, says Bertie', *Irish Independent*, 18 June 2007.
13. Stephen Collins, 'Sargent rules out coalition with Fianna Fáil', *Irish Times*, 8 August 2006.
14. Liam Reid, 'Ahern a "dead man walking" – Sargent', *Irish Times*, 7 May 2007.

15. Shane Coleman, 'From protest to threshold of power', *Sunday Tribune*, 25 February 2007.
16. Miriam Donohoe, 'Flynn agus na Fianna', *Irish Times*, 30 June 2007.
17. *Dáil Debates* 637: 133, 26 June 2007.
18. *Dáil Debates* 637: 63, 14 June 2007.
19. *Dáil Debates* 637: 71, 14 June 2007.
20. Harry McGee and Shaun Connolly, 'Sargent's huge win tinged with sadness as he resigns as leader', *Irish Examiner*, 14 June 2007.
21. Kaare Strøm and Wolfgang C. Müller, 'The keys to togetherness: coalition agreements in parliamentary democracies', *Journal of Legislative Studies* 5:3–4 (1999), pp. 255–82.
22. This compares with a 54 per cent similarity rating to the Fianna Fáil manifesto of the 2002 Programme for Government.
23. 'Draft Programme for Government 12 June 2007: Final Document', p. 20.
24. See Eoin O'Malley, 'Ministerial selection in Ireland: limited choice in a political village', *Irish Political Studies* 21:3 (2006), pp. 270–82.
25. Stephen Collins, 'Ahern now master of all he surveys', *Irish Times*, 30 June 2007.
26. Peter Mair, 'The Irish party system into the 1990s', pp. 213–19 in Michael Gallagher and Richard Sinnott (eds), *How Ireland Voted 1989* (Galway: PSAI Press, 1990).

13
Fianna Fáil and Irish Party Competition

R. Kenneth Carty

Whatever issues animate the campaigns of politicians and their parties, or mobilise and engage voters, once an election outcome is known analysts inevitably want to ask whether the election in question was one marked by continuity or by change. Of course, sometimes there is evidence of both and that has certainly been the case of judgements of recent Irish general elections. Writing of the 1997 election, Michael Laver argued it 'was remarkable more for what didn't happen than for what did', but he then went on to conclude that it ushered in a 'more or less permanent era of coalition government . . . which meant a much enhanced role for the Labour party'.[1] After the 2002 contest John Coakley suggested that 'the Irish party system arrived in the twenty-first century with few signs of age', although he also conceded that there was now 'substantial support for new political forces'.[2]

Much of this measured ambivalence seems to flow from differing interpretations of the continuing place and capacities of Fianna Fáil, whose size and position have long structured Irish electoral competition. In 1992 Peter Mair concluded that after 1989 it had 'become just another party'.[3] The next election led Laver to conclude that Fianna Fáil's vote would have to drop considerably (something he saw no evidence for) before 'the core logic of the Irish party system' changed.[4] But then, after the 2002 election, Coakley argued that it was clear that the party's 'overall direction has been one of [long-term] decline'.[5] Putting the 2007 election in context, and assessing what it tells us about the shifting nature of the country's political life, requires that we understand Fianna Fáil and the changes that are reshaping it. The party has obviously maintained its pre-eminent place in the system – after all, it has formed the government after the last six elections. But this success increasingly rests on shifting sand.

The place of Fianna Fáil in Irish party competition

Ireland's electoral politics have always revolved around Fianna Fáil. During the first decade after independence the issue was whether this self-styled slightly constitutional republican party would play by democratic rules. Then, in the decades that followed, the central political question quickly became: were Fianna Fáil electoral victories and governments inevitable? With the accession of a new post-revolutionary generation to power in the late 1960s, internal cracks in the partisan monolith began to appear which had the effect of destabilising the entire political system. In the 1970s and 1980s the party's legendary loyalty and discipline cracked: it quarrelled incessantly over its leadership and some prominent dissidents ultimately left to form the Progressive Democrats. These internal party conflicts were at the root of much of the electoral turmoil in a decade during which Irish voters were sent to the polls in five increasingly indecisive general elections. In the years since, Fianna Fáil continued to be the pivot around which Irish politics centred but, with its easy electoral dominance ended, it has had to rethink, and then relearn, how to govern.

As one of the twentieth century's most successful democratic political parties Fianna Fáil has long been accustomed to the prerogatives of office and to thinking of itself as the country's natural governing party. For decades it argued that coalitions were weak and divisive and that the only possible good government was one-party government. While this may have been an obvious electoral claim for the only party that could hope to command enough seats in the Dáil to form a government on its own, it soon became an essential feature of Fianna Fáil's belief system and political catechism. Abandoning beliefs is never easy and it eventually fell to Charles Haughey to lead the party towards a new style of coalition politics after the 1989 election. Albert Reynolds, instinctively opposed to coalitions, saw his subsequent short leadership flounder over the issue and it was left to Bertie Ahern to make it clear that the party was committed to building and maintaining stable coalition relationships. Though Fianna Fáil won 81 seats in 2002, the same number it had secured in February 1982 when it resolutely chose minority over coalition government, Ahern opted to form a potentially unnecessary and politically costly (in terms of cabinet seats, junior ministries and Seanad appointments) government partnership with the apostates who led the Progressive Democrats. In doing so he made it clear he recognised that the old days of Fianna Fáil *versus* the rest had gone and the future of government formation was now Fianna Fáil *and any of* the rest.[6]

Fianna Fáil is a leader-centred party so that struggles over the succession, and the style of resulting leaderships, have shaped the evolving character of the party. Because the six men who have led the party have also all been Taoiseach in their turn, the conduct of Fianna Fáil's leadership politics has shaped the wider party system. The years of intra-party conflict over Haughey's leadership contributed to the considerable fragmentation of the party system. In the decade after 1977, during which he moved to seize and then aggressively defend the party's leadership, the number of candidates running in general elections grew by 24 per cent and the vote for the three traditional big parties shrank from 93 to 78 per cent. The replacement of Haughey with Reynolds in 1992 did little to reposition Fianna Fáil and the latter quickly became the shortest serving leader (and Taoiseach) in the party's history. Ahern's political genius has been to take the party to a position where it now prefers, and so is able to dominate, coalition-making in a newly balanced party system.[7] Though, as Gallagher notes in chapter 6 (p. 83), he has been far from the party's most successful vote-getter, he is an extraordinarily skilful politician. By the time the 2007 election was called the 55-year-old Ahern was already the second longest serving Fianna Fáil leader and Taoiseach in the party's history. If he serves another full term, as he has publicly declared he intends to do, Ahern will come close to matching de Valera's post-1937 constitution time in office.

This overly simple sketch of Fianna Fáil moving from its politically suspect outsider status in the 1920s, to its mid-century dominance as the natural governing party, to its current place as the pivot in a restructured coalitional system, captures the essence of much of the change in the history and character of Irish political competition. Yet there is more to the nuances of the story that needs to be appreciated if we are to fully understand what has happened to Fianna Fáil in recent years and what it portends for the future of Irish party politics.

The changing destiny of Fianna Fáil

As Fianna Fáil faced the 2007 election it must have done so with at least some trepidation. Though it had governed for almost 23 years of the previous three decades, its long-term electoral trajectory was hardly encouraging. Table 13.1 illustrates the gross change in the party's electoral position after eight elections following its historic victory in 1977 when Jack Lynch led it to a rout of the Fine Gael–Labour coalition, capturing the largest parliamentary majority in the history of the state. It seems clear that Fianna Fáil had suffered a serious decline over this period. From an electorate that had grown by over 875,000 the party found itself attracting almost 41,000 fewer votes than it had 25 years earlier. Simply put, the electorate grew by over 41 per cent but the Fianna Fáil vote fell by five. Any party's immediate electoral concern is for its vote share which shapes parliamentary outcomes and by 2002 it had fallen by nine percentage points from its 1977 peak.[8]

In the 2007 general election Fianna Fáil finally saw the raw number of voters supporting it climb back above the 800,000 mark for the first time in three decades, but they did so in an electorate that was now 45 per cent larger and with no increase in its vote share over 2002. These numbers hint at the magnitude of the change that has reshaped the Irish party system and Fianna Fáil's place as the major player in it. They do not, however, tell the whole story for it is not simply one of a general, secular Fianna Fáil decline, although that, as we shall see, there certainly has been. There are a number of other important dimensions to the changes that have altered the basic patterns of the country's electoral competition.

Table 13.1 Fianna Fáil's quarter-century from 1977

	Electorate	FF vote	FF vote share (%)
1977	2,118,606	811,615	50.6
2002	3,002,173	770,748	41.5

The first of these is a significant decline in the proportion of the growing electorate which is actually voting, a change which must account for some of the reduction in the sheer numbers voting for Fianna Fáil. Electoral participation, which had long hovered just over 75 per cent, dipped a few points in the two elections of 1982. Then, in 1989 the numbers voting plunged sharply by five percentage points and continued to decline, falling sharply again in 2002 to below 62 per cent – the total drop over the three decades from 1969 was a full 15 percentage points. The modest recovery in the turnout rate during 2007 will have contributed to the increased total numbers supporting Fianna Fáil, although not by enough to increase the party's vote share.

It is tempting to speculate that the decision of so many Irish voters to become non-voters reflected their response to the internal chaos in Fianna Fáil as well as to the political confusion generated by the proliferation of candidates and minor parties that erupted into the party system during the 1980s. However, the reality is surely more complex, for virtually the same sharp decline in voter turnout occurred across the large majority of established Western democracies in those same years.[9] A large variety of competing explanations have emerged pointing to institutional and organisational dimensions of modern political processes, to changing socio-economic conditions, to new social-capital cultural realities, to new generational experiences, or to the impact of globalisation. Whatever the reason, and any comprehensive explanation would likely take many of these factors into account, the global character of this pattern suggests that the Irish turnout decline reflected more than just the immediate features of its contemporary competitive alignments. The parties, starting with Fianna Fáil, obviously felt the immediate brunt of voter abstentions, but it was not clear that they had any easy, specifically Irish, response to this significant shift in the behaviour of electorates across the established Western democracies.

Irish voters were not only turning out in reduced numbers. They were also abandoning the strong partisan identifications and allegiances that had, for decades after independence, shaped and stabilised a system that was relatively weakly rooted in distinctive socio-economic cleavages. Michael Marsh reports that studying the 2002 election reveals that only about one-quarter of the electorate felt 'close' to a particular party, although about the same numbers admitted feeling 'closer to one party than the others'. This put Ireland at the very bottom of a league table of 13 established Western democracies in the extent to which its electorate identified itself with a political party.[10]

Analysis of survey data suggests that fully one-half of the electorate now has no party identification – this in a system where socio-economic cues provide comparatively little partisan guidance. Much of the collapse in the standing partisan identifications once held by most of the electorate appears to have occurred in the past two decades. In 1981, at the start of the most tumultuous decade of political change, less than 40 per cent reported having no party attachment; by 2002, fully three-quarters of the electorate said they had none.[11] The impact of this shows up in a number of significant ways. First, the strength of intra-party transferring – the solidarity of the party vote – has been declining, with consequences for nomination strategies (it risks making over-nomination more costly) and for any vote-seat bonus that might be extracted at the constituency or national level (for more on transferring and nomination strategies, see chapters 6 and 4). Second, the capacity of parties to direct inter-party transferring is reduced where voters are less inclined to take partisan direction.[12] With parties less able to direct their voters, this makes pre-election bargaining, which in turn offers the possibility of providing electors with an effective choice of alternate governments, less viable. But, perhaps more important, the significant de-alignment of the electorate leaves the country with what Marsh has called a 'floating party system'. With no anchors stabilising party competition short-term factors, including the electoral campaigns themselves, become more important and consequently are increasingly likely to have a 'big impact' on electoral outcomes.[13]

The rhythm and dynamic of party competition, and ultimately Fianna Fáil's place in the politics of government-making, was fundamentally altered by the electoral fragmentation and volatility of the support patterns of those continuing to vote, and the slow adjustment to its consequences. Figure 13.1, which records the effective number of parties at the level of the electorate as well as the Dáil, provides a clear portrait of the changing fragmentation of the party system. It illustrates just how much the election of 1987 – in which the Progressive Democrats emerged out of Fianna Fáil, a Workers' Party challenged on the left, and Sinn Féin returned to electoral politics – was a major turning point. That contest saw the total number of individuals running for a seat in the Dáil jump by almost 30 per cent. The result of this proliferation of choices was a level of electoral fractionalisation not seen since the 1940s. The vote share of the three large established parties plunged by 16 percentage points (from 94 to 78 per cent of the vote) leading to a drop of ten points in their share of seats in the Dáil which fell below 90 per cent for the first time in two decades.

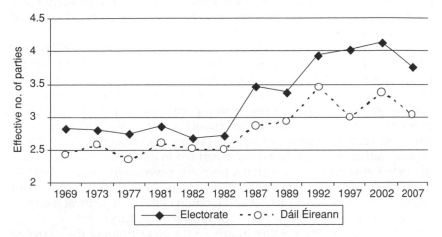

Figure 13.1 Party system fragmentation, 1969–2007

At first it appeared that Fianna Fáil had survived the electoral dislocations of 1987 more successfully than its opponents. The party's vote share declined only one percentage point from the previous election, while Fine Gael's share collapsed from 39 per cent to just over 27. That marked decline in Fine Gael support has proved difficult to reverse and the party has not won as much as 30 per cent of the vote in a general election since.[14] For its part, Labour saw its vote eroded by almost a third in 1987, but it was soon to recover and resume its traditional place in the party system with something over 10 per cent of the vote. These changes strengthened Fianna Fáil's hand as compared to its traditional opponents and allowed the party to return to office that year as a minority government. However, they also testified to the end of several decades of predictable party competition and presaged the end of Fianna Fáil's easy electoral predominance.

Two years later saw the Greens emerge as an organised partisan force in the election that witnessed the largest single drop in voter turnout. Fianna Fáil's vote share did not drop in 1989, but two other features of that election's outcome heralded the party's new reality. First, and most immediately relevant, it won fewer seats than in 1987 and this led to Haughey's surprising decision to form a coalition with the Progressive Democrats. It was surprising because many in the party blamed the Progressive Democrat leaders and TDs for Fianna Fáil's electoral problems, and surprising because one of the party's long-standing core principles had been the rejection of coalition politics. By following its leader into a coalition the party seemed to be signalling that it recognised that there had been a qualitative change in the Irish political world and its place in it. A second, perhaps less noticed but equally significant, development was the fall of Fianna Fáil's share of the electorate to below 30 per cent for the first time since the turbulent elections of the 1920s. At those levels, it would inevitably be difficult to form a single-party government whose legitimacy wouldn't be questioned.

The fragmentation of the system increased sharply again in 1992 (Figure 13.1) with the addition of a Democratic Left party and greater support for Independents as well as Labour. That election saw another jump in the number of candidates running – by 30 per cent over 1989 – but this time Fianna Fáil paid a large electoral price. Its vote share dipped below 40 per cent for the first time since 1927 and, with just 41 per cent of the seats in the Dáil, it was again reluctantly driven to accept a coalition partner. This time it looked left – to Labour – rather than right to its former partners in the Progressive Democrats, to create a government. Though the Reynolds government collapsed in two years, the experience confirmed that while Fianna Fáil's days as a dominant single-party might be over, its size and location in the Irish political spectrum gave it a pre-eminent role in a new coalition-style politics.

However, Fianna Fáil's ability to survive the vicissitudes of the changing party system and continue to hold office for most of the last two decades, an image reinforced by its ability to form yet another, different coalition in the wake of the 2007 election, masks the reality of the party's continuing long-term secular decline. Table 13.2 reveals just how far the party has fallen. During the decade of Jack Lynch's leadership the party won, on average, over 47 per cent of the vote in three successive general elections and a clear majority of the seats in the Dáil in two of them. In the subsequent Haughey years the party's average vote declined by just over two percentage points, but that, with the fragmentation of the rest of the party system, pushed its share of the Dáil down by five points. This was enough to deprive the party of a parliamentary majority in the five contests of that decade and push it into accepting the need to practise coalition politics. Then, in four elections under Reynolds and Ahern, Fianna Fáil has again seen its vote share drop, this time more sharply to just over 40 per cent. The corresponding decline in its Dáil strength was not as great, but it has led Ahern to embrace the principle of genuine partnership as the basis for coalition governments designed to

Table 13.2   Fianna Fáil's electoral and parliamentary decline, 1969–2007

		Avg. vote share (%)	Avg. share of electorate (%)	Avg. share of Dáil seats (%)
1969–77	Lynch	47.5	36.6	52.1
1981–89	Haughey	45.2	32.7	47.2
1992–2007	Reynolds–Ahern	40.4	26.4	45.8

last full parliamentary terms. Now attracting the active support of just over one-quarter of the electorate, Fianna Fáil can hardly credibly claim, as it long sought to do in its heyday under de Valera and Lemass, that it is the sole legitimate political voice of the republic.

Fianna Fáil's continuing ability to maintain its pre-eminence in the face of its vote losses has been made easier by a similar decline in Fine Gael's vote and seat shares over the same period. During the Lynch decade Fine Gael regularly won about a third of the votes and seats; in recent elections it has managed only about a quarter of the vote and a similar, but rather variable, seat share.[15] Although it remains the largest of the other parties in the system, its substantially reduced size means that forming politically viable alternative coalitions to Fianna Fáil is inherently more difficult. However, there are a number of other factors that have played an important part in maintaining Fianna Fáil's central place in Irish electoral competition. These have worked at the level of individual voters' political commitments, the party's own election strategy, and the impact of the electoral system's translation of votes into seats. Each deserves some attention.

As we have already seen, the Irish party system appears to be in a period of marked de-alignment with significantly fewer electors identifying with political parties. There are, however, definable differences across the system with most of the remaining identifiers associating with the three long-established major parties.[16] Among them Fianna Fáil does best. It has the largest number of self-identifying partisans of any of the parties and its partisans admit to having stronger and more stable attachments to their party than do those of the others. It remains true that such partisans generally constitute the most stable voters and, in particular, Fianna Fáil's partisans are more likely to vote for their party than are those who identify with the other parties. At the same time, the weaker identifications of its opponents' partisans may help account for the fact that Fianna Fáil 'does not repel transfers as it used to'.[17] Thus, while Fianna Fáil has had the most to lose with the erosion of the traditional base of the system in a set of family socialised party identifications, the course of these changes may have left it comparatively better off – at least as the process has evolved to date.

As the party's vote came under increasing pressure Fianna Fáil's national campaign managers responded by increasing central control over the candidate selection process at the heart of their electoral strategy.[18] This was perhaps most obvious in their often controversial attempts to direct the numbers and identities of local constituency teams of candidates, but no less important was the cumulative impact on the party's national electoral strategy. Figure 13.2 traces the changes in the numbers of candidates nominated by Fianna Fáil over the last four decades and it is clear that there has been a regular and deliberate pattern to it. Recognising that there are organisational and electoral costs to nominating too many candidates – in disruptive internal party competition, in vote fragmentation, and in transfer losses – the party has been systematically reducing the number it nominates in order to maximise its seat return.[19] In the last three elections the number of the party's nominees has stabilised at about two-thirds of the size of the Dáil, a ratio that has not been so low since the 1930s. The largest number the party ever nominated was in 1977 (89 per cent), when the national executive added an unusually large number of candidates to those chosen locally but, as its vote subsequently declined, Fianna Fáil responded strategically by reducing the numbers it nominated, even while the total number of all candidates contesting general elections was growing by some 12 per cent. This strategy has paid off in terms of maximising the number of seats it has won given its altered vote share.

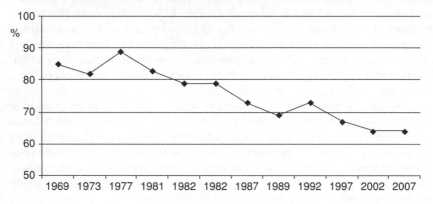

Figure 13.2   Dáil seats contested by Fianna Fáil

Virtually all electoral systems provide some advantage to the largest parties and the Irish version of the single transferable vote is no exception. It has always given some bonus to Fianna Fáil. This bonus is reflected in the 'index of proportionality', simply calculated as seats won as a percentage of votes won. With full proportionality being 100, any score over 100 represents a bonus in the sense that it indicates that a party has won more seats than proportionality would dictate it was entitled to. Figure 13.3 charts the index for Fianna Fáil over the last four decades. It indicates that the extent of the party's bonus has varied considerably from election to election but, given this was an era of often evenly balanced contests, it inevitably made a difference to the party's governing prospects. It is particularly striking that the bonuses delivered to Ahern in 1997 and 2002 were the largest ever in Fianna Fáil history; and the one he secured in 2007 was exceeded only once before – by de Valera in 1943. This jump in the bonus was skilfully engineered by the party's decision to enter into transfer pacts with potential coalition partners, which increased the inter-party transfers flowing its way.[20] Given the significant decline in the party's own vote share during this period, these especially large bonuses have been critically important for Ahern and have provided one of the pillars on which he has depended to keep Fianna Fáil in office.

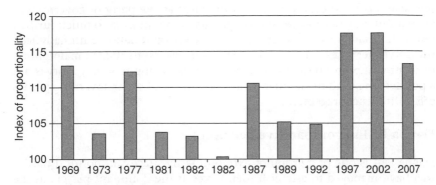

Figure 13.3 Fianna Fáil's electoral system bonus

These separate, but entwined, stories are brought together in Figure 13.4 which illustrates the general trend lines for Fianna Fáil's candidates, votes and seats over the past four decades. It reveals that they have all been continually falling as the party's dominance of the system is systematically eroded. The number of candidates has declined more sharply than its vote share, suggesting that the party's nomination strategies have been relatively

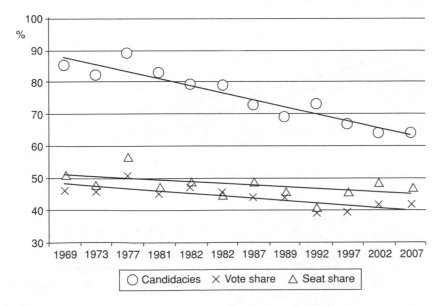

Figure 13.4 Fianna Fáil candidates, votes and seats, 1969–2007

successful at minimising the political costs of its electoral decline. That aspect of the system's competitive dynamics – bolstered, at least temporarily, in no small part by the electoral system – is reflected in the slower decline in its seat share. If it expects to maintain its status as the party of government, Fianna Fáil may need to resist dropping its nomination ratio much further, lest it stimulate a vicious cycle in which fewer candidates continually lead through fewer votes to fewer seats. Despite its success in 2007 in maintaining its dominant position in Irish politics, the party's long-term trajectory is not a positive one. And the contemporary experience of other governing parties offers little encouragement.

Fianna Fáil in comparative perspective

Fianna Fáil is one of a group of extraordinarily successful political parties that have managed to establish themselves as the dominant players in the national politics of their respective countries. This era may be drawing to a close for they all appear to be experiencing a similar long-term decline. Figure 13.5 traces the trends in voter support over the last four decades for the four most electorally successful Western European parties – Fianna Fáil, Austria's Socialists, Sweden's Social Democrats and Germany's Christian Democrats (with its partner Christian Social Union) – and two other long-dominant governing parties, Japan's Liberal Democrats and Canada's Liberals.[21] While

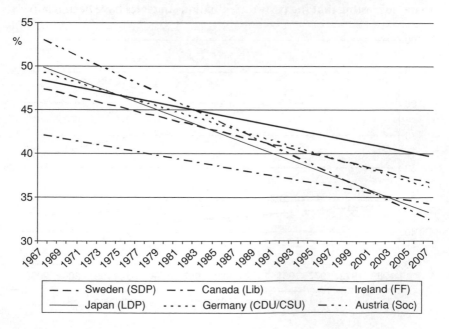

Figure 13.5   Trends in major party vote shares, 1967–2007

there is some variation in the rate of decline among the individual parties the long-term general trend across these institutionally and socially very diverse political systems is unmistakable.

Despite what we have seen about the changing cast of the Irish party system and Fianna Fáil's declining position in it, the evidence of Figure 13.5 suggests that, by comparative standards, the party has been the most successful of all in this group in meeting its challenges. Forty years ago it might have ranked fourth among these six parties, today it ranks first and appears to be in a relatively much stronger position than any of them. This seems particularly striking given Marsh's observation that levels of party attachment, assumed to stabilise support, are much lower in Ireland.[22] The looming question of Irish politics must be what might happen if Fianna Fáil becomes more like the other established, once commanding, dominant parties and shrinks to a size where it can no longer dominate party politics as easily as it has for so long.

Fianna Fáil and the party system

In forming his third government Bertie Ahern revealed just how politically promiscuous Fianna Fáil has become. In 1992 the party had coalesced with Labour, in 1997 and 2002 with the Progressive Democrats, and in 2007 it partnered with the Greens. It really has become a system of Fianna Fáil and any of the rest with simple numbers dictating just who the other party will be at any given moment.[23] Fianna Fáil's ability to dictate the shape and composition of governments now rests on its sheer size (magnified by the electoral system) as well as the lack of a really viable alternate pivot around which governments might easily form. However, if the party's slow long-term decline persists, even promiscuity and electoral system bonuses may not eventually save it.

Of course, a shrinking vote share for Fianna Fáil implies a growing share for others and historically, that would have meant Fine Gael and Labour. Yet in the years of Fianna Fáil's greatest vote decline neither of them was able to take advantage of it to reposition themselves as a more significant force in the system. Fine Gael's collapse in the late 1980s has left it much weaker than it had been in the previous decades when both Cosgrave and FitzGerald managed to form governments, and Labour has never managed to repeat its atypical 1992 election success. Indeed, the futures of both those parties are no more secure for their own partisans are, if anything, less loyal than Fianna Fáil's.[24] This suggests that if Fianna Fáil's vote does continue to decline, the major beneficiaries are likely to be, as they have been for two decades now, the minor parties and Independent candidates. None of the minor parties which now regularly manage to win seats in the Dáil has yet demonstrated any prospect of either displacing the others or emerging as a major party in its own right. But if this is the case the result is likely to be an increasingly fragmented party system. In that situation stable coalitions might become harder to build; almost certainly they would become harder to predict. Few voters in 1992 expected a Fianna Fáil–Labour government, not many more expected a Fianna Fáil–Green–PD one in 2007 (as we saw in chapter 9). This could make Irish elections far less of a choice of government than they have been in the past, a development that hardly seems likely to encourage public participation and restore voter turnout rates.

A quite different scenario might see some political issue or dynamic leader engendering a fundamental realignment of electoral divisions and the emergence of a very different party system. Alternatively, electoral reform could alter the terms of competition in a fashion that would reshape the existing parties and their competitive relationships. But both prospects seem unlikely. While the electorate's post-independence experience is one of comparatively weakly structured partisanship and it is now more de-aligned than ever, the compromises of coalition governance seem to militate against the emergence of highly divisive conflicts capable of realigning the system. Although electoral reform is on the agenda in many of the established and emerging democracies its prospects in Ireland are not bright. There is no obvious parliamentary coalition for it and Fianna Fáil has twice failed to convince the electorate of it.

But perhaps Fianna Fáil's organisation will find a way to stabilise its support and Dáil strength so that the lines in Figure 13.4 cease their relentlessly downward direction. In that case we can expect future elections to have all the order and predictability of 2007, and future governments to continue to be constructed by Fianna Fáil and one (or two) of the rest. Which of the rest will reflect the vagaries of specific electoral outcomes, depend on the political skill of Fianna Fáil's leadership, and measure the party's well-demonstrated determination to stay in office at whatever the cost.

Notes

1. Michael Laver, 'The Irish party system approaching the millennium', pp. 264–76 in Michael Marsh and Paul Mitchell (eds), *How Ireland Voted 1997* (Boulder, Co: Westview Press, 1999), pp. 264, 275.
2. John Coakley, 'The election and the party system', pp. 230–46 in Michael Gallagher, Michael Marsh and Paul Mitchell (eds), *How Ireland Voted 2002* (Basingstoke: Palgrave Macmillan, 2003), p. 231.
3. Peter Mair, 'Fianna Fáil, Labour and the Irish party system', pp. 162–73 in Michael Gallagher and Michael Laver (eds), *How Ireland Voted 1992* (Dublin: PSAI Press, 1993), p. 171.
4. Laver, 'The Irish party system', p. 275.
5. Coakley, 'The election and the party system', p. 231.
6. Paul Mitchell, 'Government formation in 2002: "you can have any kind of government as long as it's Fianna Fáil"', pp. 214–29 in Gallagher et al., *How Ireland Voted 2002*.
7. Mitchell, 'Government formation', p. 216.

8. The party's vote share had fallen even lower in the intervening period, reaching an all-time low (for a general election) of 39.1 per cent in 1992.
9. Martin P. Wattenberg, 'The decline of party mobilisation', pp. 64–76 in Russell J. Dalton and Martin P. Wattenberg (eds), *Parties without Partisans: Political Change in Advanced Industrial Democracies* (Oxford: Oxford University Press, 2000), pp. 71–5, discusses the turnout collapse in the OECD states, including Ireland. For current data see the IDEA website, www.idea.int/vt/index.cfm.
10. Michael Marsh, 'Party identification in Ireland: an insecure anchor for a floating party system', *Electoral Studies* 25:3 (2006), pp. 489–508.
11. Ibid., Table 2, p. 495.
12. For evidence of declining rates of 'party solidarity' and successful inter-party transfer direction see Michael Gallagher, 'Stability and turmoil: analysis of the results', pp. 88–118 in Gallagher et al., *How Ireland Voted 2002*, and pp. 94–5 above.
13. Marsh, 'Party identification', pp. 506–7.
14. For a recent assessment of Fine Gael's place in the party system, see Eoin O'Malley and Matthew Kerby, 'Chronicle of a death foretold? Understanding the decline of Fine Gael', *Irish Political Studies* 19:1 (2004), pp. 39–58.
15. As its vote share has declined the number of seats it has won has become more unpredictable. Over the last four elections (1992–2007) it has averaged 27.3 per cent but ranged from a low of 18.7 per cent to a high of 32.5 per cent.
16. This paragraph draws heavily on the evidence and analysis in Marsh, 'Party identification'.
17. See p. 84, this volume.
18. For a discussion of the pressures changing the candidate nomination processes in Irish parties, see Yvonne Galligan, 'Candidate selection: more democratic or more centrally controlled?', pp. 37–56 in Gallagher et al., *How Ireland Voted 2002*, and also chapter 4, this volume.
19. There is a small but lively literature on the subject of the best number of candidates to nominate. See Michael Gallagher, 'Candidate selection in Ireland: the impact of localism and the electoral system', *British Journal of Political Science* 10:4 (1980), pp. 489–503. Richard S. Katz pulls one debate together in his 'But how many candidates should we have in Donegal? Numbers of nominees and electoral efficiency in Ireland', *British Journal of Political Science* 11:1 (1981), pp. 117–22.
20. Michael Gallagher, 'The results analysed', pp. 121–50 in Marsh and Mitchell, *How Ireland Voted 1997*, pp. 128–9; Peter Mair and Liam Weeks, 'The party system', pp. 135–59 in J. Coakley and Michael Gallagher (eds), *Politics in the Republic of Ireland*, 4th edn (Abingdon: Routledge, 2005), p. 152.
21. Coakley, 'The election and the party system', p. 240, identifies these as the most successful parties in Europe in the post-Second World War period. He notes that by 2002 Fianna Fáil had become Europe's 'most consistently successful vote-getter'.
22. Marsh, 'Party identification', Figure 1, p. 494, provides comparative data for Sweden, Germany and Canada.
23. The party has always been happy to deal with Independents who could generally be bought off with particularistic benefits designed to benefit their constituencies.
24. See Marsh, 'Party identification', Table 7, p. 499, for a comparison of partisans' propensity to vote for their own party.

Appendices

Liam Weeks

Appendix 1: results of the general election, 24 May 2007

Table A1.1 Electorate, valid votes, and vote for each party

Constituency	Electorate	Valid votes	Fianna Fáil	Fine Gael	Labour	Prog. Dems.	Green Party	Sinn Féin	Others
Carlow–Kilkenny	102,016	67,654	32,272	20,031	6,324	1,073	5,386	2,568	0
Cavan–Monaghan	92,248	65,787	24,851	20,528	796	0	2,382	13,162	4,068
Clare	79,555	56,385	24,824	19,854	892	810	2,858	1,929	5,218
Cork East	84,354	53,808	20,431	16,602	11,249	0	1,572	3,672	282
Cork North-Central	67,777	42,347	15,136	11,674	5,221	0	1,503	3,456	5,357
Cork North-West	64,085	46,620	24,732	17,913	2,288	0	1,687	0	0
Cork South-Central	91,090	59,068	26,154	16,782	5,466	1,596	4,945	3,020	1,105
Cork South-West	61,577	42,497	18,093	15,299	4,095	0	2,860	2,150	0
Donegal North-East	57,244	38,545	19,374	8,711	703	0	520	6,733	2,504
Donegal South-West	60,829	39,853	20,136	9,167	1,111	0	589	8,462	388
Dublin Central	63,423	34,639	15,398	3,302	4,353	193	1,995	3,182	6,216
Dublin Mid-West	61,347	37,339	12,321	4,480	4,075	4,663	4,043	3,462	4,295
Dublin North	80,221	54,641	22,998	7,667	5,256	1,395	9,107	1,454	6,764
Dublin North-Central	53,443	36,416	16,029	9,303	2,649	0	1,891	1,375	5,169
Dublin North-East	53,778	34,929	13,864	8,012	5,294	749	2,349	4,661	0
Dublin North-West	51,951	30,964	15,124	3,083	6,286	0	853	4,873	745
Dublin South	89,464	61,204	25,298	16,686	6,384	4,045	6,768	1,843	180
Dublin South-Central	86,710	47,531	15,725	6,838	10,041	912	2,756	4,825	6,434
Dublin South-East	63,468	33,842	9,720	6,311	5,636	4,450	4,685	1,599	1,441
Dublin South-West	67,148	41,652	16,355	8,346	8,325	0	1,546	5,066	2,014

Dublin West	52,193	33,982	12,726	6,928	5,799	553	1,286	1,624	5,066
Dun Laoghaire	89,035	58,713	20,471	13,832	9,392	3,959	4,534	1,292	5,233
Galway East	81,864	55,794	22,137	21,832	1,747	3,321	1,057	1,789	3,911
Galway West	86,602	55,096	20,468	11,235	6,086	8,868	3,026	1,629	3,784
Kerry North	56,216	39,313	12,304	12,697	4,287	0	747	8,030	1,248
Kerry South	53,660	39,032	15,868	9,795	5,263	0	738	1,375	5,993
Kildare North	71,311	45,191	17,851	9,590	7,882	983	2,215	1,103	5,567
Kildare South	56,670	34,591	17,425	5,939	7,154	1,513	2,136	0	424
Laois–Offaly	103,673	71,491	40,307	19,560	1,703	4,233	812	3,656	1,220
Limerick East	76,874	49,375	24,042	12,601	5,098	3,354	1,296	2,081	903
Limerick West	58,712	40,431	19,097	16,153	2,277	1,935	969	0	0
Longford–Westmeath	83,980	54,916	22,599	16,999	9,692	2,298	960	2,136	232
Louth	86,007	55,014	23,181	16,159	2,739	0	4,172	8,274	489
Mayo	98,696	71,386	17,459	38,426	831	296	580	3,608	10,186
Meath East	67,443	43,007	18,735	11,129	5,136	957	1,330	1,695	4,025
Meath West	56,267	40,464	20,874	11,745	1,634	0	1,011	4,567	633
Roscommon–S. Leitrim	62,437	46,077	17,897	18,031	832	0	836	3,876	4,605
Sligo–North Leitrim	57,517	39,934	16,360	15,684	1,555	0	1,209	4,684	442
Tipperary North	57,084	44,431	15,245	7,061	4,561	634	495	1,672	14,763
Tipperary South	54,637	38,782	18,004	8,200	3,400	541	591	1,198	6,848
Waterford	73,434	49,528	23,025	13,552	5,610	0	1,049	3,327	2,965
Wexford	103,562	68,616	28,949	21,658	9,445	2,162	802	5,068	532
Wicklow	91,492	64,925	24,706	15,033	10,608	903	4,790	3,234	5,651
Dublin	812,181	505,852	196,029	94,788	73,490	20,919	41,813	35,256	43,557
Rest of Leinster	822,421	545,869	246,899	147,843	62,317	14,122	23,614	32,301	18,773
Munster	879,055	601,617	256,955	178,183	59,707	8,870	21,310	31,910	44,682
Connacht–Ulster	597,437	412,472	158,682	143,614	13,661	12,485	10,199	43,943	29,888
Ireland	3,111,094	2,065,810	858,565	564,428	209,175	56,396	96,936	143,410	136,900

Notes: The number of votes obtained refers to first preference figures. A further 19,436 votes were deemed invalid. In this and all subsequent tables 'Others' includes the Socialist Party (13,218 votes), People before Profit Alliance (9,333), the Workers' Party (3,026 votes), the Christian Solidarity Party (1,705 votes), Fathers' Rights–Responsibility Party (1,355 votes), Immigration Control Platform (1,329 votes), and the Irish Socialist Network (505 votes), along with Independents (106,476 votes).

Table A1.2 Turnout and percentage votes for each party

Constituency	Turnout	Fianna Fáil	Fine Gael	Labour	Prog. Dems.	Green Party	Sinn Féin	Others
Carlow–Kilkenny	67.0	47.7	29.6	9.3	1.6	8.0	3.8	0.0
Cavan–Monaghan	72.1	37.8	31.2	1.2	0.0	3.6	20.0	6.2
Clare	71.4	44.0	35.2	1.6	1.4	5.1	3.4	9.3
Cork East	64.4	38.0	30.9	20.9	0.0	2.9	6.8	0.5
Cork North-Central	63.2	35.7	27.6	12.3	0.0	3.5	8.2	12.7
Cork North-West	73.4	53.1	38.4	4.9	0.0	3.6	0.0	0.0
Cork South-Central	65.5	44.3	28.4	9.3	2.7	8.4	5.1	1.9
Cork South-West	69.7	42.6	36.0	9.6	0.0	6.7	5.1	0.0
Donegal North-East	68.0	50.3	22.6	1.8	0.0	1.3	17.5	6.5
Donegal South-West	66.2	50.5	23.0	2.8	0.0	1.5	21.2	1.0
Dublin Central	55.4	44.5	9.5	12.6	0.6	5.8	9.2	17.9
Dublin Mid-West	61.4	33.0	12.0	10.9	12.5	10.8	9.3	11.5
Dublin North	68.6	42.1	14.0	9.6	2.6	16.7	2.7	12.4
Dublin North-Central	68.8	44.0	25.5	7.3	0.0	5.2	3.8	14.2
Dublin North-East	65.6	39.7	22.9	15.2	2.1	6.7	13.3	0.0
Dublin North-West	60.4	48.8	10.0	20.3	0.0	2.8	15.7	2.4
Dublin South	68.9	41.3	27.3	10.4	6.6	11.1	3.0	0.3
Dublin South-Central	55.7	33.1	14.4	21.1	1.9	5.8	10.2	13.5
Dublin South-East	53.8	28.7	18.6	16.7	13.1	13.8	4.7	4.3
Dublin South-West	62.6	39.3	20.0	20.0	0.0	3.7	12.2	4.8
Dublin West	65.5	37.4	20.4	17.1	1.6	3.8	4.8	14.9
Dun Laoghaire	66.4	34.9	23.6	16.0	6.7	7.7	2.2	8.9
Galway East	68.7	39.7	39.1	3.1	6.0	1.9	3.2	7.0
Galway West	64.2	37.1	20.4	11.0	16.1	5.5	3.0	6.9
Kerry North	70.5	31.3	32.3	10.9	0.0	1.9	20.4	3.2
Kerry South	73.3	40.7	25.1	13.5	0.0	1.9	3.5	15.4
Kildare North	70.5	39.5	21.2	17.4	2.2	4.9	2.4	12.3
Kildare South	61.7	50.4	17.2	20.7	4.4	6.2	0.0	1.2

Laois–Offaly	69.6	56.4	27.4	2.4	5.9	1.1	5.1	1.7
Limerick East	64.8	48.7	25.5	10.3	6.8	2.6	4.2	1.8
Limerick West	69.5	47.2	40.0	5.6	4.8	2.4	0.0	0.0
Longford–Westmeath	66.1	41.2	31.0	17.6	4.2	1.7	3.9	0.4
Louth	64.7	42.1	29.4	5.0	0.0	7.6	15.0	0.9
Mayo	73.0	24.5	53.8	1.2	0.4	0.8	5.1	14.3
Meath East	64.3	43.6	25.9	11.9	2.2	3.1	3.9	9.4
Meath West	72.6	51.6	29.0	4.0	0.0	2.5	11.3	1.6
Roscommon–South Leitrim	74.4	38.8	39.1	1.8	0.0	1.8	8.4	10.0
Sligo–North Leitrim	70.1	41.0	39.3	3.9	0.0	3.0	11.7	1.1
Tipperary North	78.5	34.3	15.9	10.3	1.4	1.1	3.8	33.2
Tipperary South	71.6	46.4	21.1	8.8	1.4	1.5	3.1	17.7
Waterford	68.0	46.5	27.4	11.3	0.0	2.1	6.7	6.0
Wexford	67.1	42.2	31.6	13.8	3.2	1.2	7.4	0.8
Wicklow	71.6	38.1	23.2	16.3	1.4	7.4	5.0	8.7
Dublin	63.0	38.8	18.7	14.5	4.1	8.3	7.0	8.6
Rest of Leinster	67.0	45.2	27.1	11.4	2.6	4.3	5.9	3.4
Munster	69.0	42.7	29.6	9.9	1.5	3.5	5.3	7.4
Connacht–Ulster	69.8	38.5	34.8	3.3	3.0	2.5	10.7	7.2
Ireland	67.0	41.6	27.3	10.1	2.7	4.7	6.9	6.6

Notes: Turnout is defined as the total vote (including invalid votes) expressed as a percentage of the electorate; of those cast, 0.9 per cent were invalid. Others: Socialist Party 0.6 per cent, People before Profit Alliance 0.5 per cent, Workers' Party 0.1 per cent, Christian Solidarity Party 0.1 per cent, Fathers' Rights-Responsibility Party 0.1 per cent, Immigration Control Platform 0.1 per cent, Irish Socialist Network 0.02 per cent, Independents 5.2 per cent.

Table A1.3 Seats and candidates by party

Constituency	Total	Fianna Fáil	Fine Gael	Labour	Prog. Dems.	Green Party	Sinn Féin	Others
Carlow-Kilkenny	5–11	3–3	1–3	0–2	0–1	1–1	0–1	0–1
Cavan–Monaghan	5–10*	3–3*	1–2	0–1		0–1	1–1	0–2
Clare	4–12	2–3	2–4	0–1	0–1	0–1	0–1	0–1
Cork East	4–10	2–2	1–2	1–2		0–1	0–1	0–2
Cork North-Central	4–13	2–2	2–2	0–1		0–1	0–1	0–6
Cork North-West	3–7	2–3	1–2	0–1		0–1		
Cork South-Central	5–14	2–3	2–3	1–1	0–1	0–1	0–1	0–4
Cork South-West	3–7	1–2	2–2	0–1		0–1	0–1	
Donegal North-East	3–11	3–3	1–1	0–1		0–1	0–1	0–4
Donegal South-West	3–7	2–2	1–1	0–1		0–1	0–1	0–1
Dublin Central	4–13	2–3	0–1	1–1	0–1	0–1	0–1	1–5
Dublin Mid-West	4–11	1–2	0–1	1–1	1–1	1–1	0–1	0–4
Dublin North	4–13	2–3	1–1	0–1	0–1	1–2	0–1	0–4
Dublin North-Central	3–7	1–2	1–1	0–1		0–1	0–1	1–1
Dublin North-East	3–8	1–2	1–2	0–1	0–1	0–1	0–1	
Dublin North-West	3–8	2–2	0–1	1–1		0–1	0–1	0–2
Dublin South	5–13	2–3	2–3	0–2	0–1	1–1	0–2	0–1
Dublin South-Central	5–16	2–2	1–2	1–2	0–2	0–1	1–1	0–6
Dublin South-East	4–13	1–2	1–1	1–1	0–1	1–1	0–1	0–6
Dublin South-West	4–8	2–2	1–1	1–1		0–1	0–1	0–2
Dublin West	3–8	1–2	1–1	1–1	0–1	0–1	0–1	0–1
Dun Laoghaire	5–11	2–2	1–3	1–2	0–1	1–1	0–1	0–1
Galway East	4–14	2–3	2–4	0–1	0–1	0–1	0–1	0–3
Galway West	5–15	2–3	1–3	1–1	1–3	0–1	0–1	0–3
Kerry North	3–10	1–2	1–1	0–1		0–1	1–1	0–4
Kerry South	4–8	1–2	1–2	0–1		0–1	0–1	1–1
Kildare North	4–11	2–2	1–2	1–1	0–1	0–1	0–1	0–3
Kildare South	3–8	2–2	0–2	1–1	0–1	0–1	0–1	0–1

Constituency							
Laois–Offaly	5-16	3-4	2-3	0-2	0-1	0-1	0-1	0-4
Limerick East	5-14	2-3	2-2	1-1	0-1	0-1	0-1	0-5
Limerick West	3-7	2-2	1-2	0-1		0-1		0-3
Longford–Westmeath	4-13	2-3	1-3	1-1	0-1	0-1	0-1	0-3
Louth	4-12	2-3	1-3	0-1	0-1	0-1	1-1	0-2
Mayo	5-13	1-3	3-4	0-1	0-1	0-1	0-1	1-2
Meath East	3-11	2-2	1-2	0-1	0-1	0-1	0-1	0-3
Meath West	3-10	2-2	1-3	0-1		0-1	0-1	0-2
Roscommon–South Leitrim	3-9	1-2	2-2	0-1		0-1	0-1	0-2
Sligo–North Leitrim	3-10	2-2	1-3	0-1		0-1	0-1	0-2
Tipperary North	3-9	1-2	1-1	0-1	0-1	0-1	0-1	1-2
Tipperary South	3-11	2-3	1-1	0-2		0-1	0-1	0-2
Waterford	4-13	2-3	1-3	0-1	0-1	0-1	0-1	0-4
Wexford	5-11	2-3	2-3	0-1	0-1	0-1	0-1	0-1
Wicklow	5-15	2-3	2-2	1-2	0-1	0-1	0-1	0-5
Dublin (12)	47-129	19-27	10-18	9-15	1-10	5-13	1-13	2-33
Rest of Leinster (9)	41-118	22-27	12-26	5-13	0-8	1-10	1-9	0-25
Munster (13)	47-135	22-32	17-27	5-14	0-7	0-13	1-11	2-31
Connacht–Ulster (8)	31-89*	15-21*	12-20	1-8	1-5	0-8	1-8	1-19
Ireland (43)	166-471*	78-107*	51-91	20-50	2-30	6-44	4-41	5-108**

* Figures include Rory O'Hanlon, who as outgoing Ceann Comhairle was returned automatically for Cavan–Monaghan.

** This figure includes one Independent candidate who ran in four different constituencies, and one candidate who ran on behalf of the Christian Solidarity Party in two different constituencies.

Notes: Others: Socialist Party four candidates (none elected); the Workers' Party six (none elected); Christian Solidarity Party eight (none elected); People before Profit Alliance five (none elected); Fathers' Rights–Responsibility Party eight (none elected); Immigration Control Platform three (none elected); Irish Socialist Network one (none elected). There were 73 Independent candidates, of whom five were elected.

Appendix 2: Members of the 30th Dáil

Table A2.1 Members of the 30th Dáil

TD (constituency)	Party	Occupation	Date of birth	First elected	Times elected	First pref. votes in 2007
Bertie Ahern (Dublin Central)	FF	Accountant	Sep 1951	1977	10	12,734
Dermot Ahern (Louth)	FF	Solicitor	Feb 1955	1987	6	9,982
Michael Ahern (Cork E)	FF	Accountant	Jan 1949	F1982	8	10,350
Noel Ahern (Dublin NW)	FF	Clerical officer	Dec 1944	1992	4	7,913
Bernard Allen (Cork NC)	FG	Laboratory technologist	Sep 1944	1981	9	6,866
Barry Andrews (Dun Laoghaire)	FF	Barrister	May 1967	2002	2	8,587
Chris Andrews (Dublin SE)	FF	Catering and tourism business	Jun 1965	2007	1	6,600
Seán Ardagh (Dublin SC)	FF	Accountant	Nov 1947	1997	3	8,286
Bobby Aylward (Carlow–Kilkenny)	FF	Farmer	Apr 1955	2007	1	11,600
James Bannon (Longford–Westmeath)	FG	Farmer, auctioneer	Mar 1958	2007	1	7,652
Seán Barrett (Dun Laoghaire)	FG	Insurance broker	Aug 1944	1981	8	5,361
Joe Behan (Wicklow)	FF	School principal	Jul 1959	2007	1	9,431
Niall Blaney (Donegal NE)	FF	Civil engineering technician	Jan 1974	2002	2	6,288
Áine Brady (Kildare N)	FF	Teacher	Sep 1955	2007	1	11,245
Cyprian Brady (Dublin Central)	FF	Civil servant	Jun 1962	2007	1	939
Johnny Brady (Meath W)	FF	Farmer	Jan 1948	1997	3	8,868
Pat Breen (Clare)	FG	Farmer, former architectural technician	Mar 1957	2002	2	7,036
Séamus Brennan (Dublin S)	FF	Accountant	Feb 1948	1981	9	13,373
Tommy Broughan (Dublin NE)	Lab	Teacher	Aug 1947	1992	4	5,294
John Browne (Wexford)	FF	Salesman	Aug 1948	N1982	7	12,768
Richard Bruton (Dublin NC)	FG	Economist	Mar 1953	F1982	8	9,303
Ulick Burke (Galway E)	FG	Teacher	Nov 1943	1997	2	5,149
Joan Burton (Dublin W)	Lab	Accountant, lecturer	Feb 1949	1992	3	5,799
Catherine Byrne (Dublin SC)	FG	Housewife	Feb 1955	2007	1	4,713
Thomas Byrne (Meath E)	FF	Solicitor	Jun 1977	2007	1	7,834

Name (Constituency)	Occupation	Party	Date of birth	First elected	No.	Votes
Dara Calleary (Mayo)	Employee of Chambers Ireland	FF	May 1973	2007	1	7,225
Joe Carey (Clare)	Accountant	FG	Jun 1975	2007	1	5,818
Pat Carey (Dublin NW)	Teacher	FF	Nov 1947	1997	3	7,211
Deirdre Clune (Cork SC)	Former civil engineer	FG	Jun 1959	1997	2	5,739
Niall Collins (Limerick W)	Accountant, lecturer	FF	Mar 1973	2007	1	10,396
Paul Connaughton (Galway E)	Livestock manager	FG	Jun 1944	1981	9	6,886
Seán Connick (Wexford)	Self-employed owner/manager	FF	Aug 1964	2007	1	9,826
Margaret Conlon (Cavan–Monaghan)	Teacher	FF	Sep 1967	2007	1	9,303
Noel Coonan (Tipp N)	Auctioneer	FG	Jan 1951	2007	1	7,061
Joe Costello (Dublin Central)	Teacher	Lab	Jul 1945	1992	3	4,353
Mary Coughlan (Donegal SW)	Social worker	FF	May 1965	1987	6	10,530
Simon Coveney (Cork SC)	Manager of family business	FG	Nov 1973	B-1998	3	5,863
Brian Cowen (Laois–Offaly)	Solicitor	FF	Jan 1960	B-1984	7	19,102
Seymour Crawford (Cavan–Monaghan)	Farmer	FG	Jun 1944	1992	4	10,978
Michael Creed (Cork NW)	Farmer	FG	Jun 1963	1989	4	10,516
John Cregan (Limerick W)	Eircom technician	FF	May 1961	2002	2	8,701
Lucinda Creighton (Dublin SE)	Trainee barrister	FG	Jan 1980	2007	1	6,311
Ciarán Cuffe (Dun Laoghaire)	Architect, lecturer	Grn	Apr 1963	2002	2	4,534
Martin Cullen (Waterford)	Chief executive, Federation of Transport Operators	FF	Nov 1954	1987	5	11,438
John Curran (Dublin MW)	Company director	FF	Jun 1960	2002	2	8,650
Michael D'Arcy (Wexford)	Farmer, trainee solicitor	FG	Feb 1970	2007	1	7,692
John Deasy (Waterford)	Congressional aide	FG	Oct 1967	2002	2	7,554
Jimmy Deenihan (Kerry N)	Teacher	FG	Sep 1952	1987	6	12,697
Noel Dempsey (Meath W)	Career guidance counsellor	FF	Jan 1953	1987	6	12,006
Jimmy Devins (Sligo–N Leitrim)	Medical doctor	FF	Sep 1948	2002	2	7,102
Timmy Dooley (Clare)	Businessman	FF	Feb 1969	2007	1	10,791
Andrew Doyle (Wicklow)	Farmer	FG	July 1960	2007	1	6,961
Bernard Durkan (Kildare N)	Agricultural contractor	FG	Mar 1945	1981	8	5,340
Damien English (Meath W)	Student accountant	FG	Feb 1978	2002	2	7,227
Olwyn Enright (Laois–Offaly)	Solicitor	FG	Jul 1974	2002	2	8,297
Frank Fahey (Galway W)	Teacher	FF	Jun 1951	F1982	7	5,854
Frank Feighan (Roscommon–S Leitrim)	Newsagent, businessman	FG	Jul 1962	2007	1	9,103

Table A2.1 continued

TD (constituency)	Party	Occupation	Date of birth	First elected	Times elected	First pref. votes in 2007
Martin Ferris (Kerry N)	SF	Unemployed fisherman	Mar 1952	2002	2	8,030
Michael Finneran (Roscommon–S Leitrim)	FF	Health board officer	Sep 1947	2002	2	9,982
Michael Fitzpatrick (Kildare N)	FF	Garda, auctioneer, ministerial assistant	Oct 1942	2007	1	6,606
Charles Flanagan (Laois–Offaly)	FG	Solicitor	Nov 1956	1987	5	9,067
Terence Flanagan (Dublin NE)	FG	Accountant	Jan 1976	2007	1	4,483
Seán Fleming (Laois–Offaly)	FF	Accountant, financial director of Fianna Fáil	Feb 1958	1997	3	8,064
Beverley Flynn (Mayo)	FF	Bank manager	Jun 1966	1997	3	6,779
Pat 'The Cope' Gallagher (Donegal SW)	FF	Fish exporter	Mar 1948	1981	8	9,606
Éamon Gilmore (Dun Laoghaire)	Lab	Trade union official	Apr 1955	1989	5	7,127
Paul Gogarty (Dublin MW)	Grn	Journalist	Dec 1968	2002	2	4,043
John Gormley (Dublin SE)	Grn	Director of Academy of European languages	Aug 1959	1997	3	4,685
Noel Grealish (Galway W)	PD	Company director	Dec 1965	2002	2	5,806
Tony Gregory (Dublin Central)	Ind	Teacher	Dec 1947	F1982	8	4,649
Mary Hanafin (Dun Laoghaire)	FF	Teacher	Jun 1959	1997	3	11,884
Mary Harney (Dublin MW)	PD	Research worker	Mar 1953	1981	9	4,663
Seán Haughey (Dublin NC)	FF	Public representative	Nov 1961	1992	4	9,026
Brian Hayes (Dublin SW)	FG	Teacher	Aug 1969	1997	2	8,346
Tom Hayes (Tipperary S)	FG	Farmer	Feb 1952	B-2001	3	8,200
Jackie Healy-Rae (Kerry S)	Ind	Publican, farmer	Mar 1931	1997	3	5,993
Michael D. Higgins (Galway W)	Lab	University lecturer	Apr 1941	1981	8	6,086
Máire Hoctor (Tipperary N)	FF	Teacher	Jan 1963	2002	2	7,374
Phil Hogan (Carlow–Kilkenny)	FG	Insurance broker, auctioneer	Jul 1960	1989	5	8,589
Brendan Howlin (Wexford)	Lab	Teacher	May 1956	1987	6	9,445
Paul Kehoe (Wexford)	FG	Sales representative	Jan 1973	2002	2	8,459
Billy Kelleher (Cork NC)	FF	Farmer	Jan 1968	1997	3	9,456

Name (Constituency)	Party	Occupation	Born	Elected		Votes
Peter Kelly (Longford–Westmeath)	FF	Funeral director, retired publican	Aug 1944	2002	2	7,720
Brendan Kenneally (Waterford)	FF	Accountant	Apr 1955	1989	4	5,624
Michael Kennedy (Dublin N)	FF	Insurance broker	Feb 1949	2007	1	10,869
Enda Kenny (Mayo)	FG	Teacher	Apr 1951	B-1975	11	14,717
Tony Killeen (Clare)	FF	Teacher	Jun 1952	1992	4	8,321
Séamus Kirk (Louth)	FF	Farmer	Apr 1945	1982	7	10190
Michael P. Kitt (Galway E)	FF	Teacher	May 1950	B-1975	9	8,796
Tom Kitt (Dublin S)	FF	Teacher	Jul 1952	1987	6	8,487
Brian Lenihan (Dublin W)	FF	Barrister	May 1959	B-1996	4	11,125
Conor Lenihan (Dublin SW)	FF	Journalist, programme manager with Esat Digifone	Mar 1963	1997	3	8,542
Michael Lowry (Tipperary N)	Ind	Company director	Mar 1954	1987	6	12,919
Ciarán Lynch (Cork SC)	Lab	Adult literacy organiser	Jun 1964	2007	1	5,466
Kathleen Lynch (Cork NC)	Lab	Homemaker	Jun 1953	B-1994	3	5,221
Pádraic McCormack (Galway W)	FG	Auctioneer	May 1942	1989	5	5,419
James McDaid (Donegal NE)	FF	Medical doctor	Oct 1949	1989	5	6,724
Tom McEllistrim (Kerry N)	FF	Teacher	Oct 1968	2002	2	7,367
Shane McEntee (Meath E)	FG	Publican, farmer	Dec 1956	B-2005	2	6,766
Dinny McGinley (Donegal SW)	FG	Principal teacher	Apr 1945	F1982	8	9,167
Finian McGrath (Dublin NC)	Ind	Teacher	Apr 1953	2002	2	5,169
Mattie McGrath (Tipperary S)	FF	Plant hire contractor	Sep 1958	2007	1	7,608
Michael McGrath (Cork SC)	FF	Chartered accountant	Aug 1976	2007	1	9,866
John McGuinness (Carlow–Kilkenny)	FF	Transport company director	Mar 1955	1997	3	11,635
Joe McHugh (Donegal NE)	FG	Teacher	July 1971	2007	1	8,711
Liz McManus (Wicklow)	Lab	Writer	Mar 1947	1992	4	6,751
Martin Mansergh (Tipperary S)	FF	Government advisor, civil servant	Dec 1946	2007	1	6,110
Micheál Martin (Cork SC)	FF	Teacher	Aug 1960	1989	5	11,226
Olivia Mitchell (Dublin S)	FG	Teacher	Jul 1947	1997	3	8,037
John Moloney (Laois–Offaly)	FF	Undertaker, publican	Jun 1953	1997	3	7,242
Arthur Morgan (Louth)	SF	Company director	Jul 1954	2002	2	8,274
Michael Moynihan (Cork NW)	FF	Farmer	Jan 1968	1997	3	10,146
Michael Mulcahy (Dublin SC)	FF	Barrister	Jun 1960	2002	2	7,439
Denis Naughten (Roscommon–S Leitrim)	FG	Research scientist	Jun 1973	1997	3	8,928

Table A2.1 continued

TD (constituency)	Party	Occupation	Date of birth	First elected	Times elected	First pref. votes in 2007
Dan Neville (Limerick W)	FG	Personnel manager	Dec 1946	1997	3	8,314
M.J. Nolan (Carlow–Kilkenny)	FF	Director of chocolate company	Jan 1951	N1982	6	9,037
Michael Noonan (Limerick E)	FG	Teacher	May 1943	1981	9	7,507
Darragh O'Brien (Dublin N)	FF	Pensions consultant and senior account executive	July 1974	2007	1	7,055
Caoimhghín Ó Caoláin (Cavan–Monaghan)	SF	Bank official	Sep 1953	1997	3	13,162
Charlie O'Connor (Dublin SW)	FF	Press officer with National Youth Federation	Apr 1946	2002	2	7,813
Éamon Ó Cuív (Galway W)	FF	Cooperative manager	Jun 1950	1992	4	9,645
Willie O'Dea (Limerick E)	FF	Accountant	Nov 1952	F1982	8	19,082
Kieran O'Donnell (Limerick E)	FG	Chartered accountant	May 1963	2007	1	5,094
John O'Donoghue (Kerry S)	FF	Solicitor	May 1956	1987	6	9,128
Fergus O'Dowd (Louth)	FG	Teacher	Sep 1948	2002	2	8,387
Seán O'Fearghail (Kildare S)	FF	Farmer	Apr 1960	2002	2	8,731
Noel O'Flynn (Cork NC)	FF	Company director	Dec 1951	1997	3	5,680
Rory O'Hanlon (Cavan–Monaghan)	FF	Medical doctor	Feb 1934	1977	10	–
Batt O'Keeffe (Cork NW)	FF	Lecturer	Apr 1945	1987	6	8,040
Jim O'Keeffe (Cork SW)	FG	Solicitor	Mar 1941	1977	10	7,560
Ned O'Keeffe (Cork E)	FF	Company director, farmer	Aug 1942	N1982	6	10,081
John O'Mahony (Mayo)	FG	Teacher	Jun 1953	2007	1	6,869
Mary O'Rourke (Longford–Westmeath)	FF	Teacher	May 1937	N1982	6	8,215
Brian O'Shea (Waterford)	Lab	Teacher	Dec 1944	1989	5	5,610
Aengus Ó Snodaigh (Dublin SC)	SF	Teacher	Aug 1964	2002	2	4,825
Christy O'Sullivan (Cork SW)	FF	Livestock dealer	Nov 1948	2007	1	10,333
Jan O'Sullivan (Limerick E)	Lab	Pre-school teacher	Dec 1950	B-1998	3	5,098
Willie Penrose (Longford–Westmeath)	Lab	Barrister	Aug 1956	1992	4	9,692
John Perry (Sligo–N Leitrim)	FG	Businessman	Aug 1956	1997	3	7,910

Name	Occupation	Party				Votes
Peter Power (Limerick E)	Solicitor	FF	Jan 1966	2002	2	3,569
Seán Power (Kildare S)	Bookmaker	FF	Oct 1960	1989	5	8,694
Ruairí Quinn (Dublin SE)	Architect	Lab	Apr 1946	1977	9	5,636
Pat Rabbitte (Dublin SW)	Trade union official	Lab	May 1949	1989	5	8,325
James Reilly (Dublin N)	Doctor	FG	Aug 1955	2007	1	7,667
Michael Ring (Mayo)	Auctioneer	FG	Dec 1953	B-1994	4	11,412
Dick Roche (Wicklow)	University lecturer	FF	Mar 1947	1987	5	10,246
Éamon Ryan (Dublin S)	Tour operator	Grn	Jul 1963	2002	2	6,768
Trevor Sargent (Dublin N)	Teacher	Grn	Jul 1960	1992	4	7,448
Éamon Scanlon (Sligo–N Leitrim)	Butcher, auctioneer	FF	Sep 1954	2007	1	9,258
Alan Shatter (Dublin S)	Solicitor	FG	Feb 1951	1981	8	5,752
Tom Sheahan (Kerry S)	Company director	FG	Sep 1968	2007	1	5,600
P.J. Sheehan (Cork SW)	Auctioneer, merchant, farmer	FG	Mar 1933	1981	8	7,739
Seán Sherlock (Cork E)	Parliamentary assistant	Lab	Dec 1972	2007	1	7,295
Róisín Shortall (Dublin NW)	Teacher	Lab	Apr 1954	1992	4	6,286
Brendan Smith (Cavan–Monaghan)	Ministerial advisor	FF	Jun 1956	1992	4	15,548
Emmet Stagg (Kildare N)	Laboratory technologist	Lab	Oct 1944	1987	6	7,882
David Stanton (Cork E)	Teacher	FG	Feb 1957	1997	3	7,686
Billy Timmins (Wicklow)	Army officer	FG	Oct 1959	1997	3	8,072
Noel Treacy (Galway E)	Auctioneer	FF	Dec 1952	B-1982	8	7,524
Joanna Tuffy (Dublin MW)	Solicitor	Lab	Mar 1965	2007	1	4,075
Mary Upton (Dublin SC)	Lecturer	Lab	May 1946	B-1999	3	5,987
Leo Varadkar (Dublin W)	Doctor	FG	Jan 1979	2007	1	6,928
Jack Wall (Kildare S)	Electrician	Lab	Jul 1945	1997	3	7,154
Mary Wallace (Meath E)	Personnel executive	FF	Jun 1959	1989	5	10,901
Mary White (Carlow–Kilkenny)	Bookseller	Grn	Nov 1948	2007	1	5,386
Michael J. Woods (Dublin NE)	Horticulturalist	FF	Dec 1935	1977	10	7,003

Notes: Most TDs are full-time public representatives. For such TDs, the occupations given here are those previously followed.
Rory O'Hanlon was returned automatically as outgoing Ceann Comhairle.
There were two general elections in 1982, in February (F) and November (N). 'B-' indicates that deputy was first elected at a by-election.

Appendix 3: the government and ministers of state

The government

The Fianna Fáil–Green Party–Progressive Democrat government was approved by the Dáil on 14 June 2007. Bertie Ahern was re-elected as Taoiseach by 89 votes (comprising 77 Fianna Fáil, 6 Green Party, 2 Progressive Democrats and 4 independent TDs) to 76. The government subsequently appointed was:

Bertie Ahern (FF)	Taoiseach
Brian Cowen (FF)	Tánaiste, and Minister for Finance
Dermot Ahern (FF)	Minister for Foreign Affairs
Séamus Brennan (FF)	Minister for Arts, Sport and Tourism
Mary Coughlan (FF)	Minister for Agriculture, Fisheries and Food
Martin Cullen (FF)	Minister for Social and Family Affairs
Noel Dempsey (FF)	Minister for Transport and the Marine
John Gormley (GP)	Minister for the Environment, Heritage and Local Government
Mary Hanafin (FF)	Minister for Education and Science
Mary Harney (PD)	Minister for Health and Children
Brian Lenihan (FF)	Minister for Justice, Equality and Law Reform
Micheál Martin (FF)	Minister for Enterprise, Trade and Employment
Éamon Ó Cuív (FF)	Minister for Community, Rural and Gaeltacht Affairs
Willie O'Dea (FF)	Minister for Defence
Éamon Ryan (GP)	Minister for Communications, Energy and Natural Resources
(Paul Gallagher SC	Attorney General)

Ministers of state, their departments and special areas of responsibility

Tom Kitt (FF)	Taoiseach (Government Chief Whip and Information Society); Defence
Michael Ahern (FF)	Enterprise, Trade and Employment; Education and Science (Innovation Policy)
Noel Ahern (FF)	Finance (Office of Public Works)
John Browne (FF)	Agriculture, Fisheries and Food (Fisheries)
Pat Carey (FF)	Community, Rural and Gaeltacht Affairs (Drugs Strategy and Community Affairs)
Jimmy Devins (FF)	Health and Children; Education and Science; Enterprise, Trade and Employment (Disability Issues and Mental Health (excluding discrimination issues))
Pat 'The Cope' Gallagher (FF)	Health and Children (Health Promotion and Food Safety)
Seán Haughey (FF)	Enterprise, Trade and Employment; Education and Science (Lifelong Learning, Youth Work and School Transport)
Máire Hoctor (FF)	Health and Children; Social and Family Affairs; Environment, Heritage and Local Government (Older People)
Billy Kelleher (FF)	Enterprise, Trade and Employment (Labour Affairs)

Tony Killeen (FF)	Environment, Heritage and Local Government; Communications, Energy and Natural Resources (Environment and Energy)
Michael P. Kitt (FF)	Foreign Affairs (Overseas Development)
Conor Lenihan (FF)	Community, Rural and Gaeltacht Affairs; Education and Science; Justice, Equality and Law Reform (Integration Policy)
John McGuinness (FF)	Enterprise, Trade, and Employment (Trade and Commerce)
Batt O'Keeffe (FF)	Environment, Heritage and Local Government (Housing, Urban Renewal and Developing Areas)
Seán Power (FF)	Justice, Equality and Law Reform (Equality Issues)
Dick Roche (FF)	Foreign Affairs (European Affairs)
Trevor Sargent (GP)	Agriculture, Fisheries and Food (Food and Horticulture)
Brendan Smith (FF)	Health and Children (Children)
Mary Wallace (FF)	Agriculture, Fisheries and Food (Forestry)

Appendix 4: the Irish electoral system

Ireland uses the system of proportional representation by means of the single transferable vote (PR-STV) at parliamentary, local and European Parliament elections (the President, too, is elected by the single transferable vote). In 2007, 166 TDs were elected to Dáil Éireann from 43 constituencies each returning either three, four or five deputies. PR-STV has been in force in Ireland since 1922; elsewhere, only Malta employs it to elect the lower house of parliament, but it is also used to elect certain other bodies, such as the Northern Ireland Assembly, the Australian Senate and local councils in Scotland.

STV differs from other forms of PR in that it focuses on the candidate, rather than on parties. It operates on the simple logic of voters ranking candidates according to their preference. On the ballot paper, voters indicate their first choice by writing the number '1' next to a candidate's name (see ballot papers in the photo section at the front of the book). This is sufficient to cast a valid vote, but they can also express their lower choices by writing 2, 3, 4, and so on, beside the names of their next preferred candidates. The list of preferences functions in the sense that should a voter's first preference be insufficient or unnecessary to get their first choice elected, their vote can be transferred to assist their next preferred candidate. This highlights the fact that even though one may award as many preferences as there are candidates, each voter still only has one vote, which may be transferred so as to minimise the number of 'wasted' votes.

All valid ballot papers are counted to establish the electoral quota. The count revolves around the Droop quota, which is why this measure is employed in chapter 6. This figure represents the minimum number of votes that absolutely guarantees election. It is calculated by dividing the total valid votes by one more than the number of seats to be filled, and adding one, disregarding any fraction. For example, if there were 40,000 valid votes cast in a four-seat constituency, the quota would be 40,000/(4+1) plus 1; that is, 8,001 votes. No more than four candidates could possibly attain this figure, and thus any candidate doing so is deemed elected.

First preferences alone do not determine the outcome of the election; in 2007 only 32 candidates reached the quota on the basis of their first preference vote. Except in the highly unlikely event of all the seats being filled by the requisite number of candidates attaining the quota on first preferences, the counting process now consists of a series of 'counts' or stages, each involving the elimination of the lowest-placed candidate or the distribution of the 'surplus' votes (those over and above the quota) of a candidate whose total exceeds the quota. In 2007, the shortest counts were in Donegal SW, Dublin NW, Kildare S and Limerick W (just three counts each) and the longest was in Galway W (13 counts).

If a candidate receives more votes than the quota, their surplus votes are transferred to other candidates in proportion according to the next preference marked on each of the ballot papers. If the voter does not express a further preference, their vote is discarded, with only transferable votes being examined. It is here that the counting operation becomes complex. The surplus ballot papers examined are those from the last sub-parcel of votes received. On the second count this consists of the entire batch of votes received on the first count, but at all subsequent counts, only those from the last sub-parcel are examined. For example, if candidate A was elected on the first count with 9,001 votes, thus being 1,000 votes over the quota of 8,001, all of the 9,001 votes would be examined for their next available preference. If 20 per cent of the transferable vote in the original 9,001 contained a second preference for candidate B, 20 per cent of the surplus 1,000 (that is, 200) would be distributed to candidate B. Ballot papers are physically transferred, being those last filed in the sub-parcel, a method that is quasi-random rather than truly random and hence has the potential to affect the results. (For this reason, the counting of votes in the Seanad panel elections, where the number of votes is much smaller, is slightly different: all the ballot papers are transferred according to the calculated fraction of their value to avoid any risk of selection bias. This is known as the Gregory method.) For any candidate who reaches the quota on the second or a later count, only the parcel of votes that took them above the quota is examined; the distribution of the surplus takes place according to the same rules.

At the end of each count, if no candidate has reached the quota and there are no surpluses to distribute, the candidate with the lowest vote is eliminated, their votes being transferred to the next available preference stated on the ballot paper. 'Next available' means that when the next preferred candidate cannot receive a vote because they have already been elected or eliminated, the vote is transferred to the next choice. The returning officer can speed up the counting process – at the cost of transparency – by eliminating more than one candidate at a time if their combined vote is less than the vote of the next lowest candidate, in other words when multiple elimination cannot alter the result of the election. For example, in the constituency of Mayo at the 2007 general election, the candidates with the four lowest votes after the third count were (reading the lowest first) Cooke, Enright, Barrett and Cowley. Cooke, Enright and Barrett were all eliminated after this count, because even if all of Cooke and Enright's transfers were to go to Barrett, he would still have trailed behind Cowley and would thus have been the next to be eliminated.

Counting continues until all the seats have been filled. This occurs when a sufficient number of candidates have reached the quota, or if the number of candidates left is one greater than the number of seats to be filled and there are no further surpluses to distribute, at which stage all bar the candidate with the fewest votes are deemed elected.

Further reading

Department of the Environment, Heritage and Local Government, *Guide to Ireland's PR-STV Electoral System*, www.environ.ie/en/LocalGovernment/Voting

Michael Gallagher, 'Ireland: the discreet charm of PR-STV', pp. 511–32 in Michael Gallagher and Paul Mitchell (eds), *The Politics of Electoral Systems* (Oxford: Oxford University Press, 2008).

Richard Sinnott, 'The rules of the electoral game', pp. 105–34 in John Coakley and Michael Gallagher (eds), *Politics in the Republic of Ireland*, 4th edn (London: Routledge and PSAI Press, 2005).

Appendix 5: regulation of campaign spending

Details of the intimate relationships between businessmen and politicians that were revealed at a number of tribunals of inquiry in the 1990s resulted in a demand for closer monitoring and regulation of the activities of politicians. A number of laws were introduced to provide transparency and accountability in the relationships between politicians, parties and individuals who support them, financially or otherwise. The legislation also sought to limit expenditure at elections so as to lessen the role of money in influencing electoral outcomes and to ensure a level of equity between competing groups and parties.

The Electoral Act 1997, and the Electoral (Amendment) Acts of 1998, 2001 and 2002, provided the necessary legislation. The 2007 general election was the second at which candidates were subject to these regulations. The Standards in Public Office Commission (hereafter referred to as the Standards Commission) is responsible for the enforcement and monitoring of the legislation. Established in December 2001 by the Standards in Public Office Act, it replaced the Public Offices Commission, which had been in place since the Ethics in Public Office Act 1995. The commission scrutinises election spending in a variety of ways, including making visits to constituencies, inspecting campaign premises, and collecting samples of election material.

The aforementioned legislation has significant implications for the electoral process, though there is an important caveat. That is that while the expenditure and receipt of money is tightly regulated during the three to four weeks of the formal campaign (that is, from the dissolution of the Dáil till election day, a period of 26 days in 2007), there are no restrictions on what selected or intending candidates may do in the period before the election is called. In practice it is clear that some candidates, quite legally, spent large amounts of money in the 12–24 months before the election, which dwarfed the amounts they could and did spend during the formal campaign period. Expenditure outside this period (provided it is not in relation to goods or services used during the election period) is not subject to the limits imposed by the electoral legislation, thus benefiting larger parties (who typically have greater financial resources) and wealthier candidates, who can afford to spend extra monies before the election is called. It also means that the official expenditure returns do not paint an accurate picture of what was really spent on the election by the parties and their candidates. Obtaining this would require a definition of when the election campaign began (a difficult task in the era of 'permanent campaigns') and the acquisition of such figures from the parties, which they are under no obligation to provide.

The regulation of receipt and expenditure of money during the campaign period is as follows. Once a candidate receives a monetary donation in excess of €126.97, they must open and maintain an account solely for donations (the legislation had originally stipulated round figures in Irish pounds, which were subsequently converted into euros). All donations in excess of €634.87 must be disclosed. The term 'donation' is defined in the respective legislation as any contribution given for political purposes by any person or organisation. It includes a donation of money, property, goods, services, or even such items provided at a discount (where the donation is calculated as the difference between the price charged and the commercial price). The maximum donation that a candidate may accept from any one donor in a year is an aggregate sum of €2,539.48; this also applies to monetary donations received by candidates from a political party. Parties can receive up to €6,348.69 from one person.

Anonymous donations in excess of €126.97 must be reported and handed over to the Standards Commission. Donations of any value from non-Irish citizens resident outside the island of Ireland must be refused by candidates, and either returned to the donor or remitted to the Standards Commission. Unsuccessful candidates must disclose all election donations received in excess of €634.87 within 56 days after polling day. Successful candidates must include their election donations in an annual disclosure of donations that has to be submitted not later than 31 January of the year after the election.

During the election period, candidates are limited to spending €30,150 in a three-seat constituency, €37,650 in a four-seater, and €45,200 in a five-seat constituency. These limits were an increase (determined in line with the changes in the Consumer Price Index) on the previous election. Election expenses are defined in the legislation as those incurred during the election period to: promote or oppose a candidate or a party; present the policies of a party or a candidate, or the comments of a party or a candidate on the policies of another party or candidate; solicit votes for or against a candidate; present the policies of a candidate; influence the outcome of the election. The expenditure that parties can incur during this time is dependent on the proportion of spending limits that candidates assign to them. Because candidates are under no legal obligation to assign any of their limits to their respective parties, in theory it is possible that a party would be unable to spend any money during the official election campaign if all of its candidates refused to assign any of their spending limits to the party. However, such a scenario does not occur in practice because of the conventions of party discipline and loyalty. A final stipulation is that candidates cannot transfer their limits to another candidate.

Before 2002, the items requiring inclusion in the expenditure returns did not include the value of property, services or goods where costs are met out of public funds. However, following a court case taken by a Fianna Fáil candidate in 2002, the High Court ruled that this provided an unfair advantage to members of the Oireachtas. As a result, all candidates must include such costs (but only where they are used for electoral purposes) when submitting their expenditure returns.

Candidates are entitled to apply for reimbursement of a portion of their election expenses, provided they have been elected or their vote at any stage of the count exceeded one-quarter of the Droop quota. A quarter of the quota is approximately 4.2 per cent of the vote in a five-seat constituency, 5 per cent in a four-seater, and 6.2 per cent in a three-seater. The maximum amount for which candidates can be reimbursed is the lesser of €8,700 or their total election expenditure. Candidates elected to the Dáil are also required to submit a tax clearance certificate and a statutory declaration that their tax affairs are in order within nine months of the election. Details of all declared donations and election expenses are published on the Standards Commission's website (www.sipo.ie).

Finally, there are penalties for those in breach of the legislation. Overspending by a candidate is a criminal offence and could result in an individual petitioning the High Court to challenge the result of an election. Candidates failing to provide the required declarations, and election agents exceeding the prescribed limits, are liable to a fine, while anyone knowingly supplying false information faces a fine and/or a jail sentence.

References

Standards in Public Office Commission, *Guidelines for the General Election to the Thirtieth Dáil to be held in 2007* (Dublin: Standards in Public Office Commission, 2007), available at www.sipo.ie

Index